Collective Bargaining in American Industry

Collective Bargaining in American Industry

Contemporary Perspectives and Future Directions

Edited by

David B. Lipsky
Cornell University

Clifford B. Donn
LeMoyne College

Lexington Books
D.C. Heath and Company/Lexington, Massachusetts/Toronto

Library of Congress Cataloging-in-Publication Data

Collective bargaining in American industry.

   Papers presented at a conference held at Cornell
University on Mar. 7–9, 1986; co-sponsored by the New
York State School of Industrial and Labor Relations at
Cornell and the Institute of Industrial Relations at
Le Moyne College.
   Includes index.
   1.   Collective bargaining—United States—Congresses.
I.   Lipsky, David B., 1939–   II.   Donn, Clifford B.
III.   New York State School of Industrial and Labor
Relations.   IV.   Le Moyne College. Institute of
Industrial Relations.
HD6508.C656   1987   331.89'0973   85–45936
ISBN 0–669–12594–6 (alk. paper)
ISBN 0–669–12595–4 (pbk. : alk. paper)

Published simultaneously in Canada
Printed in the United States of America
Casebound International Standard Book Number: 0–669–12594–6
Paperbound International Standard Book Number: 0–669–12595–4
Library of Congress Catalog Card Number 85–45936

The paper used in this publication meets the minimum requirements of
American National Standard for Information Sciences—Permanence of
Paper for Printed Library Materials, ANSI Z39.48–1984.

87 88 89 90 91 8 7 6 5 4 3 2 1

Contents

Preface

This book had its origins in conversations between the editors in which we lamented the lack of studies on contemporary collective bargaining in key American industries. To be sure, scattered studies of recent developments in some industries do exist, but they are far too few to satisfy the needs of industrial relations scholars, practitioners, and students. This lack was particularly lamentable because beginning in the late 1970s collective bargaining in these industries appeared to have entered a new era—an era of change and transition that had made much of our knowledge of American labor relations obsolete.

After confirming the need for new studies on individual industries with several of our colleagues, we proceeded, with little difficulty, to obtain commitments to write the chapters in this volume from leading scholars with a special interest in the industries we selected. The authors presented initial drafts of their chapters at a conference held at Cornell University on March 7–9, 1986. Co-sponsored by the New York State School of Industrial and Labor Relations at Cornell and the Institute of Industrial Relations at Le Moyne College, the conference was supported by the Pierce Memorial Lecture Fund of Cornell's ILR School.

The conference provided a rare opportunity for collaborative scrutiny in a collected volume of this sort. A small group of industrial relations scholars and practitioners was invited to join the editors and authors at the conference to discuss the draft chapters. Those discussions proved to be not only lively and stimulating but also productive. They helped to identify numerous ways the authors might strengthen their papers. We urged the participants, including the authors, to commit their comments and suggestions to writing and, in the weeks that followed, almost all of them did so. Indeed, some of the participants provided detailed critiques of each of the papers. In some cases, we solicited appraisals from other outside readers. We then sent all of these comments and critiques to the authors, who worked to incorporate the suggestions into the final versions of the chapters that appear here. We are confident that subjecting each of the industry studies to such intensive scrutiny has helped to insure the reliability and quality of this volume.

We believe that the volume will be of great interest both to labor relations practitioners and scholars seeking up-to-date information on collective bargaining in the eight industries covered and to instructors and students in a variety of industrial relations courses. In particular, we hope the book will prove a useful companion to basic textbooks on union-management relations. Most texts in the field necessarily generalize about collective bargaining in the United States, occasionally offering illustrations and examples from specific industries. Students therefore are often unable to understand how the textbook examples have grown out of the special characteristics of the industry and the special experiences of the unions and employers in the industry. As a consequence, students do not gain an appreciation for the variation in union-management relationships throughout American industries. Moreover, scattered textbook examples do not give students a coherent view of how the various parts of a collective bargaining system fit together within a particular industry.

This book should enable the instructor to illustrate concepts and principles with examples from a specific industry, with the examples presented in the context of the entire industry, rather than in isolation. By the end of the course, the student will have been exposed to the overall system of collective bargaining in a representative cross-section of industries. Finally, we also designed the volume to be useful as a basic or supplementary text in many elective industrial relations courses, such as those on technological change, negotiating behavior, and contemporary issues in industrial relations. In sum, we hope this book will be widely used not only as a reference by academics and practitioners but also as a basic or supplementary text in a variety of industrial relations courses.

We have many people to thank for their help in collecting and editing this volume. First and foremost are the authors, whose already keen interest in their respective industries and good scholarship are well reflected in the efforts they gave to our task. We are deeply indebted to Robert E. Doherty, dean of the New York State School of Industrial and Labor Relations at Cornell University, who supported and encouraged this project at every stage of its development. We would also especially like to thank James Begin of Rutgers University for his participation in the conference and his detailed commentaries on all the draft papers and the overall project itself. Professor Begin's insights were invaluable in improving the quality of the volume. Similarly, we thank Richard Block of Michigan State University, whose extensive comments on the papers were particularly useful. We also thank the practitioners and other scholars who attended the conference and offered comments on the papers: Robert B. McKersie (Massachusetts Institute of Technology), Jack Stieber (Michigan State), Russell Allen (George Meany Center), and Donald E. Cullen, Ronald G. Ehrenberg, Tove Helland Hammer, Michele Kaplan, Jeff Keefe, and Susan Woods (all of Cornell). Jack

Golodner, Director of the AFL-CIO's Department of Professional Employees, deserves a special thanks for his comments on the chapters dealing with police officers and college faculty members. Robert Jensen and Frank Musick, both of the United Automobile Workers, offered insightful appraisals of the chapters on the automobile and agricultural machinery industries. Others who assisted the authors are acknowledged in the chapters that follow. We sincerely thank all who helped, but we offer the usual disclaimer: If any errors of fact or interpretation remain, they are sole the responsibility of the editors and authors, and none of the views expressed in the volume are necessarily the views of those who assisted in its preparation.

We would be remiss if we did not also thank Irene Grant, manager of the ILR School's Conference Center, and Nancy J. Hooge, assistant director of Le Moyne's Institute of Industrial Relations, whose able assistance insured the success of the March 1986 conference at Cornell. June Niblock provided valuable administrative and secretarial assistance with her usual efficiency, and Dianne Porter and Gail Hendrix, also of Cornell, provided additional secretarial services. Bruce Katz, our editor at D.C. Heath, was a constant source of encouragement and patience, and we are grateful for his support. We also wish to acknowledge the significant contribution made by Wendy Campbell of Research Findings in Print, who did the final editing of the manuscript. Last, but certainly not least, we thank our families for sharing our hopes and tolerating our foibles.

1

Introduction

David B. Lipsky
Clifford B. Donn

I n the 1980s collective bargaining in American industry moved through a
period of significant transition. The deregulation of several industries,
heightened international competition, a serious economic recession,
employment losses in heavy manufacturing, the shift in employment opportunities to the sunbelt states, the growth of white-collar and service occupations, and rapid technological change in some sectors were only some of the
environmental forces that served to reshape collective bargaining in many
industries. At the same time, union membership rolls dwindled (from 35.5
percent of the labor force in 1945 to 17.5 percent in 1986; *New York Times*
1987), employers redoubled their opposition to unions, which, according to
one recent study, grew by "leaps and bounds" (Freeman and Medoff 1984,
230), and the political climate grew more conservative, further fueling
changes in traditional bargaining practices in many industries.

Many of the largest American unions were on the defensive, and many
union leaders had difficulty devising strategies to counteract the problems
they were encountering. Over the years 1979–85 numerous unions made significant concessions to employers in their contract negotiations. In exchange
for economic concessions, however, some employers granted unions rights
and privileges they had not previously enjoyed. In some industries profit sharing became a part of the compensation system, while in others unions gained
representation on company boards of directors. Some employers arranged for
their unionized employees to become shareholders in the business, often
through an employee stock ownership plan. Others granted unions an influence over their capital investment decisions and a role in making other critical
decisions traditionally made exclusively by management. Many unions, urged
on by the AFL-CIO, sought a voice in determining how collectively bargained
pension monies should be invested. And finally, unions and employers in
several sectors experimented with quality-of-working-life programs and with
various participative schemes.

The forces reshaping collective bargaining in the United States over this
decade effectively reduced the uniformity of practice and experience in labor-

management relationships. Those relationships are now so diverse that it is more inappropriate than ever to characterize the United States as having a single, more or less standard system of collective bargaining. At no time since the late 1940s have labor-management relations exhibited such a vast range— from harmonious, cooperative, and participative to hostile, conflictual, and intransigent.

Although generalizations about the current nature and future course of collective bargaining in this country are certainly possible, and probably necessary, our understanding of this important social institution can certainly benefit from detailed studies of specific industries. By this means students, scholars, and practitioners can come to grips with the special and often unique characteristics of particular labor-management relationships. Accordingly, this volume provides eight studies, each describing and analyzing collective bargaining in a particular American industry. The book's chapters serve as a representative cross-section of industries: automobiles, agricultural machinery, rubber, telecommunications, airlines, professional sports, higher education, and police. The volume concludes with a chapter by the editors that proffers a synthesis not only of the major trends and common themes that emerge from the individual industry studies, but also of collective bargaining in the United States in general.

Of course, collective bargaining in this country has always been an institution rich in diversity. The nature of each collective bargaining relationship came about through a variety of influences both internal and external to the bargaining process. The internal factors include such things as the ideology of labor and management, the way the unions and employers were organized, and the history of the relationship between the parties. The external factors include the state of the economy and the nature of the laws and court decisions that regulate bargaining practices.

Nonetheless, this diversity has never been more in evidence than in the 1980s. The environmental forces mentioned above placed such strains on labor and management that bargaining in many industries was jolted out of the path it had followed since World War II. Different unions and employers responded to these pressures in different ways, however, creating more diversity than had been apparent for most of the post–World War II period.

This volume was designed with the intent of capturing that diversity. The eight industry studies illustrate the variety of ways in which bargaining is practiced as well as the diversity of forces and industry adaptations that have been reshaping collective bargaining in the United States. Thus, we present studies of industries in which collective bargaining is a well-established process (automobiles and agricultural machinery, for example) and ones in which it is not (higher education and police). We have a representative selection of manufacturing and services, private sector and public sector, white-collar and blue-collar bargaining.

In some of the industries surveyed in this volume bargaining is conducted by one major union (for example, the United Automobile Workers in autos and agricultural machinery). In other industries several or numerous unions engage in bargaining (airlines and telecommunications). In some bargaining is highly centralized (professional sports); in others it takes place entirely at the local level (police). In some industries, collective bargaining covers the great majority of employees in the industry (autos), while in others only a minority of employees are covered by collective bargaining agreements (higher education). In a majority of the studies presented here employment is exclusively in the private sector. In one, police, employment is entirely in the public sector, and in another, higher education, employment is in both the private and public sectors. Most of the industries have workplaces with fixed locations, but in at least two—airlines and police—the workplaces shift location. In several of the industries outputs can easily be produced at a variety of locations in or out of the United States (autos); in others outputs have to be created where they are used (police and higher education). Highly trained and specialized employees are needed in some industries (professional sports and higher education), whereas workers can readily acquire the requisite skills in others (autos and agricultural machinery). In some of the industries producers engage in fierce competition (airlines, at least since deregulation); in others, employers are shielded from competitive market forces (police).

Given the diverse characteristics of these industries it is not surprising that unions and employers in them responded to the changes and pressures of the 1980s in markedly different ways. The first three studies in this volume are representative of traditional blue-collar bargaining—the so-called shrinking perimeter of organized labor. The automobile, agricultural machinery, and rubber chapters are excellent examples of manufacturing industries in which well-established collective bargaining relationships have been seriously affected by heightened international competition and recent economic recessions.

The automobile industry has long been considered a pacesetter in collective bargaining. Auto bargaining has been characterized by innovations in contract settlements, and those settlements have frequently exerted great influence on bargaining processes and outcomes throughout much of the unionized sector. Increasingly in the 1970s and 1980s the UAW and the auto companies grappled with the problem of foreign imports, especially from Japan, which had the effect of significantly reducing domestic auto producers' employment levels. Foreign competition and periodic economic recessions brought about union concessions on wages and other contract terms, but those concessions were accompanied by several innovative workplace experiments, many of which were designed to increase worker participation in shopfloor decisions and to foster union-management cooperation. Uniformity in auto contracts declined in the 1980s as the companies sought agreements better tailored to their special needs. But as auto contracts became less uniform, their influence on settlements in other, related industries, such as agricultural machinery and rubber, declined.

Labor relations in agricultural machinery were characterized in the 1980s by high levels of conflict and several serious strikes. This industry was especially hard hit by the collapse of the farm economy in the 1980s. Output and employment in the industry dropped precipitously, and one major producer, International Harvester, reorganized, dropped out of the industry, and adopted a new name—Navistar. In both the automobile and agricultural machinery industries, the principal union is the UAW. Traditionally, the bargaining strategy of the UAW in agricultural machinery was to model its agreements on those it had negotiated in autos. Pattern bargaining of this sort, however, diminished in significance in the 1980s. Interestingly, the workplace innovations adopted by the parties in autos have not, in the main, been adopted by the parties in agricultural machinery. Although adverse economic conditions moved the UAW and the auto companies toward greater cooperation, similar pressures in agricultural machinery prompted an opposite response from the UAW and the companies. The already adversarial nature of the parties' bargaining relations instead intensified.

The rubber industry was also battered by the economic recession and foreign competition of the 1980s. Here, however, technological change—from bias-ply to radial tires—exacerbated the effects of unfavorable market conditions. The position of the union in the industry, the United Rubber Workers, was further undermined by the growth of domestic nonunion competition. Foreign producers, such as Michelin, opened nonunion facilities in the United States; and domestic producers, such as Goodyear and Firestone, shut down many of their unionized plants and opened nonunion plants in other locations. Other unions faced with serious membership losses have tried to recoup their losses by expanding into new jurisdictions, but the URW has made almost no attempt to organize workers outside the rubber industry. As in agricultural machinery, the URW also was influenced by the auto pattern in its settlements. But rubber is another industry in which pattern bargaining became less pronounced over the course of the decade.

The chapters on telecommunications and airlines illustrate the effects of deregulation on collective bargaining. In telecommunications divestiture—the breakup of AT&T—also had serious consequences for collective bargaining. For most of its history AT&T had maintained a virtual monopoly over long distance and local telephone services and telephone and telephone equipment production. Accordingly, the Bell system was closely regulated by government agencies. Gradually, however, technological advances undercut the corporation's control over telephone services. New companies, such as MCI and Sprint, began to compete in the long distance market; and other companies began to manufacture telephones, ending the dominance over telephone production of Western Electric, AT&T's manufacturing subsidiary. At the same time, AT&T moved into the production of more sophisticated types of telecommunications equipment.

Finally, in the 1980s long distance telephone service was largely deregulated and regional telephone companies were separated from AT&T. Deregulation and divestiture made telecommunications a much more competitive industry but had serious consequences for collective bargaining. For example, the Communications Workers of America, the dominant union in the industry, had fought for many years to establish nationwide, centralized bargaining in the Bell system. In a formal sense CWA's goal was finally achieved in 1974. But the breakup of AT&T spelled the breakup of centralized bargaining in the industry. AT&T and the CWA had trouble adapting to deregulation and divestiture: in both 1983 and 1986 the union struck the company after contract talks had reached an impasse. In the late 1980s substantial uncertainty still clouded the future direction of collective bargaining in telecommunications.

For over 40 years the airlines industry was closely regulated by the Civil Aeronautics Board, a federal agency. The CAB controlled the fares the airlines charged, the routes they flew, and the entry of new carriers into the industry. But during the Carter presidency the CAB began to deregulate the industry. The early success of administrative deregulation led Congress to pass the Airline Deregulation Act in 1978, which had the effect, in the short term, of converting a highly regulated industry into a highly competitive one and the longer term effect of weakening unions in the industry. In combination with the effects of the economic recessions of 1979–83 deregulation placed unions in airlines on the defensive. As airline profits declined or disappeared, unions representing pilots, flight attendants, and ground personnel were forced to grant economic concessions to the carriers. Often those concessions included two-tier wage agreements that not only cut the salaries of the more senior employees but allowed the carriers to establish an even lower, separate pay scale for new employees. In the face of the new competitive environment some established carriers (such as Northwest and Republic) merged, while others (such as Braniff) went into bankruptcy. New airlines entered into competition with the older airlines, and some of the new carriers (such as People Express) were nonunion. An industry in which collective bargaining was once the rule became one in which the nonunion sector began to exert significant influence on labor relations in the unionized sector.

Professional sports, higher education, and police are also service industries, but in all three collective bargaining is a relatively recent phenomenon. For the most part the macroeconomic changes that had major effects on collective bargaining elsewhere in the 1980s were not factors that shaped bargaining relationships in any of these industries.

Collective bargaining in professional sports attracted much attention in the 1980s, particularly because of serious strikes that interrupted playing schedules, in baseball in 1981 and in football in 1982. Professional athletes have been unionized for several decades, but overt conflict between the parties is new. The special characteristics of collective bargaining in professional sports distinguish it from the other industries examined in this volume, though not necessarily from other segments of the entertainment industry of which professional sports are a part. For example, in professional sports collective bargaining is used to set the minimum salary in a league, while salaries above the minimum are set by individual negotiations between players (and their agents) and owners, as is sometimes the case in the performing arts, such as screen acting and orchestras. Disputes over such issues as the reserve clause in baseball and free agency in all sports, the escalating salaries of players (especially in baseball), and drug testing of the players made headline news in the 1980s and served to heighten the tensions between players' unions and team owners.

Higher education offers an example of collective bargaining by highly trained, skilled professionals—college faculty—who carefully guard their professional prerogatives. Although bargaining in public institutions of higher learning is generally regulated by state public sector bargaining laws, bargaining in private colleges and universities falls within the jurisdiction of federal labor statutes governing the private sector. Public sector bargaining statutes passed by states in the 1960s and 1970s served to promote collective bargaining by faculty in public institutions, but a key Supreme Court decision—*Yeshiva*—seriously eroded the bargaining rights of faculty in private institutions. Moreover, the bargaining power of college faculty in the 1980s was undermined by such factors as the financial distress suffered by many colleges and by the growing numbers of part-time faculty employed to teach courses. Since skilled white-collar workers will constitute a growing fraction of the labor force in years to come, the problems faculty unions have encountered in attempting to organize college professors have important implications for the future of the labor movement.

In the 1960s unionism among government employees, such as municipal employees, state employees, and public school teachers, grew rapidly. By the 1980s the percentage of public sector employees organized for bargaining purposes exceeded the percentage of private sector employees so organized. The experience of police officers and municipalities in collective bargaining demonstrates the special and often unique issues that characterize collective bargaining in the public sector. For example, bargaining by police officers is generally regulated by state and local statutes, as it is for other state, county, and municipal employees. Those statutes vary from one jurisdiction to another, differing on such issues as the obligation of public employees and employers to bargain in good faith, the enforceability of collective bargaining contracts, the scope of topics that can be negotiated by the parties, and the type of dispute resolution techniques used to settle impasses.

Police officers, however, are usually treated differently from most of their public sector colleagues. Police (and firefighters, too) are said to provide truly essential services to their communities. Although some states have granted other public employees a limited right to strike, none has granted police officers that right. No state statute tolerates even a short work stoppage by police officers, although, of course, occasionally an unlawful police strike does occur. A major issue, then, that arises in the study of police labor relations is whether collective bargaining can be genuine or effective in the absence of the right to strike.

In toto the industry studies included in this volume illustrate virtually all the salient trends in American collective bargaining in the 1980s. In assembling the volume we might have selected a different cross-section of industries that arguably would have illustrated those trends just as well, but we were guided in our choice by two additional criteria.

First, we sought contributors who were already engaged in research on an industry of particular interest, in other words, who were up-to-date and could provide fresh perspectives on their industries. Second, we did not want to duplicate unnecessarily industry studies already available in recently published journal articles and books. For example, one of this book's contributors, Harry Katz, had recently published a well-regarded book on labor relations in the automobile industry (Katz 1985), but we thought it would be useful to have a chapter-length study of collective bargaining in autos, especially since it would give the author the opportunity to consider more recent developments in the industry. Another contributor, James Dworkin, had published an important book on collective bargaining in major league baseball (Dworkin 1981), but had not had the opportunity to pursue in print his interest in other professional sports. Other contributors had published more narrowly focused articles on their industries, and they welcomed the chance to integrate their knowledge of the industry's labor relations in the form of a longer study.

One prototype for this volume is a book containing ten excellent industry studies, edited by Somers, that appeared in 1980. Although much has happened in collective bargaining in those ten industries since then, much of the material in the Somers volume is still valid and the book continues to be widely used. With one exception, airlines, we therefore decided not to replicate any of the industry studies contained in the Somers volume. In the case of airlines, deregulation had brought about so many dramatic and significant changes in the industry's labor relations after 1980 that we decided a fresh study was needed. Still other recent books contain useful industry studies, and by and large the case studies included in those books are not duplicated here (for example, see Mills and McCormick 1985).

Each of the industry studies in this volume contains an interesting story about collective bargaining, and each can be read without the reader necessarily having any interest in the others. But clearly the editors and authors

The Bargaining Environment
  The Technological Environment
  The Economic Environment
  The Legal Environment
The Parties
  Unions
  Employers
The Structure of Bargaining
  Bargaining Units
  Pattern Bargaining
The Bargaining Process
  Historical Background
  Bargaining Issues
  Contract Administration
Labor–Management Conflict
  Historical Background
  Sources of Conflict
  Patterns of Conflict

**Figure 1–1. Chapter Format Based on Dunlop's Systems Model
of Collective Bargaining**

have a larger purpose in mind. By reading all of the studies (as well as the concluding chapter), we hope the reader will gain some appreciation for the similarities and differences that exist across bargaining relationships and for the flexibility and adaptability of the institution of collective bargaining.

One important feature of this book should help the reader in this regard. A substantial effort was made to tell each of the industry stories using a single format. Presented in the figure here, the outline is a modification of the industrial relations systems model developed nearly 30 years ago by John Dunlop (1958). The collective bargaining system in any industry consists of several different interrelated elements. It does not begin in a vacuum, but rather in the context of certain facets of the environment: (1) the technological facets, which include the methods and machines used to produce the products and services of the industry, the technological characteristics of the jobs held by workers, the skill levels required by the prevailing technologies, and the pace and diffusion of technological change; (2) the economic, which include the state of the labor and product markets, the degree of competitiveness of the industry, the overall prosperity of the industry and the economy, and the financial or budgetary constraints that affect both employers and unions; and (3) the legal, which include statutes, public policies, court decisions, and administrative decisions that set the "rules of the game" for the producers in the industry and for the parties in collective bargaining and are in turn influenced by the other two environmental facets.

The environmental context can serve to encourage and foster collective bargaining, as was the case in the 1960s when the passage of public sector bargaining statutes by many states and the growth of government services (and budgets) promoted the spread of collective bargaining among government employees. The environmental context can also discourage or restrict collective bargaining, as was the case in the 1980s when foreign competition, recession, the introduction of labor-saving technologies, and judicial decisions favoring employers reduced the numbers of employees covered by collective bargaining agreements in many manufacturing industries. It is also worth noting that the environmental context not only influences collective bargaining but is, in turn, influenced by it. For example, high wage settlements in an industry may have a significant influence on the economic environment in which the industry's collective bargaining occurs.

Another element of an industry's bargaining system is the set of parties (or "actors," in Dunlop's terminology) that are the main participants. The actors, as shown in the figure, are unions, including the workers who belong to unions and their union representatives, and employers, including the owners of enterprises, their managers and supervisors, and professionals and consultants who may also play a role in the bargaining system. In nonunion settings workers may influence the rules of the workplace, but their influence tends to be indirect and informal. Collective bargaining, by contrast, is characterized by formal employee organizations and formal joint procedures for determining and administering workplace rules.

The environmental context and the objectives, needs, and desires of the parties determine the special characteristics of an industry's system of collective bargaining. The actors establish a structure for bargaining, which needs to be compatible with the environmental context. In the figure, the structure of bargaining includes two subelements: bargaining units, which define the numbers and kinds of workers and employers covered by collective bargaining agreements; and pattern bargaining, which refers to the influence, if any, that some labor agreements have on others. Clearly, it makes a difference whether the bargaining unit is a small shop or an entire industry and whether an agreement in one relationship does or does not affect the terms of settlement in another relationship. In the 1970s the bargaining structure in many industries, especially in the manufacturing sector, was highly centralized; the key decisions were usually made at the company or industry level by top union and corporate executives. In the 1980s many observers noted that the changing environment had caused bargaining to become more decentralized—more centered on the shop, the plant, and the single employer (see, for example, Freedman and Fulmer, 1982).

Bargaining structure in turn helps shape the bargaining process. In the figure the bargaining process encapsulates not only the history of negotiations in an industry but also the substantive issues that are, or have been, of central concern in those negotiations. It also encompasses the administration of contracts, including grievance procedures and grievance arbitration. Substantive issues are both the subject matter of the negotiating process and, when codified in a collective bargaining contract or in more informal agreements between the parties, the outcomes of the system. Wages, fringe benefits, hours of work, and working conditions have traditionally been the substantive issues of greatest concern to the parties. But in the 1980s the scope of bargaining in many industries expanded to include innovative workplace reforms that had not normally been part of the bargaining process in the past.

There is always the possibility that the bargaining process between unions and employers will not lead to peaceful agreement but to some form of conflict. The figure shows labor-management conflict as the last key element of an industry's collective bargaining system. Collective bargaining can be viewed principally as a means of reconciling the opposing interests of employers and workers, but that reconciliation may not be possible short of open confrontation, usually in the form of a strike. The placement of conflict in the systems format shown in the figure implies that it is primarily an outgrowth of the bargaining process. In the U.S. system of collective bargaining, strikes, lockouts, and other types of conflict are largely tactical in nature, used by the parties to obtain more favorable contract terms, and are not a form of social protest used to change the system itself or the environment in which the system operates.

In summary, the systems approach to the study of collective bargaining provides an analytical theory or model that is useful in comparing labor relations practices and experiences across industries. As Dunlop (1958, 3) said,

> The idea of an industrial relations system implies a unity, an interdependence, and an internal balance which is likely to be restored if the system is displaced. . . . Industrial relations systems show considerable tenacity and persistence. . . . An industrial relations system was developed at one moment in time. But an industrial relations system may also be thought of as moving through time, or, more rigorously, as responding to changes which affect the constitution of the system.

It should be noted that the systems format did not perfectly suit each of the industries examined in this volume. Thus, although we insisted that the authors follow the general outline of the systems model in their chapters, we also recognized that each author had to have the latitude to focus on the special features of the industry he studied—to emphasize some and downplay others.

Our insistence on use of the systems format gave rise in the planning stages of this project to a friendly, if perhaps arcane, academic debate among the editors and the contributors. The systems model has long been widely accepted by industrial relations scholars as a useful way to study collective bargaining, but it is not the only model or approach that might have been used. In recent years some scholars have come to believe that the historically unprecedented changes that occurred in many collective bargaining relationships in the 1980s could not be adequately explained by traditional industrial relations theories and models. Some scholars suggested, for example, that the systems model was too static—that it was best suited to the study of stable, mature collective bargaining relationships. They sought new approaches that would enhance our understanding of the more dynamic aspects of collective bargaining. For example, one group of scholars proposed a "strategic" model of industrial relations, which they believed did a better job of explaining structural shifts in collective bargaining than did a pure systems model (Kochan, Katz, and McKersie 1986, especially 3–20). And at least one contributor to this volume maintained that a straightforward historical narrative of collective bargaining in his industry would be the best method of tracking the significant changes that occurred in collective bargaining.

The editors and the authors discussed these issues, considered the alternatives, and at last agreed (some more reluctantly than others) that a systems model still had great relevance and could accommodate the dynamic characteristics of collective bargaining in American industry. Clearly, however, the common use of a systems format throughout this volume does not resolve the larger debate. At the heart of that debate is the issue whether any person interested in industrial relations now has the means and the wits to understand the contemporary transformation of collective bargaining in American industry. In the end this is more than a scholars' debate because the ability to understand—and therefore to manage—this important social institution will have a direct bearing on the future welfare of workers and employers, and of the larger community of which we are a part.

References

Dunlop, John T. 1958 [reprinted in 1970]. *Industrial Relations Systems*. Carbondale, Ill.: Southern Illinois University Press.

Dworkin, James B. 1981. *Owners Versus Players: Baseball and Collective Bargaining*. Boston: Auburn House.

Freedman, Audrey, and William E. Fulmer. 1982. Last Rites for Pattern Bargaining. *Harvard Business Review* (March-April): 30ff.

Freeman, Richard B., and James L. Medoff. 1984. *What Do Unions Do?* New York: Basic Books.

Katz, Harry C. 1985. *Shifting Gears: Changing Labor Relations in the U.S. Automobile Industry*. Cambridge, Mass.: MIT Press.

Kochan, Thomas A., Harry C. Katz, and Robert B. McKersie, 1986. *The Transformation of American Industrial Relations*. New York: Basic Books.

Mills, D. Quinn, and Janice McCormick. 1985. *Industrial Relations in Transition: Cases and Text*. New York: John Wiley.

New York Times. 1987. Troubles of U.S. Labor Unions Eased in 1986. February 15, p. 31.

Somers, Gerald G. 1980. Collective Bargaining: Contemporary American Experience. Madison, Wis.: Industrial Relations Research Association.

2
Automobiles

Harry C. Katz

The auto industry has long been an innovator in American industrial relations, and it has continued to be so in recent years. It was the auto industry that introduced to American collective bargaining supplementary unemployment benefits, "30 and out" retirement systems,[1] and paid personal holidays. Furthermore, the terms promoting quality of working life programs specified in a 1973 letter of agreement between the General Motors Corporation (GM) and the International Union, United Automobile, Aerospace and Agricultural Implement Workers of America (UAW) proved to be a bellwether in the development of worker participation programs elsewhere in the country. Continuing this tradition are recent innovations in auto labor relations (some of which have set patterns for a number of other industries): the "concessionary" collective bargaining agreements negotiated at the Chrysler Corporation in 1980, those at GM and the Ford Motors Corporation in 1982 and 1984; shop-floor work teams that are composed of only a few job classifications; participation programs that encourage extensive worker and union involvement in issues strategic to the firm's management; the job security provisions outlined in the 1982 and 1984 GM and Ford agreements; and the Saturn plant agreement negotiated in 1985 between GM and the UAW. Even when the auto industry has not served as a pattern setter, it has consistently been representative of American labor relations in recent years. For instance, the auto parts supply sector, and increasingly the final assembly sector of the auto industry as well, has recently experienced sharp growth in the number of nonunion operations, as have so many other U.S. industries.

Despite the extent of these innovations, they have not been instituted without serious debate within labor and management ranks and much uncertainty about future developments. The key issue as of this writing is whether the "reform" pattern instituted, for example, in the Saturn agreement, or a more conflictual pattern (perhaps arising with the growth of nonunion operations) will become the predominant mode of labor-management relations. The issue is a focal point of debate within much of the rest of American industry as well. Of central concern in this debate is the future course of the economy and the extent to which the worldwide auto market will encourage any particular pattern of labor relations. In light of this connection between economic events and labor relations practice, it is appropriate to begin this chapter with a discussion of economic trends in the auto industry.

The Bargaining Environment

Growth Followed by Heightened International Competition

From 1946 until 1979 the U.S. auto industry experienced consistent growth and prosperity, even in the face of the industry's periodically sharp cyclical swings. Over those years domestic production of cars and trucks increased from 5 to 13 million; the number of production workers grew 20 percent, although fluctuating substantially along with vehicle production during cyclical peaks and troughs. This combination of large output growth and relatively modest employment growth was the result of significant productivity gains accomplished by the industry. Productivity and output growth helped produce strong profits for the auto companies and, as discussed in more detail later, helped support substantial real growth in autoworkers' earnings over the years in question.

In 1979 auto industry employment (including final assembly and auto parts supply) stood at 759,700 production employees and 223,100 white-collar employees.[2] If auto servicing and sales, road construction and repair, and other auto-related activities are counted as part of auto employment, the total represents a significant share of all employment in the U.S. economy. By this broader definition of national motor vehicle–related employment, the total in 1979 was 8,053,000, or 8.3 percent of the civilian U.S. labor force.[3]

From the end of World War II into the late 1970s the economic environment of the auto industry was conducive to general stability and steady improvements in labor relations. Three environmental factors were critical to that state of affairs: growth in domestic auto sales, a low level of imported auto sales, and a high degree of unionization. But by the end of the 1970s a labor-management pair that had grown accustomed to long-term growth in sales and profits began to face a number of fundamental changes in the world auto market. The most important of these was an increase in international competition. The share of imports in the American motor vehicle market rose from 14.6 percent in 1970 to 23.5 percent in 1984 (it was a record 27.8 percent in 1981). Particularly threatening were signs of significant cost and quality differentials between the U.S. producers and their Japanese competitors. The resulting disruption of the industry was exacerbated by the effects of a severe macroeconomic recession in the early 1980s. By 1981 auto employment had dropped to 61 percent of its peak in December 1978.

The immediate effect of the decline in domestic sales and the increase in foreign competition was financial troubles for auto companies. In late 1979 Chrysler was rescued from bankruptcy only with the help of government-guaranteed loans. A number of auto parts companies did go bankrupt, and by 1982 rumors were circulating in the industry that even the Ford Motor Company was rapidly running out of cash reserves and might face bankruptcy.

In mid-1983, however, domestic auto sales began to rebound strongly, and the financial status of the auto assemblers markedly improved. The Big Three—GM, Ford, and Chrysler—combined went on to earn profits of $6.3 million in 1983 and $9.8 in 1984. Some observers believed this signaled a return to the industry's former prosperity. But many industry analysts continue to warn that the American auto industry has not yet been able to match Japanese cost and quality standards and that in light of import restraints the industry's profits only mask this problem.[4]

Product Strategy and New Technology

Over the late 1970s and 1980s the worldwide auto industry was confronted by a number of other changes. Although not as obvious as the increase in international competition, those changes were no less profound in their effects on U.S. auto production and industrial relations systems. Since the end of World War II the U.S. auto industry had been a noteworthy model of the success possible in adapting mass production techniques to steady, but incremental, technological change. In fact, it was through mass production—with its large economies of scale and narrow division of labor—that the auto companies were able to adapt and ultimately prosper. In the early 1970s it had appeared that mass production techniques would be extended through the development of "world cars"—vehicles assembled with interchangeable parts manufactured all over the world. A number of aspects of the new competition in the world market, however, raised doubts about the world car strategy and the future efficacy of the mass production techniques themselves. The new economic environment placed a premium on flexibility in the production process, at the same time demanding that labor and management reorient their relations accordingly (Katz and Sabel 1985).

Factors contributing to the need for greater flexibility in the production process include new developments in the product market, new technologies, and macroeconomic events. Within the product market U.S. auto producers have moved away from a strategy of producing a wide variety of family-size cars and large volumes of each model and instead are recreating their product lines according to a strategy of specialty or "niche" vehicles.[5] From the 1940s through the 1960s the American auto companies had produced primarily family-size cars, each model in large volumes, and had made much of their profits from those cars. But by the 1970s the auto market had become more compartmentalized as consumers began to demand a wider variety of car types, such as luxury cars, recreation vehicles, and sports cars.

As the auto companies began to produce smaller volumes of each model, they looked for a labor relations system that both maintained low costs and high quality in smaller volume production and facilitated more rapid switches in car type. For example, the auto companies traditionally assembled only one basic car model in each assembly plant. But by the early 1980s they had begun to assemble a number of models of a given type in each plant, and they were drafting plans for new assembly technologies that would allow the simultaneous assembly of sedans, station wagons, and trucks in the same plant. Thus, the shop floor would have to find ways to adjust rapidly to different production volumes and vehicle types. One way that has found a place in many plants is to replace the traditional assembly line production techniques and highly formalized labor relations practices with work teams and more informal work rules.

The increasing use of robotic and microelectronic technology has added further pressure for more flexible work rules, especially since robots represent a critical advantage over earlier technologies in the relative ease with which they can be adapted to changing product lines. A machine that is frequently reprogrammed, or an assembly line that is frequently rearranged, requires workers and work rules that can just as easily adjust.

A third factor that has contributed to the industry's search for greater flexibility in labor relations is the volatility in product demand generated by macroeconomic and structural economic developments.[6] As demand began to fluctuate more sharply in the late 1970s, the auto companies intensified their search for the most efficient ways to adjust production volumes and switch between the model types produced in any plant. And the likely continuation of the structural problems that created the macroeconomic flux—oil price shocks, government policy responses to the inflation-unemployment trade-off, and the increased sensitivity of the U.S. economy to world economic events—suggests a continuation of the trend of macroeconomic instability.

In fact, the American auto companies have been facing a dual problem. While they have been racing to adjust to the new volatility in product demand and to changing technologies, they have simultaneously struggled to reduce the cost advantage held by Japanese producers. Complicating this problem is the fact that the industry is not agreed on the actual source of the Japanese productivity advantage. There is some evidence that the Japanese auto companies have had lower costs and higher quality because they have better mass production practices, particularly their "just-in-time" inventories, which lower inventory costs, and the *nenko* pay system with fewer job classifications and fewer links between specific job duties and pay, which contributes to lower production costs.[7] Moreover, these and other Japanese practices seemed to allow the flexibility in production the American firms were striving so hard to find. Thus, managers in the American firms have been unsure whether to focus their strategy on performing mass production in a less costly manner or to focus on redesigning their production system itself. Their confusion has had important consequences for the conduct of industrial relations, as discussed later in this chapter.

The Structure of the Industry

The changing nature of world auto markets has also had important effects on the organizational and spatial makeup of the U.S. auto industry. On the organizational side, the early 1980s witnessed a rash of joint production arrangements between auto companies within and across national boundaries. All of the U.S. auto assemblers rushed to forge coproduction agreements with a foreign counterpart. GM linked with Toyota, Ford with Mazda, Chrysler with Mitsubishi, and American Motors with Renault.[8] Under these coproduction agreements the partners constructed a number of new auto assembly plants in the United States. In a separate development assembly and parts plants solely owned by Japanese companies were also opened in this country. Both types of new plants have ushered in changes in auto labor relations as many instituted innovative production practices and some are unorganized (issues discussed in more detail later in this chapter).

The coproduction arrangements often extend beyond assembly plants; the companies also engage in the exchange of parts or in the formation of joint research and development projects. Throughout the U.S. auto industry this has led to more extensive linkages between the assembly companies and their parts suppliers. The assemblers have dramatically reduced the number of parts suppliers they purchase parts from and have initiated longer term contracts with their suppliers at the same time as they have increased the percentage of the parts purchased from suppliers ("outsourced") as opposed to building the parts themselves. The immediate effects on labor relations of these new assembler-supplier arrangements were to require greater cost reduction efforts on the part of both the supply plants owned by the assemblers and the independent parts suppliers. But the formation of stronger links across the assembly companies and between assemblers and parts suppliers eventually may also produce complicated problems regarding bargaining structure and union jurisdiction.

The geographic consequence of the changes under way in the world auto market has been a recentralization of auto production. In part to capture the benefits of just-in-time inventory procedures, and in part as a product of more advanced process technologies, the U.S. auto industry has taken a number of steps to centralize production. The auto manufacturers have closed plants located far from Detroit; GM has built Buick City, the Saturn complex, and others as part of plant clusters that bring together parts manufacturing, stamping, and assembly operations near one central location; and others have consolidated stamping and other preassembly operations into their assembly plants.

It is also noteworthy that a number of the new assembly plants, those either recently built or planned, are clustered in Kentucky and Tennessee and the surrounding region. Honda is in Marysville, Ohio; the Saturn complex is to be built in Spring Hill, Tennessee; the Toyota assembly plant, in Greenwood, Kentucky; and the Nissan assembly plant, in Smyrna, Tennessee. No doubt the decision to build in the South is at least partly the result of management's belief that southern workers are less willing to unionize or more willing to accept nontraditional industrial relations practices than their counterparts in other regions.[9]

The Legal Environment

Laws and regulatory policies have also made up a significant part of the environment influencing the course of labor relations in the auto industry. The federal government has long enforced safety and emissions standards for the auto industry and its products. The scope of those regulations broadened in the 1970s as part of a more general elaboration of environmental policies. The regulations influenced labor relations to the extent that they affected the price and sales of automobiles. Emissions standards in particular encouraged the auto makers to produce small cars with good gas mileage and possibly also to retain some small car production in the United States. On the whole, however, laws and regulations specifically affecting labor relations in the auto industry have been fairly stable over the past four decades, and changes in this part of the industry's environment have not had a major influence on labor relations.

There are nevertheless a few exceptions to this generalization. Over the 1970s nonunion operations in the automobile parts industry increased in importance, as shown in table 2–1 (fourth column). The UAW and other unions led numerous organizing attempts in those nonunion plants, and federal regulation of the conduct of those election campaigns became an important issue. Plant closings and unions' status in plants being closed were also at issue. As the auto parts industry came under the intense competitive pressures of the early 1980s, they responded by closing down some of their operations. In some cases the unions in those plants challenged the closings on grounds that they represented a "runaway shop" campaign to meet the competition posed by the growing number of nonunion firms.

In recent years the auto assemblers and suppliers have also tangled with the equal employment opportunity regulations. In 1980, for example, Ford and the Equal Employment Opportunity Commission (EEOC) settled a

Table 2–1
Wages and Unionization in Parts Supply Firms

Year	Average Hourly Wage, Assemblers	Average Hourly Wage, Suppliers	Suppliers' Wage as Percentage of Assemblers' Wage	Percentage of All Suppliers Unionized*	Percentage of All Suppliers Located in the South
1983	$12.13	$8.20	67.6%	60%	29%
1974	5.54	4.45	80.3	80–84	15
1969	3.82	3.24	84.8	80–84	11
1963	2.90	2.59	89.3	87	8.5
1957	2.37	2.26	95.3	95	
1950	1.63	1.61	98.8	82	
1940	.96	.84	87.5	50–55	

Sources: U.S. Department of Labor (1963, 1971, 1976, 1985).

Note: An auto parts supply firm is defined in the U.S. Department of Labor surveys cited here as an establishment with more than 50 employees that engages in manufacturing metal parts for motor vehicles. The definition excludes establishments operated by passenger car manufacturers (this exclusion was not part of the surveys for the years 1940, 1950, and 1957—see text).

*This is defined as the percentage of parts supply firms with a majority of their hourly employees covered by a collective bargaining agreement.

seven-year discrimination case against the company with damages assessed at $23 million (BNA 1980). Under the terms of the agreement Ford agreed to make $13 million in payments to minorities and women who had been refused or denied promotion opportunities. The company also promised to allot to women 20 percent of its production supervisor jobs and 30 percent of its new hires in production jobs. And in 1983 the EEOC, GM, and the UAW signed a $42 million conciliation agreement that ended a 10-year-old nationwide discrimination charge against the company (BNA 1983a). The GM settlement called for new training and educational programs including $15 million for endowments and scholarships for employee education. GM also agreed to make good-faith efforts toward meeting specific employment goals for minorities and women in various production and skilled trades jobs.

The Parties

The Union

The UAW represents the majority of the unionized workers in the auto industry.[10] The International Union of Electronic, Electrical, Technical, Salaried and Machine Workers (IUE) also represents some hourly workers in the electrical products plants of the assembly firms and along with the UAW and a number of other unions represents workers in the parts supply firms. By the late 1940s the UAW had organized all hourly workers in the U.S. and Canadian companies that assembled cars and trucks.[11] Until 1985 the union was an international, since it included Canadian autoworkers; but in that year the Canadian members voted to form a separate union, and a separation agreement was negotiated between the U.S. and Canadian parts of the UAW.

The UAW is a large and fairly centralized union. Internally it is subdivided into departments for each of the major assembly companies and into separate departments for the agricultural implements industry, for skilled trades, and for union organizing. National union staff coordinate the bargaining within each department and assist in the implementation of fringe benefit, employee assistance, health and safety, and quality-of-working-life (QWL) programs.

The central figure in the union over the postwar period was Walter Reuther, who earlier was active in the union's sit-down strikes and organizing efforts of the 1930s. Reuther served as president of the UAW from 1947 until his death in 1970, during which time he led a coalition of UAW leaders who dominated the national affairs of the union (Stieber 1962). Reuther's creative imagination and personal influence encouraged a particularly innovative spirit within auto bargaining. Moreover, under his guidance the UAW was very active in national and local politics and a strong supporter of the Democratic party. Yet, even with the dominance of the Reuther coalition, the UAW has historically had strong democratic traditions, apparent in the lively internal affairs of the local unions in each plant.

The Companies

In addition to assembling vehicles the major auto companies also manufacture a number of the parts they use. The extent to which the companies produce their own parts—or their vertical integration—varies, however. Industry analysts estimate the degree of vertical integration in 1985 was: GM, 80 percent; Ford, 50 percent; and Chrysler, 40 percent. Since the major assembly companies (at least the American-owned ones) are completely unionized, and the national (companywide) collective bargaining agreements cover both the final assembly and parts plants owned by those companies, we need not distinguish, for the most part, between the final assembly and parts plants owned by the "assembly" companies.

The Big Three have been the major employers in the industry since the 1920s. In the 1950s a number of smaller assembly companies remained in the industry, but by the 1970s the only other assemblers with operations in the United States were American Motors and Volkswagen.[12]

As already noted, Japanese auto assemblers began to open plants in the United States in the early 1980s, and by the middle of the decade many of the

Japanese firms had also announced plans to build even more (final assembly and parts) plants here. They vary in unionization: Honda's auto assembly plant in Marysville and Nissan's in Smyrna have operated on a nonunion basis, whereas among the jointly owned American and Japanese firms the Toyota-GM plant, the Ford-Mazda plant, and the AMC-Renault plant (co-owned) are all organized. As of this writing, it is unclear whether Chrysler-Mitsubishi will automatically recognize the UAW.

The Toyota-GM plant is an interesting case. At the start up of the NUMMI (New United Motors Manufacturing, Inc.) plant in Fremont, California, Toyota and GM recognized the UAW and hired a majority of the NUMMI workforce from the ranks of UAW workers on layoff from the former GM assembly at that site, although the union status of NUMMI had initially been a source of controversy between the two principals. When the agreement forming NUMMI was first announced, officials at Toyota had stated that they did not intend to recognize the UAW automatically or to hire from the ranks of laid-off GM workers. Informal talks between Toyota, GM, and the UAW ensued, after which Toyota announced a change in its views. Clearly, the UAW's threat to disrupt other GM operations if the NUMMI plant were to operate on a nonunion basis played a critical role in those negotiations (a role similar to that played by the union's threats raised in the mid-1970s regarding GM's nonunion plants in the South, discussed below).

In those deliberations the UAW agreed to have a minimal number of job classifications in the NUMMI plant (Buss and Koten 1983). The first formal collective bargaining agreement at NUMMI, negotiated in 1985, specified only a single job classification for all production workers and only three classifications for skilled trades workers. Following the same pattern Ford announced plans in 1984 to build an assembly plant in Flat Rock, Michigan, with Mazda and to recognize the UAW in the plant. This was after national officers of the UAW had stated their willingness to agree to innovative labor relations practices in the plant, including having only a few job classifications.

The major automakers had to address two other issues of union status over the post–World War II period. In the mid-1970s GM opened several plants in the South and initially operated them on a nonunion basis. The UAW tried to organize the new plants through representation elections but succeeded in only a few cases. The union was more successful when, at the national level, its leaders threatened to withdraw their support for QWL programs and use selective pressure tactics in GM's plants in the North. In 1976, as part of a new national contract, GM pledged to remain neutral in the representation campaigns taking place in its southern plants. Yet, even in the face of this official policy of neutrality, the UAW continued to lose many of the elections. Its leaders became of the opinion that GM had not in fact remained neutral during the election campaigns, and therefore they pressed

GM for revised election procedures. In the national agreement of 1979 GM agreed to an "accretion" clause whereby in any new facilities whose output was very similar to that in its existing plants, the UAW would be automatically recognized as the bargaining agent. GM went even further in 1982 when it agreed to recognize the UAW automatically—without a formal representation election—if the union could produce signatures showing that a majority of the workers in a plant favored representation by the UAW. By the end of the year the union had used those rights to organize all of GM's nonunion facilities.

Throughout the postwar period the UAW tried to expand its organization into the ranks of white-collar employees as well. The companies actively resisted those efforts and most often defeated them. Among the major assemblers, the UAW's organizing efforts were most successful—though still only limitedly so—at Chrysler.

In the parts supply sector unions were less successful in their efforts to organize blue-collar workers than they were in the assembly firms. Again, table 2–1 shows the percentages of hourly workers in the parts supply industry who worked in plants where a majority of the workers were covered by a collective bargaining agreement, for selected years from 1940 to 1983. Unfortunately, the definition of the auto supply sector changed with the 1963 survey, and so the data across those years are not strictly comparable. (Before 1963 the parts plants owned by a major assembly company were included in the supply sector; from 1963 on they were not). Nevertheless, the figures do clearly show that by 1983 the parts supply sector was significantly less unionized than the assembly firms, which, as noted, were 100 percent organized. The relationship between the extent of unionization in the supply sector and earnings there relative to earnings in the assembly firms is discussed in detail below.

The Structure of Bargaining before 1979

The Final Assembly Sector

Before 1979 the bargaining structure in the final assembly sector was notable for its high degree of pattern-following behavior both within and across the auto companies. In each national bargaining round the UAW began by targeting one assembly company for the first set of negotiations and then using the agreement reached with that company as a pattern to follow with the other companies. Over the postwar period the national agreements reached with the different companies exhibited a substantial similarity, especially in terms governing wages and fringe benefits. This structure has been characterized as "connective bargaining." According to Ulman (1974, 98) connective bargaining involves the negotiation of wages, fringes, and some work conditions between the company and one or more national unions, the latter connecting the company-wide wage settlements in an industry via pattern bargaining. Working conditions and, to a lesser degree, some pay questions are also negotiated at the plant level with local unions; and local and national unionists are sequentially involved in grievance handling.

Within the connective bargaining structure of the U.S. auto industry, compensation is set by national agreements, with each individual agreement covering all the UAW plants operated by the company. Some work rules, such as overtime administration, employee transfer rights, and seniority privileges, are also set in the national contracts. Locals of the union, in turn, negotiate with individual plants agreements that supplement the national agreement. Typically, local agreements define plant-specific work rules, such as the form of the seniority ladder, job characteristics, job-bidding and transfer rights, health and safety standards, production standards, and an array of other rules guiding shop-floor production. The local agreement does not touch on wages or fringe benefits, since those are set in the national contract. Nonetheless, local contracts can have an indirect influence on wage determination at the plant level by defining or modifying the job classifications on which wage rates are based. Local piece-rate systems can also influence wage levels; but by the late 1950s piece rates, with very few exceptions, had been eliminated from the industry (MacDonald 1963).

Local bargaining over work rules allows for the expression of local preferences and for some adjustment to local conditions. Indeed, local bargaining can engender what Kuhn (1961, 57) termed "fractional bargaining": informal bargaining among work groups with opposing interests. Shop-floor bargaining in the auto industry has most often been resolved through the grievance procedure ending in binding, third-party arbitration, although disputes concerning production standards, new job rates, and health and safety issues are not resolved through recourse to arbitration. Occasionally over the postwar years, plants in the industry have undergone strikes called as part of both local contract negotiations and informal shop-floor bargaining. In the main, however, the connective structure of bargaining has been successful in tempering labor-management disputes at the plant level.

Although the national agreements afford the UAW locals the right to negotiate a local agreement with plant management, a critical element in the connective bargaining structure is the active role the national union plays in monitoring plant-level bargaining and agreements. The formal power to do so comes from the fact that many features of local agreements such as the seniority ladder and local strikes require the approval of the national union, as specified in the national agreement.

The distinction between national compensation determination and local work rule bargaining, and the limits placed on local bargaining by the national union, ensured that local work rule bargaining was not overly influenced by the employment consequences of shop-floor work rules. Over the postwar years the recourse to either a foreign or a domestic nonunion supply of parts previously produced in union plants occasionally led to significant numbers of layoffs in some plants. This could have encouraged broader modifications in local work rules and wider divergence among plants in their efforts to lower costs, but two factors worked against these pressures. For one, the industry's long-term output and employment stayed on an upward path until the late 1970s. Business lost to an outside supplier was made up for by an expanding volume of other activities remaining in house. Second, the national agreements with the UAW granted displaced workers liberal rights to bid on new jobs in other plants of the company. As a result, and in contrast to the more recent period discussed later in this chapter, local unions were not under pressure to relax work rules in order to save jobs in firms facing foreign or nonunion competition.

With pay set strictly at the national level, the bargaining structure did not promote any linkage between pay and local work rules, and in that sense the system was not "connective." The system was very connective, however, in the extent of national union monitoring of local union affairs and its functioning as a channel of communication up and down the union hierarchy.

Connective bargaining vested the political power within the union in the national union officers. It is easy to trace a parallel course between the growth of the connective structure in the immediate postwar years and the rise and solidification of the Reuther faction within the UAW (Lichtenstein 1980; 1982). The elaboration of the connective structure in the auto industry over the 1950s also paralleled the centralization then under way within other bargaining structures throughout U.S. industry, such as in steel and trucking (Weber 1961).

By separating work rule bargaining from bargaining over compensation, this connective structure also discouraged local unions and workers from concerning themselves with business decision making, either at the corporate level or on the shop floor. For this reason the connective structure is fertile ground for "job control unionism," another key feature of postwar bargaining in the U.S. auto industry and a feature to which we will return in a later section.

The Parts Supply Sector

As of 1985 the supply sector of the U.S. auto industry comprised approximately 2,500 companies that supplied either parts or services directly to the auto assembly companies (*Business Week* 1985a). Where there was union representation the supply companies historically negotiated on a company, plant, or multiplant (within the same company) basis, although the specific jurisdiction of collective bargaining agreements varied substantially across companies. The history of contract negotiations in the supply sector also varied, although there was a strong tendency for pattern following across suppliers and a tendency for the suppliers to follow the pattern set by the Big Three assemblers (Levinson 1960).

In fact, the influence of the agreements reached in the auto assembly firms extended well beyond the auto supply industry. The UAW has historically tried, with some success, to use the auto assembly agreements as a pattern for their negotiations in the agricultural implements industry. Other unions, especially those whose members were linked to auto production, such as the rubber workers, also looked to the contracts with the auto assembly firms as pattern setters. The extent of interindustry pattern following has varied somewhat over the years, but generally it has been significant. (Chapters 3 and 4 in this volume discuss the impact of the auto assembly contracts on the agricultural machinery and tire industries.)

The Bargaining Process before 1979: Wage Rules and Job Control Unionism

In addition to its connective bargaining structure, labor relations in the auto assembly firms were shaped by the determination of wages through formulaic wage rules in multiyear national contracts and by a reliance on job control unionism premised on the contractual resolution of disagreements and the linking of worker rights to strict job definitions.

Wage and Fringe Benefit Determination

Since the historic GM-UAW agreement of 1948 auto assembly firms have used formulaic wage rules to set wage levels in their labor contracts.[13] Those contracts have been national in scope, specific to each company, and in effect for multiyear periods (since 1955 they have been three-year agreements). The formulas traditionally included in the contracts are an annual improvement factor (AIF), which since the mid-1960s has amounted to 3 percent per year, and a cost-of-living adjustment (COLA) clause, which originally provided full cost-of-living protection and in the 1970s gave roughly a 0.8 percent wage increase for every one percent increase in the national consumer price index (note, however, that the COLAs were cents-per-hour increases, whereas the AIFs were percentage increases).

The importance of these formulas is that they provided continuity in wage determination over time and continuity across the assembly companies at any particular time. Over time, except for minor adjustments, the formulas rigidly set wages at the Big Three from 1948 to 1979.[14] And across the industry national agreements followed pattern setters, and the national contract wage was not modified in local bargaining.

The COLA and AIF formulas can be viewed as a form of a "wage rule" that guided the behavior of labor and management bargainers in a manner analogous to the function served by shop-floor work rules (Katz and Sabel 1979). For national union leaders, steady adherence to the wage rules served as a ready standard for judging their performance in bargaining: the rank and file could not fault union leaders for securing wage increases that satisfied the rule during contract renegotiations. Furthermore, as time went by the wage rules became secure, continually legitimated by the efforts of the union's national leaders. Meanwhile, pattern following within the industry satisfied workers' concerns for equity. Union members could also support the wage rules because adherence to them brought the members steadily improving real wages. As evidence of that fact, table 2–2 shows that the average hourly wage of Ford assemblers has consistently exceeded the average for all production workers in the private sector since 1940 and has actually been gaining ground in that time.

On the other side of the bargaining table wage rules were appealing to management both as a means of reducing the likelihood of overt conflict with labor and as a means to predict long-term labor costs. The predictability of labor costs was especially attractive to managers in the auto industry because of the long lead time necessary to plan, develop, and invest in a new product.

Along with increases in real hourly earnings, autoworkers received steady improvements in their fringe benefit packages over the postwar years. A number of these—such as supplementary unemployment benefits, 30-and-out pensions, and paid personal holidays—were innovations that eventually spread to the auto supply firms as well as to a number of other industries. During those years fringe benefits became a larger share of total worker compensation. Table 2–3, reporting the hourly compensation costs to GM of an auto assembler, shows that between 1948 and 1981 real total compensation more than tripled.

As in the wage negotiations bargaining over fringe benefits proceeded in a predictable, formulaic manner. Fringe benefits were not negotiated flexibly in response to the short-run financial or employment conditions of the industry. Instead they were added to in sequential steps. The evolution of the fringe package was strongly influenced by demands from the UAW. The pattern was that after a long campaign by the union, a particular fringe benefit would be added to the national contract. In subsequent negotiations the union would then push for the extension and elaboration of the benefit.

The negotiation of supplementary unemployment benefits (SUB) illustrates this pattern. The demand for some form of guaranteed annual wage appeared on the UAW's bargaining platform as early as 1937 (McPherson 1940, 103–5). In 1939 GM agreed to institute an income security plan that

Table 2–2

Comparions between the Average Hourly Earnings of Ford Auto Assemblers and Those of All Production Workers in the Private Sector, 1948–1980

Year	Wage of Auto Assembler[a] (1)	Wage of Average Production Worker in the Private Sector[b] (2)	Ratio of (1)/(2)
1948	$1.58	$1.23	1.29
1950	1.58	1.34	1.18
1955	2.01	1.71	1.17
1960	2.46	2.09	1.18
1965	2.91	2.45	1.19
1970	4.25	3.22	1.32
1975	6.44	4.54	1.42
1980	10.33	6.66	1.55

Sources: Assembler data from U.S. Department of Labor (1979a) and Ford Motor Company (1979). Private sector data from U.S. Department of Labor (1983a). Reprinted with permission, from Katz (1985). © MIT Press, 1985.

[a]Hourly earnings (including COLA and AIF) of assemblers at Ford Motor Company.

[b]Average hourly earnings of nonsupervisory production workers in the nonagricultural private sector.

Table 2–3

Total Hourly Compensation Costs for a GM Assembler, 1948 and 1981

Costs	1948	1981
Base wage (includes COLA and AIF)	$1.44[a]	$11.45[b]
Fringe benefits (includes social security, insurance, holiday, and vacation costs)	.18[a]	8.20[c]
Total	1.62	19.65
Total in 1948 dollars[d]	1.62	6.28

Note: This table is reprinted, with permission, from Katz (1985), © MIT Press, 1985.

[a]This figure is from MacDonald (1963, 40).

[b]This figure is from internal statistics of the General Motors Corporation.

[c]This figure is an estimate calculated by General Motors Corporation. It is consistent with other estimates that have circulated recently in the industry press.

[d]The consumer price index rose from 72.1 in 1948 to 279.3 in 1981.

paid laid-off workers benefits financed out of their future earnings, but the union continued to find this plan inadequate. Walter Reuther repeatedly raised the demand for a guaranteed annual wage in the immediate postwar negotiations (Harbison and Dubin 1947, 28). In the early 1950s the UAW commissioned an advisory panel of academics to study the issue and offer recommendations. Acting in part on those recommendations the parties agreed in the 1955 contract negotiations to create an SUB plan (first at Ford) that went a long way in satisfying the union's demand for greater income security and stability. The plan set up an SUB fund (funded solely by corporate contributions) that provided laid-off workers a maximum of 65 percent of their previous take-home pay for up to 26 weeks. In the 1967 contract renewal the SUB benefit was extended to a maximum benefit of 95 percent of take-home pay for up to 52 weeks. (The 65 and 95 percent figures include any available state unemployment insurance benefits.)[15]

Both the wage rules and the "structured" negotiation of fringe benefit improvements had a number of more general implications for bargaining in the auto industry, as we have seen. First, the ban on local modification of nationally set contract wages was a critical part of the connective bargaining structure that fixed the distinction between national and local bargaining in the industry. Second, the use of formulaic wage rules to set compensation narrowed the range of national union participation in corporate decision making and thereby was a key factor in the contractually based, "job control" character of labor-management relations in the industry.

Third, the use of wage rules kept earnings rising steadily for workers employed in the assembly firms. At the same time, the influence of the wage rules was extended through the pattern following by the parts supply firms. Returning to table 2–1, note that from 1940 to 1957 earnings in the supply sector rose at a faster rate than earnings in the assembly sector but then declined from 1963 to 1983 relative to the assembly sector. (In these last figures parts plants that were owned by one of the assembly companies are counted in the assembly category.)

The extent of union organization in the two sectors may explain the later decline in pattern following by the supply firms. The assembly firms were all virtually completely organized by the UAW by the end of World War II, whereas the supply firms were not. It is interesting to note that the relative rise in supplier earnings occurred after that period, during which the UAW and other unions were increasing their representation in the supply sector. Note that from 1940 to 1957 the percentage of the parts supply plants with a majority of their workers covered by a collective bargaining agreement rose from around 50 percent to 95 percent and the ratio of mean earnings in the supply firms to mean earnings in the assembly firms rose from 87.5 percent to 95.3 percent. Earnings in the supply firms then fell relative to those in the assembly firms, from 89.3 to 67.6 percent, between 1963 and 1983 when the extent of union coverage of the supply firms dropped, from 87 percent in 1963 to 60 percent in 1983. Associated with this decline in union coverage was the increasing movement of the supply plants to the South, as noted in the last column of table 2–1. In this regard the auto parts supply sector was similar to other U.S. manufacturing industries over the past two decades, industries in which an increase in nonunion operations, often heavily concentrated in the South, led to declines in the relative earnings of workers in their unionized plants.[16]

Job Control and Arm's Length Relations between Labor and Management

Both nationally and on the shop floor the labor relations system in the U.S. auto industry relies on contractually defined procedures to regulate disagreements between labor and management. Those procedures are heavily focused on "job control";[17] that is, wages are explicitly tied to jobs and not to worker characteristics or individual job performance. In addition, much of the detail within the contract concerns the specification of an elaborate job classification system, with many rules governing the exact requirements of each job and the seniority rights that are tied to a job ladder, which in turn guides promotions, transfers, and layoffs (Piore 1982).

In this system labor and management negotiate over compensation levels and work rules. During negotiations over compensation the parties depend on rules to keep them away from discussing either company pricing or profits. This was an explicit motivation for adopting the AIF and COLA formulas in 1948, when Charles Wilson, then president of General Motors, was searching for a way to answer and avoid Walter Reuther's request to discuss company profit and pricing policies (Reuther 1976: 248–56; Harbison and Dubin 1947). At the national level the use of wage rules and job control unionism also discouraged discussion of other broad corporate concerns, such as investment planning, outsourcing, and the problems associated with the introduction of new technologies. At the local level job control unionism discouraged shop-floor discussion of business and production decisions. In short, the reliance on the formal grievance procedure for dispute resolution and the extreme job control focus together leave little room for alternative forms of worker participation in decision making.

The dominance of job control unionism in autos did not lead to a complete stabilization of shop-floor labor-management relations. Labor and management have often engaged in struggles over the exact terms of working conditions and the bounds of union or worker involvement in decision making. Frequently, those issues were addressed through informal day-to-day relations between workers and their supervisors, but occasionally unresolved disputes found an outlet in authorized and unauthorized local strikes.

Furthermore, the combination of connective bargaining and job control unionism did not produce standardization in the tenor or results of shop-floor labor relations because the focus of connective bargaining was on standardizing *contractual terms*. Significant variation emerged in the tenor and practical conduct of shop-floor relations across plants and across work groups within individual plants. In some plants the relationship between the parties was consistently acrimonious, while in others the parties developed a more cooperative style. This wide diversity in relations has been demonstrated by the variation in plant-level industrial relations performance indicators from two GM divisions: for example, in 1980 the grievance rate in both divisions varied by a factor of 20, and the absentee rate was twice as high in one plant as it was in another.[18]

For the automakers this labor relations system well served their goal of containing the union's and workers' influence over issues the companies deemed to be managerial prerogatives. Indeed, as Harbison and Dubin (1974, 48–88) noted, containment of the union's influence was a central objective of auto management in the union's early years. The labor relations system that developed largely removed that concern by limiting the bargaining agenda to issues of job control.

For the UAW, although the limited bargaining agenda did not satisfy all of Reuther's initial goals, it did satisfy important political needs of the union.[19] In particular, the national union was placed in firm control of what periodically had been restive local unions and workers (Lichtenstein 1980). The multiyear agreements signed after World War II also satisfied the important union goal of contractually ensuring union security (Harbison 1950).

The intensity and scope of shop-floor relations varied significantly over the postwar period, but it is possible to trace some broad patterns in those relations. In the prewar and war years the initiative for workplace bargaining lay in the hands of the UAW, strengthened by the rapid spread of union representation. By the late 1940s and the 1950s that initiative had shifted to management, a turn of events that characterized many other unionized industries as well (Harris 1982; Strauss 1962). Specifically, auto management over those years tried hard (in many instances with success) to limit the influence of workers and the UAW over such key "managerial prerogatives" as production standards (Herding 1972, 28–31; Lichtenstein 1982, 220). Nonetheless, this managerial offensive did not foreclose the UAW's success at regularizing its influence over many workplace issues during the late 1940s and 1950s. For example, the administration of the grievance procedure and arbitration became more formal and stable throughout the 1950s.

The economic expansion of the mid- and late 1960s and the social upheavals of the time led to a new era in auto bargaining from the mid-1960s through the early 1970s.[20] This era was marked by shop-floor militancy and local strike waves (*Business Week* 1964). The number of written grievances per 100 blue-collar employees in the plants covered by the GM-UAW national agreement rose from 50.4 in 1960 to 71.9 in 1973. Heightened shop-floor militancy found its counterpart in more contentious and difficult local contract negotiations. For example, the number of union demands submitted in local contract negotiations at GM rose from 11,000 in 1958 to 39,200 in 1973.[21]

Shop-floor militancy also led to more frequent and intense local strikes. The percentage of total working time lost to strikes in the motor vehicle and equipment industry had varied between 0.21 and 0.28 in the years between 1959 and 1963, during which time a new national contract was not being negotiated, whereas in the late 1960s the percentage of work days lost rose, to 0.74 in 1968 and 0.94 in 1969 (also years between contract negotiations) (U.S. Department of Labor 1979a). The lengthy strike at GM's Lordstown plant in 1972 came to symbolize this era of worker militancy (Rothchild 1973).

During this era both management and the UAW national leadership were struggling to reassert the more disciplined regularity that had characterized shop-floor labor relations in the 1950s. This led Walter Reuther in some instances to guide the settlement of local contract negotiations and not allow local strikes (Selekman et al. 1964, 551–52).

To some extent it was inevitable that tension should develop between the national and local unions over their respective influence and authority over union affairs. The important fact about the challenges to national union control that did emerge over the postwar period is that they were met through minor adjustments in the existing connective bargaining structure. In fact, it was only recently that the parties instituted any major modification of the connective bargaining structure (discussed later).

High rates of absenteeism, production slowdowns, and the unsettled nature of shop-floor labor relations in the late 1960s led auto management to seek these minor adjustments, particularly improvements in worker-supervisor relations and new motivational tools. QWL programs were developed in part to respond to worker militancy and to improve the tenor of labor-management relations in those plants that perennially were relatively poor performers. In their early years the parties viewed the QWL programs as supplements to the existing job control system, to be kept separate from other collective bargaining procedures. As a result, although the QWL programs became a significant part of auto labor relations, the new programs, like the local unions' challenges to national union control, were accommodated through amendments to the existing labor relations system and were not fundamental alterations in the basic structure of the system.

Thus, various shifts and strains in labor-management relations across plants and over time in the auto industry exercised a critical influence on working conditions and the balance of power between labor and management. At the same time, however, the importance of the wage and fringe benefit rules and of job control unionism severely limited worker and union involvement in business decisions and any fundamental change in the bargaining process.

From the late 1940s through the late 1970s the applications of wage rules and job control unionism provided steadily rising real wages and benefits to auto workers as auto employment and production continued to grow. At the time imports were a limited part of total auto sales, and thus the bargaining process took place within geographic boundaries of union organization that closely matched the relevant product market. That the bargaining process closely mirrored the economic environment was one of the primary reasons the system continued to appeal to both labor and management. And of course, stability and continuity in auto negotiations processes served important political functions for both labor and management.

The Bargaining Process after 1979: "Shifting Gears"

Final Assembly Sector

By the late 1970s the economic environment of the world auto industry had changed substantially from its former pattern, and labor and management strove to respond to a number of new economic pressures. Although the decline in auto sales was enormous, its most unusual aspect was its length. The industry had experienced sharp cyclical flux over the postwar period and had made the necessary adjustments. Management had adjusted its inventory and purchasing policies, and in labor relations the parties had instituted contractual recall and layoff rights and the SUB system to respond to cyclical flux in employment levels. But neither labor nor management was accustomed to or prepared for the prolonged decline in sales that started in 1979. As the slump deepened, the SUB funds were depleted and SUB payments were reduced. Autoworkers' hopes of recall diminished as the ranks of the laid off exceeded the recall rights allowed in the national UAW contracts. With auto production heavily concentrated in the north-central states hardest hit by the deep recession in the national economy, many laid-off autoworkers around the turn of the decade were forced to move to the South or West in search of employment. For the auto companies themselves the prolonged sales slump and the attendant financial losses raised doubts about their ability to raise capital and their future economic viability.

Wage Concessions. Modifications in the wage rules traditionally used to set auto compensation levels were among the first responses to the crisis facing the industry, initially as part of efforts to avoid bankruptcy at Chrysler in 1979, then as part of the agreements reached at GM and Ford in March 1982, and later in the 1984 agreements at Ford and GM.

In the 1979 Chrysler negotiations the threat of bankruptcy and pressures from the federal government, which was providing loan guarantees to Chrysler, led the parties to defer payment of the annual improvement factor and the scheduled cost-of-living payments, though otherwise retaining the wage formulas. Under further direct pressure from the federal government in 1980, the parties agreed to extend the deferrals and also substantially reduce the number of paid personal holidays. When Chrysler's financial difficulties continued, labor and management returned to the bargaining table in January 1981 for yet a third time and agreed to cancel the remaining AIF and COLA increases. The total effect of all these concessions on the part of the union was to render the hourly pay of Chrysler workers $2.50 below the pay received at Ford and GM.

The sustained decline in auto sales also led to extensive layoffs and a significant number of plant closings at Ford and GM in 1980 and 1981.[22] The companies and the union were therefore willing to open new contract negotiations early, in March 1982 instead of September 1982 when the existing 1979–82 national agreements were due to expire.[23]

As at Chrysler, the compensation concessions agreed to at Ford and GM represented major modifications in the traditional wage rules. The Ford and GM agreements eliminated the AIF increases scheduled for 1982 and 1983. Three quarterly COLA increases were deferred for eighteen months, though after December 1982 regular COLA increases of one cent per 0.26 point increase in the consumer price index were to continue. Additionally, all paid personal holidays (nine per year in the 1979–1982 agreement) and one regular holiday were eliminated. The net effect of the elimination of the holidays was to raise annual work hours 4 percent.

To soften the blow of the wage concessions, management agreed to add profit-sharing plans in the new contracts. When the industry later recovered, as will be discussed in more detail below, the profit-sharing programs paid out to the average eligible worker in 1983, 1984, and 1985, respectively, $402, $1,993, and $1,262 at Ford and $606, $515, and $328 at GM.

The 1982 contracts at Ford and GM included a number of other new programs that improved the income security and job security of auto-workers. Under a new "guaranteed income stream" benefit program, permanently laid-off workers with more than 15 years' seniority would receive 50 percent of their last year's earnings (and an additional one percent for each year of seniority beyond 15 up to a maximum of 75 percent of their last year's pay) until they reached normal retirement age.[24] A joint national employee development and training program at each company, funded by company contributions (10 cents per worker hour at GM, for example) was also created to provide counseling, training, and tuition assistance to laid-off and employed workers.[25]

The 1982 agreements proposed the initiation of experiments with employment guarantees at selected plants (four at GM and three at Ford). In those plants 80 percent of the existing work force were to be guaranteed employment during the term of the agreement (until September 1984).[26] In addition, management promised not to close any plants for 24 months for reasons of "outsourcing the components manufactured in the facility," although plant closings would be permitted for reasons of production volume or company consolidation of operations. The companies also pledged to try to maintain existing employment levels and make their best efforts to replace any jobs lost because of outsourcing. They made lump-sum contributions to the SUB funds, which had become sorely depleted, and made it possible for workers with more than ten years of seniority to receive up to 104 weeks of SUB pay. The new guaranteed income stream program, the plant-closing moratorium, SUB funds, and related contractual changes were announced as the job security components of the new contracts.

Those job security measures served two purposes. On the one hand, they functioned as partial compensation to the union and its members for the pay concessions. But they also appeared to serve a symbolic function by offering some explicit assurance to the workers that the pay concessions would in fact lead to an improvement in their job security. By reducing their compensation, it was argued, autoworkers would improve the cost competitiveness of U.S. cars and UAW labor on the international market, which in turn would increase U.S. vehicle sales and U.S. auto employment. It is not clear that the companies' 24-month moratorium on plant closings caused by outsourcing was something the automakers would not otherwise have done given the pay concessions agreed to in the 1982 contract, since those concessions alone would reduce the economic incentive for outsourcing. Whatever its actual significance, the moratorium put the companies' views on security on record and also enabled the union leadership to tell their members that something had been gained in exchange for the pay concessions. It seems that this sort of explicit linkage between concessions and employment security is often necessary to convince workers of the value of any such concessions.

Although the "concessionary" agreements (the UAW terms them "survival" agreements) included a number of new programs and significant changes in scheduled wage increases, throughout the process of pay modification labor and management pursued a course that maintained the basic structure of the traditional wage rules. The pattern was, first, to delay the implementation of increases generated by the wage rules and, later, only after more severe economic pressures, to cancel temporarily those pay increases. The concessionary agreements at Chrysler, for example, provided for the later full restoration of the traditional AIF and COLA formulas, and the 1982 agreements at GM and Ford provided for full restoration of the traditional COLA formulas before the expiration of the contracts. The union leaders could therefore claim that the formulas had not been abandoned but only temporarily deferred.

Fringe Benefit Concessions. Changes in fringe benefit packages at the Big Three also took place in a very structured pattern of events. The major adjustment made to fringe benefits in the Chrysler agreements and in the 1982 Ford and GM agreements was elimination of paid personal holidays.

Paid personal holidays in the auto industry had first appeared in the 1976 agreements and consequently represented the latest major extension of the autoworkers' fringe benefit package. By eliminating those most recent additions the parties were pursuing a course that entailed the least disruption of the basic structure of the benefits package. Their behavior can be explained in part by the fact that the benefits package had developed incrementally over the years in response to long campaigns by the UAW. Once included in the agreement, each new benefit then acquired standing as an entitlement or principle. When economic pressure forced a reduction in the benefits package, the logical target for elimination was thus the latest benefit added to the package. For workers whose seniority rights protected them from any net employment decline resulting from the lengthening of work hours, the elimination of paid personal holidays did not engender any change in total annual income. The reduction of the benefits package in that manner therefore also reflected the interests of senior autoworkers.

The total net effect of the 1982 wage and fringe benefit concessions negotiated was to reduce the rise in total hourly labor costs in GM and Ford after March 1982 from the approximately $5.50 it would have been in the absence of the concessions to an actual rise of approximately $3.50 by September 1984.

The Effects of the Post-1983 Recovery. Starting in early 1983 auto sales and profits were buoyed by a strong macroeconomic recovery and by the continuation of informal import restrictions on Japanese cars. By the end of the year GM, Ford, and Chrysler had posted respective profits of $3.7 billion, $1.9 billion, and $700 million, and in 1984 they tallied profits of $4.5 billion, $2.9 billion, and $2.4 billion. By mid-1984, constrained by the earlier plant closings, the Big Three were all running at or near full capacity, with capacity particularly strained in plants producing large cars.

At Chrysler this recovery led to the reinstatement of the traditional wage rules in its new labor contracts. A one-year agreement signed in December 1982 provided an immediate wage increase equivalent to the traditional 3 percent AIF formula increase, fully restored the traditional COLA formula and provided 47 cents in COLA catch-up, and eliminated the profit-sharing plan introduced in 1981. A September 1983 contract reopener granted further increases, and in a new three-year agreement reached in September 1985 Chrysler workers received substantial upfront increases (an "equity recovery" amount of $2,120 for past sacrifices), a continuation of the COLA, and a reinstitution of profit sharing. Perhaps most important, the agreement called for the traditional 3 percent AIF wage increase in 1987, the last year of the contract.

In 1984 GM and Ford also negotiated new contracts in an environment that had shifted at least some bargaining power back to labor's advantage. The union's bargaining stance was further strengthened by workers' angry response to the substantial bonuses awarded executives at Ford and GM as part of their 1983 compensation packages. For example, Philip Caldwell, then chairman of Ford, received a combined salary and bonus in 1983 of $1.4 million and earned $5.9 million through the appreciation of stock purchased in his long-term compensation package (*Business Week* 1984).

The 1984–87 agreements at GM and Ford provided first-year wage increases of one percent to assembly workers and up to 3.5 percent to certain skilled trades workers, with average increases of 2.25 percent. In the second and third year of the agreement workers were to receive lump-sum payments amounting to 2.25 percent of their annual wages. In contrast to the first-year increases, these lump-sum payments would not be included in the base wages used to determine pensions, overtime, and other benefits payments. Each worker also received $180 upon ratification of the settlement and a continuation of the profit-sharing program initiated in the 1982 national contract. The wage settlement also continued the COLA formula, although 24 cents of COLA-generated increases were diverted to cover the rising fringe benefits expenses.

The GM and Ford wage packages represented a compromise between the union's desire for full restoration of the traditional wage formulas and the company's desire to provide lower increases and a more direct link between future wage increases and company performance. On the one hand, the settlement restored the COLA formula intact, but on the other, it eliminated the traditional annual improvement factor. At 2.25 percent the scheduled average annual increases were somewhat lower than the traditional 3 percent AIF; they varied in size depending on the job classification; and they further modified the traditional pattern by not building all of those increases into the base rates. In effect, the parties substituted profit sharing and lump-sum increases for the traditional AIF formula wage increase. And by retaining profit sharing the parties ensured autoworkers' annual incomes would vary across the Big Three at least in part as a function of company performance.

The most innovative feature of the 1984 settlements was a new job security program, the Job Bank program, covering workers with one year or more of seniority who in the future become displaced from their jobs because of technological advances, corporate reorganizations, outsourcing, or any other negotiated productivity improvements. Under the new program workers displaced for any of those reasons would be placed into a reserve pool—the Job Bank—and receive full pay while waiting to be transferred or retrained for jobs elsewhere in GM. The company set aside a $1 billion fund for the program, which was set to last six years—three years beyond the duration of the other terms of the contract. The Job Bank was not to cover workers laid off because of reductions in sales volumes, and a labor-management committee was given the difficult task of ruling whether any given layoff is covered by the program.

The new job security program compensates workers displaced by technological change or outsourcing and thereby creates a financial disincentive for the company to initiate action that creates such displacement. But the program does not explicitly limit management's rights to outsource or to introduce any new technology, reflecting the UAW's long-standing acceptance of technological change. Nor does the program commit management to any specific future employment level. The design of the job security program is similar to that of the supplementary unemployment benefits program by compensating workers, creating financial penalties for layoffs, and relying on fund financing.

Summary. The wage adjustments made in the 1984 contracts reflected the autoworkers' reluctance to allow any further modifications in the wage rules even though employment levels were significantly below previous peaks. In particular, UAW negotiators did not want to lose the ground they had gained in earlier years. Table 2–2 shows that from 1950 to 1970 a steady ratio was maintained between autoworkers' hourly earnings and the mean earnings of all production workers in the private sector in the United States. And in the 1970s that ratio increased. Consequently, although the use of wage rules over all three decades clearly brought stability to the negotiations process, it is not as clear how the use of the wage rules affected wage outcomes. One could argue that even in the absence of the rules, autoworkers' earnings would likely have followed increases in mean private sector earnings.

Yet the autoworkers' resistance to modifying the wage rules further in the face of the massive layoffs after 1979 provides clear evidence of how the industry's wage rules did affect wage outcomes. Furthermore, the fact that the wage reductions introduced in the Big Three agreements after 1979 preserved the structure of the wage rules provides additional evidence of autoworkers' persistently strong attachment to the wage rules and illustrates how the wage rules affected the bargaining process.

More generally, the auto industry illustrates how wage-setting procedures, once adopted and used in one economic environment, are not easily modified in the face of changes in that environment. The COLA and AIF wage rules were introduced and then extended in the auto industry over a 30-year period in an economic environment of long-run growth in employment and auto sales. After so many years of their use, it was difficult for autoworkers to accept the fact that the economic environment of the 1980s might no longer countenance continuation of the rules.

The Parts Supply Sector

Concessionary bargaining was by no means the exclusive preserve of the assembly sector. The parts supply firms faced all the pressures that were impinging on the assemblers, but, worse, they lacked the financial resources of the assemblers and faced more substantial growth in their domestic non-union competitors. Because the labor relations history and the response to the new economic pressures of the supply firms have been so diverse, it is impossible to summarize briefly the course of concessionary bargaining among the parts suppliers. Instead, I will focus on recent events at the Budd and Dana Corporations, two of the largest parts suppliers in the industry.[27] The UAW is the dominant union at both of those companies, although it does not represent all production workers in their auto parts plants.[28]

Both Budd and Dana generally followed the pattern-setting agreements at GM and Ford in 1979. Then, in 1982 the two suppliers negotiated concessionary agreements with the UAW, although some of the terms represented greater concessions by the union than those negotiated at GM and Ford in the spring of that year. At Dana, for example, COLA increases scheduled for after March 1982 were eliminated (they had been only deferred at GM and Ford). The 1982 Dana contract also did not include the guaranteed income stream benefits initiated at GM and Ford.

In 1984 and 1985 the contracts negotiated at Budd and Dana began to exhibit substantial differences. The 1982 contract at Dana had been of shorter duration than the 1982 GM and Ford agreements, which enabled Dana in 1983 to negotiate an agreement that differed from the assemblers' pattern. Even though by 1983 employment at Dana had recovered to match previous levels, the company was able to negotiate a contract that included a number of unique features and overall was less favorable to its work force than the agreements negotiated at Chrysler in 1983 and at GM and Ford in 1984. A company official at Dana stated that the firm had "drifted away from the automotive-type market" and that it was "probably more appropriate that we strike out on our own" (BNA 1983a). In doing so, Dana was not unlike many other firms at the time: A change in its business strategy (a movement out of the auto parts supply industry) was leading to changes in the conduct of its labor relations.[29]

At Budd, in contrast, employment had continued to decline after 1983. As a result, 1985 contracts between the UAW and Budd included additional concessions and did not follow the 1984 pattern-setting agreements at GM and Ford. The 1985 Budd-UAW contract eliminated three-quarters of COLA increases, lowered scheduled pension increases, gave no improvements in supplementary unemployment benefit funds, and did not include the training and Job Bank programs initiated at GM and Ford.

Negotiations at these two supply companies illustrate the roles that both economic pressures and business strategies can play as determining forces in collective bargaining. As those roles changed, collective bargaining in the various supply firms diverged, no longer following a single, pattern-following path.

The Erosion of Connective Bargaining

In autos the pay concessions and the move to contingent compensation schemes that tie wages to company performance increased the variation in employment conditions across the auto assembly and supply companies. In addition, the interindustry pattern bargaining that had linked auto agreements to those in the rubber and agricultural implements industries also began to erode. (Again, see chapters 3 and 4 in this volume.) At the same time erosion of the old connective bargaining structure across the plants within the auto firms began to break down the traditional similarity in their work rules.

During the economic downturn of 1980–83 the threat of further employment losses resulting from either the further outsourcing of parts production or further reductions in production volume led labor and management to modify local work practices within both the assembly and the parts plants. At their core those modifications represented efforts to lower labor costs. The pressure for interplant work rule variation came from the same source as the pressure for intercompany pay variation: the fact that even greater employment losses would result if the tradtional rules were maintained.

More specifically, some of the work rule changes involved increases in the "effort bargain" through a tightening of production standards. Other changes included efforts to lower production costs by increasing management's ability to deploy labor flexibly, by, for example, consolidating job classifications and limiting job-bidding rights.

Work rule revisions were first sanctioned by local unions whose members had experienced severe layoffs, with informal sanctions provided by the national union. Later, in the 1982 Ford and GM contracts the national union formally empowered local unions to modify work rules when they faced a serious threat from new outsourcing by the company. The relevant wording of the Ford-UAW agreement reads:

> In the event that changes in labor costs can make a difference in the reasons for a major outsourcing action, the Union shall have 30 days from the notice [of such action] to propose any changes in work practices or any local deviation from the Collective Bargaining Agreement that might make it feasible for the company to continue to produce without being economically disadvantaged (Ford Motor Company 1982: 39).

This new clause legitimized a wider range of interplant work rule variation than had been allowed in the past, but it did so in a way that illustrates the national union's desire to preserve as much as possible of the old bargaining structure. For instance, note that the new clause appeared in a letter of understanding on outsourcing that supplemented the national agreement—not in the contract itself which delineates national and local responsibilities. In practice the narrow application of the clause did not hold. My own field interviews have revealed that employment declines became so severe after 1980 that many local unions made significant work rule changes even when there was no impending decision to outsource production.

The UAW's 1984 agreements with GM and Ford went a step further by empowering plant-level, regional, and national bipartite committees to "waive, modify or change National Agreement provisions when such actions would result in the preservation or increase of job opportunities" (General Motors Corporation 1984, 194). Nonetheless, any such exceptions to the national agreement had to be approved by the UAW leadership and by the corporate vice presidents who supervise administration of each company's contract.

As mentioned above, in many plants the modification of work rules has been instituted concomitantly with ongoing worker participation programs. Thus, along with those programs, the erosion of the connective bargaining structure has shifted the bargaining process in the auto industry away from the traditional job control unionism that characterized its postwar years.

Worker and Union Participation in Managerial Decision Making

Broader worker involvement in managerial decision making began in the auto industry through participation programs that were viewed as supplements to collective bargaining. The recent expansion of those programs and the introduction of team forms of work organization in some plants have since led, however, to a significant turning away from the traditional job control orientation of shop-floor labor relations.[30]

The earliest worker participation programs in the U.S. auto industry were the QWL programs at GM. Irving Bluestone, a former vice president of the UAW and one of the chief designers and proponents of the programs, has written that a guiding principle of QWL is that "the provisions of the national agreement and of the local agreements and practices remain inviolable" (Bluestone 1980, 40). He went on to say that where QWL is introduced, "the local [union] understands that normal collective bargaining continues" (p. 40).[31]

In the early QWL efforts those guidelines were observed by maintaining a clear and sharp separation between QWL program activities and normal collective bargaining issues and procedures—those efforts were a supplement to and not a fundamental alteration of the existing collective bargaining system. In particular, the early programs were conceived as experimental means of addressing workers' concerns with their work environment and the climate of their relations with their supervisors.[32] Labor and management were expected to continue their basic focus on contractual issues of job control.

But as the industry continued to face economic decline, the distinction between QWL activities and "normal collective bargaining" often disappeared, at the corporate level and on the shop floor. In many cases worker and union involvement became inextricably linked with other aspects of labor relations. In the process labor and management took significant steps away from their traditional job control orientation and thereby contributed even further to the erosion of the former outlines of bargaining in the industry.

At the corporate level these steps included placing Douglas Fraser, then President of the UAW, on the Chrysler Board of Directors; "mutual growth forums" at Ford and GM, joint meetings at which top managers and UAW leaders discussed such broad business decisions as investment and outsourcing; and an informal exchange of information between national officials of the company and the union. Activities initiated at the local level have included worker involvement in shop-floor quality circles and wide-ranging discussions between plant managers and union officials concerning outsourcing, new technologies, and production problems.

The range of issues subject to worker influence now varies widely across plants. In some a majority of the hourly work force participates regularly in quality circles. A more extensive form of worker involvement has been established in the 12 GM plants (including five new assembly plants) organized under the "operating team" concept, whereby there are few job classifications or in some cases only a single job title for production workers and a "pay for knowledge" compensation system that rewards workers for learning a wider variety of jobs.[33] The teams receive early warning about new technology and production plans; they can voluntarily create job rotation schemes; and they are involved in decisions on the layout of work areas. Some Ford and Chrysler plants employ variants of this team system. At the same time, however, in some other plants at the Big Three labor-management relations are much as they were years ago.

The Future

Three Alternative Paths

The auto industry (and many others in the United States) is now asking fundamental questions about the design and conduct of its industrial relations system. The answers labor and management provide to those questions will shape the future course of U.S. industrial relations. Constraining the range of choices available to the parties is the complex interconnectedness of their system. I believe the parties in the auto industry are facing three basic choices, which I will label the status quo path, the conflict path, and the reform path. Each is encouraged by different economic developments, but the unions as well as management nonetheless retain the ultimate choice of which path to follow.

The Status Quo Path. One strategic alternative for the parties in auto labor relations is to reintroduce the traditional labor relations system—wage rules, connective bargaining, and job control unionism—or, more simply, the status quo. The 1985 contract at Chrysler, which reinstated the 3 percent annual improvement factor, took an obvious step in this direction. The advantages of this route for the union (and workers) are many: The traditional system provides a clear definition of union and worker roles and formal mechanisms such as job classifications and seniority rules to protect workers from any adverse consequences of managerial discretion. The drawback of this system is that in light of the new economic environment of the world auto industry, adherence to the traditional system hampers economic performance and hastens a long-run decline in employment in the industry. The UAW's support for domestic content legislation (legislation to require that a certain percentage of the components of all cars made in the United States also be manufactured in this country) and its recent opposition to work restructuring and participation programs in some plants represent steps in the direction of this status quo path.

The Conflict Path. Confronted by the prevalence of outsourcing and by declines in employment, the UAW could instead choose a more active or militant strategy, thereby leading labor relations down a path to conflict.[34] In addition to trying to limit management's ability to outsource or introduce labor-saving technological change, the union might press for wage increases greater than the traditional formula increases. This strategy holds out the advantage of higher wages (though most likely lesser employment) for autoworkers. But since the union's bargaining power has seriously eroded with the decline in industry health and employment, the union is poorly positioned to promote this strategy. Furthermore, even if the strategy were pursued, in the end it would likely produce even more serious problems for both the union and workers than they now face. One risk is that increased militancy, by creating costly work disruptions, would encourage management to press more vigorously for outsourcing of parts, offshore production of vehicles, or technological change to avoid those costs. And the conflict path has the same drawback (and worse so) as the status quo path: It would produce a labor relations system that would make a poor fit with the new economic conditions in the world auto industry. As discussed earlier, the heightened competition in the world auto industry demands production systems that can flexibly and quickly adapt to changing product demands and technologies. But a conflict bound labor relations system would not be a flexible one.

The Reform Path. The third alternative available to the industry is to reshape the basic design of its labor relations system, following in the steps of recent innovations in relations at the Big Three. The traditional system—characterized by arms-length, formal relations between labor and management, rigid and numerous job classifications, a seniority-based layoff system, formulaic wage setting, and a high degree of standardization of employment conditions across work groups, plants, and firms—has demonstrated its limitations in the present economic environment. A reformed system could reverse those practices and at the same time allow greater worker and union participation in decision making, team forms of work organization, employment security, compensation that is contingent on worker, plant, or company performance, and diversity and experimentation across work groups and plants.

The Saturn Corporation:
Following the Reform Path

In July 1985 GM and the UAW reached tentative agreement on the design of a new labor relations system for the new GM subsidiary, the Saturn Corporation. Saturn is the first new subsidiary of GM created since 1918. The new firm will operate in a complex of plants to be built in Spring Hill, Tennessee, and produce approximately 250,000 small cars starting in 1989. The Saturn labor agreement comprises many features that follow the reform path and is therefore worthy of careful consideration.

The organizational structure of Saturn will consist of a number of committees, each of which will include worker or union representation (Saturn Corporation 1985). On the shop floor will be work units made up of 6 to 15 workers, following GM's operating team system discussed earlier. There will be few distinct job classifications, and the plan is to have workers perform a variety of tasks in their work area and also some of the planning and control tasks traditionally carried out by supervisors. At the top level of Saturn a "strategic advisory committee" will engage in long-run business planning and will include an advisor from the UAW leadership.

All employees of Saturn will be paid on a salary basis. Production workers are to receive base wages that are 80 percent of the average wage received by other GM employees and autoworkers in a set of comparison firms. Workers also can receive a bonus to reflect their work group's performance and the economic performance of the overall Saturn Corporation, among other things. The bonus could lift Saturn workers' earnings substantially above the earnings received by their counterparts in other parts of GM. The specific form the bonus will take, as well as many other features of the Saturn agreement, will be determined in subsequent negotiations and agreements.

The new labor relations system at Saturn sets out to provide a more permanent form of employment security for its work force than the traditional layoff system in the industry. Eighty percent of the Saturn work force are protected by a pledge that layoffs will not occur "except in situations arising from unforeseen or catastrophic events or severe economic conditions" (Saturn Corporation 1985). The remaining 20 percent of the work force will be "associate members" and not receive this protection. Needless to say, the practical meaning of the employment security pledge and the mechanisms to be used to decide when and if a catastrophic event or severe economic conditions have occurred have yet to be resolved.

The Saturn agreement also includes pledges to resolve labor-management disagreements through "consensus" and to allow for renegotiation of the terms of any labor-management agreement at any time the parties so desire. How those pledges will operate in practice remains to be seen. My guess is that it will be impossible to make all or even most decisions through means of consensus and impossible to avoid fixed-term agreements. Nevertheless, the spirit of the Saturn agreement represents a sharp break with traditional labor relations in the auto industry.

The motivation behind the Saturn agreement seems to be to create a more flexible (and hence informal) labor relations system and one in which direct worker involvement in decision making contributes to cost reduction and ready adaptability to change. In particular, the need for flexibility in labor relations stems from Saturn's plan to use modular production techniques. The plan is for parts (many to be produced with mass production techniques) to be assembled into various modules and the modules then recombined or altered when market demands or technology changes. Yet, as with the specific operation of the labor relations system, the precise technologies and production methods to be used in Saturn remain to be seen.

The decision by the Executive Board of the UAW to approve the Saturn agreement illustrates the union's willingness to experiment with radical reforms in labor relations practices when those reforms promise to result in a clear gain in employment. The promise lies in the fact that it was the plan to institute the innovative labor relations practices itself that helped convince GM management to build Saturn in the United States rather than to build it abroad or to depend even more on Japanese or Korean small cars marketed by GM.

The plans for Saturn thus represent a significant change in strategy by the UAW and GM management. Saturn will not start production until 1989, however; and it will take a number of years to develop clear evidence on the nature and effectiveness of the new labor relations practices.

The more pressing issue confronting labor and management in the industry (and their counterparts throughout U.S. industries) is whether they can reform labor relations in the *existing plants* along the lines of Saturn and other recent workplace experiments. Here, it is important to note that the Executive Board of the UAW was willing to endorse Saturn to only a limited extent, and the U.S. labor movement as a whole is still engaged in a keen debate over the wisdom of adopting reforms like those in the Saturn agreement. The UAW Executive Board approved the Saturn agreement only after a letter was appended to the agreement specifying that the union "views Saturn as a special project designed to maintain small car production" and that the UAW does not consider the Saturn labor agreement as a "precedent regarding the Union's policy at any other facility" (Saturn Corporation 1985).

A number of other labor leaders have already voiced their strong disapproval of the Saturn agreement. Some have expressed concern that Saturn's reform and similar ones elsewhere eliminate the need and role for a union.[35] They view the various committees in Saturn's organizational structure as a coopted rather than a true form of worker participation in decision making.[36] For example, in his opening speech to the 1985 Canadian autoworkers convention, President Robert White warned that the Saturn agreement was a dangerous step toward enterprise (and weak) unions (CAW 1985, 39). Victor Reuther, brother of the late Walter Reuther, has warned that by linking worker compensation to economic performance, Saturn will bring a return to the piecework system (Serrin 1985).

In the face of the American auto industry's strong financial performance from mid-1983 through 1986, many national union leaders could postpone making a public judgment on the Saturn reforms. But the fundamental nature of the economic restructuring occurring in the industry worldwide and the associated increase in international competition make it likely that within only a few years the American auto industry will again be witness to substantial layoffs and plant closings. At that point union leaders will have to decide whether they are willing to redesign labor relations or pursue the status quo, with steps toward conflict when the pressures grow severe enough.

The Japanese-American Plants: Further Pressure to Reform

A significant new pressure for labor relations reform in the auto industry is making itself known in the auto plants operated or being constructed in the United States by Japanese parent companies. Those plants all use team forms of work organization, involve production workers in production decision making to some degree, and rely on a labor relations system that looks more like the Saturn style rather than the traditional auto pattern (although these "Japanese-American" plants lack the formal role for union representation on strategic planning committees called for in the Saturn agreement). As discussed earlier, the number of plants constructed or planned by Japanese companies is substantial and includes some plants to be owned jointly by an American auto company and a Japanese auto company. By the year 1990, if current plans are carried out, approximately 1.4 million vehicles will roll off the lines of these plants—a figure that represents over 17 percent of the total U.S. production of cars in 1984 of 8 million, or over 23 percent of U.S. car production of some 6 million cars in 1982, a bad year for the industry. Again, Saturn alone is projected to assemble approximately 250,000 vehicles. Together, these figures mean that by the early 1990s the UAW will be confronted by the fact that almost 25 percent of the cars assembled in the United States are being made in plants whose labor relations practices differ markedly from the traditional system in the industry. (This percentage is a conservative estimate because it excludes other plants inside GM, Chrysler, and Ford operating with similarly reformed labor relations practices.) Thus, even if the overall economic health of the American auto industry continues to stabilize, it will be increasingly difficult for the UAW to avoid pressures to redesign labor relations practices at the Big Three. Or at the very least, those pressures will force national and local union leaders throughout the industry to come to a decision on the path they prefer for labor relations.

In general, leaders of the national unions in this country have long maintained an ambivalent attitude toward increased worker and union participation in business decision making (see Kochan, Katz, and Mower 1984). The dilemma facing many union leaders in the mid-1980s was that even if they favored increasing union and worker participation, management would agree to participation schemes only as part of a broader package of labor relations reforms. Furthermore, union leaders were often unsure of the implications of that broader package of reforms.

Industrial Adjustments: Two Views

We can interpret recent economic pressures on the world auto industry in one of two very different lights. On the one hand, the recent pressures, in particular, those for flexibility, can be viewed as a reflection of the auto industry's participation in a more general movement toward flexible manufacturing. Piore and Sabel (1984) have claimed that the market economies are in the grip of a basic transformation away from mass production forms of work and corporate organization and toward "flexible specialization." They argue that heightened macroeconomic volatility, the shift to specialized and "niche" markets, and microelectronics have all combined to induce that transformation. The important implication for labor relations of Piore and Sabel's theory is their corollary that flexible specialization will be most successful in plants where workers have learned a variety of skills and are granted a high degree of autonomy in the production process. Exhibiting some signs of both these economic pressures and these responses, the auto industry could easily be cited as an example of this transformation. Following this line of argument, the reforms under way in auto labor relations illustrate how greater worker participation in decision making is an outgrowth as well as a necessary concomitant of flexible production techniques.

On the other hand, a very different interpretation is offered by those who view the recent changes in the auto industry as reflecting an extension of, not a transformation away from, mass production techniques. According to this perspective the auto industry is following the course predicted by "product life cycle" theories, having now matured to the point that labor costs are the critical factor in industry competition.[37] Consonant with these theories is Braverman's (1974) viewpoint that management introduces technology for the express purpose of deskilling the work force, leaving workers less powerful and management more in control of production. Together these theories lead to an interpretation of recent concessionary bargaining as simply management's latest effort to speed up the production process and lower production costs at labor's expense. The proponents of the deskilling view agree, for example, that there is some sign of recentralization in present-day auto manufacturing, but they believe this recentralization pales in comparison to the industry's efforts to use outsourcing or multiple parts sourcing as a device to undercut labor's bargaining power.[38] The deskilling position holds that it is the "world car" strategy in one variant or another, and not flexible specialization, that represents the likely future course of auto manufacturing. Moreover, the consequence of any further technological change will be a further deskilling of the work force as production techniques are even further refined to control the production process and limit workers' influence.

The two viewpoints are therefore diametrically opposed. Whereas the flexible specialization theorists envision the emergence of adaptable production techniques that require and thus foster worker autonomy and skills, the product life cycle theorists, along with Braverman, would predict the extension of mass and world car production techniques that require docile and deskilled workers.

Conclusions

My own view is that the auto industry represents a case closer to the flexible specialization story than the deskilling scenario. I interpret the Saturn agreement, the recent market shifts within the world auto industry, and the shop-floor experiments in worker participation in decision making as evidence that the industry is moving (or at least trying to move) toward a manufacturing and labor relations system that requires a much higher degree of flexibility than the traditional industry practices. Furthermore, the evidence available seems to point to an overall increase in worker skill levels, not deskilling, and to a greater degree of real worker participation in decision making. I have observed several of the new team systems, for example, and found that the teams themselves are a device through which production workers learn a variety of tasks, many of which demand that they broaden their skills. Craft workers also are being asked to learn a broader variety of skills, often including some aspect of computer programming or sophisticated electronic repair. Although there are some cases of jobs being deskilled in the auto industry, and although new technologies generally do require fewer workers, I have seen no concrete evidence of a broad deskilling of the auto work force.

Looking at all the aspects of labor relations in autos, what is most interesting about the industry is that labor relations appears to be so critical to its future economic success. The evolving nature of production techniques and labor relations in industry is food for thought precisely because it provides so much rich information on the nature of developments in the broader economy. Scholars will long be debating whether it is deskilling or flexible specialization that is taking place, just as they will continue to disagree over whether worker participation experiments amount to real participation or subtle cooptation. In so debating, these scholars will look to the auto industry to support their claims.

Notes

1. The "30 and out" retirement systems allow workers to retire and receive pension benefits after 30 years of service no matter what the employee's age.

2. The industry is defined here as code 371 in the Standard Industrial Classification. The data are from U.S. Department of Labor (see under "various years").

3. This figure includes the following: 1,117,000 in vehicle and parts manufacturing; 2,740,000 in automotive sales and servicing; 3,100,000 in truck driving and warehousing; 362,000 in passenger transportation; 456,000 in petroleum refining and production; and 278,000 in road construction. These data are derived from U.S. Department of Transportation (1982, table 17).

4. See, for example, Abernathy, Clark, and Kantrow (1981) and Altshuler et al. (1984).

5. These shifts in the American product market can be traced to a worldwide erosion of distinct national auto markets (Altshuler et al. 1984).

6. See Piore and Sabel (1984) for a more elaborate discussion of these effects of macroeconomic and structural changes.

7. For a description of labor relations and work organization practices in the Japanese auto industry, see Cole (1971; 1979).

8. In the case of Renault and American Motors the coproduction arrangement

took the form of co-ownership. By 1986 Renault owned 47 percent of American Motors.

9. Another reason for locating in the Kentucky-Tennessee region is its convenience as a distribution point.

10. For an analysis of the internal political operation of the UAW, see Stieber (1962).

11. For lively accounts of the early history of the UAW, see Reuther (1976) and Howe and Widick (1949). An interesting account of the UAW during World War II appears in Lichtenstein (1982).

12. The history of collective bargaining in the independent companies over the 1950s is recounted in MacDonald (1963).

13. The history of wage setting in the U.S. auto industry is discussed in more detail in Harbison (1950), Reder (1949), Ross (1949), and Katz (1985).

14. Chronologies of postwar bargaining in the U.S. auto industry can be found in BNA (see under "various years") and U.S. Department of Labor (1969).

15. Further discussion of the "structured" nature of fringe benefit determination is provided in Katz (1985, 22–27).

16. See Kochan, Katz, and McKersie (1986, 47–80) for a discussion of the growth of the nonunion sector and its general effects on unionized plants.

17. Job control unionism is not synonymous with "business unionism," which refers to the political philosophy of the labor movement. Some labor movements, such as the Japanese, could be characterized as business unionism movements but not as relying on job control unionism.

18. Katz (1985, 105–32), which gives further evidence of the variation in industrial relations performance across plants and the impact of this variation on the economic performance of the plants.

19. Lichtenstein (1985) provides an analysis of the postwar political agenda of the UAW.

20. As with the earlier era, it is important to realize that events on the shop floor in autos at that time were similar to those in many other unionized industries in the United States.

21. These figures on grievances and local union demands come from unpublished internal files of General Motors Corporation.

22. By 1983 Ford had closed seven major plants and GM, five.

23. In January 1982 Douglas Fraser, then president of the UAW, and Roger Smith, chairman of the board of GM, reached a tentative agreement that any later negotiated wage concessions would be linked to reductions in the price of GM cars. This agreement later broke down, but it does provide further illustration of the union's and workers' desire to make an explicit link between pay concessions and the employment stimulated by cost and price reductions. The tentative agreement is described in BNA (1982b).

24. The agreements limited each company's potential total liability under the guaranteed income stream program to $175 million at GM and $45 million at Ford.

25. An interesting feature of those programs is that they provided training and tuition assistance for programs that place laid-off auto workers into jobs *outside* the auto industry. For details of the Ford program, see UAW-Ford National Development and Training Center (1982).

26. The failure of most of those experiments is discussed in Katz (1985, 164).

27. The largest supply firms are the Budd, Dana, Rockwell, Eaton, and Bendix (Allied) Corporations.

28. At both Dana and Budd union organizing drives at their nonunion plants have at times been a source of much controversy. At one point, in the aftermath of a union organizing drive held at one of its plants in 1980, Dana was ordered by a court injunction to follow the neutrality pledge it had signed with the UAW in 1976. See BNA (1982a).

29. For more on the relationship between business and labor relations strategy, see Kochan, Katz, and McKersie (1986).

30. For a discussion of how developments in this country compare with those in auto plants in West Germany, Italy, and the United Kingdom, see Katz and Sabel (1985).

31. Bluestone has since argued that the scope of issues addressed in worker participation programs should be broadened to include changes in work organization and strategic business decisions. See, for example, Bluestone (1986).

32. An evaluation of the impact of these QWL programs on industrial relations and economic performance at the plant level appears in Katz, Kochan, and Gobeille (1983); Katz, Kochan, and Weber (1985); and Katz (1985, 105–32).

33. The pay-for-knowledge schemes typically have six steps; workers receive roughly 10 cents per hour more as they move up each step by proving competence in a wider number of jobs in the work area. In one plant the steps were (1) one job, (2) three jobs, (3) six jobs, (4) nine jobs, (5)) all jobs in the work area, and (6) assistant team coordinator.

34. The option here is to follow a strategy similar to the one used by the British mineworkers in their well-publicized strike of 1984.

35. Peter Kelley, president of UAW Local 160 and a frequent critic of official union policies, argued that in Saturn the union was "climbing into bed" with management and abrogating its duty as representative of the workers (*Business Week* 1985b, 65). It was Kelley who first leaked the Saturn agreement to the press as part of his effort to rally local union leaders to oppose endorsement of the agreement by the UAW's executive board.

36. See Katz and Sabel (1985) for a discussion of the issues worker participation programs raise regarding the role of unions.

37. For a discussion of product life cycle theories, see Wells (1972).

38. For the argument that recent technological change has produced deskilling, with frequent reference to evidence from the U.S. auto industry, see Shaiken (1984).

References

Abernathy, William J., Kim B. Clark, and Alan M. Kantrow. 1981. The New Industrial Competition. *Harvard Business Review* (September-October): 68–81.

Altshuler, Alan, et al. 1984. *The Future of the Automobile.* Cambridge: MIT Press.

Bluestone, Irving. 1980. How Quality of Worklife Projects Work for the United Auto Workers. *Monthly Labor Review* (July): 40–41.

———. 1986. Changes in U.S. Labor-Management Relations. In *Proceedings of* the *Thirty-Eighth Annual Meeting, December 28–30, 1985, New York,* ed. Barbara D. Dennis, 165–70. Madison, Wis.: Industrial Relations Research Association.

BNA (Bureau of National Affairs). 1980. Ford Motor, EEOC Settle Nationwide Job Bias Action. *Daily Labor Report,* November 25, A-3, A-4.

———. 1982a. Auto Workers Held Entitled to Enforcement of Neutrality Pact with Dana Corporation. *Daily Labor Report,* June 8, A-3, A-4.

———. 1982b. General Motors Accepts Union Proposal to Pass Labor Costs Savings to Consumers. *Daily Labor Report,* January 12, A-11.

———. 1983a. Autoworkers Accept New Contract at Dana as Parties Sever Link with Auto Pattern. *Daily Labor Report,* December 12, A-1.

———. 1983b. EEOC, General Motors Sign $42 Million Agreement to Settle 10-Year-Old Charge. *Daily Labor Report,* October 10, A-3–A-5.

———. Various years. Collective Bargaining Negotiations and Contracts: Wage Patterns. Washington, D.C.

Braverman, Harry. 1974. *Labor and Monopoly Capital.* New York: Monthly Review Press.

Business Week. 1964. Brush Fires Plague Auto Industry. November 14, p. 54.

———. 1984. Executive Pay: The Top Earners. May 7, pp. 88–95.

———. 1985a. Detroit Raises the Ante For Parts Suppliers. October 14, p. 94–97.

———. 1985b. How Power Will Be Balanced on Saturn's Shop Floor. August 5, p. 65.

Buss, Dale D., and John Koten. 1983. GM-Toyota Proposed Venture May Face Output Delays as It Awaits FTC Ruling. *Wall Street Journal.* September 23, p. 1.

Cole, Robert E. 1971. *Japanese Blue Collar.* Berkeley: University of California Press.

———. 1979. *Work, Mobility and Participation.* Berkeley: University of California Press.

Ford Motor Company. 1979. Agreements Between Ford Motor Company and the UAW. Detroit.

———. 1982. Letters of Understanding Between the Ford Motor Company and the UAW. Detroit: February 13.

General Motors Corporation. 1984. Agreement Between General Motors Corporation and the UAW. Detroit.

Harbison, Fredrick H. 1950. The General Motors–United Auto Workers Agreement of 1950. *Journal of Political Economy* 58 (October): 397–411.

Harbison, Fredrick H., and Robert Dubin. 1947. *Patterns of Union-Management Relations.* Chicago: Science Research Associates.

Harris, Howell John. 1982. *The Right to Manage.* Madison: University of Wisconsin Press.

Herding, Richard. 1972. *Job Control and Union Structure: A Study on Plant-Level Industrial Conflict in the United States.* Rotterdam: Rotterdam University Press.

Howe, Irving, and B.J. Widick. 1949. *The UAW and Walter Reuther.* New York: Random House.

Katz, Harry C. 1985. *Shifting Gears: Changing Labor Relations in the U.S. Automobile Industry.* Cambridge: MIT Press.

Katz, Harry C., Thomas P. Kochan, and Kenneth R. Gobeille. 1983. Industrial Relations Performance. Economic Performance, and QWL Programs: An Interplant Analysis. *Industrial and Labor Relations Review* 37 (October): 3–17.

Katz, Harry C., Thomas A. Kochan, and Mark Weber. 1985. Assessing the Effects of Industrial Relations Systems and Efforts to Improve the Quality of Working Life on Organizational Effectiveness, *Academy of Management Journal* 28 (September): 509–26.

Katz, Harry C., and Charles F. Sabel. 1979. Wage Rules: A Theory of Wage Determination. Paper presented at the Ninety-Second Annual Meeting of the American Economic Society, Atlanta, Ga., December, 28–30.

———. 1985. Industrial Relations and Industrial Adjustment in the Car Industry. *Industrial Relations* 24 (Fall): 295–315.

Kochan, Thomas A., Harry C. Katz, and Robert B. McKersie. 1986. *The Transformation of American Industrial Relations.* New York: Basic Books.

Kochan, Thomas A., Harry C. Katz, and Nancy Mower. 1984. *Worker Participation and American Unions: Threat or Opportunity?* Kalamazoo: W.E. Upjohn Institute for Employment Research.

Kuhn, James W. 1961. *Bargaining and Grievance Settlement.* New York: Columbia University Press.

Levinson, Harold M. 1960. Pattern Bargaining: A Case Study of the Automobile Workers. *Quarterly Journal of Economics* 74 (May): 296–317.

Lichtenstein, Nelson. 1980. Auto Worker Militancy and the Structure of Factory Life, 1937–1955. *Journal of American History* 67 (September): 335–53.

———. 1982. *Labor's War at Home.* London: Cambridge University Press.

———. 1985. UAW Bargaining Strategy and Shop-Floor Conflict, 1946–1970. *Industrial Relations* 24 (Fall): 360–81.

MacDonald, Robert M. 1963. *Collective Bargaining in the Automobile Industry.* New Haven: Yale University Press.

McPherson, William H. 1940. *Labor Relations in the Automobile Industry.* Washington, D.C.: Brookings Institution.

National Automobile, Aerospace and Agricultural Implement Workers Union of Canada (CAW). 1985. Unpublished transcript of Robert White's speech to the UAW of Canada National Convention, September 4, in author's possession.

Piore, Michael J. 1982. American Labor and the Industrial Crisis. *Challenge* 25 (March-April): 5–11.

Piore, Michael J., and Charles F. Sabel. 1984. *The Second Industrial Divide.* New York: Basic Books.

Reder, Melvin W. 1949. The Structure of the 1948 General Motors Agreement. *Review of Economics and Statistics* 31 (February): 7–14.

Reuther, Victor G. 1976. *The Brothers Reuther and the Story of the UAW: A Memoir.* Boston: Houghton Mifflin.

Ross, Arthur M. 1949. The General Motors Wage Agreement of 1948. *Review of Economic and Statistics* 31 (February): 1–7.

Rothchild, Emma. 1973. *Paradise Lost: The Decline of the Auto-Industrial Age.* New York: Random House.

Saturn Corporation. 1985. Memorandum of Agreement Between Saturn Corporation and UAW. Detroit: General Motors Corporation, July.

Selekman, Benjamin M., et al. 1964. *Problems in Labor Relations,* 3d ed. New York: McGraw-Hill.

Serrin, William. 1985. Saturn Labor Pact Assailed by a UAW Founder. *New York Times,* October 28, p. 18.

Shaiken, Harley. 1984. *Work Transformed.* New York: Holt, Rinehart & Winston.

Stieber, Jack. 1962. *Governing the UAW.* New York: Wiley.

Strauss, George. 1962. The Shifting Power Balance in the Plant. *Industrial Relations* 2 (October): 65–96.

UAW-Ford National Development and Training Center. 1982. Establishing a Local UAW-Ford Employee Development and Training Program—A Guide for Local Unions and Management. Detroit: September.

Ulman, Lloyd. 1974. Connective Bargaining and Competitive Bargaining. *Scottish Journal of Political Economy* 21 (June): 97–109.

U.S. Department of Labor, Bureau of Labor Statistics. 1963. Industrial Wage Survey: Part I—Motor Vehicles, Part II—Motor Vehicle Parts. Bulletin 1393, (April), Washington, D.C.: GPO.

———. 1969. Wage Chronology—General Motors Corporation, 1939–68. Bulletin 1532. Washington, D.C.: GPO.

———. 1971. Industry Wage Survey: Motor Vehicles and Parts, April 1969. Washington, D.C.: GPO.

———. 1976. Industry Wage Survey: Motor Vehicles and Parts, 1973–1974, Bulletin 1912, Washington, D.C.: GPO.

———. 1979a. Collective Bargaining in the Motor Vehicle and Equipment Industry. Report 574. Washington, D.C.: GPO.

———. 1979b. Ford Motor Wage Chronology, Bulletin, 1994, Washington, D.C.: GPO.

———. 1983. *Handbook of Labor Statistics.* Washington, D.C.: GPO.

———. 1985. Industry Wage Survey: Motor Vehicles and Parts, May 1983, Bulletin 2223. Washington, D.C.: GPO, March.

———. Various years. *Employment and Earnings.* Washington, D.C.: GPO.

U.S. Department of Transportation. 1982. *National Transportation Statistics,* Washington, D.C.: GPO.

Weber, Arnold. 1961. Introduction. In *The Structure of Collective Bargaining,* ed. A. Weber. New York: Glencoe.

Wells, Louis T. 1972. *The Product Life Cycle and International Trade.* Boston: Division of Research, Graduate School of Business Administration, Harvard University.

3
Agricultural Machinery

Ronald L. Seeber

The 1979 round of negotiations between the International Harvester Corporation (IH) and the International Union, United Automobile, Agricultural Implement and Aerospace Workers of America (UAW) foreshadowed events that were soon to become routine in bargaining between the giant U.S. manufacturing corporations and the major industrial unions. IH sought UAW concessions over a host of work rules that had been secured by the union in a more permissive bargaining environment. Company managers desired significantly more freedom to employ UAW members as they saw fit, and they sought to achieve that freedom by removing contractual restrictions on shift scheduling, transfers between jobs, and overtime work. The UAW firmly rejected those demands, and the result was a six-month strike. By the time the strike ended, the bottom had begun to fall out of the farm machinery market, and since then the company has never fully recovered. At the time, the strike was the longest the UAW had ever waged at a major company during its 43-year history. That dubious record would not stand for long, however: Only three years later the UAW's 36,000 members at the Caterpillar Corporation stayed on strike for 205 days.

During an era when each year brought a new postwar low in private sector strike activity, two successive rounds of negotiations within the same industry resulted in conflicts of record duration. This anomaly alone makes the agricultural machinery industry a sector worthy of close scrutiny by observers of industrial relations. The industry's recent history of bargaining presents a pattern that should be familiar in content to students of the current era of labor concessions. At the same time, however, the causes of the UAW concessions in this industry are strikingly different from those in other industries, such as autos, steel, air transport, and meat packing. Competition

I would like to thank the participants in the Pierce Memorial Conference; Dick Shoemaker and Frank Musick of the UAW; and James P. Begin of Rutgers University for their helpful comments on an earlier draft of this chapter. David Walsh provided excellent research assistance, and Melissa Harrington and Joyce Orzino ably provided typing services. Any remaining errors are my own.

from lower cost imports has not been an insignificant challenge to the industry, but its impact has so far been minimal. Nor has any significant nonunion sector arisen in agricultural machinery to provide domestic competition because the capital expenditures necessary to establish a farm machinery plant discourage new entrants to the industry. Instead, it is almost solely the continuing crisis in the farm economy that has caused the decline in the machinery sector and prevented any recovery in agricultural machinery. Thus, any return to bargaining in a more permissive economic environment seems unlikely. Future rounds of negotiations look to be just as interesting, and potentially conflict-ridden, as the results in the late 1970s and early 1980s.

Before examining industrial relations in the industry in more detail, I should offer a note on terminology. Although most of the chapters in this volume describe industries clearly defined by their product or an occupational title, the industry in question here is not as simply defined. In fact, the industry goes by three separate names, depending on the interested party. Business services and the business press typically refer to the industry as the agricultural *equipment* industry, whereas publications that categorize industries by the Standard Industrial Classification (SIC) system refer to it as the agricultural *machinery* industry. Finally, the union that has organized the industry, the UAW, carries on its collective bargaining activities with the employers in this sector through its agricultural *implements* division. For our purposes in this chapter *agricultural machinery* will be used as equivalent to the other terms.

The Bargaining Environment

The Product Market and Industrial Organization

The U.S. agricultural machinery industry manufactures equipment and implements for use in agricultural production in this country and abroad. Industry products are classified in three basic categories. First are multipurpose farm tractors; second are combines used solely in harvesting one kind of crop, be it corn, soybeans, cotton, or others; and third is a wide range of implements used either in combination with the tractors or combines, or separately. Firms in the industry are defined as either full line, meaning that they produce all three of the categories of farm machinery, or long line, meaning that they specialize in one category or only a subcategory of farm machinery. The number of full-line farm machinery firms is small and declining; the number specializing in only one or a few machines in a single category is somewhat larger, but still small. The bulk of the firms therefore are long-line firms, although the full-line firms dominate the market.

The industrial organization of the farm machinery industry is therefore similar to that of other large, capital-intensive, manufacturing industries in the United States, in which the few major corporations accounting for a large proportion of the goods sold within the industry. This has not always been the case, however. In the nineteenth century individual entrepreneurs and small firms developed a single product, and companies proliferated to produce and market that product. The turn of the twentieth century marked the beginnings of the consolidation of the industry into "monopolistic combinations under single corporate control of the principal companies previously making particular lines of implements" (U.S. Federal Trade Commission 1948, 33). For example, between 1902, the year it was formed, and 1946 IH purchased 15 specialty companies that produced either tractors or another line of farm machinery. Between 1911 and 1947 John Deere acquired 16 other firms, and Allis-Chalmers Manufacturing Company bought 15 other firms over the years 1901–1938 (U.S. Federal Trade Commission 1948, 35–49). Today the product market is dominated by the competition among these full-line conglomerates, challenged only weakly by the few small, specialty product manufacturers that continue to exist.

Table 3–1 lists the principal manufacturers of farm machinery as of the late 1970s. The structure of the industry has been remarkably stable since its consolidation came to a halt after World War II. The three largest employers are International Harvester,[1] Caterpillar, and John Deere. Those firms not only dominate the product market but also set the pattern for the collective bargaining that takes place throughout the rest of the industry. (The UAW traditionally targets one of these three for the pattern-setting negotiations in each round of bargaining in the industry.) Although many of the other firms have played a significant role in the historical development of the industry and its industrial relations practices, it is the pattern setters that will be the focus of our attention in this chapter.

The 1980s have witnessed a near-collapse of what previously in this century had been a healthy and ever-growing industry. Table 3–2 presents figures on unit sales and dollar value sales of two- and four-wheel drive tractors over the years 1979–84. The all-time peak of farm machinery sales (in dollar value of shipments) was in 1979 when the industry sold almost 140,000 tractors. This number dropped precipitously during the early 1980s to just under 67,000 units in 1984, a fall of over 50 percent. The figures for the sales of combines and balers show an even starker decline in the industry. Combine sales plummeted from a peak of just over 32,000 units in 1979 to just over 11,000 in 1984, a decline of almost two-thirds. Baler sales declined by over 50 percent as well. Data on the sales of other types of farm machinery

Table 3–1
The Major Producers of Agricultural Machinery, 1977

		Product	
Company	Tractors	Other Agricultural Machinery	Other Products
Allis-Chalmers	x	x	Power and construction equipment
Caterpillar	x	x	Power and equipment equipment
Clark Equipment		x	Construction equipment
John Deere	x	x	Construction equipment
FMC		x	Power and construction equipment
Ford	x		Automobiles
Hesston		x	—
International Harvester[a]	x	x	Construction equipment, trucks
Hoehring		x	Construction equipment
Massey-Ferguson	x	x	Power and construction equipment
Sperry-Rand (New Holland)	x	x	Diversified conglomerate
Steiger Tractor	x		—
Tenneco (J.I. Case)	x	x	Diversified conglomerate
White Consolidated	x	x	Power and construction equipment

Source: *Standard and Poor's* (1977, M17).
[a]International Harvester sold its farm equipment division to Tenneco's J.I. Case Division in January, 1985. Harvester also changed its name to Navistar in 1986.

are not as easily compared, but numerous industry observers have suggested they tell the same story.

The debilitated market for agricultural machinery is inexorably linked to the crash of the farm economy in the 1980s. Throughout the previous decade, as commodity prices in the United States rose and land values spiraled, farmers had an incentive to invest in farm machinery as well as the cash to do so. But in the early 1980s both of those trends dramatically reversed. Exports of U.S. commodities first leveled off and then declined in the early part of the 1980s, depressing commodity prices. Land values were quick to follow. Together these events left farm operators without either the need for new equipment or the means to purchase it.

Coupled with this decline in demand has been a shift toward greater demand for smaller tractors, which are exclusively imports. By 1977 U.S.

Table 3–2
Unit Sales and Dollar Value Sales of U.S. Farm Equipment, 1979–84

Year	Tractor Sales (thousands)			Value of Tractor Sales (millions)	Combine Sales (thousands)	Baler Sales (thousands)	Net U.S. Farm Equipment Sales (millions)
	Two-Wheel Drive over 40 hp	Four-Wheel Drive	Total				
1979	127.5	11.5	139.0	$3,425.0	32.2	18.8	$11,748
1980	108.4	10.9	119.3	3,183.3	25.8	14.0	10,639
1981	94.1	9.7	103.8	3,479.3	26.8	13.6	10,221
1982	70.4	6.8	77.2	2,433.4	16.2	8.9	7,981
1983	66.2	5.1	71.3	2,212.6	12.8	9.0	7,617
1984	62.7	4.0	66.7	—	11.4	8.3	—

Source: *Standard and Poor's* (1985, 58).

manufacturers had moved the production of all small tractors (under 40 horsepower) overseas (*Standard and Poor's* 1984, 537). Thus, the U.S. farm machinery market, which as recently as 1975 had been a net exporter of almost $1.8 billion in goods, became a net importer by 1983. Industry analysts give no suggestion that this trend is likely to reverse itself in the near future.

The farm machinery economy shows almost no sign of improving any time soon. It does seem likely that the continuing debt crisis facing farmers will force them, at such time as their income improves, either to retire or to reduce their debt rather than invest in new equipment. Thus, any future recovery in the U.S. farm economy will take some time to bring forth a revival of the agricultural machinery industry.

The Labor Market

It was only natural for the UAW to have organized the agricultural machinery industry in addition to the auto industry. The production processes and the jobs in the two industries have many parallels.

Farm machinery factories are large and often fully integrated, requiring from outside the facility only the steel and other raw materials necessary to produce cast iron; all the parts necessary for assembly are manufactured in house. The long and continuous production process, like that in auto plants, takes place in three separate locations in the plant. First, the foundry forges cast iron and molds engine blocks and transmissions. Second, the machine shop, which employs the most workers in the operation, prepares parts for assembly. The third stage of production occurs in the subassembly and assembly lines, which usually employ the smallest number of workers in the complex. Although the factories may comprise only one or two of these divisions, most do not specialize—they comprise all three—and it is here that they differ from auto plants. Very few engage in only one step in the process.

Production facilities in the industry are therefore extremely large, by any industry's standard. John Deere Corporation, for example, has at times employed over 15,000 workers at its Waterloo, Iowa, site, the largest tractor-making facility in the world. In the 1950s McCormick Works (which later became International Harvester) had several plants of the same magnitude in the Chicago area. Even the smallest plants in the industry employ more than 1,000 workers. In the 1979 bargaining round John Deere reportedly employed over 30,000 UAW members at only nine sites; Caterpillar, nearly 40,000 UAW members at only ten sites; and International Harvester, some 35,000 employees at fifteen sites.

Because the production process is highly integrated, the skills required of their workers are diverse. Roughly 15 percent of the members of the large, companywide bargaining units work in skilled trades that are equivalents of the traditional building trades occupations of electrician, plumber, and carpenter. The remaining 85 percent work in a broad range of occupational categories ranging from unskilled laborer to highly skilled machinists and pattern makers. The proportional mix of skilled and unskilled workers has remained fairly stable since World War II.

Over the years the large plants have achieved economies of scale that, as mentioned, have discouraged other (nonunion) firms from entering the industry. At the same time, the existing firms are limited in their own ability to restructure their output: Moving a plant's operations (for example, to a less unionized region of the country) is generally out of the question, and closing a plant can mean eliminating an entire product line of the firm (*Standard and Poor's* 1984, 540). Thus, the primary threat to employment, at least in the major farm machinery firms, is neither nonunion competition nor plant closings, as in many industries, but simply the economic health of the industry as a whole.

Thus, the recent labor market in the industry mirrors the condition of the product market; it is now exhibiting its greatest relative decline since the birth of farm machine technology. As shown in table 3–3 overall employment in the industry reached an all-time peak in 1979 with an annual average of over 182,000. Production employment also reached a peak that year with an annual average of over 129,000 workers. The decline shown in the later years for the industry as a whole was also experienced at the three major employers. At the opening of bargaining in 1979 the UAW represented an estimated 29,000 employees at John Deere; 40,000 at Caterpillar; and 35,000 at International Harvester (BNA 1979). By 1983 Deere employed only 17,500 workers; Caterpillar, only 24,000; and at International Harvester the situation was even graver. In late 1983, when the company succeeded in negotiating a group incentive plan covering 3,200 workers at three plants in order to stave off plant shutdowns, International Harvester's worldwide employment had declined from over 90,000 just four years earlier to just over 30,000 employees, and the number of those represented by the UAW dropped to 12,000 (BNA 1983b).

The Legal Environment

The process of collective bargaining in the agricultural machinery industry is governed by the National Labor Relations Act (NLRA) and its amendments. Although there were numerous attempts to unionize the McCormick Works in the late 1800s, and its successor International Harvester Corporation in the early years of this century, none succeeded in establishing any permanent organization until the passage of the NLRA in 1935. Workers in the industry were not to realize any true gains from unionism until after the NLRA took effect and the Congress of Industrial Organizations (CIO) was formed, in

Table 3-3
Average Annual Employment in the Agricultural Machinery Industry, 1979-84
(in thousands)

Year	All Employees	Production Workers	UAW-Deere	UAW-Caterpillar	UAW-Harvester
1979	182.3	129.2	29	40	35
1980	169.1	115.8	—	—	—
1981	155.3	103.9	—	—	—
1982	122.7	79.1	27	36	20
1983	108.1	70.2	17.5	24	12
1984	116.5	77.8	—	—	13

Source: *Employment and Earnings* (various years), under SIC code 352. Company employment figures are derived from reports in the *Daily Labor Report, Business Week,* and the *Wall Street Journal.*

1938. Students of industrial relations are familiar with the coverage and policies developed by the National Labor Relations Board to implement the provisions of the act and they need not be expanded upon here.

The Parties

Unions

Although there are some small craft unions at some plants of the major companies, it is fair to say that there is only one important union in agricultural machinery—the UAW. The union has succeeded in maintaining a high level of organization within the industry; data collected between 1968 and 1972 revealed that an average of 57 percent of all workers in the industry (SIC coded 352) were unionized (Freeman and Medoff 1979, 150). The same sampling showed 77 percent of the industry's production workers were unionized. Data collected throughout the decade of the 1970s revealed some slippage in that figure, however, to between 47 and 48 percent of all workers (Kokkelenberg and Sockell 1985, 524). All signs point to the fact that most of the nonunion production workers are at the smaller firms in the industry.

The history of union organization in this industry is, like that of the U.S. labor movement as a whole, a series of advances and retreats until the establishment of "permanent unionism" following World War II. In his history of labor relations at International Harvester, Ozanne (1967, 5) traces the rise of trade unions at the McCormick Harvester Machine Company during the Civil War inflation of 1862. Molders engaged in at least six strikes at McCormick during the war. The fortunes of the union rose and fell during the following twenty years, until it was crushed during the period following the

1886 Haymarket affair in Chicago. Unionism at the newly named International Harvester Corporation strongly revived in 1903 and again in 1919 (Ozanne 1967, 44–70, 96–103). But works councils designed to channel worker discontent away from independent unionism were established during World War I forestalling any organizing success at the company until the mid-1930s. It was through efforts by the newly formed CIO in 1936 that formal negotiations, fixed-term contracts, and permanent representation of workers by unions of their own choosing began.

CIO leaders chose International Harvester as a major target of their organizing efforts beginning in 1938. The CIO's Steel Workers Organizing Committee gained control of the works council at the company's Chicago works in 1938 (Ozanne 1967, 195).

That same year the Farm Equipment Workers Organizing Committee was established at the Chicago plant but it had relatively little success. A series of union-initiated legal challenges resulted in a 1941 decision by the National Labor Relations Board that the Harvester's works councils were company dominated organizations in violation of the NLRA. Once the councils were dissolved, the Farm Equipment Workers immediately struck for recognition at all the Harvester plants, even though the committee formally represented only a small minority of the employees. Secretary of Labor Francis Perkins then insisted on an immediate NLRB election. The committee won four of the six contested plants in the election, with the remaining two going to local unions affiliated with the American Federation of Labor (AFL) but unaffiliated with any national unions.

The Farm Equipment Workers and Harvester subsequently signed a contract, and in 1942 the committee was chartered by the CIO as a national union in its own right, the United Farm Equipment and Metal Workers of America (FE). The postwar years saw successive rounds of deeply contested negotiations between the two parties; in only one of the annual rounds of bargaining between 1946 and 1954 was a contract negotiated without a strike at International Harvester (Fink 1977, 91).

Over those years the FE was not the only union operating in the industry. The UAW had begun organizing workers manufacturing farm machinery in 1939, succeeding in gaining union recognition and eventually collective bargaining agreements with Allis-Chalmers, J.I. Case, John Deere, and some of the International Harvester plants. After World War II the UAW and the FE entered a bitter battle over which would organize the remaining nonunion plants in the industry.

The CIO leadership tended to side with the UAW in the battle. In fact, as early as 1940 the CIO had recommended that the FE merge with the UAW. But the FE rejected that recommendation; and after the union continued to ignore CIO orders to cease its struggle, merge with the UAW, and dispel its image as communist-dominated, the CIO expelled the union. At the time the

FE was paying dues to the CIO for 43,000 members, making it one of the larger unions within the organization. The Farm Equipment Workers later merged with the United Electrical Workers, after that union was also expelled from the CIO.

Although the FE-UAW competition in representation and negotiations of collective bargaining agreements in the industry continued, the Farm Equipment Workers strength began to wane in the early 1950s. Internal challenges to FE leadership began in 1954 as several of the locals openly sought to shift their representation to the UAW. And the success of UAW challenges in 1954 representation elections sparked the rapid demise of the Farm Equipment Workers.

Meanwhile in the mid-1950s the UAW was steadily and successfully organizing most of the other plants within the industry. Indeed, by the time of the AFL-CIO merger in 1955, the UAW's gains left it the only union of importance in the industry.

All of the major employers within the U.S. farm machinery industry have long roots in history. As noted earlier the roots of International Harvester date to the onset of industrialization in the United States. Likewise, the John Deere Corporation was started in the latter part of the nineteenth century, and it had already grown to its present form well before World War II. The Caterpillar Tractor Company was also firmly established by the time of the CIO organization of the industry during and immediately following World War II. And the smaller companies in the industry have a similar history.

Thus, well established before the industry's bargaining structure took hold, the employers in agricultural machinery have never found it necessary to create a formal employers' organization to coordinate their bargaining efforts. Nonetheless, the firms have coordinated their bargaining efforts to a degree in response to pattern bargaining by the UAW (discussed in the next section). Despite the fact that of the three major employers, only John Deere's business is entirely within the agricultural machinery industry, International Harvester and Caterpillar are considered, at least for the purposes of collective bargaining, to operate entirely within the industry (*Forbes* 1985, 156). That is, because there is no nationwide or industrywide bargaining structure in the construction equipment and power equipment industries—the other sites of Caterpillar and Harvester's business—their principal bargaining activities take place in the farm machinery industry. The firms also have a geographical connection: all are headquartered in Illinois; and most of their plants are located in the midwestern farm states.

The Structure of Bargaining

The formal bargaining units in the agricultural machinery industry, without exception, are companywide. Each contract negotiated by the UAW covers all the union's members at one company, with additional local supplements negotiated in individual plants of the firm. The companywide agreements address the economic terms and conditions of employment, while the local supplements generally specify work rules peculiar to the plant. The timing of negotiations is such that the economic pattern at the firm is established at the same time as the local bargaining is taking place, although the actual settlement of local issues is often deferred until the parties reach agreement on the companywide economic pattern. John Deere, however, has consistently insisted that its local agreements be concluded before the companywide pact (Shoemaker 1986). Thus, it is possible for a companywide strike and settlement to be followed by another strike over local issues.

The companywide bargaining units are obviously large. At the onset of collective bargaining in 1979 the UAW represented 40,000 workers at Caterpillar, 35,000 workers at International Harvester, and 29,000 workers at John Deere. The remainder of the industry's employers, which also bargain on a companywide basis, are significantly smaller than the Big Three.[2]

The bargaining structure is thus a direct outgrowth of the employer and the union structures. At some of the plants of each of the corporations, other small units of craftsworkers are also represented, but the dominant mode is for the UAW to represent all the production workers at a site. An interesting result of this arrangement is that the UAW thus has also been successful in organizing many of the diversified holdings of Caterpillar and International Harvester—their plants outside the farm machinery industry. As noted earlier, these two corporations have become less singularly involved in the industry than John Deere is. As a result many of their employees in the other industries—such as trucks, engines, and construction machinery—are covered by UAW labor contracts. During their growth periods of the 1950s and 1960s it generally was to International Harvester and Caterpillar's benefit to do their negotiating on a centralized basis for all of their unionized employees. In the case of John Deere only one of its operations, a plant in Wisconsin that produces consumer products, is not engaged in producing agricultural machinery.

The bargaining structure, as it has developed over the years since World War II, also closely reflects the structure of the UAW. Divided into 18 geographical regions within the United States, the international has six vice presidents, each of whom is assigned on a permanent basis, (although not constitutionally required) the responsibility for heading up the negotiations within a major industrial sector. Three of the vice presidents have responsibility for negotiations with one of the three major auto manufacturers: General Motors, Ford, and Chrysler. The other three head up operations within, respectively, the aerospace industry, the farm machinery industry, and the remainder of miscellaneous industries having some contracts with UAW locals. In recent years, the leadership on the union side of the farm machinery bargaining table has been quite stable. UAW vice president Pat Greathouse served as director of the union's Agricultural Implements Department from 1962 until 1979, representing the union in negotiations with each of the three major companies. From 1980 to 1983 the vice president was Steven Yokich, and as of this writing Bill Casstevens serves as leader of the division.

Stability of leadership and centralization of bargaining control did not always characterize UAW bargaining in the industry. McKersie (1961) detailed the sometimes tortuous path the UAW followed in instituting a centralized structure at International Harvester in the 1950s. Once the UAW-FE rivalry was resolved in favor of the UAW, the union had moved to centralize control over farm machinery contracts, to ensure economic terms that followed the pattern set in the auto industry. At the same time—and, in fact, even earlier, in the late 1940s—Harvester had moved to centralize control on its side of the bargaining table, and its managers did see certain advantages in this new arrangement (McKersie 1961, 291–94). The transformation to centralized control occurred more easily at John Deere and Caterpillar, where bargaining had not been fractionalized by the UAW-FE rivalry in the late 1940s and early 1950s.

Centralized control and the reliance on the auto pattern seem to have made the agricultural implements division a secondary player within the UAW. Very little new ground is broken in agricultural machinery that has not been tested previously in auto negotiations (Mitchell 1980, 192). The initial pattern is set at the major automobile companies during negotiations every three years. Collective bargaining agreements in the auto industry traditionally expire 15 days before those in the agricultural machinery industry. (Of all the farm machinery firms only J.I. Case has not shared the common expiration date.) Usually the UAW completes bargaining with at least the major pattern-setting auto company before attempting to transfer the pattern to the agricultural machinery industry. In several bargaining rounds, however, the UAW has delayed negotiations with the agricultural machinery firm the union has targeted to be the industry's pattern setter until all three of the major contracts have been negotiated in autos.

The existence of strong pattern bargaining over the 1960s and 1970s has been well documented (Mitchell 1980, 192). The pattern covered the entire economic package of wages and benefits. Wage agreements over those two decades almost always included the standard auto agreement of a 3 percent annual improvement factor (AIF), at all of the large and small employers in the agricultural machinery industry. The contracts also customarily specified an exact cents-per-hour across-the-board wage increase. If differentials among the firms existed, they were more likely to be in the across-the-board increase than in the standard 3 percent AIF. But pattern transferral from autos to agricultural machinery and within agricultural machinery did not end with wage negotiation. Cost-of-living and pension clauses took very similar shape within both industries. For example, the UAW's 1964 success in its crusade for retirement with full pension benefits after 30 years of service in the automobile industry was soon transferred to the farm machinery industry.

After this long period of almost routine pattern bargaining in the agricultural machinery industry, the practice began to break down in the 1979 negotiations. Although the economic settlements in that round eventually represented a strong pattern in the industry, International Harvester had made a concerted effort to break away from industry norms by making work rules the major issue, a strategy that led to a long and bitter strike (BNA 1984, p. 18:121). By 1982 only one bargaining round later, the pattern had almost entirely disintegrated. International Harvester requested early bargaining to obtain relief from intense economic pressure. The company succeeded in negotiating an agreement with the UAW that called for major work rule, wage, and fringe benefit concessions by the union. When John Deere and Caterpillar began their normally scheduled round of bargaining during the summer of 1982, the UAW declared it had no intention of accepting the same terms as those in its Harvester contract. Although the terms eventually settled on were not the same, they bore a close resemblance: Both specified a three-year wage freeze and other concessions on benefits and work rules (BNA 1983a). Thus, the pattern was broken for the first time in over 20 years. Contracts were signed—at Caterpillar, only after a very long strike—providing for a new, historically off-season expiration date of June 1, 1986. Obviously, this date broke the linkage not only with the bargaining cycle in the industry, but also with International Harvester, now a full year off cycle. Early in 1985 Harvester sold what remained of its farm machinery division to J.I. Case, a second-level pattern follower in agricultural machinery. It remains to be seen whether J.I. Case will become the new third partner in the Big Three pattern of agricultural machinery negotiations. It also remains to be seen whether the UAW will be able to reestablish common expiration dates of the three major collective bargaining agreements. The 1986 round of bargaining saw a roughly equal pattern between Caterpillar and John Deere continue, with J.I. Case remaining as a secondary partner.

The Bargaining Process

The collective bargaining process in the industry has remained the same since the consolidation of the bargaining structure in the 1950s. Once the UAW gained primacy in the industry, it first concentrated its efforts on signing new members at all of the major firms and then sought to coordinate the expiration of the major bargaining agreements into what was to become the standard three-year cycle of negotiations in the industry. By the early 1960s both the structure and the process of bargaining were fully established, and collective bargaining began to adopt a form that was to become routine for over twenty years.

In all of the three major corporations the management bargaining team is usually headed by a vice president of industrial relations or human resources. The vice president is assisted by various personnel department staffers with knowledge of special aspects of the contract and by representatives from each plant covered by the agreement.

On the union side of the table, each plant local that is a party to the companywide bargaining agreement sends a delegation to an intracorporation bargaining council. The company council is charged with formulating contract demands and is assisted in this by international representatives from UAW headquarters and a head of the company council.

In the pre-1982 bargaining cycle negotiations typically began in early summer for a September 30 expiration date, although they generally did not reach a point of continuous and regular meetings until early September. When the pattern agreement was set in the auto industry, the companies in agricultural machinery and the UAW began hard bargaining. Often the union announced its strike target not only to place pressure on the company that would be the target but also to begin to focus its bargaining efforts and implicitly announce a delay at the other two major companies. The union traditionally settled the contract at the pattern company and then moved on, one by one, to follow the pattern at each of the other two major companies and finally at the smaller companies. The UAW did not necessarily carry out its strike threat at the pattern setting company. In most bargaining rounds over the late 1960s and the 1970s Caterpillar and John Deere were the targeted pattern setters, not so much because International Harvester was the toughest bargainer of the three but rather because strikes at Harvester were historically almost inevitable and the UAW wished to see the pattern established before the conflict.

Bargaining Issues

Pattern bargaining in the industry has focused exclusively on the economic package. The centralized bargaining structure has produced relatively high wages for workers in the industry. Cost-of-living protection was negotiated as early as 1950 and remains in force today. Table 3–4 compares the average hourly wage levels of production workers in farm machinery, autos, and all manufacturing industries over the years 1972–85. Until 1981 the relative wages of farm machinery workers remained stable at a level 17 to 23 percent higher than the all-manufacturing average and 8 to 15 percent lower than the auto average. Since 1981 their relative wage position has eroded, as their wages have remained almost unchanged and in real terms have declined dramatically.

Table 3–4
**A Comparison of the Average Hourly Wage of Production Workers in
Farm Machinery, Automobiles, and All Manufacturing Industries, 1972–85**

	Average Hourly Wage in:			Farm Machinery Wage as a Percentage of Wage in:	
Year	Farm Machinery (SIC 352)	Motor Vehicles and Equipment (SIC 371)	All Manufacturing	SIC 371	All Manufacturing
1972	$4.47	$5.13	$3.82	87%	117%
1973	4.74	5.46	4.09	87	116
1974	5.27	5.87	4.42	90	119
1975	5.92	6.44	4.83	92	123
1976	6.26	7.09	5.22	88	120
1977	6.71	7.85	5.68	85	118
1978	7.34	8.50	6.17	86	119
1979	7.96	9.06	6.70	88	119
1980	8.78	9.85	7.27	89	121
1981	9.75	11.02	7.99	88	122
1982	9.84	11.62	8.49	85	116
1983	9.54	12.12	8.83	79	108
1984	9.68	12.73	9.19	76	105
1985	9.87	13.42	9.53	74	104

Source: U.S. Department of Labor (various years).

The UAW was also successful in negotiating supplemental unemployment benefits (SUB) in 1955 at International Harvester and shortly thereafter at the other major farm machinery companies. Pension plans were negotiated at Harvester in 1950 and passed along throughout the pattern.

Wage bargaining in the industry has typically resulted in contractually negotiated wage rates for each labor grade. All occupational groupings of employees are covered in one or another of the labor grades. As in most industrial union contracts the employer has very little discretion in wage setting because the contract specifies both minimum to maximum wage rates within each range. Moreover, at John Deere and Allis-Chalmers the contract still retains incentive systems for a large proportion of the workers in the bargaining unit.

Other than the usual bargaining over routine wage, benefit, and pension improvements, the union and the companies have sought to establish a number of operating principles within its collective bargaining. Although these principles are not unique to the industry, they provide an insight into the character of collective bargaining within the industry.

For years the UAW has sought to install a number of contract provisions designed to increase its institutional security. First, since many of the farm machinery firms have plants in both states with "right to work" laws and those without, the question of a single union security provision covering all the workers has been of some concern. Particularly at John Deere, which operates six plants in Iowa and four plants in Illinois, this has been an issue. In particular, the union has sought to negotiate provisions that minimized the impact of the right to work statute. The UAW's union security clause calls for a union shop in plants not located in a right-to-work state. In those plants located in a right-to-work state the employer has to provide union dues checkoff, and if any change in the right-to-work status of that state should occur the union security clause would automatically escalate to the highest permissible by law.

Second, many union locals within all of the major companies have succeeded in negotiating provisions calling for mandatory union attendance at any orientation meetings for new employees. Many of the locals have produced films on union history, which they showed at those meetings. Through this and other means the UAW has managed to sustain high membership levels at the major manufacturers even at those plants not covered by the union-shop security clause.

Third, the UAW has been very successful in requiring that the company pay for full-time union representatives. The grievance committee structure, by which the company pays for approximately one full-time union grievance representative per 1,000 workers, is well established at each of the major agricultural machinery employers.

Absenteeism, a perennial problem in American industry, had run rampant by the late 1960s and 1970s in the agricultural machinery industry. Coupled with a heavy growth in demand for the final product of the industry, as well as a younger, newly hired work force, the industry was particularly burdened by absenteeism. In this case the parties were able to negotiate a unique solution. The agreement signed at John Deere in 1970 provided that each employee who worked a 40-hour week without an absence, lateness, or leaving early received a half-hour of bonus time off. In keeping with the UAW's tradition of attempting to get more and more time off the job for its members, the earned bonus hour plan met two goals. First, it provided a direct incentive to workers to maintain perfect attendance, and that incentive seemed to work quite well. Second, workers who did attend their job routinely were able to generate, over the course of the year, several days of paid time off in addition to vacation time.

The pattern soon spread to the other major companies, all of which were able to chart substantial declines in absenteeism and as many as five to ten additional days off the job for workers who posted a perfect attendance year. And as with many other contract terms, once this provision was included in the agreement, it was only a matter of time before the union sought to improve on the formula. Routine advancements to an hour and a half, and in one contract two hours, of perfect attendance per week were agreed to in 1976 and 1979. It was not until the first concessionary round of bargaining in 1982 that the formula was reduced and in some cases abandoned.

Over the past few years UAW leaders have become very concerned about the employment security of their members in the agricultural machinery industry. Again, that concern is certainly not unique to the industry, but some of the collective bargaining solutions that have been arrived at have been unusual. International Harvester Corporation and the UAW negotiated a mini "domestic content" provision during their bargaining in 1984.[3] During a trial period from April 1984 to April 1985 the company calculated the number of UAW worker hours that went into truck production. The union was guaranteed for the duration of the contract that the number of UAW hours would be proportionately consistent with the 1984–85 calculation or Harvester would owe the union a work debt through an hours bank (BNA 1985). A second solution tried at International Harvester has been plantwide group incentive arrangements (BNA 1983). Once again, production was monitored over a specified number of weeks to establish a production standard. If production surpassed that standard in any subsequent week, bargaining unit members were to be paid a bonus proportional to the production increase. Likewise if production decreased in any week after the base period, workers' wages were to be reduced by a proportional amount not to exceed 20 percent of their normal wage. This plan was negotiated at three of the Harvester plants in an attempt to forestall plant closings threatened by the company.

Each of the major firms also negotiated early warning systems for plant closings. In the 1982 round of bargaining International Harvester agreed to give the UAW six months' notice of permanent plant closings and 60 days' notice of an outsourcing decision that would result in the layoff of 10 percent or more of the UAW members in a plant. Discussions between the union and the management are then to be held (BNA 1982b). The April 1983 Caterpillar-UAW contract called for 180 days' notice of a full plant shutdown and 60 days' notice of a partial plant closing. Similar provisions were negotiated at John Deere (UAW 1983). All of these discussions over closings and their implications for UAW members are advisory in nature, but allow the union some input into these decisions.

"First dollar" profit sharing was also negotiated at International Harvester. This form of profit sharing is not the usual variety: a percentage of *all* profits goes to bargaining unit members instead of the more common practice of a percentage of profits beyond a specified rate of return on investment. Moreover, the company agreed to pay profit sharing for 1984 regardless of firm performance, resulting essentially in a lump sum payment to employees who worked during 1984—a year the company posted no profits. The profit sharing plan was to continue in existence throughout the duration of the contract that was due to expire in 1986 (UAW 1983).

One bargaining issue notable by its absence in the industry is work rule reform. Many union-management pairs during the concessionary era of the 1980s have attempted to meet external economic threats through the reorganization of workplace relations (see, for example, chapter 2 in this volume). Designed to lower labor costs, various joint labor-management experiments to alter work rules and shop floor practices have been attempted in many industries, but only limited efforts along these lines have been made in the agricultural machinery industry. To some observers it may seem as if the union and the companies are simply waiting out the industry's decline until the return of better days, when they can resume their earlier patterns of bargaining. In fact, the record of bargaining issues addressed by the parties in recent years suggests that the transformation taking place in U.S. industrial relations has had little or no effect on the bargaining relationships in agricultural machinery.

Contract Administration

Contracts in the industry are administered and enforced through a very rigid grievance procedure. Each of the major collective bargaining agreements specifies a four-step grievance process, each step of which requires participation by one of the UAW's full-time, paid officials. In the first step the employee discusses the complaint with the union steward. Before the grievance is filed, however, a grievance committee member whose services are paid for by the company assists the employee and the steward in writing up the complaint, as required by the collective bargaining agreement; there is an average of one committee member per 350 workers and one per about 30 stewards in each of the plants in the agricultural machinery chain. The second step of the grievance procedure is a meeting at which the committee member presents the formal grievance to the grievant's supervisor. If the grievance is not resolved at that step, it is taken to the industrial relations manager of the plant and the shop chairman, who is the leader of the plant's grievance committee members. If still not resolved, the grievance goes to the fourth step, a meeting of the international representatives of the union and labor relations representatives of the overall firm. Finally, any grievance unresolved at the fourth step are examined by a council of local shop chairmen and international respresentatives of all of the plants in the particular company's chain, who meet to decide whether to send the case to arbitration.

The arbitration process specified in the UAW's agricultural machinery agreements exclude several major bargaining issues. In particular, union members have the right to strike over health and safety issues; and thus those issues are not arbitrable unless both the company and the union agree to make an exception for a specific grievance. The union must notify the company if it intends to take a strike vote and then if it intends to strike on a specific date over a health and safety grievance. Although no such centrally authorized strikes over health and safety issues have ever been called, the *threat* to strike has frequently been used to spur negotiations over these grievances.

At the two firms with a significant number of workers who receive incentive wages—John Deere and Allis-Chalmers—the application of incentive standards is also generally not arbitrable. Rather, the union has the right to train and employ, at company expense, a full-time measurement expert whose services can be called upon whenever disputes over incentive standards arise. Although the union's measurement experts play no official role in changing incentive standards, serving as they do in only an advisory capacity, they seem to have served as a check upon arbitrary management decisions in this area.

This highly centralized grievance process developed some serious bottlenecks early on in its history. By 1955 International Harvester and the UAW had a desperately high level of unresolved grievances. The union had traditionally preferred the strike to arbitration as a means of settling contractual disputes; and the company had been reluctant to implement the terms of arbitration decisions (Ozanne 1967, 229). The problem was at least partially solved through joint union-management committees and a companywide union council set up to screen out unmeritorious grievances. This process, though modified in the other firms, became the standard in the industry and led to a maturation of contract administration process at all of the firms.

Labor-Management Conflict

Conflict between labor and management in the agricultural machinery industry has long been not only intense but almost routine. As was reported earlier, the Farm Equipment Workers, in its nine rounds of negotiations with International Harvester between 1946 and 1954, was able to settle a contract only once without engaging in a strike. Likewise, in 1955 and 1958 the UAW, in its first companywide contracts with Harvester, also went out on strike. Not until 1961 was the first contract negotiated between Harvester and the UAW without any form of overt conflict (Ozanne 1967, 230).

Following the establishment of pattern bargaining in the early 1960s, industrial conflict became more routinized. Table 3–5 lists the UAW strikes and targeted pattern setter companies for the six rounds of bargaining conducted between 1967 and 1982. In each of the rounds, there was at least one strike at the major companies and in one case (1979) strikes at all three companies. In only two of the six bargaining rounds was the pattern-setting agreement signed without a strike; and only once (1982) was the pattern agreement passed on to the other two firms without a strike. Each round of

Table 3–5
Strikes at the Major Farm Machinery Companies,
1967–82 Bargaining Rounds

Contract Expiration		Pattern Setter	Strike	
			Location	Length (days)
September 30,	1967	Caterpillar	Caterpillar	50
			John Deere	49
September 30,	1970	Caterpillar	Harvester	19
September 30,	1973	John Deere	Caterpillar	15
			Harvester	14
September 30,	1976	John Deere	John Deere	39
			Harvester	3
September 30,	1979	John Deere	Caterpillar	80
			John Deere	21
			Harvester	172
September 30,	1982	Caterpillar	Caterpillar	205
June 30,	1985	Caterpillar	Caterpillar	
			John Deere	

Source: Bureau of National Affairs, *Daily Labor Report* (various issues).

bargaining has typically been accompanied as well by conflict in the smaller firms following the establishment and passing on of the pattern among the major three. When J.I. Case and the UAW signed their agreement in the summer of 1980, it marked the first time in five rounds of bargaining that the negotiations at that firm had been settled without a strike (BNA 1980). Thus, by any available comparative measure the frequency of strikes in the agricultural machinery industry is much higher than average; according to one source, the frequency of strikes among large bargaining units in manufacturing ranged from 5 to 30 percent annually from 1954 to 1975 (Kochan 1980, 252).

The duration and intensity of strikes in the industry tends to be high as well. By virtue of the industry's centralized bargaining structure, each strike is necessarily a large one. And although the strikes were, at least until 1979, not particularly long, ranging on average from 15 to 30 days annually (Kochan 1980, 249), their size and intensity made them very costly. In 1979 at John Deere and in 1982 at Caterpillar the UAW conducted strikes of record length. Interestingly enough, it has rarely been the simple establishment or passing on of the economic pattern that served as the source of conflict, but rather issues peculiar to the individual firm. In 1979 and 1982 it was UAW resistance to the firms' demands for specific concessions demands that sparked the conflicts. And in the future the union is likely to continue to pursue establishment of guaranteed employment levels for its members while at the same time resisting any major work rule concessions.

Why is industrial conflict so intense here? Three broad reasons stand out as possible explanations. First is the long history of militant and competitive unionism in the industry. The UAW, like the FE at International Harvester, has never had a reputation for shying away from conflict. Both the UAW and the FE were borne out of worker militance, and both owed their initial successes to strikes—the UAW at General Motors and the FE at Harvester. The competition between the two unions for worker loyalty did nothing to dampen their militance from 1945 to 1954 (McKersie 1961, 281–83). Moreover, the expectations of union members themselves have traditionally been high—based on their desire to achieve the same gains as those made in the auto industry. Members have commonly translated those expectations into a willingness, often an eagerness, to strike. In the early days of bargaining in the industry the employers were also more than willing to resist the unions with a militance of their own. Like most of the employers organized by the CIO, International Harvester and the others in the industry did not easily adapt to the presence of strong unions. In fact, Harvester was brought before the NLRB in the early days of its unionization for its tactics in avoiding its statutory obligations to bargain with the union (Ozanne 1967, 179). This employer militance reemerged in the late 1970s and early 1980s as well.

A second reason for the sustained and intense conflict between the UAW and the employers in the industry lies in the timing of negotiations. The desire of the UAW leaders to place maximum pressure on the automobile companies led them to coordinate expiration contract dates to the new car model year, a strategy that has indeed given the UAW a great deal of bargaining power. But in linking the expiration dates in autos to those in farm machinery, the UAW could not claim the same bargaining power because of the seasonal nature of the demand for agricultural machinery. Domestic demand is concentrated between April and October, with 85 percent of all farm machinery sold during that seven-month period (*Standard and Poor's* 1984, 538). Thus, just when demand is fully supplied, contracts expire and strikes begin. In that low-demand period the companies can afford to hold out for more favorable contract terms, and so strikes are prolonged. The linkage between the contract expiration dates in the two industries therefore may have assisted in the transferral of the auto pattern to farm machinery but it has also in all likelihood caused strikes to be longer than necessary to effect that transferral. Furthermore, the pattern-following behavior of the negotiations probably complicates them and promotes conflict, for while the union formulates its demands almost exclusively based on what occurs in Detroit, the companies focus on their own individual business conditions as well as the industry's as a whole. These differing sources for specific contract demand would make for extremely difficult bargaining in any industry.

Finally, the parties do not appear to have reached any consensus on the future of the industry. Unlike in many other contemporary bargaining situations, no strong competition from outside the domestic unionized sector of the industry exists. Foreign competition has been a limited threat, and no significant nonunion challengers have arisen. Therefore, company efforts to restructure labor relations have been met with a firm, and directly opposite, conclusion by the union about what should be done in labor relations.

Conclusions

Collective bargaining in the agricultural machinery industry has produced a history of sustained, intense conflict since the centralization of the bargaining structure and the establishment of pattern bargaining in the 1950s. The industry is both a strong pattern follower and a pattern setter for a wide variety of tertiary industries and employers. Strong parallels exist to collective bargaining in the automobile industry. Both industries have three major employers that dominate production and sales within the industry and then a smaller set of firms that follow the agreements signed by the larger three.

The bargaining system within the agricultural machinery industry has performed reasonably well until recently. During the industry's growth years bargaining processes and outcomes were similar to those in most other mass production industries. The union successfully took wages out of competition by organizing almost all the production workers in the industry and then equalizing labor costs across the firms. The system has, however, been marked by an above-average level of conflict and, in the last two rounds of bargaining, by two of the most severe strikes in the history of U.S. industrial relations. It seems as if the industry and the UAW have had an unusually hard time reaching agreement during the concessionary era of the 1980s. Whether their difficulty should be traced to employer or union intransigence is not at all an easy question to answer. In fact, the blame may best be placed on the very nature of the farm crisis in the United States and the fact that the parties cannot transfer responsibility for the crisis to nonunion competitors in the South or to a foreign shore. The UAW and the companies have no common enemies. One of the major problems in bargaining may stem from the fact that the two parties are in fundamental disagreement on the source of their financial difficulties. If this is merely a cyclical downturn, albeit a severe one, the parties may simply be bargaining hard to prepare themselves for the coming surge in demand. If, on the other hand, the problems are structural, the UAW and the companies may be doing a major disservice to the workers in the industry. Each of those interpretations leads the reader to a different conclusion about the state of bargaining: difficult and unfortunate, or irrational. Whatever else might be said, it does seem clear that neither the union nor management is winning this battle.

One would suspect that collective bargaining in this industry will continue to present difficulties to the parties involved into the foreseeable future. Despite declines in real wages in the industry (caused by wage freezes over the years 1983–86) the demand for the final product has continued to decrease. We can predict, therefore, that the companies will press further for work rule flexibility and lower labor costs and the UAW will continue to resist.

Notes

1. Although International Harvester sold what remained of its agricultural machinery line to Tenneco's J.I. Case Division in January 1985, I refer to the company by its former name throughout this chapter because the significant developments in industrial relations occurred under the stewardship of the original owner.

2. During the 1979 round of negotiations it was reported in various sources that there were approximately 3,000 UAW members in the Allis-Chalmers bargaining unit; 2,100 at Massey-Ferguson, and 7,700 at J.I. Case.

3. The UAW has engaged in a wide variety of strategies to maintain bargaining unit employment at high levels. The use of the term *domestic content* here should not be confused with the union's political efforts to require that a certain proportion of products sold in the United States be produced domestically.

References

Bacon, Lawrence S. 1980. *Bargaining for Job Safety and Health.* Cambridge, Mass.: MIT Press.

BNA (Bureau of National Affairs), *Daily Labor Report.* 1979. No. 190, September 28, p. A–6.

———. 1980. No. 130, July 3, p. A–9.

———. 1982a. No. 8, January 13, p. A–9.

———. 1982b. No. 88, May 3, p. A–8.

———. 1983a. No. 80, April 25, p. A–8.

———. 1983b. No. 159, August 16, p. A–2.

BNA (Bureau of National Affairs). 1984. *Collective Bargaining Negotiations and Contracts.* Washington, D.C.: BNA.

Fink, Gary. 1977. *Labor Unions.* Westport, Conn.: Greenwood Press.

Forbes. 1985. 37th Annual Report on American Industry. January 14, p. 156.

Freeman, Richard B., and James L. Medoff. 1979. New Estimates of Private Sector Unionism in the United States. *Industrial and Labor Relations Review* 32 (January): 143–74.

Kochan, Thomas A. 1980. *Collective Bargaining and Industrial Relations.* Homewood, Ill.: Richard D. Irwin.

Kokkelenberg, Edward C., and Donna R. Sockell. 1985. Union Membership in the United States, 1973–1981. *Industrial and Labor Relations Review* 38 (July): 497–543.

McKersie, Robert B. 1961. Structural Factors and Negotiations in the International Harvester Company. In *The Structure of Collective Bargaining,* ed. Arnold Weber, 279–303. New York: Glencoe.

Mitchell, Daniel J.B. 1980. *Unions, Wages and Inflation.* Washington, D.C.: Brookings Institution.

Ozanne, Robert. 1967. *A Century of Labor-Management Relations at McCormick and International Harvester.* Madison, Wis.: University of Wisconsin Press.

Shoemaker, Richard. 1986. Correspondence with the author.

Standard and Poor's. 1977. *Standard and Poor's Industry Surveys,* vol. 2. New York: Standard and Poor's, April.

———. 1984. Agricultural Machinery. In *Standard and Poor's Industry Surveys.* New York: Standard and Poor's, October.

———. 1985. *Standard and Poor's Industry Surveys,* vol. 2. New York: Standard and Poor's, July.

Taft, Philip. 1964. *Organized Labor in American History.* New York: Harper and Row.

UAW Agricultural Implement Department. 1983. *Contract Highlights of Proposed New Agreement, 1983–1986.* Detroit: International Union, United Automobile, Aerospace and Agricultural Implement Workers, June.

U.S. Department of Labor, Bureau of Labor Statistics. Various years. *Employment and Earnings.* Washington, D.C.: GPO.

U.S. Federal Trade Commission. 1948. *Report of the Federal Trade Commission on Manufacture and Distribution of Farm Implements.* Washington, D.C.: GPO.

4
Tires

Mark D. Karper

After a long hiatus the tire industry has recently reappeared as the subject of a number of studies on collective bargaining. Those recent studies have focused on key aspects of employee relations such as concessionary bargaining (Cappelli 1985), work rules (Kochan, McKersie, and Cappelli 1984), and plant dispersion and the changing bargaining structure (Jeszeck 1982; 1986). Jeszeck's dissertation is the most comprehensive study of the tire industry to date, and in large part this chapter is indebted to his work. As these individual case studies have attested, recent economic developments have made the tire industry unique among the major U.S. manufacturing industries. The industry has had to retool completely to allow production of radial tires, but unlike other manufacturers facing similar challenges in recent years, it has managed to do so without federal financial assistance, import protections, price increases, or wage cuts. In fact, the dramatic increases in labor productivity made through retooling the industry may ultimately allow U.S. tire manufacturers to fight off foreign competition while at the same time making U.S. rubber workers the highest paid manufacturing employees in the nation.

Tire building is the major activity of the broader U.S. rubber industry, with tire sales accounting for 60 percent of total rubber sales in 1985 (U.S. Department of Commerce 1985). This chapter focuses exclusively on the tire building sector, because it serves as the pattern setter for the larger industry. Specifically, beyond a topical review of the bargaining environment, the parties involved in the bargaining process, the structure and history of collective bargaining, and the major issues in contract administration, we will also

I wish to acknowledge C. Stephen Clem, Director of Research and International Affairs, United Rubber Workers, and Ted Schaefer, Manager of Industrial Relations Research, Goodyear Tire and Rubber Company, for their assistance and interviews; Lisa Dittrich, who assisted in the research; and Charles Jeszeck, whose unpublished works provided much of the background information needed for this chapter. I take sole responsibility, however, for the opinions and any errors in this chapter.

examine recent changes in the rubber industry brought about by the energy crisis. It was this crisis that led to major technological innovations in the industry and that opened the door for stiff on-shore and off-shore foreign competition in the U.S. tire market.

The Bargaining Environment

The basic procedures employed to build tires in the 1980s are very similar to those used in the 1940s. Production proceeds in seven steps. First is the receiving and storage of large amounts of bulk materials. The next step is the mixing of those materials into uncured rubber in large machines known as Banburies. The development of the Banbury mixer in the 1930s allowed replacement of the huge vats, typical of production in the 1920s, that necessitated production in extremely large batches, as in steel production (Nelson 1982). The calendaring room represents the third step in the process, whereby the uncured rubber is pressed onto fiberglass, polyester, or steel fabric. From there the rubber-coated fabric goes to extruding machines that produce the component parts of tires: sidewalls, treads, and belts. Those components are then assembled in the tire building room on a machine that contains a spinning drum to help fuse the component parts together. (Radial, as opposed to bias-ply, tires must be machined twice with a second-stage tire building machine that molds the tire into the radial configuration.) The "green" tires are then shipped to the vulcanizing department where they are dried at a controlled rate. The final step is the smoothing, finishing, grading (as required by the federal government), and shipping of tires (Jeszeck 1982).

The tire building process is thus highly sequential, and each step in the process has its own department. Workers do not exchange jobs between departments, and as a result, each department has a highly defined work group. Among the implications of this structure is that it allows any single work group to shut down the entire facility by walking off the job.

Although the steps in the process of building tires are much the same today as they were in 1940, both the tire itself and the facility in which it is produced have changed dramatically. In 1940 tires were typically built in huge multistoried complexes employing more than 10,000 employees. In 1980 the typical plant was a single-story facility employing 2,000 or fewer workers. The radial tire of the 1980s takes longer to build (and lasts longer) than the bias-ply tire manufactured in the 1940s.

Historically, changes in the types and location of facilities and technological changes in the types of tires produced can be divided into four time periods: 1910–35, 1936–60, 1961–73, and 1974 to the present. Before 1910 the rubber industry was yet to be dominated by automobile and truck tire production; it was the years 1910–35 that witnessed the birth and development of the tire industry as we recognize it today. Around 1910 automobile and truck tires were still being produced in small facilities. One of the earliest producers of tires (for bicycles) was B.F. Goodrich, which moved its production facilities to Akron in the late 1880s and began producing auto and truck tires in the early 1900s. Four other small producers also began their tire operations in Akron in the early 1900s by pirating skilled workers and technology away from one another.

In 1910 some 80 percent of all rubber production was still in nontire products, most of which were made by the U.S. Rubber Company (later Uniroyal; Jeszeck 1982). This situation quickly changed between 1910 and 1920 as the mass production of automobiles and trucks began and the demand for tires then skyrocketed. This initial demand was met by the five Akron tire producers' continually expanding their operations and by U.S. Rubber's building a giant new tire facility in Detroit. As the demand for tires expanded even further in the 1920s, economies of scale—particularly a reliable supply of natural rubber and large-batch techniques—became a major factor in the production of tires. By 1935 96 percent of all U.S. tire sales accrued to only the four largest tire companies: B.F. Goodrich, U.S. Rubber, Firestone, and Goodyear (Nelson 1982). Since the facilities of three of these "Big Four" companies were located in Akron, Ohio, that city became the geographic center of tire production; in 1935 two out of every three tires made in the United States were manufactured there.

The 1936–60 period was the second expansion phase of the rubber industry. During that time the rubber industry began its decentralization away from Akron. Studies by Sobel (1951), Knox (1962), and Jeszeck (1982) have investigated whether this movement, which was to the South and the Far West, was motivated by the manufacturers' desire to escape the militant unionism that had begun in Akron in the 1930s or whether it was simply for economic and technological reasons. Jeszeck, in particular, concluded that the desire to escape militant unionism was the chief factor in the decentralization of the tire industry. Oddly, the success of the United Rubber, Plastic, Cork and Linoleum Workers of America (URW) in organizing the new facilities at the other locations did not serve to stem the withdrawal from Akron. In fact, the Akron facilities did not actually decline in size until the 1950s, and so the real question is why the rubber industry did not expand *in Akron* as it had in the 1920s and 1930s. The decentralization process was completed by 1984, when B.F. Goodrich closed the last tire-producing facility in Akron (Modern Tire Dealer 1985). Table 4–1 shows the extent of decentralization away from Akron since 1920, and table 4–2 lists the plants closed between 1960 and 1986.

The years 1961–72 represented a period of further expansion into new facilities but it was also the period during which the industry sowed the seeds of what the business press came to call the "great tire shakeout"—the exten-

Table 4–1
New Plant Locations of the Thirteen Largest U.S. Tire Makers, 1920–86

Company	Location	Year
Goodyear	Los Angeles, Calif.	1920
B.F. Goodrich	Los Angeles, Calif.	1922
Firestone	Los Angeles, Calif.	1922
Uniroyal	Los Angeles, Calif.	1929
Goodyear	Gasden, Ala.	1926
Kelly Springfield	Cumberland, Md.	1920
Armstrong	Natchez, Miss.	1938
B.F. Goodrich	Oaks, Penn.	1937
Firestone	Memphis, Tenn.	1937
Goodyear	Jackson, Mich.	1937
Uniroyal	Chicopee Falls, Mass.	1939
Uniroyal	Eau Claire, Wisc.	1933
Armstrong	Des Moines, Iowa	1943
General	Waco, Tex.	1944
Firestone	Des Moines, Iowa	1945
Firestone	Pottstown, Penn.	1945
B.F. Goodrich	Miami, Okla.	1945
Goodyear	Topeka, Kans.	1946
B.F. Goodrich	Tuscaloosa, Ala.	1946
Mohawk	West Helena, Ark.	1956
Mansfield	Tupelo, Miss.	1959
General	Mayfield, Ky.	1959–60
Gates-Arm	Nashville, Tenn.	1959–60
B.F. Goodrich	Ft. Wayne, Ind.	1962
Armstrong	Han, Calif.	1962
Kelly Springfield (Goodyear)	Tyler, Tex.	1962
Firestone	Decator, Ill.	1963
Kelly Springfield	Freeport, Ill.	1963
Firestone	Salinas, Calif.	1962
Uniroyal	Opelika, Ala.	1963
Cooper	Texarkana, Ark.	1964
Firestone	Blooming, Ill.	1965
Goodyear	Danville, Va.	1966
General	Charlotte, N.C.	1967
General	Bryan, Ohio	1967
Goodyear	Union City, Tenn.	1968
Firestone	Albany, Ga.	1968
Mohawk	Salem, Va.	1969
Firestone-Dayton	Oklahoma City, Okla.	1969
Dunlop	Huntsville, Ala.	1969
Kelly Springfield	Fayetteville, N.C.	1969

Table 4–1 continued

Uniroyal	Ardmore, Okla.	1970
Goodyear	Madisonville, Ky.	1972
Firestone	Nashville, Tenn.	1972
Firestone	Wilson, N.C.	1974
General	Mt. Vernon, Ill.	1974
Goodyear	Lawton, Okla.	1978
Goodyear	Gasden, Alaska	1978
Bridgestone	Lavorgne, Tenn.	1981
Cooper	Tupelo, Miss.	1981

Sources: Jeszeck (1982, 33–34) and Modern Tire Dealer (*Annual Facts Directory* 1980, 1981, 1982, 1983, 1984, 1985).

Notes: All the Akron facilities were built before 1920. Michelin, the French tiremaker, opened five other plants (not shown above) between 1977 and 1981; they are located in Greenville, S.C., Spartanburg, S.C., Dothan, Ala., Lexington, S.C., and Lubbock, Tex.

sive reorganization of the industry — of the 1970s and 1980s. Two decisions made during this period were especially disastrous. The first was the decision to continue to expand production capacity at a time when the industry was already witnessing the effects of overcapacity — an overcapacity caused by the unique way in which tires are marketed. Although the four major tire producers controlled the bulk of the market, they have nonetheless been fixed in a fierce price competition with one another, always attempting to increase or at least maintain their market share. The industry's uniqueness stems from the fact that the Big Four all competed as original equipment suppliers to the auto industry, which required the tire firms to guarantee delivery of massive orders at the lowest possible price. As a result, any company that did not continually expand its capacity ran the risk of defaulting on orders and being pushed out of the original equipment market. All companies became, in short, very cost-efficient producers. Even the larger replacement tire market was also cost competitive, since 89 percent of the tires sold in this market were not marketed directly by the tire manufacturers but rather by small, independent retailers dealing in several brands (Modern Tire Dealer 1985).

The resulting narrow profit margins in the industry may have contributed to its second disastrous decision, made in the 1960s. That was the decision not to convert from the single-ply tire to the radial tire but instead to convert to bias-ply tires, which, unlike radials, did not require new tire building machines. Although the superior safety, durability, and gas mileage of radial tires were well recognized by that time, the tire manufacturers believed that radial tires provided an inferior ride and would therefore be unacceptable to automakers and consumers. But the oil crisis of 1973 was soon to change the automakers' minds: as radial purchases grew from 6 percent of original equipment in 1972 to 66 percent in 1975, Detroit was better

Table 4–2
Plant Closings in the U.S. Tire Industry, 1960–86

Years	Company	Plant
1960–71	None	
1972–79	Gates	Littleton, Colo.
	Goodyear	Akron, Ohio no. 1
	B.F. Goodrich	Akron, Ohio
	B.F. Goodrich	Los Angeles, Calif.
	Goodyear	Akron, Ohio no. 2
	Firestone	Akron, Ohio no. 2
	Mohawk	Akron, Ohio
	Uniroyal	Los Angeles, Calif.
	Goodyear	Los Angeles, Calif.
	Manfield	Tupelo, Miss.
	Mohawk	West Helen, Ark.
1980–86	Uniroyal	Detroit, Mich.
	Uniroyal	Chicopee Falls, Mass.
	Firestone	Akron, Ohio
	Firestone	Dayton, Ohio
	Firestone	Los Angeles, Calif.
	Firestone	Salinas, Calif.
	Armstrong	West Haven, Conn.
	Firestone	Akron, Ohio
	Firestone	Memphis, Tenn.
	Firestone	Nashville, Tenn.
	Firestone	Pottstown, Penn.
	Dayton	Dayton, Ohio
	Seiberling	Barberton, Ohio
	General	Akron, Ohio
	B.F. Goodrich	Akron, Ohio
	B.F. Goodrich	Oaks, Penn.
	Goodyear	Jackson, Mich.
	Firestone	Albany, Ga.
	Firestone	Des Moines, Iowa
	General	Waco, Tex.
	B.F. Goodrich	Miami, Okla.

Sources: Jeszeck (1982, 42) and *Annual Facts Directory* 1985; 1986).

able to meet corporate average fuel efficiency standards for cars, mandated by the Environmental Protection Agency. Although the demand for radials in the replacement market lagged behind the demand in the original equipment market, by 1984 almost 75 percent of the larger replacement market was also radial tire sales (Modern Tire Dealer 1985). In fact, industry projections predict that at the present rate of conversion to radials, overall U.S. production should be almost 100 percent radial by 1990, having taken over the U.S. market in twenty years (radials were only 3 percent of the market in 1970).

The delayed and then rapid conversion to radial production hurt U.S. manufacturers in many ways. First, since radial tires could not be produced in plants designed to produce bias-ply tires without complete retooling, all U.S. manufacturing facilities—the old and the new—were rendered obsolete in a short span of time. Second, while the U.S. manufacturers were racing to retool their plants, the U.S. market turned to foreign tire manufacturers, which had been producing radials for over 20 years, to meet the initial surge in demand for radial tires in the early 1970s. The Michelin tire company of France benefited in particular, as it was already the world's leading producer of radial tires when the oil crisis began. Third, at the same time as the domestic tire industry was facing the huge expense of retooling, overall tire sales were falling because both new car sales and the number of miles being driven were declining in response to higher energy prices and gasoline shortages. Finally, since radial tires lasted on average up to four times longer than bias-ply tires, even the future of the replacement market held out no great rewards for the expensive adjustments being made in the industry.

The result of all of these developments was the great tire shakeout: as shown in table 4–2, 32 U.S. plants closed between 1972 and 1986, leaving only 39 production facilities open in 1986. How the parties adjusted to this rapid economic and technological change is the subject of several of the following sections of this chapter.

The Parties

The Union

Early attempts at organizing workers in the rubber industry can be traced back to the Knights of Labor, which in 1887 rejected a trade charter for a New Jersey local composed of rubber workers. Despite this rejection interest in organizing among East Coast rubber workers continued, and in the last years of the century rubber workers joined federated locals of the American Federation of Labor (AFL) (that is AFL affiliates with no specific occupational jurisdiction). In 1902, after more than ten years of organizing activity, the AFL chartered the first national rubber union, the Amalgamated Rubber Workers Union, to unite rubber workers in those federated locals. That union was destroyed by a series of debilitating strikes during 1904 and was eventually suspended from the AFL in 1906 for a lack of dues-paying members. During those years rubber industry employers had begun to form employee associations and company unions to discourage further organizational efforts. Employer hostility to unions intensified even further after a spontaneous strike by Akron rubber workers in 1913, a strike that was ultimately led by the IWW, the Industrial Workers of the World. After that strike was crushed, rubber workers did not again enter into local unions in any significant numbers until the passage of the National Industrial Recovery Act in 1933. Encouraged by section 7(a) of the act, which afforded workers the right to organize, workers in the rubber industry flocked into federated locals of the AFL. In 1933 AFL President William Green gave Coleman Claherty, an organizer on leave from the Boilermakers Union to assist in AFL organizing campaigns, the task of starting a new national union in the rubber industry. It was during the mid-1930s that the existing plant locals joined together to form the National Council of Rubber Workers (NCRW), but the locals—militant and fiercely independent (which they remain to this day)—rejected Claherty's two organizational principles: craft separation where possible, and strikes only as a last resort. When, in 1935, an AFL charter for a new union, the United Rubber Workers of America (URW), was presented to the NCRW convention by William Green, he recommended Coleman Claherty as its first president. The convention promptly rejected Claherty for any office and instead elected Sherman Dalrymple as the first president of the URW. By 1936 the URW had completed its break from the AFL when it chose to affiliate with the Congress of Industrial Organizations (CIO) and was suspended from the AFL (see United Rubber Workers 1985b).

Despite strong internal divisions among the locals and strong employer opposition, the union flourished under Dalrymple. From 1936 to 1941 the union engaged the tire makers in a bitter organizational struggle; in fact, the famous sitdown strikes of the period originated in the rubber industry and only later spread to the auto industry. By the time of Dalrymple's resignation in 1946, URW membership had grown to over 130,000, as shown in table 4–3. Dalrymple's resignation was the product of sharp intra-union rivalry between the major locals in the Akron area and URW locals outside the area over bargaining goals in the rubber industry. He left his post under pressure from CIO national leaders who hoped that his successor, L.S. Buckmaster, could unite the two warring groups. Buckmaster was also to be haunted by this rivalry, however, and the militant Akron faction succeeded in having him suspended from the presidency in May 1949 for interfering in local union affairs. But Buckmaster won reelection after his suspension ended October 1949, effectively muting the Akron faction's attempt to control the union; and he continued to hold the presidency until 1960, when he was replaced by George Burdon.

Burdon had won as an independent, after the untimely death of URW vice president Joseph Childs prevented the obvious successorship. The Burdon administration was also characterized by internal problems, including a disagreement between the president and vice president Peter Bommarito over internal finances. Burdon decided to retire in 1966 rather than continue the struggle against the popular Bommarito, who replaced him that year with only one dissenting vote from the union's executive council.

Table 4–3
URW Average Monthly Dues-Paying Membership, 1939–85

Year	Membership	Year	Membership	Year	Membership
1939	33,828	1955	163,270	1971	181,735
1940	40,023	1956	178,017	1972	182,949
1941	50,270	1957	172,053	1973	184,865
1942	69,743	1958	165,274	1974	190,523
1943	86,733	1959	157,123	1975	188,393
1944	112,948	1960	171,689	1976	175,371
1945	132,351	1961	156,124	1977	154,902
1946	130,862	1962	158,344	1978	177,997
1947	165,056	1963	165,509	1979	173,234
1948	162,360	1964	160,611	1980	166,415
1949	157,131	1965	165,922	1981	140,056
1950	140,577	1966	171,743	1982	132,141
1951	157,536	1967	179,905	1983	116,818
1952	168,229	1968	170,842	1984	116,907
1953	173,805	1969	189,287	1985	121,600
1954	171,230	1970	189,126		

Source: Correspondence from URW Research Department, Akron, Ohio, 1986.

Bommarito's tenure saw the URW's first national strike, in 1976, during the time the tire firms had begun their extensive series of plant closures. Earlier, as the industry's decline led to a rapid decline in the number of dues-paying members from its peak in 1974 (see table 4–2), Bommarito was forced to solve the resulting financial difficulties of the union by internal consolidations; he even resorted merger talks with the United Automobile Workers (UAW) in 1975. By reducing the ranks of paid union staff through a redistricting plan, the union slowly regained financial health, which in turn ended its interest in merger talks. After Bommarito had survived this crisis, he retired and was replaced by Milan (Mike) Stone, who won the presidency, with Bommarito's endorsement, in 1981.

Since Mike Stone's ascendency in 1981, the URW has had to rethink its approach to bargaining. In particular, in light of plant closings, layoffs, and foreign competition in the tire industry, the union's leaders recognized they could no longer afford costly strikes such as that of 1976. As noted above, the late 1970s and early 1980s saw 32 URW-organized tire plants close (almost one half of the tire industry); and perhaps more important, eight of the nine new plants that were opened during those years remained nonunion, cutting union penetration of the tire industry to 81 percent by 1986, a considerable drop from the 93 percent the union had enjoyed in 1967 (Jeszeck 1986). These factors coupled with a twofold increase in tire imports between 1978 and 1984 to a record high of 20 percent of the replacement market would have made continuation of the earlier militant posture suicidal (Modern Tire Dealer 1985). Nevertheless, the URW has not abandoned its key bargaining goals, and the rubber companies still face a union that intends to remain a dominant force in the industry. If anything has changed, it is that the URW has begun to examine a broader range of methods to achieve its goals.

Throughout its first 50 years, the URW was characterized by a strong grassroots democracy. From its inception its local unions, in particular the large Akron locals during the early years, have been able to maintain a degree of independence that is almost unmatched by other industrial unions. It was the militant Akron locals that had rejected the AFL leadership at the union's founding convention, and on numerous occasions since then they have rejected their own national leadership. Thus, the internal structure and overall goals of the union reflect both the benefits and the drawbacks of strong internal democracy. And, as will be shown later in this chapter, the strong independence of the locals has been a primary factor in the bargaining structure of the industry.

On paper the structure of the URW looks similar to that of other international unions. By constitutional mandate, however, the International Executive Board must have a majority of unpaid union officers. Although in recent years the executive board has been less militant, in the past it was known for its hard-line policies, one dramatic example being the suspension of URW President Buckmaster in 1949. The URW constitution also mandates the bargaining procedure of the tire industry, a unique process known as bargaining chains, which for many years allowed for domination by the militant Akron locals. (This concept of bargaining chains will be explained in greater detail in the section on bargaining structure.) This combination of a lay executive board and unique bargaining procedures has given the URW a particularly keen orientation toward the needs of ordinary tire workers.

As of this writing the URW remains basically healthy, despite the recent events in the tire industry. As shown in table 4–3, the URW membership of 120,000 in 1985 was only slightly below what it was in 1945. Even during the 1950s, when overall union membership in the industrial sector was reaching its peak, URW membership was only 50 percent greater than its present level. The continuing viability of the union reflects its concentration on the rubber industry, and more specifically the tire industry, which remains the union's top organizing and bargaining priority to this day. The expansion of URW jurisdiction (and its formal name) to plastic, cork, and linoleum workers in 1945 did not really change that orientation. Thus, in analyzing any URW decision, it is important to take account of how the union believed its decision would affect the majority of its members (tire workers), since historically those members have had the greatest influence of all members on the international leadership's organizational and bargaining goals.

The Employers

In the early history of the U.S. rubber industry, from 1840 to 1900, the majority of the manufacturers produced footwear and clothing, typically in very small plants. From the beginning of this century through World War I the industry was transformed by the emergence of tire production as its cornerstone and by the growth of the Big Four tire firms. The years 1917–73 were when the Big Four extended their domination over the industry, with the number of U.S. tire manufacturers dropping from 200 to 13 by 1973. Again, as noted above, it was after the energy crisis of 1973 that the Big Four were forced to restructure their operations, culminating in the merger of Uniroyal's tire operations with B.F. Goodrich's in 1986 — making the Big Four now the Big Three (*Business Week* 1986b).

The basic bargaining structures and relationships in the industry were formed in the 1917–73 period, during which the four rubber firms competed successfully. Nevertheless, because it is over the period 1973–86 that the industry has faced such wide-ranging challenges to what had been an extremely stable bargaining environment, this section will concentrate on the behavior of the individual companies in this most recent period. Table 4–4 summarizes annual sales and profit data for the Big Four for the years 1974–84.

Table 4-4
Sales and Profits of the Big Four, 1974–84

Year	Net Profits (as a percentage of sales)				Tire Sales, Worldwide (in billions)			
	Firestone	Goodyear	B.F. Goodrich	Uniroyal	Firestone	Goodyear	B.F. Goodrich	Uniroyal
1974	4.2%	3.0%	2.5%	1.9%	3.60	5.32	2.11	2.30
1975	3.6	3.3	1.1	1.1	3.72	5.55	2.04	2.18
1976	2.4	2.4	0.7	0.9	3.93	5.96	2.12	2.31
1977	2.5	3.3	2.5	1.3	4.31	6.85	2.36	2.58
1978	−2.8	3.2	2.7	0.2	4.75	7.85	2.59	2.73
1979	2.1	2.3	2.8	−4.6	5.13	8.90	2.98	2.57
1980	−2.2	3.4	2.0	−.3	4.69	9.30	3.07	2.29
1981	3.5	3.6	3.4	2.3	4.36	10.32	3.18	2.26
1982	0.2	3.4	−1.1	1.3	3.86	9.58	3.05	1.96
1983	2.9	3.1	0.6	3.3	3.86	9.73	3.19	2.04
1984	2.6	4.0	1.8	3.7	4.00	10.24	3.40	2.10

Source: United Rubber Workers (1985a).

Of all the Big Four companies Goodyear was probably the least affected by the great tire shakeout of the 1970s. Goodyear was the largest tire producer and the largest company in the industry in 1978, and it remains so today. In 1986, as in 1978, it competed in every segment of the tire market and maintained worldwide operations. The company's size and large, international operations have served to protect its profitability throughout the 1970s and 1980s while the three other firms all experienced varying degrees of serious financial difficulty. Goodyear has restructured its tire manufacturing operation, but it has not had to diversify into other markets to maintain its profit levels or to prevent hostile corporate takeovers.

On the other hand, Firestone, the second largest tire producer, began losing its sales position in the industry in 1977 when the U.S. Department of Transportation ordered the recall of the company's 500-series tire, which at the time was the leading bias-ply tire in the United States. Firestone's insistence that the tire was safe despite the recall probably damaged the company's credibility as a quality tire producer long after the 500 series was discontinued. For this reason, among others, the firm cut back operations and netted serious losses in 1978 and 1980 (United Rubber Workers 1985a). Still, in 1986 Firestone remained an independent company that, like Goodyear, competed in every segment of the tire market and relied on tire manufacturing as its major product. What remains unclear in 1986 is whether Firestone will continue to concentrate on the tire market in the future.

The other two Big Four companies instituted more dramatic changes in recent years as both fought off hostile corporate takeover attempts—but with different results. In its successful defense against takeover by Northwest Industries, B.F. Goodrich managed to improve profitability, but it did so by dropping out of the original equipment tire market and embarking on diversification into the chemical industry. Uniroyal also managed to fend off a takeover attempt by Carl Icahn through a leveraged buy-out by management, but after a dramatic turnaround in profitability, the company finally had to dismember itself to meet its short-term debt obligations, becoming a holding company. The 1986 merger of its tire operations with B.F. Goodrich will effectively end Uniroyal's role in the rubber industry, where it had once been the number one producer (in the first decade of this century). It is still too early to speculate how this "new" company will do in the competitive tire market. Goodrich-Uniroyal Tire Company has announced its intention to market both brands (Goodrich and Uniroyal) of tires (*Business Week* 1986b).

Table 4–5 outlines basic business and wage indicators for the U.S. tire industry over the years 1975–84. The data show that tire production varied widely during those years, from a peak of 231 million tires in 1977 to a low of 159 million tires in 1980. By 1984 tire production had returned to 209 million units, just over the level of 1979. Thus, as the industry has settled in to radial tire production, the key question now is whether U.S. production

Table 4–5
Economic Indicators for the U.S. Tire Industry, 1975–84

Year	Tires Produced (millions) (1)	Plant Utilization Rate (2)	Imports as Percentage of U.S. Replacement Tire Market (3)	Productivity (4)	Average Hourly Wage[a] (5)	Tire Prices[b] (6)
1975	186.7	68.6%	8.1%	10.8%	$5.68	148.5
1976	186.0	68.9	10.3	-5.5	6.37	161.5
1977	231.6	85.7	10.1	7.1	7.23	169.9
1978	223.4	84.3	9.6	2.0	7.82	179.2
1979	206.7	82.3	12.4	.7	8.59	205.9
1980	159.3	68.7	12.9	11.6	9.74	236.9
1981	181.8	84.6	14.0	11.5	11.05	250.6
1982	178.5	83.7	13.0	6.6	11.66	255.2
1983	187.0	84.6	17.2	7.0[c]	12.35	245.3
1984	209.0	89.7	20.8	7.0[c]	12.97	243.8

Sources: Figures compiled from data reported in Jeszeck (1986) and United Rubber Workers (1985a). The figures include data on all 13 major tire producers (see table 4–1).

[a] Average hourly wage for entry-level production workers.

[b] The numbers in this column are index values based on 1967 = 100.

[c] Estimate, in *Business Week* (1985a).

will increase in the last half of the 1980s, and in particular whether any increase in the demand for tires in the replacement market will be met by more efficient domestic production or by an increase in the import share of that market. The import share had risen from 8.1 percent in 1975 to 20.8 percent in 1984, as shown in table 4–5, column 3.

The estimated 40 percent increase in tire industry productivity between 1980 and 1984 has led some analysts to believe that the import share may in fact drop (*Akron Beacon Journal* 1986). Several factors account for that productivity increase, chief of which is the increase in plant capacity utilization that has occurred since 1980. This increase has come about through the numerous plant closings as well as through agreements between individual plants and URW locals that expanded tire production to 24-hours-a-day, 7-days-a-week operations. In addition, as noted earlier, all the plants that remain have recently been retooled to produce radial tires and thus can boast of the most modern production facilities.

The combined effect of all these influences on productivity is well reflected in the lower tire prices of 1983 and 1984 (table 4–5, column 6), as well as in the industry's higher wages (table 4–5, column 5) and higher profits (table 4–4). The industry is optimistic that if productivity increases can continue, the U.S. producers can recapture the share of the replacement market they lost to foreign producers in the 1970s and 1980s. If they do so, we may well see the end of the great tire shakeout and of plant closings in the industry.

The Structure of Bargaining

In the early years of the URW collective bargaining agreements in the rubber industry were negotiated on a single-plant basis. During World War II the National War Labor Board encouraged greater centralization of bargaining to curtail the militancy of the Akron locals, and by the end of the 1940s all contracts in the tire industry were companywide. The parties negotiated separate subjects on a cyclical basis—with five-year contracts on pensions and medical benefits, two-year contracts on the terms of employment, and three-year contracts on wages (with a possible reopener every year)—such that negotiations took place every year. Between 1946 and 1948 the parties made two attempts at industrywide bargaining similar to the bargaining structures that existed in trucking and steel, but those efforts collapsed under the weight of differences in bargaining goals both within the union and among the companies. Companywide bargaining remains the practice to the present. The next major change in bargaining practice was a three-year bargaining cycle established in 1967 when all issues were finally included in a single contract that expired after three years.

In each bargaining round the URW looked to one target agreement to set the pattern for other negotiations, but this pattern bargaining took a slightly different form in the rubber industry from that in, for example, the auto industry because the URW placed greater control in the hands of the locals than did the UAW. As mentioned earlier, each company negotiates with a URW bargaining committee representing all the locals in the company—a bargaining chain. The chain makes all the critical decisions at the bargaining table, including whether to strike or to settle, a system that also gives each local the right to enter into supplemental agreements covering its particular plant within the company. The bargaining structure therefore has elements of centralization at the company level but is, relatively speaking, a decentralized one, which illuminates why special efforts were necessary to coordinate the industrywide strike of 1976.

In addition to that one nationwide effort, the URW has been involved in international efforts to coordinate collective bargaining in the U.S. tire industry with collective bargaining in its European and Japanese counterparts. Those efforts have so far produced no concrete results other than increasing good will between U.S. and foreign rubber workers' unions. Divergent economic forces, in particular, have prevented any effective cooperation in dealing with the multinational companies, such as Goodyear, Michelin, and Bridgestone. But it should be recognized that those multinational tire companies—and tire production in general—remain concentrated in the highly industrialized countries, where unions are a viable force and wages among all the competing countries are at least roughly comparable. Any shift in worldwide tire production to the sparsely unionized, low-wage climes of the less developed nations would pose a much greater threat to U.S. rubber workers, and thus would demand much greater energies spent by the URW in its international efforts to coordinate bargaining.

The Bargaining Process

Historical Background

The past relationship between the tire companies and the URW can only be described as stormy. Strikes over contract negotiations were so common in the tire industry that it is difficult to recall any set of negotiations, until recently, in which strikes have not been a factor. Between 1947 and 1979, 25 strikes took place in the rubber industry, all of which were companywide strikes, with the sole exception of the national strike of 1976. In many ways conflict was a natural result of the bargaining structure described above, which in fact was designed to facilitate striking. It was only in 1982 and 1985 that the URW and the companies with which it negotiates both faced domestic nonunion (primarily from Michelin) and foreign competition that was stiff enough to force them to modify their relationships to avoid strikes.

Recall that the URW was borne out of bitter conflict in the 1930s. The union achieved its first contracts with individual plants in 1938 and managed to organize the rest of the rubber industry by the end of World War II. But rather than continuing its past practice of negotiating individual plant contracts, the URW adhered to the War Labor Board regulations requiring companywide bargaining. By war's end the union had formulated a general wage plan as the first step in enhancing its economic position and as a step toward industrywide pattern bargaining. The plan called for a 30-cents-an-hour wage increase as well as a standard 30-hour workweek with overtime for Saturday and Sunday work. Although not all the specific goals of the plan were reached, a series of URW strikes in 1946 and 1947 succeeded in establishing agreements at each company that constituted an industry pattern. It was also during the immediate postwar years that attempts at industrywide bargaining began, experiments that proved to be a total failure on the part of both sides. The companies, long competitors, did not hesitate to launch into individual negotiations with their locals whenever the opportunity presented itself. And frought with its own internal divisions, the URW ceased its push for industrywide bargaining. By late 1947 the efforts had died.

The frequent strikes between 1947 and 1979 were principally over issues of wages and fringe benefits, but until the oil crisis of the 1970s the major financial problem facing the industry was not so much labor costs as overcapacity and the resulting cut-throat competition among firms. Indeed, when competitive conditions changed in the tire industry after the 1976 contract, bargaining procedures changed as well.

Bargaining Since 1967

In 1967, as noted earlier, the parties agreed to place all bargaining issues in a single, three-year, companywide contract. This new arrangement necessitated changes in the URW's approach to contract negotiations, namely, to provide for greater coordination among the bargaining chains than in the past. The process that developed, which continues today, begins with a national policy meeting at the URW international convention one year before scheduled negotiations. At that time the four bargaining chains representing members at each of the Big Four manufacturers coordinate their goals for the coming bargaining round. They also select the tire company they plan to strike to set the pattern for the other three chains. Each chain within the union has the task of selling the national goals to its local memberships.

The URW had, as part of its policy dating from the 1950s, sought wage settlements that matched or exceeded those in the auto industry, and the wage goal in 1967 was no exception. The companies, in turn, had always vigorously resisted these wage demands, and in that year they formed a mutual assistance pact designed to counter the URW's traditional whipsawing strike tactics. The ironic result of both parties' efforts to coordinate their approaches to bargaining was a settlement that was achieved only after a series of strikes at all the major producers except for General Tire, but it nevertheless was a settlement that maintained parity with the auto industry.

The 1970 negotiations again focused on the issue of wage parity with the auto industry, but this time the cost-of-living-adjustment (COLA) provision achieved by the UAW in 1969 was added to the list of URW demands. And again, despite URW efforts at greater internal coordination of bargaining strategy, negotiations gave way to several strikes, rather than the single pattern-setting strike the union had planned. Those strikes failed to achieve a COLA clause, and as a result URW wages fell over the 1970–72 contract period from 102 percent to 95 percent of UAW average wages (Jeszeck 1986).

The 1973 negotiations were clouded by the Nixon administration's 1973 wage and price controls. Since this was one of the first negotiations held under the new set of anti-inflation guidelines, the URW was reluctant to engage in lengthy strikes for fear of government retaliation. Accordingly, the 1973 agreement again contained no COLA clause, which resulted in further erosion of URW wages to 88 percent of auto wages by 1975 (Jeszeck 1986).

The 1976 negotiations were marked by the first-ever national strike in the industry, a strike that closed down 60 percent of all U.S. tire-making capacity. The industrywide strike was coordinated by a multi-employer bargaining chain committee (the only time such a committee was created) within the URW, which had as its goals regaining wage parity with the UAW and securing a COLA clause. URW leaders believed that a national strike was the only effective weapon against the industrywide mutual assistance pact of the employers. At last, the union did succeed in coordinating the efforts of its chains: The union regained wage parity with the autoworkers and secured a COLA clause in the contract. Although URW members were very satisfied with these results, the cost of the strike was nonetheless very high for both sides.

The 1976 negotiations were the last until 1985 to be held under prosperity in the tire industry, as it was in 1978 that the great tire shakeout began. As noted above, the economic slump was initially evident in the decline in tire sales. But it was soon accentuated by the rapid shift to radial tire production for the replacement market, which led to the closing of many of the older, URW-organized, bias-ply tire plants.

Collective bargaining for national agreements in 1979 well reflected the contradictions inherent in the great tire shakeout. For the first time large numbers of the older plants were being closed, but at the same time profits were sufficient to allow the major producers to agree to substantial wage increases. As a result, the 1979 contracts provided for large wage increases along with a continuation of the COLA clause in order to prevent a costly stoppage like the 1976 strike. These provisions masked the fact, however, that individual locals were agreeing to concessions in plant-level bargaining. With threats of plant closings the companies played one plant against another to achieve work rule concessions. Their managers reasoned that the higher labor productivity possible by the work rule concessions would more than offset the cost of the wage increases called for in the national agreements. It was only at Uniroyal that the concessions were not exclusively at the plant level. To help bail the company out of its financial distress, the URW's Uniroyal chain agreed to a contract reopener in 1980 that resulted in wage reductions of $1.58 per hour. The URW also acquiesced to wages' remaining below the industry pattern in the 1982 negotiations with Uniroyal, giving the company a wage advantage similar to that which the Chrysler Corporation had enjoyed during its bailout in the late 1970s (see chapter 2 in this volume). Once restored to financial health, Uniroyal rejoined the bargaining pattern in the industry in 1985.

The companies' strategy of individual concessionary agreements at the plant level, rather than a wage concession at the companywide level, resulted in 1982 national agreements that called for a wage freeze but continuation of the COLA clause. The companies were able to achieve a freeze on wages because U.S. tire shipments in 1982 were at their lowest point since 1967 (Jeszeck 1986). Local concessions were still the rule, as 22 of the 35 unionized plants in the industry negotiated individual concessionary agreements on work rule issues. The most common concessions were to allow a move to continuous operations without paying a wage premium and to eliminate output quotas. The net effect of the 1982 companywide and individual plant concessionary agreements, along with the closing of any facilities that did not agree with concessions, was an increase in capacity utilization that caused both labor productivity and profitability within the industry to increase dramatically by 1985.

In the face of the actual and threatened plant closings of these years, the URW sought to address job security issues in the 1982 negotiations, achieving provisions for severance pay and early notice of any closings. The union had hoped that the latter provisions would give locals the time to enter negotiations to prevent plant closings, but there is little evidence that the early warning mechanisms had the desired effect. Tellingly, no company ever agreed as a matter of policy to retool instead of relocate its ailing plants.

Negotiations for the 1985 agreements took place under conditions similar to those of 1976, with the industry once again enjoying good profits. The 1985 round was dramatically different from that in 1976, however, as the negotiations concluded without a single strike and produced moderate settlements that maintained and in some terms surpassed parity with autoworkers. There are two possible explanations for these peaceful and moderate negotiations. First, wage increases in the auto industry at the time were themselves moderate, thus making moderate settlements palatable to both sides in the tire industry; and second, the local concessionary agreements had been so successful from the tire companies' standpoint that the firms saw no reason to change their tactics. But whatever the circumstances surrounding the 1985 negotiations in tires, the fact that the URW agreed to a wage package below its original proposal and did so without a strike is remarkable indeed. It is unique in the history of bargaining in the industry and may bode a more lasting turn toward moderation in future bargaining.

Contract Administration

Contract administration has long been a major source of difficulty between the parties in the tire industry. The production process, with its highly segmented and sequential steps, lends itself to highly structured work rules, which in turn translate into conflicts over the precise interpretation of those rules. Negotiated work rules to prevent speedups and require strict adherence to the rules in the contract have always been a top priority for the URW. More specifically, the URW locals have negotiated numerous restrictions on job duties and work quotas, as well as other shop-floor practices. Conflicts over interpretation of the rules found their way into numerous grievances, especially at the older facilities, where the parties have a long tradition of using the grievance procedure for this purpose. In fact, Jeszeck (1982) has hypothesized that the reason the companies chose to rebuild their facilities outside of Akron was that it was easier to do that than to change work rules and implement new ones in the Akron facilities.

Over the years the parties have developed sophisticated grievance procedures to handle the large number of disputes over their complex work rules. The procedures vary between three and four steps, depending on the local contract. The first step is typically handled by the company foreman and the union shop steward and provides three days from the time of the contested incident to file a written grievance and three days after for the foreman to answer. The second step involves the production superintendent and the URW division chair (an international official who serves as the representative for the particular URW chain) and again allows only three days for scheduling a meeting once the union makes that request and three days for a reply from the superintendent. If this second step fails to yield a resolution, the grievance goes to the local union president and the plant's manager of industrial relations (at which point other union and management officials can also be involved), who are required to reach an agreement within 30 days or else the grievance goes to an impartial umpire chosen from an established list of seven umpires selected by both parties. The umpire has 90 days to hold a hearing and 7 days to issue a decision, unless one party or both desire a fully documented opinion, in which case the deadline is extended to 30 days. The grievance provisions in the contract also contain a disclaimer that allows for extensions if a backlog of grievances develops. Because of its short deadlines the tire industry's grievance mechanism has worked efficiently in resolving the large numbers of highly complex grievances.

Any dissatisfaction with contract administration that has arisen appears to have been focused on the work rules themselves and on the parties' inability to resolve grievances at the early steps. Those problems have been resolved to some extent by recent changes in some work rules negotiated at the plant level and by the closure of many of the plants with the worst grievance records. More specifically, the fear of plant closings on both sides has reduced grievance activity and also encouraged the parties to reach agreement on work rule changes that will cut production costs. In short, the 1980s have witnessed some fundamental changes in contract administration, with the tire industry's system now more closely matching the more stable systems of, for example, the auto and steel industries.

Conclusions

Collective bargaining in the tire industry has recently been altered by the changing economic environment affecting all heavy manufacturing industries in the United States. The energy crisis of the 1970s, on-shore and off-shore foreign competition, technological change, and a financial environment in which all U.S. firms must guard against hostile corporate takeovers have forced both labor and management in the tire industry to take a close look at the efficiency of their traditional structures and processes of bargaining—and to change those aspects that are maladaptive.

But the environmental developments of the 1970s and 1980s changed the parties themselves more than their relationships. Most notably, Uniroyal was completely restructured and left the tire industry, and Firestone and B.F. Goodrich decided to withdraw from certain segments of the industry. As this already highly competitive industry came to face even greater competition from foreign sources, the remaining Big Three companies have been forced to consider labor costs as a critical element of any strategy to remain competitive.

Most notable on the union's side is the fact that 32 URW-organized plants closed over this period, laying off over half the union's tire-building members in the process. In the past the URW had had some success in organizing new tire facilities outside the Akron area, but more recently it has managed to organize only one of the nine plants built between 1978 and

1984 (five of those nine are Michelin plants; *Modern Tire Dealer* 1985). The crucial challenge for the URW today is to boost its organizing success rate and face the fact that a majority (60 percent) of tires sold in the United States are made by nonunion workers (Jeszeck 1986, 240). For a union that had maintained a 95 percent organization rate in the industry up to the 1970s, this has been a dramatic change indeed.

In fact, it is amazing, given these changes in the parties themselves, how little their bargaining relationships have changed. Wages and fringe benefits (with a few exceptions) increased from 1976 to 1986. The resurgence in industry profits in 1983 and 1984 was not founded on a new labor-management relationship or a completely restructured work environment, such as the Saturn arrangements now being introduced by General Motors Corporation (see chapter 2 in this volume). Instead, the resurgence relied on the massive improvements in labor productivity made possible by the retooling necessary for radial tire production and by the parties' willingness to institute new work rules. Although the URW's concessionary agreements with individual plants have dramatically improved productivity, the contract administration process itself has not fundamentally changed. And although the strikeless 1985 negotiations may suggest a new, less militant URW, there is no evidence that the union has given up on any of its long-standing collective bargaining or organizing goals.

What is ahead for the tire industry critically depends on the ability of the major producers to continue to increase productivity. Of course, factors out of the control of either management or labor, such as the value of the U.S. dollar in international markets, will also have a major influence on the industry's health. But in light of the significant productivity increases achieved between 1980 and 1984, the outlook from the mid-1980s seems more than favorable for an expansion of employment and of domestic tire sales. As the challenge for tire industry management is international competition, the challenge for the URW is to organize nonunion tire plants, especially the five facilities opened by Michelin since 1977. Those plants did not appear to hurt the URW negotiating posture in 1985, but they threaten the future bargaining power of the union and thus could conceivably alter the future bargaining relationship between the parties.

Finally, we are left with the question why the tire industry was able to adapt to the changing market conditions of the 1970s and 1980s more quickly than many other industries, particularly the auto industry. The tire companies have been able both to retool and to fight off foreign competition without federal subsidies or wage cuts. The most obvious answer to this question is that the increases in labor productivity that accompanied the retooling led to a resurgence of the industry, unlike the faltering attempts to play catch-up with competitors, as was the case in autos. The less obvious answer is that because the tire industry was always more competitive than the auto industry, it was already more adept at responding rapidly to changing market conditions by the time it came to face its most serious challenges. Thus, at the very least the industry and its union serve as a unique example of the kind of adaptability possible even in labor-management pairs historically characterized by relatively hostile relations. Their experience belies the common contention that the blame for the recent decline in U.S. industrial strength should be placed solely with union leaders and members who refused to adapt to changing market conditions.

References

Akron Beacon Journal. 1986. Outlook for Tire Industry Improves. July 26, p. 16.

Business Week. 1986a. Productivity in the Tire Industry. April 22, p. 104.

————. 1986b. Uniroyal: The Road from Corporate Giant to Corporate Shell, July 14, p. 29.

Cappelli, Peter. 1985. Plant-Level Concession Bargaining. *Industrial and Labor Relations Review* 39 (October): 90–104.

Dick, John. 1979. The Effect of Technological Innovations on the Structure of the Tire Industry, master's thesis. Akron: University of Akron.

Jeszeck, Charles. 1982. Plant Dispersions and Collective Bargaining in the Tire Industry, Ph.D. dissertation. Berkeley: University of California.

————. 1986. Structural Change and Collective Bargaining in the U.S. Tire Industry. *Industrial Relations* 25 (Fall): 229–49.

Knox, Robert. 1962. Workable Competition in the Rubber Tire Industry, Ph.D. dissertation. Chapel Hill: University of North Carolina.

Kochan, Thomas A., Robert B. McKersie, and Peter Cappelli. 1984. Strategic Choice and Industrial Relations Theory. *Industrial Relations* 23(Winter): 16–37.

Modern Tire Dealer. 1985. *Nineteenth Annual Facts Directory,* vol. 59, January.

Nelson, Daniel. 1982. Origins of the Sitdown Era. *Labor History* 23 (Spring): 198–225.

Sobel, Irwin. 1951. The Economic Impact of Collective Bargaining in the Rubber Tire Industry, Ph.D. dissertation. Chicago: University of Chicago.

United Rubber Workers. 1985a. United for Freedom 1985 Collective Bargaining Policy, pamphlet in author's possession.

————. 1985b. A URW Golden Anniversary History, pamphlet in author's possession.

U.S. Department of Commerce. 1985. *U.S. Industrial Outlook 1985.* Washington, D.C.: GPO.

5
Telecommunications

Wallace E. Hendricks
with research assistance by
Susan Sassalos

T elecommunications literally means "communications at a distance."
Under this definition the telecommunications industry today encompasses a wide variety of services. In this chapter we focus on that
portion of the industry traditionally associated with telephone companies and
their close competitors. The major exclusion is the broadcasting industry
(radio and television). It should be emphasized, however, that rapid changes
in technology make distinctions between the various components of the telecommunications industry more nebulous as time passes; for example, cable
television companies may in the future attempt to compete for certain types
of local services now provided exclusively by local telephone companies
(NTIA 1985, 111–12). These changes in technology, combined with deregulation, will have a substantial influence on the bargaining environment in
telecommunications over the next few years.

The Bargaining Environment

Technological Environment

For many years the telephone industry has offered its customers both a wide
variety of voice and data transmission services as well as the telecommunications equipment that made the use of those services possible.[1] Before the
1960s virtually all service was bundled such that the customer had to lease
equipment from the telephone company in order to buy service. The major
company in the industry, American Telephone and Telegraph (AT&T), was

This chapter has benefited tremendously from comments by Ronnie Straw and Morton Bahr,
both of the Communications Workers of America; by J.R. Smith and Thomas Cox, of Illinois
Bell; by members of the Illinois Telephone Association Committee on Labor Relations; and by
Peter Feuille of the University of Illinois. We owe a special citation to Jeffrey Keefe, a doctoral
candidate at Cornell University and a former chief steward at C&P Telephone, for providing us
with a number of ideas, insights, and corrections. The views expressed here, however, do not
necessarily represent those of these persons.

fully vertically integrated, from the manufacture of telecommunications equipment (by its subsidiary Western Electric) through the sale of local service (AT&T owned over 90 percent of the stock in the Bell System operating companies) and long distance service (AT&T Long Lines).

As we will discuss in more detail below, regulatory changes and changes in technology radically altered this environment. In 1956 AT&T controlled 85 percent of the local telephone service in the United States and thus also controlled 85 percent of the market share for terminal equipment; since the Bell companies bought only from Western Electric, Western Electric controlled 85 percent of the terminal equipment market (Brock 1981, 235). Later regulatory changes that allowed customers to purchase their own equipment had a profound effect on those markets. A large number of electronics firms have since entered the markets for both residential and business equipment. By the end of 1973, for example, business customers had a choice of 39 KTS systems (only three of which were from Western Electric) manufactured by 15 different companies, and 163 different PBX systems (only 13 of which were from Western Electric) from 28 different manufacturers.[2] This new competition reduced the price of competing systems and increased the product variety available (Brock 1981, 245).

The unbundling of terminal equipment from basic telephone services, along with changes in technology, has also altered the types of products available to the consumer. For example, most telephones now have a modular assembly, with components that can be plugged in and out. This reduces the time and skills needed for telephone repair. In addition, consumers now can install their own equipment or have an independent servicer install it. This change has significantly reduced the ranks of telephone installers, whose function had previously been the exclusive domain of the telephone companies.

Changes in technology have also transformed the provision of basic telephone service. Telephone communication is essentially a combination of two processes: call switching and signal transmission. The major breakthrough in call switching was the electronic switching system (ESS). ESS and other computer-based technologies increase the system's capacity while requiring little if any additional labor (BLS 1979, 29–30). Since the introduction in 1965 of electronic switches controlled by computer software, the cost per voice circuit has fallen from $1,100 to $250 (NTIA 1985, 9). Computers effectively eliminate the need for intercept operators, and they also perform maintenance and quality control operations. As a result, the number of operators in the Bell System has continually declined from its peak of 138,600 in 1971. Although the introduction of computer technology has therefore shifted the telephone work force toward central office crafts, the shift has not been as dramatic as expected. Computers have had a minimal impact on the traditional crafts of cable splicing and line work, except dispatch functions.

Moreover, several technological changes have reduced the need for central office (CO) technicians as well. ESS has lowered the demand for CO switching technicians because remote adjustment procedures and improved diagnostics in many cases obviate the need for an attending CO technician. In addition, mechanized loop testing (LMOS/MLT) has significantly reduced the demand for testers, a job formerly performed by the CO switching technicians but which has now been downgraded to a clerical job. Finally, the introduction of remote switching units will extend the service range of central offices from their current five-mile radius. Each of these technologies reduces the need for skilled central office personnel but has little impact on the skilled labor who work outside on the lines.

The technological changes that have most altered the shape of the industry are those in signal transmission. When telephone wires (cables) are required to transmit signals from one customer to another, there are good economic reasons for granting a monopoly to a single firm. If two or more firms were allowed to provide service, unnecessary duplication of facilities would result, costs would rise, and the customer would pay a higher price for service.[3] But when signals can be sent using microwave transmissions, the case for a "natural monopoly" is less compelling. Regulatory changes during the 1960s (discussed below) and the new microwave technology ultimately spelled the end of AT&T's monopoly over long distance service. And satellite communications further hastened that end. Satellites, which serve, in effect, as extremely tall microwave towers, can receive, amplify, and retransmit signals to provide communications to a wide area (Brock 1981, 256).

Satellite technology, combined with computer technology for switching, multiplexing, and terminal equipment, has established a viable alternative to traditional analog communications technology. The new digital technology to integrate voice and data service (expected to make up one-third of all new transmission by 1990) represents a considerable blurring of the lines between traditional telephone companies and traditional computer companies such as IBM and Xerox (Brock 1981, 275). Between 1960 and 1980 the cost per channel for transmission fell from $1,200 to $400, and between 1950 and 1976 the cost of both microwave transmissions and coaxial cables also fell dramatically, by 80 percent and 76 percent, respectively (NTIA 1985, 12). Those cost reductions combined to triple the number of calls processed per telephone company employee over the last 30 years. Whereas six hours of work were required for one month of telephone service and 100 calls in 1940, only one and one-half hours were required for the same service in 1980 (NTIA 1985, 15).

Although the primary impact of microwave technology has been in the long distance market, there is also potential for a similar impact on the local service markets. The local service network is generally considered a natural monopoly, since it would not be economical for all customers to have microwave receivers. Nonetheless, some extremely large customers, such as businesses in downtown Chicago, could potentially cut their telephone bills significantly by building microwave facilities to transmit calls between their plants and offices, even locally. This is known as "system bypass." System bypass is a serious problem for local service companies because a large percentage of their revenues is achieved from a relatively small percentage of high-use customers. For example, 5 percent of New York Telephone customers supply nearly 70 percent of the company's revenue. If some of those customers were to leave the network, the fixed costs of the system would have to be borne by the remaining customers, causing a potentially large increase in their bills. Moreover, regulatory agencies and the operating companies cannot simply allow system bypass and then respond to the problem later. Once customers have invested in expensive equipment to bypass the local network, it will be very difficult for the companies to lure them back. The regulatory agency must either prohibit bypass or change the rates so that bypass is no longer economically attractive. The mere threat of bypass is therefore as important as the actual bypass itself. Thus, technological change in signal transmission is already having an influence on local markets in addition to its more generally recognized effect on the long distance market.

A further transmission innovation, fiber optic cables, may be the wave of the future. A single fiber optic filament can carry up to 240,000 calls simultaneously. Furthermore, the quality of transmission by fiber optics makes the technique ideal for high-speed data transmission. Since the microwave spectrum is already crowded, fiber optics may supplant microwave transmission in the long distance market. This would certainly be an ironic reversal. Technological change brought on by microwave transmission transformed the long distance segment of the industry from a natural monopoly to a highly competitive structure. Fiber optics could reverse this structure, since fiber optical cable is most cost effective when large quantities of information are sent.

It may be too early to tell what impact fiber optics will have on the demand for skilled workers in the industry. On the one hand, far more calls can be handled through existing conduits, reducing construction costs tremendously. On the other hand, with further technological innovation fiber optics may become economical for local service. If this were to occur, copper and coaxial cable would have to be replaced, thereby increasing the demand for line personnel, though only temporarily.

In sum, extensive technological changes over the past 40 years have had a substantial impact on the telecommunications industry. The relationship between technology and regulation is such that regulatory policy both determines and is determined by technological innovation. This is evidenced by the expansion of the PBX and KTS markets after changes in regulatory policy and by the recent policy decisions to deregulate the long distance market brought about by technological advances in signal transmission. Finally, technological changes will affect the labor requirements of the telecommunications industry, which in turn will affect both the composition of the work force and the labor relations policy of the firms in the industry.

The Economic and Legal Environments

It is very difficult to disentangle the economic and legal environments of the telephone industry because throughout this century the degree of competition in the industry has largely been determined by economic regulation. In fact, it is also not easy to separate these two from the technological environment, since, as noted above, many regulatory changes were spurred by technological innovation. In this section we will give a short history of the regulatory and economic environments to establish the basis for the current deregulation of the industry. We will then attempt to evaluate how these events have intertwined to influence collective bargaining in telecommunications.

Historical Background. Alexander Graham Bell invented the telephone in 1876, and in 1877 he and others founded the American Bell Telephone Company. Between 1877 and 1894 American Bell had a monopoly over telephone service because of its patent rights. Also during this time, through corporate reorganization, American Bell became American Telephone and Telegraph (AT&T) and purchased most of the stock in Western Electric Corporation. Between 1894 and 1907 a large number of independent telephone companies emerged to compete with AT&T. AT&T responded by attempting to buy the stock of those companies and by refusing to interconnect them with the Bell System (Owen and Braeutigam 1978, 198–99).

The duplication of services brought on by the direct competition for local service, as well as AT&T's refusal to interconnect with independent companies, brought on regulation by both the states and the federal government. In 1910 Congress passed the Mann-Elkins Act, which extended the jurisdiction of the Interstate Commerce Commission to telecommunications. AT&T did not fight regulation. In the company's view, regulation was the price to be paid for reduced competition and exclusive territorial operation (Owen and Braeutigam 1978, 199–200). At the same time, the U.S. Department of Justice initiated its first inquiry into the industry. In a pattern that was to preview future Justice Department cases, AT&T settled the case by agreeing to divest Western Union (accomplished in 1914) and to interconnect with independent companies.

By 1934 AT&T and its subsidiaries controlled 79 percent of all telephone service. In that year Congress passed the Communications Act, which set up the Federal Communications Commission (FCC) to regulate telecommunications but which otherwise did not alter the rules of regulation. AT&T retained a sole monopoly over all long distance service.

During the 1940s several technological developments generated a renewed demand for entry into the telecommunications field. The invention of the transistor, the introduction of microwave technology, and the expansion of television all gave rise to new companies that looked to compete with AT&T. The FCC ruled that only the common carriers, AT&T and Western Union, could provide service. AT&T refused to interconnect with Western Union and thus remained the monopoly in the telephone industry (Owen and Braeutigam 1978, 206–8). Nonetheless, the Department of Justice again filed an antitrust suit, which was settled eight years later, in 1956, with a consent decree that essentially forbade AT&T from entering the fledgling computer business.

AT&T's monopoly over the terminal equipment and long distance markets began to unravel during the late 1950s and the 1960s. Prior to 1956 AT&T's tariff did not allow connection of "alien equipment" (equipment provided by other companies) to the Bell System. But in that year the U.S. Court of Appeals in Washington, D.C., ruled in the famous Hush-A-Phone case that the tariff rules did not apply. The door to equipment competition was left permanently open by the FCC when in 1968 it ruled that the Carterfone (a mobile unit) was also allowable.

As noted above, many service companies wanted to enter the long distance market; they were supported in their efforts by electrical equipment manufacturers that wanted to provide telephone equipment. The FCC first granted entry into the long distance market in 1959 with its Above 890 decision, which allowed customers to use radio frequencies above 890 megahertz for private service but which disallowed the building of facilities to sell service to multiple users (that is, entry into the common carrier market). In 1963 MCI Corporation petitioned the FCC for the right to provide common carrier service between Chicago and St. Louis and to nine intermediate points. The final decision in the case, in 1969, granted MCI's petition. Within one year the FCC had 30 more applications. The Execunet decisions in 1977–78 further allowed resale of common carrier services. The door to long distance competition was now ajar, and interexchange competition grew exponentially, as shown in tables 5–1 and 5–2.

The combination of these regulatory and technological changes left the industry in considerable disarray by the 1970s. Equipment was being sold by both regulated telephone companies and unregulated electrical manufacturers. Long distance service could be provided by private line carriers, specialized common carriers like MCI, or AT&T. Over the years the battles waged at the FCC over the appropriate tariff structures for long distance service were long and numerous.

The regulatory response to this disarray was threefold. First, in 1974 the Department of Justice once again filed an antitrust suit, this time to restructure the industry by forcing AT&T to separate intercity service from local

Table 5–1

Percentage Increase in Demand for Interexchange Telecommunications Service between 1978 and 1984

(in $ billions)

Type of Service	Demand in 1978	Demand in 1984	Percentage Increase
Intrastate	$9.41	$20.36	116
Interstate	13.13	29.04	121
International	.98	2.20	124
Total	$23.52	$51.60	119

Source: NTIA (1985, 84, table 4–1).

Table 5–2

Market Share and Toll Revenues of AT&T, Independents and Competitive Carriers, 1978 and 1984

Carrier	1978		Carrier	1984	
	$ Billions Revenue	Market Share (Percentage)		$ Billions Revenue	Market Share (Percentage)
AT&T/BOCs[a]	$19.62	83.4	AT&T	$33.25	63.5
Independent telcos[b]	3.70	15.7	Local exchange companies[c]	13.40	25.6
Competitive carrier[d]	.20	0.9	Competitive carriers	4.95	9.4
			Private microwave	.80	1.5
Total	$23.52	100		$52.40[e]	100

Source: NTIA (1985, 84–85, tables 4–2 and 4–3a).

[a]BOCs are Bell operating companies.

[b]Independent telcos are regulated telephone companies not owned by AT&T, such as GTE and Contel.

[c]These are the BOCs and independent telephone companies.

[d]These are the competitive long distance companies, such as MCI, Teleconnect, and Allnet.

[e]This total differs from that in table 5–1 because the total here includes private microwave revenues.

service and to separate Western Electric and part of Bell Laboratories (AT&T's research arm) from the Bell System. Second, during the 1970s Congress attempted to rewrite the Communications Act of 1934 to reflect the changes in the industry. Finally, the FCC attempted to restructure the industry. The commission's 1980 Computer II Inquiry totally deregulated the sales of on-premises equipment and enhanced services (for example, by the computer processing of data in transportation). The inquiry also allowed AT&T

to enter the computer business, but only through an independently operated subsidiary (later termed "Baby Bell" by journalists).

The Justice Department antitrust suit was brought to trial in 1981 and settled with a consent decree announced in January 1982, with an effective date of July 1982. AT&T was charged with monopolizing telecommunications services and products. The consent decree was designed to separate AT&T's competitive business interests from the remaining Bell monopoly. The decree required AT&T to divest its 22 local operating companies while retaining its long distance business, its equipment manufacturing capability, and its research arm (Shooshan 1984, 18). In addition, the decree required the local operating companies to provide all long distance carriers with "equal access" to their "bottleneck," or switching, facilities. AT&T was also ordered to submit a plan of reorganization to the Justice Department within six months, to be effective 18 months from January 1982 (BNA 1982a, C-1).

Federal District Judge Harold Green temporarily blocked the consent decree to require a public comment period. During that period the Communications Workers of America (CWA) submitted comments and briefs indicating that the union supported the proposed decree but was concerned that national bargaining not be precluded by the reorganization of AT&T. Judge Green responded, "There is nothing in the proposed decree or in general principles of law which would preclude or interfere with such bargaining, and there accordingly is no reason whatever why, following the entry of the decree and the reorganization, such bargaining cannot continue as in the past."[4] After the public comment period Judge Greene did modify the decree to allow the divested regional companies to provide directory advertising and cellular mobile service and to market (but not manufacture) telephone equipment. This modification also barred AT&T from engaging in electronic publishing (Shooshan 1984, 19).

AT&T filed its reorganization plans in December 1982 and announced that an initial determination of the proportion of each work group to be assigned to each corporate entity would be completed by March 31, 1983 (BNA 1982b, A-7).

The details of the consent decree, including the plan for reorganization, will have a substantial impact on bargaining in the industry for years to come. We will discuss that impact in more detail later in this chapter. First, however, we want to analyze how past regulatory policies may have influenced bargaining in the industry.

Regulatory Policies and Labor Market Competition. In 1913, 24 percent of the homes in the United States had telephones (Owen and Braeutigam 1978, 199). Today, over 97 percent have telephones. This growth was in part a direct outcome of the regulatory doctrine known as "universal service," which dictated that residential prices for basic telephone services should be kept low enough to allow everyone to afford them. The doctrine was carried out through three general policies. The first was "value of service" pricing. Under this policy the prices for individual services were based on the value of the service to the customer rather than the cost of providing the service. Thus, rates for business phones were higher than rates for residential service. Long distance rates were also set to subsidize local rates. The second policy was "average" pricing, under which calls of equal distance were charged equal prices whether they occurred over a high volume, low cost route or a low volume, high cost route. Thus, calls between two rural areas would cost the same as calls between two urban areas of equal distance, even though the costs of providing the rural service were much higher than those of providing the urban service. Finally, the prices of nonbasic services (such as Trimline phones or call-waiting) were set above cost to subsidize the basic services.

The universal service doctrine created a complicated system of subsidization across both types of services and areas of the country. This cross-subsidization can be maintained only if the telephone company has such a large cost advantage over potential competitors that even the high-priced services do not offer a possible profit for new entrants or if regulatory policies simply forbid entry by competitors. Competitors will naturally attempt to enter markets for those services priced above cost and avoid those markets being subsidized. In the regulation literature this behavior is known as "cream skimming." If the regulatory policies allow entry, prices in the subsidized market will have to rise in the long run because the telephone company's profits will be smaller in the markets with entry and because the subsidies will be concomitantly smaller.

As we have seen, technological change and changes in regulatory policy have resulted in considerably more competition in the telephone industry in recent years. Thus, even without the breakup of AT&T brought about by the 1982 consent decree, the prices of subsidized services were bound to increase. In fact, the breakup was a natural extension of FCC policy to introduce more competition in telecommunications.

Under the traditional pricing in the industry, the costs of providing a service were only a minor factor in the pricing of that service. The prime factor in pricing was whether *total* revenues covered *total* costs of all services and thus provided a reasonable rate of return on investment. Detailed costing of specific services was therefore not as important as it is when competition forces prices for individual services to reflect their costs. For example, telephone companies used to provide installation and maintenance services cheaply by spreading their costs to other services. But when the subsidies from other services diminished, companies first had to initiate a scheme to assess actual costs and then had to set prices to cover those costs. In this example, as consumers can attest, installation and maintenance prices have risen dramatically. And as those prices rose, the installation and maintenance markets attracted new competitors.

Regulatory policy came to influence bargaining in the industry in two general areas.[5] First, regulation limited the number of competitors in the product market by granting monopolies. When new entrants were rare, unions had no need to organize new firms; they could simply grow with the existing firms. To the extent that regulation caused less competition in both the product market and the labor market, union power may have been higher than it otherwise would have been as a result. We label this the "structure" hypothesis. Second, regulation may have lessened the incentive of firms to contain labor costs, since costs could be passed along to customers in the form of higher rates and telephone companies did not price individual services according to their actual costs. We label this the "pricing" hypothesis.

The validity of the structure hypothesis depends on the validity of two propositions. First, less competition in the product market or higher levels of unionization, or both, must lead to greater union power. Empirical evidence on this question in studies across a wide variety of industries indicates that increases in the percentage unionized do lead to increased union power. Evidence on the influence of product market competition (the "concentration" proposition) is less clear. Some studies find an influence, while others do not. Second, regulation must lead to a change in structure for the regulatory impact to be important. This proposition is more difficult to investigate because we can only guess what the structure of the industry might have been in the absence of regulation. On the one hand, FCC and state regulatory agencies did limit entry into the industry. But on the other, policies of cross-subsidization of many services produced a market for many more potential entrants than would otherwise have existed in the absence of the policies. It is therefore no simple task to determine whether regulatory policy or technological change was the primary reason for the changes in bargaining structure we observe today. That is, it is difficult to estimate whether the telephone industry would be 90 percent unionized today in the absence of regulation.

The pricing hypothesis rests on the complicated interaction of regulatory agency price setting and management incentives to be "tough" bargainers. Suppose, for example, that the agency sets prices such that they guarantee the company an allowed rate of return above costs. If the agency does not question costs, managers may have little incentive to keep costs low as long as they can maintain the allowed rate of return. In a unique study Ehrenberg (1979) tried to determine if regulatory agencies do in fact question labor costs. Of 49 commissions studied, some had questioned upper-level *management* salaries and about 30 percent had focused on the more general labor cost issue. Ehrenberg concluded that as of 1977 about one-half of all commissions accepted union wage scales as just and reasonable but the standards used to analyze labor costs were not well defined and the level of analysis was

Table 5–3
Average Hourly Wage Rates in Selected Industries, December 1985

Industry	Wage
Combination utilities	$15.24
Motor vehicles	13.83
Electric utilities	13.32
Telephone	12.70
Gas production and distribution	12.38
Primary metals	11.83
Intercity highway transportation	11.12
Telephone and telegraph apparatus	10.84
Durable goods manufacturing	10.21
Manufacturing	9.61
Nondurable goods manufacturing	8.84
Total private industry	8.72

Source: USDOL (1986, 88, table C-2).

quite simplistic (Ehrenberg 1979, 21). Essentially, the regulatory agencies studied did not question the outcome of bargaining. Thus, there may be a prima facie case for the pricing hypothesis. On the other hand, regulated companies cannot always maintain their allowed rate of return. When their rate of return falls below the allowed rate, managers do have the incentive to lower costs. As with the structure hypothesis, the validity of the pricing hypothesis is an empirical question.

Wage data suggest that the telecommunications unions have done quite well for their members. In December 1985 the average hourly wage was $12.70 for workers in the telephone service portion of the industry and $10.84 for workers in the manufacturing portion of the industry. Table 5–3 illustrates that these rates compare favorably with wages paid at other utilities and in highly unionized segments of the broader manufacturing industry. As is the case in all industries, wage rates in telecommunications vary considerably across occupational groups and seniority levels. For example, the hourly wages of the highest seniority group in each of four major occupations at Illinois Bell in March 1986 were crafts, $15.84; service representatives, $12.65; clerical, $11.13; and operators, $10.37.[6] (These four occupational groups represented about 70 percent of the workers at Illinois Bell, and 90 percent of the workers in each occupational group were in the top wage group.)

These wage data offer a prima facie case for a regulatory impact on union power, but high wages could exist for any number of reasons. Closer study is necessary to isolate those reasons. The only major study of this question for the telephone industry is on wages and other benefits at New York Telephone. In 1976 the New York Public Service Commission, under the leadership of Alfred Kahn, began an investigation of labor costs at New York Telephone. Ronald G. Ehrenberg, under contract to the commission, investigated a large amount of data and concluded, "As of the end of 1976, NYT's employees' earnings, on the average, were 15–20% above the level I had defined to be just and reasonable" (Ehrenberg 1979, 40). In this case, he defined "just and reasonable" as the wage paid employees with equal skills in the New York labor market. It should be noted that the average of the wages paid to *all* comparable workers in New York is considerably below the average of wages paid to comparable workers at the large, unionized firms in New York. Thus, Ehrenberg specifically rejected the concept of comparing NYT wages to wages paid by comparable firms in favor of the broader labor market comparison. By this comparison, many firms would be paying excessive wages.

Ehrenberg's results, although only for a single company, probably can be generalized to most companies in the industry, since the Bell System companies bargained on a nationwide basis at the time. They suggest that union power was high under regulation, but they do not provide an easy answer to the issue of the impact of regulation on union power. NYT might have been a large, unionized company even in the absence of regulation. A 15 to 20 percent wage differential over the average wage in the labor market would therefore not be unexpected.

Ehrenberg's results are interesting for another reason. Based on those results, the staff of the Public Service Commission recommended that part of NYT's rate request be disallowed because the company's wages were too high. But by this time Alfred Kahn had left the commission; and after public hearings before the full commission, at which the unions were allowed to present their case, the commission ruled that the negotiated wage increases should be passed along to NYT's customers. In fact, the commission completely repudiated Ehrenberg's study. Thus, the first major attempt of a regulatory agency to intervene in the bargaining process was effectively muted by the interested unions.

This episode brings up an important issue. As Ehrenberg (1979, 154–63) argued, regulatory agencies have the responsibility to question all costs associated with the operation of a public utility. Yet federal law requires both parties to a labor contract to bargain in good faith. If an agency rules that only a certain level of additional labor costs can be passed on to customers in the form of increased rates, the effect on bargaining could be chilling. Such a ruling might not even be allowed by the courts. The New York Public Service Commission was certainly unwilling to open this Pandora's box.

A similar incident turned out to be the spark for the famous AT&T-EEO consent decree in 1973.[7] In 1970 the Equal Employment Opportunity Commission (EEOC) filed a petition with the FCC opposing a rate increase for AT&T on the grounds that AT&T discriminated in employment. Although the FCC denied the EEOC's request to intervene, the FCC did schedule separate hearings to investigate employment practices at AT&T. At the time of those hearings AT&T was also developing an affirmative action program for the General Services Administration (GSA). The EEOC challenged the program, which was approved by the GSA. This action brought both the Department of Labor and the Department of Justice into the case. The challenge was settled by a consent decree within a few months.

The AT&T-EEO consent decree covered the period between 1973 and 1979. It provided for affirmative action in hiring, upgrading, and transferring and for pay adjustments for covered groups. The affirmative action goals raised a problem, however: They were in direct conflict with seniority provisions in the company's labor contracts. The consent decree contained an "affirmative action override provision" that rendered seniority a secondary consideration when the affirmative action goals could not be met through the normal system. The AT&T unions naturally challenged this provision through grievance procedures, arbitration, and the courts. The company not only denied the grievances but also refused to accept arbitrator decisions that upheld the contracts, in about half the cases. In the end the courts settled the cases in favor of the company. Between 1973 and 1976 the override was used for about a fifth of all job openings. Interestingly, the company continued to pursue most of the procedures set by the consent decree when it lapsed in 1979, but it discontinued use of the affirmative action override.

The pay adjustments made may also have had an impact on collective bargaining. In particular, white male employees generally resented the adjustments. At least one source has suggested that the contracts negotiated over that period represented a payoff to placate those not favored by the decree, since collective bargaining "yielded more substantial results both on a real and comparative basis following the decree than it had before" (Northrup and Larson 1979, 15).

Whether or not one accepts the pricing and structure hypotheses about union power in the industry, it is reasonable to conclude that the regulatory policies outlined above have had a major impact on the structure of bargaining in the industry. Without regulation of entry, AT&T could not have dominated the industry to the degree it did. More competitors would have existed, and considerably less centralization of employer decision making in the industry would have developed. The average-pricing policies of the regulatory commissions, moreover, provided less incentive for wage levels to reflect different levels of productivity. In essence, wages were taken out of competition by policies that did not price individual products and services at their costs.

As a consequence the centralization of employer power and of pricing decisions created extremely strong incentives for unions in the industry to mirror this structure by centralizing their own structure and demanding centralized (national) bargaining. Schacht (1985) provides convincing evidence that this is the key to understanding the development of the CWA and the bargaining structure in the industry.

In summary, past regulatory policy in telecommunications may have established an environment that gave unions in the industry more power than they would have had were the industry not regulated. Policy almost certainly influenced the structure of unions and of bargaining in the industry. Divestiture, on the other hand, has abruptly and fundamentally altered the bargaining relationship. Before tackling that topic, however, we will present a more detailed description of the parties involved in bargaining in the industry and of the bargaining structure.

The Parties

Unions

There are two major unions in telecommunications. As of 1985 the Communications Workers of America (CWA) had approximately 175,000 members at AT&T; 487,000 members in the regional holding companies; 37,000 at General Telephone (GTE); and 20,000 in the remaining independents. The union is by far the largest in the industry. In 1985 the International Brotherhood of Electrical Workers (IBEW) represented approximately 55,000 manufacturing employees at AT&T Technologies; 56,000 operating company employees, with large units in New England, Illinois, New Jersey, and Pennsylvania; 4,000 employees at AT&T Communications; and workers at some independent companies.

Employees in the Bell System were originally organized into employee associations.[8] Those associations officially severed their ties with the telephone companies in 1937 to comply with the provisions of the National Labor Relations Act. Meetings of representatives of the associations resulted in creation of the National Federation of Telephone Workers (NFTW) in 1939. Highly decentralized, the NFTW was more a union of autonomous unions than a federation of local unions (Fink 1977).

The membership of the NFTW grew from 45,000 in 1939 to 170,000 in 1945. The postwar period witnessed a large number of strikes, and in the spring of 1946 NFTW president Joseph Beirne threatened a national strike (Fink 1977, 64). At that time all long distance calls were operator assisted and fewer than 60 percent of all telephones had direct-dial capability; a stoppage therefore could have shut down telephone service (Koch, Lewin, and Sockell, forthcoming). Although AT&T committed itself to a national agreement to avoid the strike, it later refused NFTW's demand for industrywide bargaining. It thus became clear that the decentralized structure of the NFTW was ineffective in dealing with AT&T. This was the impetus needed to restructure the union. By 1949 the union had developed a more centralized structure, taken on the name Communications Workers of America, and joined the Congress of Industrial Organizations (CIO). To affiliate with the American Federation of Labor, the union would, it was told, have had to merge with the IBEW, whereas the CIO offered it full (inter)national status (Koch, Lewin, and Sockell, forthcoming).

The IBEW had been the first union to organize telephone workers around the turn of the century. The union was generally opposed, however, to admitting female operators to full membership, and the IBEW therefore established an autonomous division for women, the Telephone Operators Department. Much of the union's later progress was hurt by the formation of employee representation units (company unions) after World War I and also by the union's refusal to create an autonomous department of male telephone workers in 1920 (Fink 1977, 83). As a result, the IBEW was to lose many potential members to the CWA and to local independent unions. Its major stronghold today, as noted above, is at AT&T Technologies (formerly Western Electric).

Independent unions in the industry formed the Telecommunication International Union (TIU) in 1974 to take advantage of national bargaining. At first the organization was simply an affiliation of locals, but around 1980 it switched to being locals of a single union. TIU attempted to affiliate with the AFL-CIO, but its application was rejected because of opposition from the rival IBEW. Then, as an alternative to direct affiliation, TIU attempted to merge with the American Federation of State, County and Municipal Employees (AFSCME). A court battle ensued in which the CWA and the IBEW tried to have their names placed on the ballot as well. Although they lost that battle, they won the war when the TIU membership turned down the merger in 1985 (BNA 1985a, 2). This spelled the end of the TIU. In that year the union lost most of its New York members to the CWA, and its largest local in Connecticut disaffiliated from the union. Membership in TIU went from 50,000 to zero within a year, and the union was dissolved in March 1986 (BNA 1985b, A-13; BNA 1985c, A-16; BNA 1985g, A-9; BNA 1985h, A-13; BNA 1986, A-12). It seems likely that the six remaining independent locals will merge with the CWA, the IBEW, other AFL-CIO unions, or the Teamsters. TIU president John Shaughnessy resigned in 1985 over these merger issues.

It is easy to predict that most of the independent unions will ultimately merge with the CWA or the IBEW, removing them as a third union force in the industry. The Teamsters, however, might emerge as a third union in the industry, having formed a communications division and announced plans to organize MCI. This union may also prove to be a force in organizing the small contractors that have entered the market for telephone installation and repair.

The future of unions in the industry may also be influenced by strategic policy decisions made within the CWA. The union abandoned its National Training Fund in 1985, while at the same time attempting to organize government employees in New York and employees at Trans World Airlines (BNA 1985c, A-15). CWA leaders have consistently expressed their commitment to organize the information industry. All told, these new organizing projects and the cuts in funds for training suggest the union is spreading itself thin.

Changes in technology may also have an influence on the leadership composition and constituencies of the CWA. When the union was formed a vast majority of its members were operators or skilled workers; but the number of operators has been declining over the past 30 years, and the number of skilled workers now accounts for less than 30 percent of the membership. Female clerical workers now constitute over 50 percent of the CWA membership, but most national and local leaders are still drawn from the ranks of skilled workers. It will be interesting to see if a gradual change occurs, with the clerical workers taking a more active role in the union.

Employers

Before divesting the 22 Bell operating companies in 1984, AT&T was the largest nonfinancial corporation in the world. Today it remains the largest company in the industry, with approximately 370,000 employees; there are 574,000 employees in all the regional companies combined and 186,000 employees in the independent telephone companies. AT&T is now divided into five major divisions: AT&T Communications (domestic and international long distance communications, formerly AT&T Long Lines); AT&T Bell Laboratories (research, formerly Bell Telephone Laboratories); AT&T Technologies (telephone equipment, formerly Western Electric); AT&T Information Systems (electronic and computer equipment and enhanced services, formerly American Bell); and AT&T International (marketing AT&T products abroad, not affected by divestiture) (Baumol and Willig 1985). All the divisions will continue to bargain on a centralized, national basis with the major unions.

At divestiture all of the stock of the 22 operating companies (known in the industry as the BOCs or Bell operating companies) was obtained by seven regional holding companies (known as the "seven sisters" or the RBOCs—for Regional Bell Operating Companies). In addition, the seven sisters jointly own Bell Communications Research, Inc. (BELLCORE), which provides many of the services formerly provided by Bell Labs, Western Electric, and AT&T general departments. Plans call for a BELLCORE staff of approximately 8,000 and an annual budget of $750 million (*Telenews* 1983, 14). AT&T had also owned minority shares in Cincinnati Bell and Southern New England Telephone (SNET). Both of these companies are now totally independent and are not part of any RBOC.

As shown in table 5–4, the RBOCs range in size from approximately 70,000 to 100,000 employees. In addition to their stock in the BOCs, each of the holding companies has also set up unregulated companies to enter other sectors of the industry, as well as other industries. The unregulated subsidiaries of Ameritech, for example, are Ameritech Communications (supplies telecommunications equipment nationwide), Ameritech Publishing (publishes directories), Ameritech Development (invests in and develops new ventures), Ameritech Mobile Communications (supplies cellular mobile radios), and Ameritech Credit (finances equipment sales for customers) (*Bell Communications Research News* 1985, 1 and 4). These unregulated subsidiaries are in most cases nonunion.

There are approximately 1,400 independent telephone companies. According to the United States Telephone Association (Snyder 1985) the ten largest are GTE Corporation; United Telephone System, Inc.; Continental Telecom; Southern New England Telephone Company; Centel Corporation; ALLTEL Corporation; Cincinnati Bell; Puerto Rico Telephone Company, Rochester Telephone Corporation; and Century Telephone Enterprises, Inc. In addition, Western Union has approximately 14,000 employees, and Northern Telecom (the Western Electric of Bell Canada) has 20,000 employees in the United States. With the exception of Western Union, all bargaining with these independents is local. Northern Telecom is nonunion.

The Structure of Bargaining

Although the telephone industry has been dominated for years by a single company, AT&T, and a single union, CWA, the industry has always been officially structured into a large number of local bargaining units.[9] Before divestiture AT&T had 163 different labor contracts. Beginning with the first agreement between AT&T and the NFTW in 1940, the union has continuously attempted to nationalize bargaining, matched in its efforts by ongoing opposition from the company.

As noted above, the NFTW's attempt to gain national bargaining in 1947 failed and precipitated the restructuring and renaming of the union as the CWA. The first inroads to national bargaining were accomplished in the 1950s with "cluster bargaining," through which two operating companies bargained together. In the later 1950s and early 1960s the union established pattern bargaining along the lines of the previous clusters. In 1965 CWA succeeded in linking wages to cost-of-living increases throughout all settlements in the Bell system. The union also adopted a policy of "an equal standard of living for equal work." Thus, there was a great deal of coordination of bargaining prior to the first nationally bargained contract signed in 1974. In fact, the previous contract, in 1971, was settled only after a five-day national strike (described below). One could reasonably argue that the 1974

Table 5–4
Number of Employees and Number of Union Members at the Major Telecommunications Companies in 1985–86

Company	Total Number of Employees	CWA Members	IBEW Members	Independent Members
AT&T	370,000	149,187	34,479	
Regional holding companies				

Nynex
  New York Telephone
  New England Telephone
	98,000[a]	39,915	19,050	2,800

Bell Atlantic
  New Jersey Bell
  Bell of Pennsylvania
  Diamond State Telephone
  Chesapeake & Potomac Telephone
	80,000[a]	38,588	10,904	571

Bell South
  Southern Bell
  South Central Bell
	96,000[a]	64,563	0	0

Ameritech
  Illinois Bell
  Indiana Bell
  Michigan Bell
  Wisconsin Telephone
	80,000[a]	37,000	13,000	0

Southwestern Bell . Southwestern Bell	72,000[a]	45,707	0	0

U.S. West
  Northwestern Bell
  Mountain Bell
  Pacific Northwest Bell
	71,000[a]	39,535	1,000	700

Pacific Telesis
  Pacific Bell
  Nevada Bell
	77,000[a]	44,562	2,505	0

Major Independents				
Cincinnati Bell	5,200[b]	0	0	0
Southern New England Telephone	13,269[b]	0	0	9,700
GTE Corporation	201,000[b]	37,000	—[c]	—[c]
Northern Telecom	20,000[b]			
Western Union	14,000[b]	10,400[d]		

Note: The first column presents totals of all employees (including supervisors and managers) and therefore should not be taken to represent the potentially organizable portion of the work force for each company. Totals for union members in the other three columns were obtained (except where noted) either from the personnel departments of the companies or from the CWA. The numbers were obtained in telephone interviews in the summer and fall of 1986.

[a]Bell Communication Research News (1985, 4).

[b]Standard and Poor's (1985, various pages).

[c]Breakdowns for IBEW and independent unions not available.

[d]This number includes the United Telegraph Workers union, which is scheduled to merge with the CWA.

contract was simply a recognition of the de facto national bargaining that had taken place for years. The 1974 contract was reached without altering the established bargaining units. Instead, the individual operating companies signed "enabling clauses" that allowed AT&T to bargain in their behalf. They still remained the actual signators to the contracts with the individual locals, however (although in bargaining with the CWA, the international president actually signed the local contracts).

While attempting to nationalize wage schedules with AT&T, the CWA and the other unions have also attempted to induce the independent companies to follow the AT&T pattern. Bargaining has remained on a local basis, and only moderate pattern following among the independents has been apparent. In 1963 there was a 150-day strike against General Telephone of California because General would not follow the Bell "pattern" (Brooks 1977, 224). Though the CWA was successful in that case, Bell System contracts have typically had only a moderate impact on local negotiations involving the independents.

The period of national bargaining beginning in the 1960s, codified in 1974, and extending up to the divestiture in 1982 was characterized by a high degree of centralization. As noted earlier, this centralization was probably a direct outgrowth of regulation. But divestiture changed the bargaining arrangements considerably. The 1983 agreement was the last agreement signed on a nationwide basis. Because the structure of the CWA was in a large part explained by the structure of the industry and its dominant company, we would have expected the union to change. The union's first response to decentralization was to set up two bargaining councils: one for AT&T and one for the Bell System operating companies. At first, the latter council demanded that the RBOCs bargain together nationally (although the companies would actually sign separate agreements, as was done in basic steel until 1985). When it became obvious that the RBOCs intended to resist this demand, the CWA restructured its districts in 1985 so that they mirrored the geographic boundaries of the seven regional holding companies. The union then proposed that the RBOCs bargain on a regional basis.

Before the 1986 negotiations five of the seven holding companies agreed to "coordinated" negotiations in which representatives of all BOCs in the holding company would sit down together with the union. Ameritech and U.S. West refused to accept coordinated bargaining, preferring instead to bargain on an individual company basis.

Thus, although the CWA had earlier evolved to negotiate through a highly centralized bargaining structure, three separate types of structures are likely to develop in the future as a result of divestiture: national bargaining with branches of AT&T; regional coordinated bargaining with most RBOCs; and local bargaining with some BOCs and the independent companies.

The Bargaining Process

Historical Patterns

Before 1974 all bargaining in the industry, technically speaking, took place at the local level. In the case of AT&T, the company met with representatives of the IBEW and the CWA to set the range of bargaining issues prior to local negotiations. The CWA would then attempt to pick a single local company (often Ohio Bell) as its pattern setter.

Although bargaining later remained local for the independent telephone companies, the 1974 bargaining round centralized negotiations at AT&T. Three bargaining tables were established: one for the CWA, one for the IBEW, and one for the TIU. Recall that it was at this time that the independent unions had loosely affiliated under the TIU to take advantage of national bargaining. Their president was allowed to be a spokesperson for the individual unions only in this special case. For its part, the IBEW formed the Telephone Coordinating Council One (TCC1), made up of the president of each local; and the TCC1, in turn, chose five representatives for its bargaining team. Only the presidents of the locals, however, could actually sign the agreements. In addition, all IBEW contracts had to be reviewed by the international in case some of its principles were violated. In 1983, for example, the CWA and the TIU had both agreed to a ten-hour, four-day week. Those terms were rejected by the IBEW international because they violated the union's principle of no ten-hour days, which applied to all IBEW contracts. The CWA had already formed the Bell Bargaining Council. Typically, bargaining would begin, bargaining would be recessed for the CWA convention, and then serious bargaining would take place. In the CWA the international holds the contracts, so the President, Glen Watts, signed each one.

In theory, national bargaining with each of the three unions was supposed to occur simultaneously. In addition, local bargaining was to start around the same time and be completed one or two weeks after the national settlement. The original understanding in 1974 was that national bargaining would cover only wages and benefits, but in later years it was expanded to cover other contract issues as well.

The 1974 agreement essentially froze wage differentials among the Bell operating companies. There was still some bargaining, however, at the local level over a portion of the wage increase. During the period of national bargaining, between 0.4 and 0.6 percent of the increase for each bargaining unit was negotiated as "local money." This local money was typically spent on job upgrades, town upgrades, changes in travel and living allowances, and so on. There was no requirement that all local money had to be disbursed, but the usual policy was to spend the entire allocation, sometimes in exchange for work rule concessions by the union.

This process changed substantially after divestiture. Before, in seeking to settle a national contract with AT&T the CWA had found it advantageous to have all contracts expire at the same time. But after divestiture the union realized that it would be spreading its resources too thin if it attempted to negotiate all AT&T contracts and all contracts with the RBOCs at the same time. Since all AT&T contracts and contracts with individual BOCs were scheduled to expire in August 1986, AT&T and the CWA agreed to move up bargaining to May 1986.

One interesting development surfaced at the RBOCs. President Bahr of the CWA indicated that if Ameritech would not agree to coordinated bargaining, the union would attempt to set the pattern at Ohio Bell and would accept no less at the other companies (Richards 1986). This had been the same company targeted for pattern setting before the first national contract. As with bargaining structure, therefore, the bargaining process may follow a road previously traveled.

Issues in Bargaining

As noted above, for many years the major issue in bargaining was the union's demand for national bargaining and uniform wages and AT&T's opposition to that demand. This issue was resolved in 1974. Nonetheless, divestiture has made this a major topic for future negotiations.

Technological change and deregulation together made workers in the industry much more cognizant of the need for job security. To a large extent, they have achieved security both through bargaining and through the unions' contributions to Judge Green's reorganization plan for AT&T. Unlike the airline unions, which dealt with deregulation problems only *after* deregulation (see chapter 6 in this volume), the telephone unions were farsighted enough to bargain for employee protection in their 1980 agreement—several years before the breakup. At that time the unions signed a Memorandum of Agreement with AT&T (Straw 1985) that provided protections for transferred employees. This memorandum was amended and supplemented in 1982 and 1983 when details of the divestiture became clearer. The revised agreements, labeled the New Entities Agreements I and II (or together as the Modified New Entities Agreement), specified the preservation of wages and the net credited service of transferred employees for five years after transfer; no reduction of pension, health, or other benefits as a result of transfer; payment of reasonable travel and moving expenses for transfer; continued application of the collective bargaining agreement in effect in the previous location; preferential hiring rights for transferees; advance notice to the union of any work group transfer; and the subsidiaries' or affiliates' continued recognition of the CWA as the exclusive bargaining agent of the transferees (Straw 1985).

Several issues raised by the divestiture were important enough to be first bargained and then later incorporated in the AT&T reorganization plan (much of the wording on labor issues was drawn directly from the New Entities Agreements). First was the question of which contract would cover workers when they were transferred between companies. The general concept was "the people follow the work, and the contract follows the people." This meant workers might work side-by-side doing the same job and be covered by different contracts. For example, 130 to 140 switchmen were transferred from Illinois Bell to AT&T Communications (AT&T COM). The Illinois Bell workers were covered by the IBEW, while the AT&T COM workers had a national contract through the CWA. In this case AT&T COM petitioned the NLRB for unit clarification, and the IBEW workers were incorporated into the CWA agreement. Thus, the contract did follow the people, but only partway there. This issue remains a problem.

There is another loophole in the concept that the contract follows the people. If a new subsidiary is set up and existing workers are not transferred to that subsidiary, the company can hire off the street while at the same time laying off people in the old divisions. This is a serious issue between the unions and the firms.

The second major concern was over pensions. Before the divestiture, the Bell System fringe benefits package was maintained either on a national basis by AT&T for all the Bell System or on a local basis by each company. At divestiture the reorganization plan provided that the national benefit plans would be split among the remaining AT&T companies, the new regional companies, and the new central services organization (BELLCORE), while the various local benefit plans would continue at each existing company and also be adopted by any new organization. The reorganization plan also specified that, at divestiture, all employees, regardless of the company to which they were newly assigned, would receive benefits that were generally comparable to those they had received before divestiture. In addition, employees who had retired prior to divestiture would continue to receive the same pension and other benefits as before divestiture from the company from which they had retired, or from the company's parent organization.

These provisions of the plan, referred to as the "divestiture interchange agreement," provided pension portability, or the "mutual reciprocal recognition of service credit, between and among AT&T, the divested Bell operating companies and the other parties to that agreement" (U.S. House of Representatives 1984). The divestiture interchange agreement, however, was limited to calendar year 1984. Employees transferring during 1984, according to this plan, would take their service credit with them; employees transferring after 1984, however, would not be eligible to carry with them their accumulated service credit.

Two months after the reorganization plan was filed, the CWA formally objected to the pension plan changes AT&T had proposed because the plan allowed only a one-year "true up" for pension portability (that is, 1984) and because, the union argued, the separate pension plans contravened the principles of the divestiture order and that any such contraventions should be decided on through collective bargaining. The court did not accept those arguments. Concern over potential problems with the transfers prompted the unions to lobby for legislation that would provide pension portability beyond 1984, and eight separate bills were subsequently introduced in the House and Senate. But disagreements over other issues raised by the reorganization stopped their passage. In the end, the union's lobbying efforts succeeded in having a pension portability provision tacked on to the Deficit Reduction Act of 1984 (H.R. 4170), which was signed into law on July 18, 1984. This legislation permanently extended the pension portability provision after 1984 for workers earning less than $50,000 annually (adjusted for cost of living), and it specified no time limit on the recognition of service credit. In addition, an employee does not have to have worked continuously for a company (subject to the modification of the final judgment)[10] to be considered a covered employee. For example, suppose a telephone worker, employed with a covered company before 1984, continued to work for the company through 1984 and 1985 and then left in 1986 for a job with a firm that was not a covered company. If, at any later date, that person returns to employment with any covered company, the new employer must recognize the employee's service credit accrued at the other covered company before he or she left in 1986 (U.S. House of Representatives 1984).

Finally, in a Letter of Understanding, the CWA and AT&T agreed to red circle rates, titles, and pension plans for the life of the 1983 contract for workers assigned to the lower rated jobs (Straw 1985).[11]

The issues raised by divestiture in telecommunications are in some ways unique to the industry but in other ways they are not unlike the problems caused by mergers and acquisitions. Although some predictable problems have arisen, the parties have been able to forge a relatively smooth transition with a minimum of outside interference, in sharp contrast to the handling of deregulation in the airlines. Nonetheless, the transition in telecommunications has only just begun.

Contract Administration

Specifications for the joint administration of certain aspects of union-management relations are contained in Bell System contracts. One provision is the Common Interest Forum, where leaders of the union and the corporation meet to discuss and decide upon a broad expanse of issues concerning the corporation. Other joint committees are charged with examining issues of cost containment and training and retraining. In the Technological Change

Committee, for example, union and management representatives address the problems of potential job displacement in advance of actual changes in the work force. The Bell System also sponsors joint quality-of-working-life (QWL) steering committees for resolving problems at the workplace.

When grievances arise, they are typically processed by advancing the grievance to successively higher levels of management and the union. The actual procedures vary across Bell companies and within AT&T. At Illinois Bell, for example, the initiator of the grievance brings up the issue with the first-line supervisor. If it is not resolved, the union steward is brought in to discuss it with the foreman. An unresolved grievance is then taken to the second-level manager, the foreman's superior. If agreement is not reached, the union sends in its business representative, a higher level union officer, who meets with a third-level manager. The company's labor relations staff is responsible for any grievance taken beyond this stage. Chesapeake and Potomac Telephone, as another example, has a three-step procedure. In the first step, if the shop steward cannot settle the complaint informally with the supervisor, a formal grievance is filed. The grievance meeting is conducted by the chief steward, and the company is represented by two first-line managers. At the second step, the union is represented by the vice-president of the local and the company, by the district manager (bypassing the second-level manager). At the third step, the ranking person for the union is the district staff representative, while the district labor relations manager as well as either a fourth-level (division) or fifth-level (department or assistant vice president) manager represents the company.

Arbitration is the final step in the Bell System's grievance procedure. It typically does not set precedents for contract interpretation. An examination of GTE's total grievances for 1984 shows that the most prevalent categories of grievances were those over issues of suspensions (28 percent), work jurisdiction (7 percent), and overtime (7 percent).[12] A similar pattern holds for the CWA in general; over half its grievances are over disciplinary action, and the second largest category is promotions and transfers.

Industrial Conflict

Two significant peculiarities of telecommunications have had a major impact on strike activity in the industry. First, historically most negotiations have taken place at the local level; most strikes have therefore affected only a relatively small number of workers and a limited geographic area. Second, the level of automation in the communications segment of the industry has made it relatively easy for the companies to continue operations during a strike. This is especially true for AT&T. Before the divestiture AT&T could call in management personnel from throughout the nation when a local strike occurred. But this is less true in the manufacturing segment of the industry (Western Electric). Nonetheless, because the individual plants of Western Electric had local agreements (which followed a very strong pattern), AT&T could in some instances maintain output when an individual plant went on strike. In any event there was little chance for lost customers, since the only customers of Western Electric were the AT&T operating companies. Thus, the impact of strikes on industry output has always been minor. Today, however, AT&T may be more vulnerable to a strike. Shutting down AT&T Technologies could put the company out of business, except for the long distance trade, which could suffer as well if the strike were protracted and the supply of parts ran out.

There have been four national strikes against AT&T. The first, in 1947, was called by the NFTW over its demand for national bargaining. The strike called out 345,000 workers and lasted for one month (Brooks 1977, 106). In the end the workers won wage increases but lost the national bargaining issue. In 1968 the union held its second nationwide strike against AT&T. The strike was called after little progress had been made in negotiations over wage-reopening provisions scheduled under the 1966 agreements. It was settled after 18 days by writing a new three-year basic agreement. The third, in 1971, called out 440,000 workers for five days (Brooks 1977, 232). The major issues this time were wage increases, a union security clause, and ironing out the male-female wage differentials that existed in some geographic areas. After the settlement some locals continued to stay out. Workers at New York Bell were on strike for 217 days. They finally settled for essentially the same wage terms; but they were able to achieve a union shop, whereas the other locals had settled for modified union security provisions (these modified provisions typically provided for grandfathering clauses for current non-members who were hired prior to 1971). Union leaders believe that this general strike was a major cause of AT&T's agreement to national bargaining in the next negotiations.

The fourth national strike, in 1983, was the first under national bargaining. The major issues were health insurance benefits and pay increases. Approximately 635,000 workers stayed out for 22 days, making this the second largest strike by any union in U.S. history and the largest in 37 years (BNA 1983, A-5). Nevertheless, its impact on customers was negligible, with only some delays for new equipment and maintenance and reduced long distance operator service. Local operations were largely unaffected. During the strike a spokesperson for AT&T indicated that the company could return operations to normal within two weeks of the end of the strike (BNA 1983, A-5). Thus, even though this last strike was major, output losses were minor.

There have been many more local strikes, especially at Western Electric.

The issues in those strikes have changed over the years. At first the primary goal of the unions was recognition. Later, in the 1950s, a number of strikes were called over changes in the pension system and over company attempts to weaken arbitration provisions. One unique aspect of those strikes was their so-called hit-and-run nature. The strikes would focus on one Bell operating company at a time and typically would last for 11 days. In most instances they were called to dramatize a grievance or force bargaining to a conclusion (Brooks 1977, 164).

A number of current conflicts could lead to more strike activity in the near future. First, although divestiture has effectively eliminated national bargaining, the unions will attempt to maintain this process and the companies will resist. Second, although the CWA fought hard to eliminate regional wage differentials realizing a good deal of success in the 1960s and 1970s, the Bell System companies are likely to attempt to reinstate those differentials. Third, employment in the traditional crafts in the industry has been declining, in part because of the competition of the new nonunion companies. Job security is therefore an important issue. Finally, Bell System companies have been expanding their operations by adding nonunion subsidiaries. There is a potential for a great deal of conflict over control of jobs at those locations.

Maintaining low labor costs, in particular, is one way the new, nonunion firms are challenging the unionized companies. To reduce this labor cost differential, AT&T, in a Common Interest Forum held during the 1983 contract negotiations, proposed establishing a profit-sharing system and a job bank (offering lifetime employment) for employees in return for the elimination of automatic wage increases and deferred cost-of-living adjustments. No agreement was reached on those issues.[13] Bell System companies are also cutting labor costs with layoffs. Ameritech, for example, proposed to lay off between 750 and 5,030 employees in 1986.[14] The corresponding strategy of the unions is to organize the new companies, thereby taking wages out of competition. The number of nonunion firms is large, however, and most have a small work force, making organizing difficult (*Business Week* 1985).

In addition to the possibility that strike activity will increase because of conflicts over specific issues, there is also the possibility that agreements will be difficult to reach simply because the level of uncertainty in negotiations has increased. Profit levels may not be as easy to predict in the new, more competitive markets, making it more difficult to plan for wage increases in long-term agreements. Moreover, both the companies and the unions will be undergoing internal organizational changes—changes that may lead to errors in judgment that will be difficult for the other side to interpret. Finally, the new bargaining structures will mean that both sides may be less certain about the other's position simply because conditions and personalities have changed dramatically.

Conclusions

The most salient features of bargaining in telecommunications have been the dominance of the industry by one firm (AT&T) and by one union (CWA), the role of regulation in maintaining this dominance, and the impact of technological change directly on regulatory policies and indirectly on the economic structure of the industry and the power of unions. It took many years for the union to achieve its primary objective of national bargaining with AT&T. And this system seemed to work fairly well: AT&T received good and stable profits; workers were well compensated; relatively little output was lost due to strikes; and the telephone system provided a high-quality product at a reasonable price. Technological change, changes in regulatory policy, and divestiture have combined to change this picture. At first, the actors seemed to adjust to the change quite readily. Collectively bargained provisions for a transition period were accomplished with only limited problems; and unlike the experience with deregulation in airlines and trucking, the parties were able to negotiate an agreement that was mutually beneficial. But as the threat of new, nonunion competition has become more real, new problems have emerged on the horizon.

It should be emphasized that telecommunications is still far from completely deregulated. *Computer II* and consent decree constraints on the leading U.S. firms still hinder their entry into many information-processing markets. For example, local companies would like to sell their services to electricity companies to monitor their clients' energy consumption, thereby saving the electric companies millions of dollars now spent on meter readers, but the telecommunications firms are probably restricted from doing so under the *Computer II* decision. Some of these issues will be taken up in the FCC's new *Computer III* investigation. U.S. firms are also being hurt by their inability to compete on an equal basis with foreign firms. Foreign firms have unfettered access to U.S. markets, while U.S. regulatory policies and foreign trade restrictions limit U.S. firms' entry into foreign markets. It is estimated that by 1990 the market for telecommunications equipment will reach $831 billion worldwide and $201 billion in the United States alone. Thus, the growing trade imbalance, as shown in table 5–5 is cause for concern.

AT&T has announced plans to move all production of residential telephones to Singapore (BNA 1985d, A-10). For the first time, telecommunications unions are facing the threat of runaway plants. In addition, many RBOCs are becoming double-breasted with union and nonunion operations. In some cases they (as well as many independent companies) are threatening to transfer work to nonunion affiliates or simply eliminate a line of work entirely. Some companies, for example, are considering eliminating repair and installation crews and leaving the field to local (most likely nonunion)

Table 5-5
U.S. Trade Balance with the World in Electronic Products, 1980 and 1984
(in $ millions)

Service or Product	Balance in 1980	Balance in 1984
Communications	968	−608
Computers	6,309	5,936
Components	625	−2,968
Consumer products, office products, and instruments	−526	−8,520
Total balance	7,376	−6,160

Source: NTIA (1985, 158, table 8-1) (based on official Bureau of Census statistics of April 1985).

contractors. This will put considerably more pressure on unions to accept lesser compensation packages.

In addition to the problems they face in firms that are already organized, unions—as well as employers—are now facing significant competition from new, nonunion firms. For instance, IBM has purchased MCI and Rohm, indicating that it will become much more active in the communications field. Since IBM is committed to remaining a nonunion company, this poses a new problem for the unions. CWA president Morton Bahr has indicated that his union will "develop a strategy to begin a world coordinated organizing campaign against IBM" (BNA 1985e, A-8).

The next decade will complete the transition of the telecommunications industry from a regulated monopoly to a highly competitive industry. It is likely that the degree of unionization in the industry will decline as small, nonunion firms enter to compete in very limited product lines or geographic areas. The information industry as a whole is only 35 percent organized today, whereas the old, regulated telecommunications industry is approximately 90 percent unionized. As management attempts to cut costs to meet this new competition the potential for conflict between unions and management is considerable. This conflict will occur over issues of both bargaining structure and compensation packages. Import penetration has increased from 2 percent of the telecommunications market in 1982 to 14 percent in 1984. The CWA estimates that as many as 120,000 unionized jobs in the industry were lost between 1982 and 1985 (*AFL-CIO News* 1985a, 1). And, AT&T recently announced plans to eliminate 24,000 jobs at AT&T Information Systems (including 7,000 managerial jobs) over an unspecified period (*AFL-CIO News* 1985b, 3).

It would be easy to predict that the turmoil in telecommunications will match that we have witnessed in airlines. This may turn out to be the case. Nonetheless, the parties have had a relatively pacific history of effectively negotiating their differences in the past, and their mutual acceptance may well carry over into the future.

Notes

1. NTIA (1985, 7–32) provides a much more detailed analysis of the issues contained in this section.

2. KTS stands for key telephone sets and PBX stands for private branch exchanges. Both are business systems that allow the customer to transfer calls within a local hookup. PBX systems typically have a private operator within the building.

3. Some would argue that this applies only to local service.

4. 522 F.Supp. 131 (1982).

5. For more detail on bargaining effects, see Hendricks (1977).

6. These data were obtained from J.R. Smith, Vice President for Personnel, Illinois Bell.

7. For more detail on the decree, see Northrup and Larson (1979).

8. See Brooks (1977) for a more comprehensive history of the unions.

9. Koch, Lewin, and Sockell (forthcoming) provide a detailed analysis of bargaining issues.

10. This provision has been challenged in court by the companies. At this writing a final judgment has not been made.

11. In telecommunications the term used is "green circle" rather than red circle, to make it clear that this agreement refers only to the workers and not to the jobs.

12. These data were obtained from GTE.

13. A number of nuances of the AT&T plan made it unacceptable to the union leaders, and they therefore did not carry the plan back to their members for approval.

14. The original announcements of 11,000 workers to be laid off (*Business Week* 1985) were apparently incorrect. Our figure is from Fred Peters of Ameritech.

References

AFL-CIO News. 1985a. "CWA Slates 'Day of Protest' on 'Mess' from Bell Breakup." Vol. 30, no. 31, August 3, p. 1.

———. 1985b. "CWA Voices Outrage at Massive Jobs Slash." Vol. 30, no. 34, August, 24.

Baumol, William J., and Robert D. Willig. 1985. "Telephones and Computers: The Costs of Artificial Separation." *Regulation* (March–April): 23–32.

Bell Communications Research News. 1985. Vol. 2, no. 2, January 23.

BNA (Bureau of National Affairs), *Daily Labor Report.* 1982a. No. 19, January 28.

———. 1982b. No. 243, December 17.

———. 1983a. No. 115, June 14.

———. 1983b. No. 168, August 29.

———. 1984a. No. 152, August 7.

————. 1984b. No. 153, August 8.

————. 1985a. No. 44, March 6.

————. 1985b. No. 88, May 7.

————. 1985c. No. 116, June 17.

————. 1985d. No. 131, July 9.

————. 1985e. No. 137, July 17.

————. 1985f. No. 139, July 19.

————. 1985g. No. 166, October 10.

————. 1985h. No. 197, October 10.

————. 1986. No. 40, February 28.

Bolter, Walter G. 1984. Restructuring in Telecommunication and Regulatory Adjustment. *Public Utilities Fortnightly,* July 5, pp. 15–22.

Brock, George. 1981. *The Telecommunications Industry: The Dynamics of Market Structure.* Cambridge, Mass.: Harvard University Press.

Brooks, Thomas R. 1977. *Communications Workers of America.* New York: Mason/Charter.

Business Week. 1985. After the Bell Breakup: A Different Ball Game for Unions. May 13, pp. 50–52.

Ehrenberg, Ronald G. 1979. *The Regulatory Process and Labor Earnings.* New York: Academic Press.

Fink, Gary M., ed. 1977. *Labor Unions: The Greenwood Encyclopedia of American Institutions.* Westport, Conn.: Greenwood Press.

Hendricks, Wallace. 1977. Regulation and Labor Earnings. *Bell Journal of Economics* 8 (Autumn): 483–96.

————. 1986. Collective Bargaining in Regulated Industries. In *Advances in Industrial and Labor Relations,* vol. 3, ed. David B. Lipsky and David Lewin, 21–42. Greenwich, Conn.: JAI Press.

Koch, Marianne, David Lewin, and Donna Sockell. Forthcoming. The Effects of Deregulation on Bargaining Structure: The Case of AT&T. In *Advances in Industrial and Labor Relations,* vol. 4, ed. David Lewin, David B. Lipsky, and Donna Sockell. Greenwich, Conn.: JAI Press.

Northrup, Herbert R., and John A. Larson. 1979. *The Impact of the AT&T-EEO Consent Decree,* Labor Relations and Public Policy Series no. 20. Philadelphia: Industrial Research Unit, Wharton School, University of Pennsylvania.

NTIA (National Telecommunications and Information Administration). 1985. *Issues in Domestic Telecommunications: Directions for National Policy,* NTIA Special Publication 85-16. Washington, D.C.: U.S. Department of Commerce.

Owen, Bruce M., and Ronald Braeutigam. 1978. *The Regulation Games: Strategic Use of the Administrative Process.* Cambridge, Mass.: Ballinger.

Richards, Cindy. 1986. Union Names Ohio Bell "Pattern" for Pact Talks. *Chicago Sun Times,* February 19.

Schacht, John N. 1985. *The Making of Telephone Unionism, 1920–1947.* New Brunswick, N.J.: Rutgers University Press.

Shooshan, Harry M., ed. 1984. *Disconnecting Bell.* New York: Pergamon.

Snyder, C.S. 1985. *Statistics for the Telephone Industry,* vol. 1. Washington, D.C.: United States Telephone Association.

Standard and Poor's Register of Corporations, Directors and Executives, vol. 1. 1985. New York: Standard and Poor's.

Straw, Ronnie J. 1985. The Effect of Divestiture on Collective Bargaining. In *Proceedings of the Thirty-Seventh Annual Meeting, December 28–30, 1984, Dallas,* ed. Barbara D. Dennis, 447–54. Madison, Wis.: Industrial Relations Research Association.

Telenews. 1983. In Search of an Industry: The New CSO. October 22, pp. 14–15.

USDOL (U.S. Department of Labor, Bureau of Labor Statistics). 1979. Technology and Labor in Five Industries, Bulletin 2033. Washington, D.C.: GPO.

———. 1986. *Employment and Earnings* 33 (February).

U.S. House of Representatives. 1984. Deficit Reduction Act of 1984, Report 98-861, 98th Cong., 2d sess. Washington, D.C.:

USTA (United States Telephone Association). 1984. *Statistics of the Independent Telephone Industry.* Washington, D.C.: USTA.

6
Airlines

Peter Cappelli

The system of industrial relations and collective bargaining in the airline industry is unique, the result not only of the technology of the industry and the specialized skills of airline employees, but also of the elaborate set of regulations, especially product market regulations, placed on the industry by the government. The elimination of those regulations beginning in the late 1970s serves as a natural experiment we can observe to assess the general role played by competitive markets in collective bargaining. In addition, the variety of occupations and unions throughout the industry make it an especially apt example to use in assessing how different bargaining situations adapt to such major environmental changes as deregulation. An understanding of those adaptations is necessary for any predictions for the future of this heavily unionized industry that now finds itself in volatile circumstances indeed.

The Bargaining Environment

Technology and the Development of the Industry

The elaborate system of regulations that both restricted and protected the industry was initiated by the federal government at a time when the free market gave every sign of being incapable of developing a system for air transport.[1] The government, through the U.S. Post Office, saw the potential value of air transportation before the industry existed, and it was the Post Office that began the first scheduled flights, which carried only mail. Private contractors eventually took over the routes, but they fared poorly and many went bank-

I am grateful to the Airline Industrial Relations Conference (AIRCon) its members, and especially to Jerry Glass, its Research Director, for providing much of the material used in this study. Thanks also to the Industrial Research Unit, the Wharton School, University of Pennsylvania, for the use of its files; to Sheldon Kline, Research Director, National Mediation Board; Keith Prouty, Labor Specialist, Department of Transportation; Norm Weintraub, Research Director, the Teamsters; and Herbert R. Northrup and Mark L. Kahn for helpful comments. This study benefited from continuing research on airline industrial relations conducted with Robert B. McKersie and from a substudy of events at Western Airlines, conducted with Kirsten Wever and Peter Sherer.

rupt. As a response to the pending collapse of the air transport system, the Hoover administration created the Watres Act of 1930, which gave the Post Office the power to subsidize carriers and reduce what appeared to be ruinous price competition. Unfortunately, the contractors lost even more money as the industry grew.

Passenger traffic had gradually developed and was becoming a more important source of revenue than mail for some carriers.[2] With passenger growth came greater concern for air safety, intensified by a series of spectacular crashes in the 1930s, one of which took the life of a U.S. Senator. The Roosevelt administration held that the concerns for safety and for economic health should be addressed together, in part because of the circumstantial evidence available at the time that poor economic performance created pressures to skimp on safety. The economic regulations proposed were guided by New Deal– and Depression-inspired views of competition: unbridled competition was harmful because it led to price cutting, bankruptcies, and unstable market structures.[3]

The Civil Aeronautics Act of 1938 set about establishing a market structure that would eliminate the problems associated with unlimited competition and thus help stabilize the industry. Competitive bidding for routes was abolished. The Civil Aeronautics Board (CAB), which administered safety and economic regulations under the act, granted routes not on the basis of costs but on the basis of the board's goal of integrating carrier networks. As Bailey, Graham, and Kaplan (1985) pointed out, the CAB never awarded a major route to a carrier that was not already established. The number of certificated carriers soon dropped to fifteen, four of which became the dominant long-distance carriers—Trans World (TWA), American, and United Airlines on the east-west routes, and Eastern Airlines on the north-south routes. Mail rates provided subsidies that would help carriers extend service and stabilize their operations in hard times. To prevent price wars, the CAB also set uniform fares for carriers flying the same routes. At the same time, to prevent collusion, the CAB had the power to approve all mergers, changes in routes, and agreements between the carriers. In short, the New Deal architects of the air transport system imposed regulations to restrain the competitive forces that had appeared to be hindering the development of the air transport system. Fifty years later, that assumption would be reversed by the proponents of deregulation.

The Legal and Economic Environments: The System of Regulations

The development of a system of market regulations helped shape the major developments in labor relations. Pilots were the most important employee group in the industry, and their relations with management were generally peaceful until the late 1920s, when private contractors took over from the Post Office.[4] The hard times and price cutting facing carriers in those years coincided with a post–World War I pilot surplus. In a move that would be a harbinger of things to come, E.L. Cord, head of Century Airlines, took the company out of business, forced Century pilots to resign, and then reorganized the airline and rehired the pilots at half their previous pay. Cord's success in that action led other carriers almost simultaneously to cut their pilots' pay and, in turn, led to the creation of the Air Line Pilots Association (ALPA) in 1931. ALPA formed a temporary alliance with the other major carriers against Cord and drove him, also temporarily, out of the business.

The government took its first step in regulating airlines when the New Deal's National Labor Board agreed to arbitrate an industrywide pilot pay dispute as part of the interest, as expressed in the National Industrial Recovery Act of 1933, in establishing wage rules. With the introduction of larger, faster planes, such as the DC-3 on the horizon, the formula for determining pilot pay became a very important issue. Hourly rates would mean a drop in earnings as pilots came to fly faster planes over a given route, whereas mileage-based rates would give them substantial increases for the same amount of flight time. In its Decision Number 83 the Labor Board established a compromise formula basing pay on seniority, hours flown, and the average speed of the plane.

The pilots' union successfully lobbied Congress in 1934 to require compliance with Decision 83 as a condition of holding an airmail contract. ALPA also managed to secure similar language in the Civil Aeronautics Act of 1938. Decision 83 therefore not only established the formula by which pilot pay is determined but mandated its use with legislative protections; failure to abide by the pay formula would cause the rescinding of the carrier's certification. Although these protections ended with deregulation, the pay formula itself remains the basis for pilot pay today.[5]

The Railway Labor Act. ALPA secured an equally impressive legislative victory in 1936 when Title II of the Railway Labor Act (RLA) was signed, bringing the airline industry under the coverage of that act. And as with Decision 83, ALPA managed to secure language in the Civil Aeronautics Act of 1938 requiring airline compliance with the RLA as a condition of certification. The practical consequence of this decision was to involve the Civil Aeronautics Board directly in enforcing the RLA and in ruling on labor relations issues.[6]

The Railway Labor Act was, of course, designed for the railroads, which share at least two important characteristics with airlines. First, both operations are spread geographically over a routing system. It was argued, therefore, that bargaining units and the bargaining process should be systemwide rather than restricted to a given geographic area, as under the National Labor Relations Act (NLRA). Systemwide units prevent employers from shifting to nonunion locations but may make it more difficult for unions to rally support from members in isolated geographic areas. Second, employees in both industries tend in general to fall into readily distinguishable occupations, termed crafts or classes in the RLA. Because of this the National Mediation Board (NMB), which enforces the RLA, has interpreted the act to require that bargaining units be based on occupational crafts.[7]

Union representation under the RLA also differs from its form under the NLRA. Under the RLA supervisors can be included in bargaining units; employers are not party to representation proceedings and cannot call for elections; and unfair labor practices carry criminal penalties, though they are difficult to enforce. Furthermore, the act specifies no formal procedures for decertification. In 1983, however, an NMB decision did establish a de facto procedure. Failure of any union to secure a majority of votes in a representation election will cause the board to certify "no union." In the three years since the NMB decision, approximately 1,000 workers have had their unions decertified under this procedure.[8]

Perhaps the most notable aspects of the RLA are its procedures for handling disputes. The act established that the parties have a virtual duty to settle differences peacefully. The National Mediation Board, which combines rulemaking and mediation functions, requires mediation in contract disputes and may require the continuance of mediation efforts until the board is convinced that an impasse has been reached. Once the board releases the parties from mediation, they must observe a 30-day "cooling off" period before they can strike. If such a strike would disrupt essential transport services for at least a section of the country, the President may appoint an emergency board to examine the facts of the case and issue recommendations. Although the recommendations are not binding on the parties, the force of public opinion may create pressure for acceptance. If there is still no settlement, the parties must again wait 30 days before engaging in strikes or lockouts.[9]

Some observers have argued that the use of emergency boards "chilled" bargaining, as bargaining positions froze until board reports were issued, and also politicized the process by involving the government (Northrup 1971). Indeed, the appointment of emergency boards is closely associated with administrations sympathetic to labor—common in Democratic administrations, uncommon in Republican terms. The appointment of boards seems to have fallen out of fashion in recent years; only one airline board has been appointed since 1968.[10] Rehmus (1977) argued that heavy reliance on mediation has reduced strikes in airlines, possibly because the mediation process allows the parties more time to settle their disputes than they would otherwise have. Moreover, Rehmus noted, over the years there have been at least 350 cases in which the parties have submitted interest disputes to binding arbitration, an option under RLA procedures. As in other industries, however, the largest and most important disputes still seem to end up in strikes.

Product Market Regulation. As noted above, CAB route and fare regulations established a product market free from many of the competitive pressures that helped shape collective bargaining in other industries. There was much less incentive in airlines to cut labor and other costs because cost reductions could not be turned into lower fares and a competitive advantage. Airlines, like Northwest, that did hold down costs certainly increased their profits; but they could not lower fares and take business away from their competitors, nor could they enter new markets. Fare structures could rise with cost increases, however, as they did automatically from 1973 to 1978.[11] This policy further decreased employer resistance to wage increases because they could easily be passed on to consumers. Unions faced no employment trade-off for higher wages, first, because there was no cost-revenue trade-off in the product market. Second, it is very difficult for the carriers to substitute capital or lower wage employees at least for skilled airline personnel because the Federal Aviation Administration (FAA) not only requires skilled employees to be certified but effectively establishes staffing levels through the use of elaborate safety regulations.

Moreover, carriers seldom faced the kind of financial trouble that would require layoffs. Because fares were set to maintain a "fair" rate of return, profit levels over the years under regulation were reasonably stable even if considerably below those in other industries.[12] This stability also meant relatively fewer business crises that would demand employee sacrifices to keep the carrier going. In the years before deregulation, if a carrier was threatened with closing, the CAB typically stepped in to arrange a friendly merger with another carrier.[13] More important, when the CAB arranged friendly mergers, it issued labor protection provisions (LPPs), which preserved the seniority rights and other interests of the employees whose companies were merging.[14]

In short, under regulation employment levels did not vary along with employment costs. Unions had little to lose by pushing up labor costs, and the carriers had little reason to resist their doing so because industry average costs were passed on to consumers through fare increases. Although holding the line on labor costs would have improved profits, airline managers typically thought that profit increases would not be worth the costs of a potential strike; because there are no inventories in air transport, all business is lost during a strike and is difficult to regain afterward. Further, because bargaining took place independently for each craft or class of workers, the proportion of labor costs to total costs in any given negotiation was very small.[15]

Together these factors reduced management's costs of granting wage increases and, in turn, increased union bargaining power.

The Process of Deregulation

Many observers believe that deregulation in the late 1970s marked the beginning of a realignment of airline labor relations. To see to what extent deregulation was the cause of that realignment, it is necessary to examine in some detail the changes introduced by deregulation. Deregulation was largely an experiment, the impetus for which came not from the parties but from the research community. Consumers, management, and labor had exhibited no particularly overt dissatisfaction with the previous system; indeed, both labor and the carriers on balance objected to the changes.[16] Even among consumers, any criticism of the regulated system seemed to pale before the range of complaints about deregulation that surfaced afterward.

The case for deregulation was based largely on a counterfactual argument about consumer interests that was current in the research on regulation in the early 1970s. As noted in more detail in the next section of this chapter, it was argued that fares and service could be much more responsive to consumer concerns in the absence of government regulations. As Dunlop (1985) has noted, the proponents of deregulation gave little if any consideration to other consequences of deregulation, such as its effects on financial performance and, most important in this context, the effects on labor relations and collective bargaining.

Although deregulation was almost entirely directed at consumer issues, it nevertheless contained some specific language on labor relations. In fact, the Airline Deregulation Act of 1978 (ADA) yielded several important gains to the airline union. First, the act abolished the carriers' Mutual Aid Plan, a strike insurance plan, and placed such severe restrictions on any such industry plans in the future as effectively to eliminate them.[17]

Second, the ADA provided some income and employment protections against potential structural changes caused by deregulation. The failure of those protections in practice illustrates the government's decision to disengage completely from labor matters once deregulation occurred. Section 43 of the ADA provided income protection for laid-off airline workers in cases where deregulation was the major cause of the layoffs and where the carrier had furloughed at least 7.5 percent of its employees within a 12-month period. Although 13 carriers have met the latter criterion—*average* industry employment dropped 6.5 percent in 1982 alone (Clark 1985)—no worker has ever qualified for coverage because the CAB has never found deregulation to be the "major" cause of even one layoff.[18] Instead, the government cited changing markets or competitive pressures as the major cause, the proximate causes of which were of course set in motion by deregulation. Using the arguments of the CAB in these cases, it is impossible to imagine any layoffs that could qualify for coverage because deregulation *per se,* almost by definition, has no direct effects on employment.

Section 43(d) of the ADA also established preferential hiring rights at the trunk carriers for those employees who lost their jobs after deregulation. That coverage was to remain in effect for ten years, through 1988. But because the rules governing those rights were not issued until January 1986 (in part because of court challenges), the program will in fact operate for only a little more than two years (BNA 1986). Further, eligibility was limited to those with at least three years' seniority at the time of deregulation. Given all these problems, few if any workers will ever be eligible for coverage.[19]

Decisions by the CAB, and later by the U.S. Department of Transportation, have since gone further, making it reasonably clear that the agency would no longer address the labor issues that result from its economic decisions. In the Texas International, Pan American, and National Airlines merger decision (which approved the merger of the last two), the CAB said that labor should no longer expect any special labor protection provisions in the case of mergers. This general principle was reaffirmed when no LPPs were issued in the transfer of Pan Am's Pacific routes to United. The CAB's retrospective rationale for this change was that the board had been involved in labor matters in the past only if they had threatened to disrupt the air transport system; because the CAB no longer manages that system, it should no longer be concerned with such disruptions and, in turn, no longer has an interest in labor matters.[20]

The Parties: Deregulation and New Entrants

The Case for Deregulation

The arguments for taking the government out of airline product markets were based largely on theoretical assertions about how imperfect product markets might function without government regulations.[21] Those arguments culminated with the theory of contestable markets, which proposes that the threat of entry by new competitors may, under certain conditions, lead to economic outcomes consistent with perfect competition even in markets too small to support many competitors.[22] Proponents of these arguments were heavily represented at the CAB, and they pressed for reductions in regulations even before the ADA was passed. Administrative deregulation, especially of fares, was in full swing by 1977. In particular, the board quickly took steps to make it easier for carriers to enter new markets.[23] Following the contestable markets theory, this was seen as a way of keeping fares down even in the small, less competitive markets.

Beginning around 1979 the industry witnessed a wave of "new" entrants into the trunk markets, generating considerable media attention and unfortunately creating a number of false impressions about the changing air transport system. First, there were few truly new carriers in the trunk markets and even fewer that have survived;[24] in the main the new competition was primarily made up of local, charter, and intrastate carriers that had expanded their reach. Second, most of the new competitors are unionized. Indeed, Piedmont and USAir, which have recently been the industry's fastest growing and most profitable carriers, not only have unions but also have labor costs well above the industry average.

Table 6–1 outlines the major unions and employers across the industry. Table 6–2 describes the major U.S. carriers by listing their profits and various measures of size—revenue passenger miles (RPMs), the most common measure; aircraft; employees; and passengers—for the year 1985. Table 6–3 lists the number of employees in the various airline crafts. Delta is the only major carrier that is not heavily unionized (only its pilots and dispatchers are organized), but it is by no means a low-wage carrier. Delta's work rules are thought to be less restrictive than those in the other airlines, but its pay rates are among the highest in the industry. The only nonunion carrier of any size was People Express (now part of Texas Air). Measured by RPMs People was roughly one-seventh the size of United. The entire nonunion sector of the industry's trunk markets accounted for only 4.3 percent of total U.S. RPMs in 1984.[25]

A third and related misconception about the evolving industry is that the new entrants have been driving the established carriers out of their markets. Again, although the market share of the trunk carriers has shrunk, from 87 percent to 73 percent of RPMs between 1978 and 1984 (GAO 1985), the largest component of that loss was to the established local carriers like USAir and Piedmont. With the exception of New York Air, the nonunion carriers like People, Midway, and Muse[26] generally operated from secondary airports and tried to stay out of the large carriers' markets. Indeed, the new carriers appeared particularly vulnerable to the vagaries of competitive markets; of the 60 airline bankruptcies since deregulation, only two, Braniff and Continental, have been at the trunk carriers (Duffy 1983), and both of those are still flying. In the smallest two-thirds of the commuter market, where the new carriers predominate, an estimated 40 percent of the carriers will go bankrupt *each year* (Molloy 1985). The only new carrier to have shown a profit on average in the years since deregulation is People Express.

The nonunion, low-price carriers have, however, had an impact on the industry that is disproportionate to their size. Bailey, Graham, and Kaplan (1985) estimated that fares are significantly lower in markets where those carriers operate because the competitors must match their fares. Those markets are also ones where many carriers operate, and so the fare cuts spread quickly among the competitors.[27]

The new, nonunion carriers have also had a disproportionate effect on labor relations in the industry, largely because their pay scales and work rules serve as invidious comparisons for employers in the union sector.[28] Furthermore, the growth of some of the nonunion carriers helps support management demands for concessions at the unionized operations. People Express has provided the most important comparisons, not so much because of its lower salaries but because of its innovative work arrangements and compensation plans. For example, all People employees are called managers, employees are cross-assigned to almost all positions (for example, from ticket agent to baggage handler to clerk) so that no employees have been hired strictly for administration, and the compensation plan calls for mandatory stock ownership and profit sharing.[29] Many industry observers wonder, however, whether these innovations will endure as the airline expands and as both the new air transport system and the work force mature. They point to cases, as at PSA, in which costs gradually rose as the carrier grew, unions then gained a foothold, and operations generally grew to resemble those at trunk carriers (May 1983).

Why the Major Carriers Have Prevailed

To understand why the new, low-cost carriers have not displaced the higher-cost trunk carriers requires an understanding of the underlying economics of air transport that have become more obvious with the removal of governmental regulations. Certainly part of the explanation is that the new carriers do not have equal access to markets. Landing rights, for example, remain with the established carriers. The four largest airports in the United States permit no new flights, while many others do not have enough gates and facilities to service additional carriers. Moreover, the computerized reservation systems are all owned by the trunk carriers, giving them a variety of marketing advantages over their competitors.[30]

Perhaps the most significant advantage for the trunk carriers is their established route and schedule system. Every route is a separate market, and there may be several markets within a given route, differentiated by levels of service and schedules. Graham, Kaplan, and Sibley (1983) found that those carriers with more extensive schedules and routes can charge more, even on the same trips, than other carriers. The trunk carriers have learned to match the low fares of the new carriers using restrictions (such as early booking rules) on business travelers. With a base of higher fare business passengers, a carrier can fill up its plane with lower fare, discretionary flyers and thus compete on fares with the low-cost carriers.[31] Programs such as frequent flyer plans then help keep the business passengers with the carrier.[32]

The recently developed hub-and-spoke route systems that feed passengers from relatively uncompetitive, regional markets onto connecting flights in more competitive markets have also served to maintain the domi-

Table 6–1
Unions Representing Occupational Groups at the Major and Other National Carriers, as of October 1, 1985

Airline	Pilots	Flight Engineers	Flight Attendants	Flight Dispatchers	Mechanics and Related Personnel	Clerical and Agent Personnel
Major Carriers						
American	APA	FEIA	APFA	TWU	TWU	–
Braniff	ALPA	–	AFA	ATDA	IBT	IBT
Continental	ALPA	–	UFA	TWU	IAM	–
Delta	ALPA	–	–	PAFCA	–	–
Eastern	ALPA	–	TWU	IAM	IAM	–
Northwest	ALPA	–	IBT	TWU	IAM	BRAC
Pan American	ALPA	FEIA	IUFA	TWU	TWU	IBT
Piedmont	ALPA	–	AFA	TWU	IAM	–
Republic	ALPA	–	AFA	TWU	IAM	ALEA
Trans World	ALPA	–	IFFA	TWU	IAM	–
United	ALPA	–	AFA	IAM	IAM	–
USAir	ALPA	–	AFA	–	IAM	IBT
Western	ALPA	–	AFA	TWU	IBT	ATE

Other National Carriers

Carrier						
AirCal	ALPA	—	TWU	—	TWU	—
Alaska	ALPA	—	AFA	—	IAM	IAM
Aloha	ALPA	—	AFA	TWU	IAM	IAM
Flying Tigers	ALPA	ALPA	AFA	IAM	IAM	ALEA
Frontier	ALPA	—	AFA	TWU	IAM	IAM
Hawaiian	ALPA	—	AFA	TWU	IAM	IAM
Midway	ALPA	—	—	—	—	—
Ozark	ALPA	—	AFA	TWU	AMFA	IAM
PSA	ALPA	—	IBT	SDA	IBT	IBT
Southwest	SAPA	—	TWU	SAEA	IBT	IAM
Transamerica	ALPA	IBT	AFA	—	—	—
World	IBT	IBT	IBT	TWU	IBT	—

Source: *Aviation Daily* (1985).

Legend:

AFA	-	Association of Flight Attendants	
ALEA	-	Air Line Employees Association	
ALPA	-	Air Line Pilots Association	
AMFA	-	Aircraft Mechanics Fraternal Association	
APA	-	Allied Pilots Association	
APFA	-	Association of Professional Flight Attendants	
ATDA	-	Air Transport Dispatchers Association	
ATE	-	Air Transport Employees	
BRAC	-	Brotherhood of Railway and Airline Clerks	
FEIA	-	Flight Engineers International Association	
IAM	-	International Association of Machinists	
IBT	-	International Brotherhood of Teamsters	
IFFA	-	Independent Federation of Flight Attendants	
IUFA	-	Independent Union of Flight Attendants	
PAFCA	-	Professional Airline Flight Control Association	
SAEA	-	Southwest Airline Employee Association	
SAPA	-	Southwest Airline Pilots Association	
SDA	-	Southwest Dispatchers Association	
TWU	-	Transport Workers Union	
UFA	-	Union of Flight Attendants	

Table 6–2
Size and Profits of the Largest U.S. Scheduled Airlines, 1984

Airline	Number of Aircraft	Number of Employees	Number of Passengers	Revenue Passenger Miles (000)	Net Profit (Loss)/($000)
AirCal	26	2,169	3,990,000	1,548,506	11,151
Alaska	27	2,734	2,543,000	1,841,212	23,908
Aloha	8	842	2,346,000	392,421	(1,857)
American	260	38,333	34,123,000	36,702,296	208,606
Best	2	121	87,000	27,354	2,097
Braniff	20	1,844	2,176,000	1,885,619	(75,419)
Continental	108	9,040	11,115,000	10,923,395	53,669
Delta	237	36,898	37,341,000	27,040,102	258,641
Eastern	284	39,514	38,081,000	29,359,288	(37,927)
Evergreen	39	386	—	—	4,636[a]
Federal Express	61	30,575	—	—	63,896
Flying Tiger	32	6,404	96,000[b]	747,900[b]	60,783
Frontier	56	5,144	7,048,000	4,464,168	(13,748)
Hawaiian	16	968	3,022,000	403,857	5,810

Jet America	6	513	538,000	824,731	(3,676)
Midway	19	1,201	1,464,000	747,428	(21,967)
Muse	14	826	1,980,000	925,083	(17,042)
Northwest	121	14,884	13,216,000	19,772,356	56,101
Ozark	47	3,987	4,949,000	2,693,866	12,723
Pacific Southwest	36	3,602	7,830,000	3,047,338	(4,796)
Pan American	119	28,217	13,913,000	28,066,826	(206,836)
Piedmont	108	9,585	14,274,000	6,227,641	58,175
Purolator Courier	107	16,673	–	–	–
Republic	160	13,652	15,177,000	8,509,948	29,511
Trans World	166	27,453	18,487,000	28,296,956	29,885
United	319	45,019	41,010,000	46,037,064	252,416
United Parcel Service	148	–	–	–	–
USAir	133	12,213	17,047,000	8,190,589	118,331
Western	78	10,460	10,538,000	9,396,580	(29,165)

Source: Adapted from Air Transport Association (1985).

[a]Includes nonscheduled service.

[b]12 months ended Sept. 30, 1984.

Table 6–3
Craft Employment in the U.S. Scheduled Airlines, 1974, 1983, and 1984

Airline Craft	1974	1983	1984
Pilots and copilots	26,046	28,108	29,962
Other cockpit personnel	7,420	6,852	7,035
Flight attendants	41,437	55,739	60,251
Communications personnel	1,777	855	764
Mechanics	46,589	40,395	42,558
Aircraft and traffic servicing personnel	89,686	95,080	100,621
Office employees	60,192	70,157	72,369
All others	34,171	31,462	31,519
Total employment	307,318	328,648	345,079

Source: Adapted from Air Transport Association (1985).

nance of the trunk carriers. Not only do such systems help fill the planes, but profits from the former routes can be used to keep fares low on the more competitive legs of a route system. Cross-subsidization among routes allows carriers to price below their marginal costs on routes where low-cost competitors operate or to threaten credibly that any fare cuts will be matched if the competitors try to take their markets with lower fares. (Republic Airlines President Daniel May has argued that if any other industry were to engage in this form of predatory pricing, it would be in violation of federal antitrust laws; May 1983, 326.)

As a result, airline labor costs—indeed all costs—may be less important than other factors in determining the competitive position of a carrier. Furthermore, the threat of new entrants has not forced the major carriers to cut fares and costs to the extent that the proponents of deregulation had expected.[33] Instead, the pressures to cut costs and reshape labor relations have been specific to the varying circumstances across individual firms.

The Double-Breasted Strategy

One new entrant that has had a lasting impact on the industry is New York Air. Taking a page from Century Air's corporate reshufflings in 1931, the firm was the result of a new idea in air transport: the nonunion subsidiary. Texas International (TI) had made a decision to enter the competitive East Coast shuttle market and to do so as a low-cost, low-fare carrier. But because collective bargaining coverage under the Railway Labor Act is systemwide, TI would have had to operate in that market under its existing union contracts, even though the new routes were geographically isolated from its Texas route system. Instead, in 1980 TI created New York Air (originally called Big Apple Airways) as a subsidiary to operate in the shuttle markets and Texas Air as a holding company owning New York Air and TI. The subsidiary operated without TI's unions or their contracts, its managers arguing that it was a separate company and not bound by TI's agreements. ALPA and other unions argued that New York Air was not in fact operated independently from TI and that the corporate restructuring—including shifting TI's assets through the holding company to New York Air—was done simply to avoid dealing with TI's unions. The courts have refused to rule on these issues and have turned them back to the NMB, where they have yet to be decided.[34]

A large number of carriers soon followed the first step of TI's strategy and established holding companies, as demonstrated in table 6–4, and three have gone on to establish separate, nonunion airlines.[35] These alter ego or double-breasted operations are the equivalent of nonunion "greenfield" sites in manufacturing, with the holding companies providing the means to shift airline company assets to nonunion operations (they may serve other purposes as well). It is not surprising, therefore, to find unions responding to this strategy by securing restrictions on its use through collective bargaining agreements, as shown in the last column of table 6–4.

The Structure of Bargaining, 1938–1978

The economic environment under governmental regulation created incentives for a bargaining structure that was very decentralized, carrier by carrier. The Railway Labor Act created the basis for this decentralization by establishing separate bargaining units for each craft or class of workers. Nothing in the act, however, prevented bargaining units from negotiating together within the same airline. But the unions did not need to coordinate their negotiating efforts because each bargaining unit individually could shut down the airline with a strike. Indeed, union efforts to coordinate bargaining would only increase management's resistance at the bargaining table by increasing the number of workers covered by an agreement and, hence, the costs of agreeing to contract improvements.

Within each airline, unions had everything to gain by fragmenting negotiations and strike liabilities. The traditional goal associated with negotiating across employers is to take wages out of competition by enforcing uniform terms and conditions of employment on all competitors (Commons 1909). But this goal was already met by the system of regulations outlined above: higher wage carriers were not at a competitive disadvantage because their prices could not be undercut; and low-cost carriers could not enter their markets.

Instead, unions negotiated with each carrier individually and took advantage of the airlines' vulnerability to strikes by engaging in whipsawing. A

Table 6-4
Airline Holding Companies, Their Principal and Double-Breasted Subsidiary Airlines, and Contract Restrictions on Double-Breasting

Holding Company	Year Holding Company Formed	Primary Airline	Double-Breasted Airline	Restrictions on Double-Breasting Imposed by the Primary Airline's Union Contract, 1980–86
Air Wisconsin Services	1983	Air Wisconsin		
Aloha, Inc.	1984	Aloha		
AMR Corp.	1982	American		
Dalfort	1983	Braniff		
Capital Holding Corp.	1983	Capitol Air	Global International	
Texas Air Corp.	1980	Continental	New York Air	
Eastern Airlines, Inc.	1938	Eastern		Yes[a]
Tiger International	1969	Flying Tigers		
Frontier Holdings	1982	Frontier	Frontier Horizon	
HAL, Inc.	1985	Hawaiian		
Mid Pacific Air Corp.	1984	Mid Pacific Air		

NWA, Inc.	1984	Northwest		
Ozark Holdings	1984	Ozark		
PSA Inc.	1973	PSA		
Pan Am Corp.	1984	Pan American		
Piedmont Aviation, Inc.	1975	Piedmont		Yes[b]
—		Republic		Yes[c]
Transamerica Corp.	1928	Transamerica	Trans International	
Trans World Corp.	1979	Trans World*		
UAL Inc.	1968	United		
USAir Group	1983	USAir		
Western Airlines, Inc.	1928	Western		Yes[c]

Source: Corporate reports and AIRCon data.

*Sold by Trans World Corp. in 1984.

[a] Restrictions on the holding company's ability to form an airline subsidiary.

[b] Piedmont Aviation, Inc. (holding company) may acquire—but not create—an airline subsidiary, but that subsidiary cannot be integrated into Piedmont Airlines operations.

[c] Restrictions on the carrier's ability to form an airline subsidiary.

strike at a single carrier not only stopped its traffic but shifted its passengers to other carriers, possibly permanently. In thinly covered routes the CAB would even allow other carriers to move onto the route just for the duration of the strike. Moreover, the NMB prevented simultaneous strikes on the same route by holding some disputes in mediation until the strike at the other carrier was settled.[36] In addition, a strike at a single carrier posed no threat to the nation's air system and thus was unlikely to cause either a consumer backlash against the union or the appointment of an emergency board.

The international unions staggered their negotiations across the carriers and used the previous settlement with one airline as the starting point for negotiations with the next carrier. This method of bargaining was particularly important where several unions were competing to represent the bargaining units in the craft, because, as Ross (1948) argued, their competition helped escalate their demands. Kahn (1971) noted that demands based on interfirm comparisons were encouraged by emergency board recommendations, which, although infrequent, nonetheless relied on the comparisons. In addition, given the uniformity in revenues across carriers, it was hard for carriers to argue against a settlement that their competitors had already accepted. A further consequence of this whipsawing was that the carriers tried hard to position themselves at the end of the bargaining round to delay the increases as long as possible and to avoid being the target of a strike.

The carriers first challenged this practice in 1945 when they were collectively facing the introduction of larger, four-engine planes and the possibility of massive pilot pay increases under the existing Decision 83 formula. They formed the Airline Negotiating Committee to negotiate this issue on behalf of the industry. ALPA refused to negotiate with the committee and struck TWA over the pay issue; TWA eventually broke from the committee to settle the dispute; and the committee soon fell apart.[37] The IAM briefly negotiated with six carriers in 1953 and again in 1966, resulting in the largest strike in industry history in 1966. Thereafter, the union abandoned multiemployer bargaining.[38] Only 6 of the 34 emergency boards appointed have addressed disputes with more than one carrier or more than one union.

In response to the union successes with these whipsawing tactics, the carriers established a new program—the Mutual Aid Plan, a strike insurance plan—in 1958.[39] Unterberger and Koziara (1975; 1980) found evidence suggesting that as MAP coverage and benefits increased over time, strikes in the industry grew longer. As Northrup (1977) pointed out, however, strike duration is not the only relevant criterion for assessing the plan's effects. The MAP did increase the bargaining power of management, but it also may have reduced the number of strikes, other things equal, by having discouraged unions from undertaking them in the first place.[40]

The evidence is overwhelming that it was through pattern bargaining that contract changes came about. Virtually every important change in contract terms was secured first at one carrier and then spread one negotiation at a time across the industry. This was the case not only for union gains but also for contract changes benefiting management.[41] Although minor differences in contracts persisted, the extensive use of comparisons as criteria for bargaining goals resulted in virtual uniformity among agreements in any one bargaining round.

The Bargaining Process

Historical Background

The contracts established during the period of governmental regulations were by all standards very beneficial to union members. Any such judgment is typically made relative to a comparable group, such as the benefits received by comparable workers in similar nonunion jobs and industries. It is difficult to find a comparison group for flight and cabin crews as they have almost no counterpart in the nonunion sector. Few would disagree, however, that cockpit crews were extremely well compensated; they were, and still are, typically the best paid employees in their corporations, short of the top officers; and senior pilots now earn as much as $160,000 per year. Salary increases for pilots have been funded by tremendous technological changes (larger and faster planes) over the years, improvements that have dramatically increased output per employee. The pilots were able to capture some of those gains in advance through contract language like that in Decision 83. But cabin crews have been considerably less successful in reaping gains from productivity increases, more, perhaps, because of the nature of the work force and the structure of their unions than because of any inherent weakness in their bargaining positions (as will be discussed in more detail later in this chapter).

Hendricks, Feuille, and Szerszen's (1980) study of compensation in airlines, mainly focusing on ground personnel, found that airline wages and contract terms were superior to those for similar jobs elsewhere and were superior in the more regulated sector of the industry.[42] Their study also suggested that contract language in airlines was more favorable to unions, again especially in the more regulated sector of the industry, than the language found in other union contracts. A more detailed discussion of work rules by craft is presented below, but there is no doubt that airline unions have secured very favorable work rules. This was especially true for cockpit crews. ALPA managed to reduce drastically the number of nonflight working hours in the 1950s by establishing restrictions on various aspects of scheduling; the union saw similar success in the 1960s in efforts to reduce actual flight time (Kahn 1971; see the section on pilots below).

Financial Crisis. As in the period before airline regulation in 1938, the period after deregulation in 1977 unleashed competitive pressures that led to price cutting and financial instability at some carriers and, in turn, to a realignment of labor relations in the industry. With deregulation and especially the end of subsidies in their smaller markets, the major carriers abandoned short routes and concentrated on what were thought to be the more profitable long-haul markets. American Airlines, for example, pulled 45 planes out of its northeast regional markets—the equivalent of a good-sized airline. American did so at least partly because of equipment mismatches: Because fares had been fixed, the trunk carriers had competed during the regulated years by attracting passengers with their biggest and most comfortable planes—not necessarily those best suited to the market in question. Once subsidies ended and fares could fall, it no longer was cost-effective to fly those planes, typically jets, in the smaller markets. Once these markets were abandoned to the new entrant carriers, they served as one of the primary places for the smaller carriers' expansion.

The planes freed from regional markets thus became concentrated over the long-haul routes. By the end of 1979 fuel price increases had begun to hurt profits, and the deepening economic recession reduced demand for air travel. Indeed, the 1980–81 recession represented the first sustained absolute decline in the demand for air transport in the history of the industry, a decline that occurred despite widespread fare cuts. The trunk carriers had excess capacity, and they reacted individually with further fare cuts to fill the empty seats, cuts that were soon matched by their competitors—a classic game-theoretic problem.[43] Those destabilizing fare cuts were exactly what the New Deal planners had hoped to prevent by regulating the industry. The result was that the 1981 fiscal year was the worst the industry had ever seen, with almost every major carrier in the red.[44]

Some changes in labor relations had been under way even before the industry's financial crisis.[45] At most carriers, however, bargaining went on more or less as usual through 1981 when Braniff, Western, and Pan Am came close to bankruptcy. Unlike during the regulated period, no friendly mergers were arranged that would protect the jobs and seniority of workers at the vulnerable carriers. All three carriers secured roughly 10 percent wage cuts in all their labor contracts negotiated that year to help prevent bankruptcy. By the end of the year unions at Continental, Eastern, and Republic had also granted wage concessions. By the standard measures of financial solvency, such as cash reserves and the ratio of current assets to current liabilities, all of these carriers were clearly in trouble; but by the same measures, the rest of the trunk carriers were relatively stable, and none managed to secure concessions during this period.[46]

The financially weak carriers sought and secured twice as many wage concessions as they did work rule changes.[47] Wage cuts generate immediate savings, which addressed the cash-flow problems at these carriers. Work rule changes, on the other hand, reduce costs on average only if there is business expansion, which was not the case, or if there are layoffs, in which case the unions are unlikely to agree to them. The wage cuts at the troubled airlines eventually forced the healthier carriers to seek matching concessions from their unions, giving rise to whipsawing—now on the part of employers that sought to match or exceed the cuts achieved by their competitors. In contrast to the six weakened carriers listed above, the six financially strongest carriers had to wait at least a year before securing concessions, at which time they sought and secured work rule concessions over wage cuts by a margin of three to two.[48] Because the healthier carriers had prospects for growth, their unions were more inclined to accept work rule changes because it was less likely that any productivity gains resulting from the changes would be translated into layoffs.

The wage and work rule concessions at the major airlines initially had little if anything to do with the low-cost, nonunion competition. The concessions also lagged deregulation by four years. Nonetheless, deregulation did contribute to the concessions. By removing the restrictions that formerly had prevented a downturn in the industry from jeopardizing individual carriers, deregulation threatened existing employment levels and so made it much more costly for union to attempt to raise wages.

Without the protections of regulation the decentralized bargaining structure inherited from the period of regulation became disfunctional. Under decentralized structures and without protective regulations, unions cannot take wages out of competition and therefore cannot protect wages against threats to employment. In short, it was the combination of the financial crisis possible under deregulation and the decentralized bargaining structure inherited from the previous era that led to the concessions.

New Strategies for Cutting Costs. The period of concessionary bargaining produced two new and distinct management approaches to reduce labor costs, costs which some industry experts suggest account for as much as 60 percent of controllable costs in air transport. The first approach, undertaken at Continental, was to use bankruptcy proceedings to cut labor contracts unilaterally. Texas Air Corporation (the holding company behind the double-breasted strategy with New York Air and Texas International) acquired Continental in 1981 over the vociferous objections of Continental's employees, who were leery of TI's previous policies toward unions. The employees had attempted—but failed—to obtain a controlling interest in the company through an employee stock ownership plan and thus prevent the takeover.[49] Despite wage concessions and loan guarantees from Texas Air, Continental veered closer to bankruptcy after the takeover. In its August 1983 negotiations with the International Association of Machinists and Aerospace

Workers (IAM), management withdrew an earlier offer, citing worsening financial circumstances, and the union then struck the carrier at the end of the 30-day cooling-off period. Continental continued to operate, however. Other unions—and many Machinists as well—crossed the picket lines; and management permanently contracted out many of the nonmechanic jobs held by IAM members.

Continental then attempted to open pilot and flight attendant contracts early and to win concessions from the two groups in return for a stock ownership and profit sharing plan. Meanwhile the carrier continued to lose money, and management threatened both unions that it might pursue bankruptcy if they did not make concessions. The unions refused to reopen negotiations, and in September 1983 Continental filed for Chapter 11 protection. Unlike at Braniff, which had petitioned for Chapter 11 status in 1982, the cash crisis at Continental was not as immediate, and observers still speculate whether the bankruptcy at Continental was the result of circumstances beyond management's control or the result of its deliberate strategy to cut labor costs. Also unlike Braniff, Continental unilaterally imposed new wage rates and work rules after filing for bankruptcy, which cut labor costs by about 50 percent.[50] Reduced fares and an expanded schedule followed immediately.

On October 1, 1983 pilots and flight attendants both struck the carrier to protest the unilateral wage cuts and work rule changes. Continental continued operating, however, with workers who crossed the picket lines[51] and replacements for those who refused to return to work. The mechanic, flight attendant, and pilot strikes technically remain unresolved as of this writing, although they have essentially been broken, and the various issues behind the disputes have degenerated into a mass of lawsuits.[52]

Since Continental filed for Chapter 11 protection, the bankruptcy laws have been amended (by the Bankruptcy Amendments and Judgeship Act of 1984), to require employers to make more thorough attempts to revise labor contracts through negotiation before doing so unilaterally. It remains to be seen whether this amendment will substantially alter the process of revising contracts. As Dunlop (1985) has observed, it is difficult to predict how judges will rule on labor matters. Although no airline has tried to use Chapter 11 protections to alter labor contracts since the Continental example, a great many have threatened to do so. And as ALPA President Henry Duffy noted, since the Continental episode management demands at the struggling carriers have closely followed this pattern: Protestations of an inability to pay eventually yield to threats to pursue Chapter 11 protections, which in turn are followed by a visit from the carriers' bankers who assure the union negotiators of the financial necessity of concessions (Duffy 1983, 513).

The second set of new tactics for reducing labor costs made its appearance at American Airlines in 1983. In some ways the approach is the opposite of that pursued at Continental.[53] American had begun to pursue union concessions after its competitors had secured them—especially after the pilot work rule changes at United in 1979 and Continental's wage cuts in 1982 and 1983. Perhaps because American was one of the strongest carriers financially, its unions rejected the company's demands for concessions in both 1981 and 1982. In negotiations beginning in 1983 American essentially tailored its business strategy to help achieve concessions. Management threatened to shrink the airline if costs could not be cut, and to make that threat credible it made arrangements to sell some of its aircraft. More important, management negotiators offered lifetime job security to current union members and the promise of an immediate expansion of bargaining units and membership—if costs were cut. The concessions proposed by management were entirely in work rules, with the exception of a reduced pay scale for new hires. All the unions eventually ratified all these concessions, without a strike.

American's approach is worthy of note because it succeeded in achieving very substantial labor-cost concessions at a time when it was neither under threat of bankruptcy nor in financial difficulty—and it did so through collective bargaining and without the serious confrontation experienced at Continental. What became the most copied part of American's approach, however, was the creation of a two-tier wage agreement, one that retained the pay schedule for current employees and established a lower one for workers hired after a certain date. As new workers are hired, average costs go down, creating strong incentives for business expansion. For unions two-tier agreements are attractive because they cost current members nothing. Table 6-5 shows that most other carriers were quick to follow American's example. (Continental and Braniff are not included in this table because their new pay scales are comparable to the bottom tier of a two-tier schedule). The idea of separate scales for new and current employees has since spread quickly to other industries as well.

One important question about two-tier agreements is whether they eventually merge with the current seniority pay scales and, if so, at what time. Most two-tier scales in airlines merge after five to twelve years, at which point no employee is covered under the former schedule, with the scale lowering the starting point and increasing the steepness of seniority progressions. The seniority-based divisions in pay thus become very sharp, and they may lead to conflicts among employee groups and within their unions.[54] Many observers view the fact that workers receive different pay for the same jobs as the source of these problems, but the concept was already well established in the existing seniority-based pay scales. Disputes between new hires and longer service employees have historical precedents, especially among pilots. In the 1960s, for example, union efforts to restrict hours helped create new jobs and speed advancement for younger workers but held back total earnings for senior pilots.

At least some of the pressure to secure two-tier agreements seems to have

**Table 6–5
Two-Tier Wage Scales in Effect or Under Negotiation at the Major and
Other National Airlines, 1986**

	Two-Tier Plan in Effect (*) for:			
Airline	Pilots	Flight Attendants	Mechanics	Agents and Clerical Employees
Majors				
American	*	*	*	*
Braniff				
Continental				
Delta	*	*	*	*
Eastern	*	*	*	*
Northwest		*	*	*
Pan American		*	*	negotiating
Piedmont	*	*	*	*
Republic	*	*	*	*
Trans World	*	*	*	
United	*	*	*	*
USAir	*	*	*	*
Western	*	*	*	*
Other Nationals				
AirCal	*	*	*	
Alaska		*	*	*
Aloha	*		*	*
Flying Tiger			*	
Hawaiian		*	*	*
PSA		*	*	*
World	negotiating	negotiating	negotiating	negotiating

Note: The two-tier plans merge with the established seniority pay scales typically in five to seven years.

come from outside the industry, mainly from the financial community, which endorsed the agreements as a sign of effective management. Carriers that are not growing, for example, clearly have little to gain from two-tier plans; they seem to have pursued them merely for their symbolic value. Recently, however, many other carriers have introduced early retirement programs to encourage turnover and allow the hiring of new workers at the lower pay scale. As shown in table 6–6, the occupation generally not covered by these programs is pilots, in part because they are in relatively short supply.

Table 6–6
Early Retirement and Severance Plans at Ten Major Airlines, as of 1985

Airline	Pilots	Existing Plan (*) for: Flight Attendants	Mechanics	Agents and Clericals
American		*	*	*
Eastern			*	*
Northwest		*		
Pan American			*	
Republic	*			
Trans World				*
United	*	*	*	*
USAir		*	*	
Western		*	*	

Source: AIRCon contract file.

Diversity Among the Carriers. Although all the airlines faced the same competitive environment after deregulation, their individual responses to that new environment—including their business strategy decisions—differed widely. It is important to understand those differences because they help explain why collective bargaining also came to exhibit much greater diversity across the carriers than in the past.[55]

On the one hand, the business strategies of such carriers as Northwest, Piedmont, and USAir have been designed to avoid the severe competition faced elsewhere. As a result, labor relations at these airlines have been stable, following the patterns of the years before deregulation. On the other hand, carriers such as Braniff, Continental, and Eastern plunged headlong into very competitive markets, suffered large losses, and thus had to cut their labor costs. It is these carriers that have secured extensive concessions from their unions. Yet the explanation is not as simple as "hard times lead to changes." American, for example, was one of the healthiest airlines and yet managed to achieve some of the most extensive concessions in the industry, while TWA and Pan Am have faced several financial crises but until recently secured almost no concessions.

Instead, the explanation for the differences in labor relations appears to lie largely with the product market strategies pursued by each airline. American, United, and some other healthy airlines were able to confront their unions with immediate job losses unless the unions made concessions (that is, both threatened to sell off planes) and to promise at least some effort to maintain job security contingent on those concessions. Other carriers, such as TWA and Pan Am, threatened job loss only in the longer run (bankruptcy) and could not offer job security. More specifically, only those like American, Delta, and United that offered job security were able to secure extensive work rule changes; those threatened with financial collapse, such as Braniff, Eastern, Frontier, and Western, secured wage cuts instead to ease their immediate cash-flow problems. In addition, the unions were able to secure significant quid pro quos—such as membership on boards of directors—only in cases where the carrier was faced with collapse. In those cases unions have some power over management because their approval of concessions is critical to the future of the firm (Cappelli 1984), as will be discussed further later in this chapter.

The pace of concessionary bargaining in airlines has slowed in recent years as wage and cost levels have come closer to market rates, especially at the carriers with two-tier plans. Bargaining has therefore shifted from addressing wage issues to addressing work rules, especially at those carriers with good prospects for growth. Between 1981 and 1983 almost every labor contract in the industry called for some kind of a wage reduction; in 1984, 19 of the 35 agreements at the major and national carriers specified a wage cut; but by 1985 only one of the 20 contracts signed that year had a cut.[56] Specific work rule changes for each of the main airline crafts are discussed below, but table 6–7 summarizes the major changes in three general areas: management's right to subcontract union work, to employ part-time workers, and to cross-assign employees among different jobs.

Bargaining at the Craft Level

A comparison of the collective bargaining experience across the different crafts allows us to extract from the financial and business circumstances the business strategies unique to the individual carriers. Through this comparison, therefore, we can examine how different union structures and labor markets have adjusted to the pressures that have followed deregulation.

Pilots. Pilots are, obviously, highly trained for their jobs, and their skills are almost completely idiosyncratic to the airline industry. The pilot labor market is equally idiosyncratic. Airlines hire trainees who already have commercial pilot licenses and ideally have further credentials as well. Most in demand are pilots with military experience, which offers the best available training.[57] As a result, the hiring of pilots traditionally followed a cycle that corresponded with the retirements of military pilots after World War II, the Korean War, and finally the Vietnam War. In fact, pilots trained by the military historically accounted for as much as 75 percent of the cockpit crews at the trunk carriers; recently, that figure has declined to about 40 percent, as military pilot training, and subsequent "retirements" to the carriers, had declined.[58]

Table 6–7
Work Rule Changes Instituted at 13 Large Airlines, as of 1985

	Contract(s) Specifies Management Right to:		
Airline	*Subcontract Union Work*	*Employ Part-Time Workers*	*Cross-Assign Employees*
Alaska		*	U
American	*	*	U
Continental		*	U
Eastern			L
Frontier		*	
Northwest		*	L
Pan American		*	L
PSA		*	
Republic	*		L
Trans World			
United		*	
USAir		*	
Western		*	

Source: AirCon contract file.

Note: Part-time work is specified only in mechanic and related contracts. All carriers can employ part-time workers in agent and clerical jobs; there are no part-time pilots or flight attendants. *U* = unlimited management right to cross-assign employees; *L* = limited right to cross-assign.

With this decline in the supply of military pilots, the carriers have turned to the commuter airlines for their pilot trainees. Because the World War II generation of pilots has begun to retire from the airlines at the same time as the industry is expanding, pilots are now in short supply. As a result, the commuter airlines are having serious difficulty retaining their pilots, with some reporting pilot turnover rates as high as 100 percent per year (*New York Times* 1986). The commuter carriers serve as the initial training ground for commercial pilot licenses and, in turn, as the stepping stone to a job at the major carriers. Because the larger trunk carriers have paid pilots extremely well, they have been able to attract trainees who already have many of the necessary qualifications away from other employers and thus to shift the cost of acquiring those qualifications to the initial employers—first the military and now the commuter carriers.[59]

The idiosyncrasies of the labor market are well reflected in the pilot seniority system that has evolved over the years. That system effectively ties pilots not only to the industry but also to their airline for their entire career. Specifically, pilot seniority is not transferable among carriers, and seniority-based pay and benefit progressions are so steep that a pilot can lose as much as $100,000 in annual salary by moving from one carrier to another.

One obvious consequence of this seniority arrangement is that it ties pilots to their carrier. For the purposes of collective bargaining, pilots' interest in protecting their current job within the seniority system was best served by the ability to negotiate airline by airline, which was in fact the case with the decentralized structure of the pilots' union, ALPA. ALPA leaders gave advice and direction, but the bargaining units were free to ignore them. ALPA's decentralized structure had resulted in part from a membership backlash against the authoritarian style of the union's first president, David Behnecke (see Hopkins 1971), and in part from the early regulatory environment. Unions normally need centralized control to enforce uniform contracts that take wages out of competition; their locals must be prevented from making concessions that can erode the industry pattern. But because government regulations had done this for the unions in air transport, ALPA had no real need for centralized authority. Instead, the international directed most of its efforts toward lobbying, at which it was highly effective.

When the carriers began to threaten layoffs after deregulation, it was therefore not surprising to find that pilots, who had the most to lose, not only were the first to make concessions but gave up the most of any craft group. The international union could not prevent concessions by locals at the struggling carriers, and pilot concessions soon became the rule across the industry. Table 6–8, which lists the annual percentage increase in cockpit crew costs for representative ranks by aircraft, shows that starting in 1981–82 pay increases dropped significantly for the crews as a whole. Those declines represent not only slower growth in pay but also changes in work rules that have increased the proportion of flight time to paid hours. Interestingly, the declines lagged deregulation by several years and also lagged behind the financial decline of the industry. Pilot concessions therefore seem to have been driven more by the breakup of pattern bargaining and by the employers' whipsawing demands than by hard times in the industry.

In addition to wage and benefit cuts, pilots have been pressed to make concessions in the elaborate system of work rules that was established during the period of regulation. Perhaps the most vulnerable of these have been the rules that restrict work schedules. Pilot contracts traditionally placed limits on total hours flown, as well as on how those hours could be scheduled, such as requiring specified amounts of days off between flights and counting travel to the airport, or "deadheading," as paid work time. Those scheduling rules together represented the equivalent of a 10 percent increase in staffing requirements for cockpit crews (Kahn 1971). Before the concessionary period airlines were thought to have done well when their pilots flew at least 60 percent of their credited monthly maximum hours. Five major carriers now have absolutely no contractual restraints on pilot scheduling; their work rules simply duplicate the FAA maximum schedule limits.[60] Management reports suggest that pilots at other carriers now fly about 90

Table 6–8
A Comparison of Percentage Increases in Annual Wage Costs of Cockpit
Crews and Private, Nonfarm Labor, 1979–85

		Pilots		
Fiscal Year	*Total Cockpit Crew (737s)*	*Captain (747s)*	*Second Officer (747s)*	*Private, Nonfarm Labor*
1978–79	9.4%	8.4%	8.3%	6.6%
1979–80	12.3	11.9	12.6	7.1
1980–81	11.5	12.4	12.9	8.3
1981–82	6.4	1.7	1.0	2.8
1982 83	1.4	6.1	6.0	3.0
1983–84	1.2	5.4	7.4	3.2
1984–85	0.5	4.0	3.5	—
1978–85	6.7	7.1	7.4	—

Sources: For cockpit crews, AIRCon data for the major and national carriers. For private, non-farm labor, U.S. Department of Labor (1985, table 104).

Notes: The AIRCon data are based on wage costs for a specific aircraft and therefore reflect not only compensation changes but also changes in work rules. Data on total crews were available only for Boeing 737s; data for captains and second officers were available only for Boeing 747s. Data by airline, instead of by aircraft, are not available. The data on private, nonfarm labor are based on the average wage increases in major collective bargaining agreements (those covering 1,000 or more workers).

percent of their maximum hours. In addition, almost all the major carriers now have the freedom to schedule beyond the 75-hour monthly maximum for flight time under certain circumstances (sometimes with premium pay).

Another important pilot work rule undergoing change is the seniority bidding requirement for the larger aircraft. Because most pilot pay formulas specify higher compensation for flying larger and faster planes, the positions on those planes are more desirable and are allocated by seniority. When a pilot retires and leaves a seat on a large plane, a replacement moves up from a smaller plane, creating an upward bumping process throughout the carrier. This process has been a problem for management, which has to train, certify, and maintain the skills of pilots for each different type of plane the airline flies—an expensive and time-consuming process. Each upward move there-fore generates a series of retraining needs as pilots change planes up through the seniority hierarchy. (This is also one reason why carriers that fly only one or two types of planes have a cost advantage over other carriers, and it also helps explain why carriers agonize over purchasing any new type of plane.) The airlines have long sought to solve this training problem by, for example, restricting pilots to one type of plane for a fixed period and by limiting senior-ity moves (Kahn 1971), and they have intensified this effort in recent years.

Recent agreements at Western, for instance, eliminated most pay differences between different airplanes, thereby eliminating both the incentive to change jobs and the retraining problem.

One historically devisive issue between pilots and management that no longer appears to be so is technological change. As Kahn (1971) thoroughly documented, the development of aircraft technology first created new tasks and positions (such as flight engineer, radio operator, and navigator) and then eliminated them as new equipment automated many of these cockpit functions. The jurisdictional disputes and other problems associated with creating and then eliminating these positions appear at least for the near future to be over. Cockpit crews have gradually shrunk, and all new aircraft, including the new Boeing 747-400 series, are certified for a cockpit crew of two pilots only.[61]

Flight Attendants. Flight attendants are similar to pilots in that their occupation is idiosyncratic to air transport; but in their case the requisite skills for the job are unique to the passenger air transport industry. Like pilots' pay, flight attendants' pay is determined by carrier-specific seniority pay schedules, although they are less steep than pilots' schedules. Flight attendant bargaining has therefore also been inextricably linked to the individual airline. One important difference, however, is that cabin crews are much more easily replaced than cockpit crews. FAA regulations require flight attendants as a condition of passenger service (indeed, the staffing level required is a function of the number of seats, whether they are occupied or not); but unlike pilots or mechanics flight attendants do not have to be certified by the FAA. And although their job is often demanding, especially of interpersonal skills,[62] flight attendants have never been difficult for the airlines to find, and the necessary training for the job can be done relatively inexpensively and quickly. TWA's success in replacing striking attendants in 1986 made it clear that even a large carrier can break a flight attendant's strike.

This weakness in attendants' bargaining position was exacerbated by the particular interests and characteristics of the attendants themselves and their unions. Until recently flight attendants typically did not view their jobs as a career; most left the industry after a short period, averaging less than two years at many carriers. Because of this high turnover, unions of flight attendants faced special difficulties in building strong organizations. The first flight attendant union, the Air Line Stewardesses Association (ALSA), formed in 1945 at United, was eventually usurped by the Air Line Steward and Stewardesses Association (ALSSA), which later affiliated with ALPA and was dominated by it. The ALSSA went on to represent most of the flight attendants at the trunk carriers. The union left ALPA in 1960 and merged with the Transport Workers Union.[63] Flight attendants made few gains relative to those won by the other airline crafts over the 1950–77 period.[64]

Since then the union organization and the bargaining position of flight attendants have changed dramatically. In the late 1970s many flight attendant locals sought independence from the internationals: the Association of Flight Attendants, which replaced ALSSA under ALPA in 1960, and especially the Transport Workers Union (TWU). Attendants from Pan Am, TWA, and American all broke from the TWU in the late 1970s and formed independent unions.

As Ross (1948) argued, representational rivalry contributes to an increase in bargaining demands and an improvement in contract outcomes. This seems to have been true for the attendants over the past decade. At the same time as the job became better paid and less restrictive in its work rules, women began seeking careers in greater numbers. As a result, this job, which traditionally had been filled primarily by women, became more attractive as a career.[65] Throughout the concessionary period of the past several years attendants made few concessions (especially as compared to pilot concessions) given their relative lack of economic bargaining power. Several factors may be responsible for that paucity of flight attendant concessions.

First, airline management may not have pursued its demands for concessions as aggressively with flight attendants as it did with pilots because attendants' labor costs account for a relatively small percentage of total costs, and in turn any concession by them would represent a small potential saving. Second, because flight attendants still have relatively high rates of turnover, lower pay, and more gradual seniority progressions than pilots have—in short, less to lose—they may be less inclined to make sacrifices to reduce potential layoffs; their potential costs of job loss (measured by opportunities elsewhere) are obviously far below those of pilots. Finally, the interunion rivalry and general move to independence may have made flight attendant unions relatively more militant than their counterparts in the other crafts.

Annual pay increases for flight attendants nonetheless show the same general decline as pilots' increases, and they also lagged the industry's financial downturn.[66] Their decline is more consistent since 1979 than that for any other airline craft and sharper than the decline in increases in the economy as a whole. What is most striking about the attendants' agreements is the sharp increase in their variance across carriers, as shown in table 6–9. Early into deregulation the largest increases in a given year were less than 20 percent larger than the smallest; by 1984 the largest increase was over 100 percent larger than the smallest rise. As among pilots the work rule concessions made by flight attendants have primarily concerned scheduling: increasing monthly hours and expanding management's rights to assign hours.

Mechanics and Related Ground Personnel. Mechanics and airline employees in related ground occupations have the most bargaining power of any airline employees. Aircraft mechanics are highly skilled and must be certified by the

Table 6–9
Mean Percentage Increases in Earnings for Selected Airline Crafts and Private, Nonfarm Labor, 1978–85

Reporting Year	Mechanics and Related Occupations		Flight Attendants		Agents and Clerical Employees		Private, Nonfarm Labor
1978–79	10.5%	(2.14)	11.6%	(6.1)	10.1%	(4.62)	6.6%
1979–80	8.0	(2.54)	13.2	(22.6)	9.6	(5.86)	7.1
1980–81	9.4	(2.07)	11.9	(12.3)	12.0	(10.3)	8.3
1981–82	8.6	(31.6)	7.9	(43.9)	8.2	(10.6)	2.8
1982–83	6.2	(43.0)	6.8	(8.7)	4.8	(21.8)	3.0
1983–84	1.3	(52.5)	1.6	(39.8)	−2.5	(70.9)	3.2
1984–85	4.6	(26.0)	2.8	(18.4)	3.8	(19.5)	—
1978–85	58.5	(234.2)	48.0	(1307)	56.4	(313.9)	—

Sources: For the airline crafts, the author's computations from AIRCon data on the 13 major carriers; for the private, nonfarm labor, U.S. Department of Labor (1985).

Notes: Wage rates for mechanics and private, nonfarm labor are computed on an hourly basis, whereas data for flight attendants and agents are calculated on an annual basis. The numbers in parentheses indicate the variance in the estimates.

FAA, making them difficult to replace. Moreover, mechanics lack the steep seniority schedules that discourage moving to other carriers in the industry. The demand for their skills outside of the airline industry is also very strong; some estimates suggest that pay for similar work outside of air transport is only about 15 percent below the airline rate. Furthermore, mechanics unions represent almost the entire airline product market. Even the traditionally nonunion and new entrant carriers have their aircraft maintenance done by union employees at union rates because virtually all maintenance is subcontracted to the major carriers and specialized maintenance firms. Airline mechanics therefore have less interest in making sacrifices at the bargaining table to reduce their chances of job loss, and carriers may be less interested in securing concessions from them because the costs of mechanics' labor are standard across the industry, placing no single carrier at a competitive disadvantage. Card (1986) calculated that real wages at the trunk carriers have declined only slightly since deregulation. The real change, however, has been a shift in employment of five to seven thousand jobs from the trunk carriers to other carriers in the industry.

The mechanics' union structure under the IAM also contributes to their bargaining power. First, the IAM, which represents the majority of airline mechanics, has a highly centralized structure; the international has the power of approval over local contracts. Since deregulation leaders of the Machinists have taken a strong position against concessions and have used the international's internal power to restrain locals from making concessionary agreements.[67] Second, the international has a special reason to want to prevent concessions: its labor contracts outside the airline industry are similar to its airline contracts, making it important to prevent concessions in airlines so that they do not spill over to those other contracts. In addition, by negotiating master agreements covering the five major carriers in the 1960s the IAM was able to create a tight contract pattern for the industry, a pattern that has endured. Finally, further adding to the pressures to keep contract settlements favorable is the sharp rivalry between the IAM, the TWU, and the Teamsters for representation of airline mechanics.

Not surprisingly, therefore, it is the mechanics who have made the fewest and least significant concessions, and typically any concessions that have been granted have been at those carriers threatened with bankruptcy. The uniformity of mechanics' pattern agreements has nevertheless been breaking up. Figure 6–1 plots the maximum rate for each mechanic settlement since 1975 and illustrates clearly the sharp increase in the variance among these settlements in recent years. Pay increases for mechanics have followed the same general decline as those for other groups since deregulation. The decline in mechanics' increases is less severe, however, and has rebounded since 1984. The mechanics' concessions may therefore be viewed as more the result of hard times in the industry and less the result of permanent changes in bargaining power than were the concessions made by the other crafts.

Partly because of the strong demand for mechanics, management demands of this craft group have recently shifted away from wage cuts toward work rule concessions. There appears to be more room for variation in mechanics' work practices and therefore more potential savings from work rule changes than is the case for cockpit and cabin crews (many of whose rules are set by the FAA) or for agent and clerical employees, whose jobs are more clearly defined.

The job of mechanics and ground crews is typically to service arrivals and departures that are not evenly spaced throughout the day. Airline management has therefore increasingly relied on part-time scheduling of mechanics as a way to meet the uneven work load. With the exception of Eastern, Republic, and TWA all the major carriers now have won contract language that allows them to use part-time employees in these positions. Perhaps the most important single work rule pertinent to mechanics' scheduling is that governing the "pushback" of the plane from the gate. In years past mechanics not only were present during this procedure but in some cases were stationed one by each wing to walk with the plane out of the gate, possibly doing some informal inspection as they went. American, Continental, Eastern, Frontier, Pan Am, Republic, and Western have cut back on this staffing requirement to a minimum of one mechanic, and in some cases they assign lesser skilled employees exclusively.

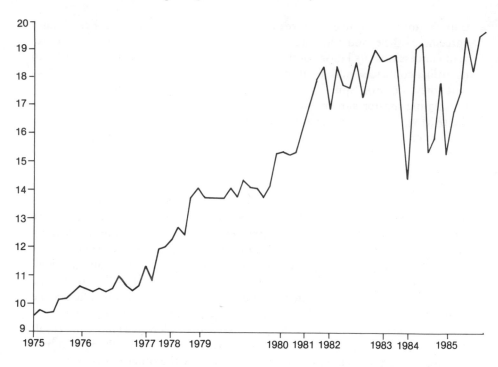

Source: AIRCon contract files.

Note: Each angle in the line represents a different collective bargaining agreement. Intervals for the years vary because the number of contracts settled varied each year.

Figure 6–1. The Maximum Hourly Rates for Airline Mechanics, as Set in Industry Contracts Negotiated from 1975 to 1985

One serious charge raised against deregulation is that its effects have forced airline management to skimp on maintenance and therefore on aircraft safety. As noted at the outset of this chapter one of the main reasons the New Deal legislators mandated airline regulation was their fear that unregulated, competitive markets would do just that—force management to save dollars at the expense of safety. Those operators that choose to fudge on safety probably do so more based on their probability of not being caught or heavily fined by the FAA than based on competitive pressures, however. Recent charges of safety violations, especially at the struggling carriers, are indeed troubling,[68] but it is difficult to assess the extent to which those violations were caused by the pressures generated by deregulated markets.

Agents and Clerical Employees. Reservation and ticket agents and clerical employees are the least unionized of any group in the airline industry; in fact, only six of the thirteen major carriers have unions of agents and clerical employees (see table 6–1). These workers have diverse skills and job duties and sometimes have little in common other than being in the same bargaining unit. This lack of a craft identification has no doubt hindered the development of aggressive unions among these occupations. But these positions and clerical jobs in general are not unionized to any great degree outside the industry either, and so it is not surprising to find that they are also relatively unorganized in air transport.

Agent and other clerical positions are very similar to their counterparts outside the industry, as are the terms and conditions of their employment. The primary reason for the lack of a substantial union impact on the wages and working conditions of this class of airline employees is simply that the group is sparsely unionized; their unions therefore were never able to take labor costs out of competition or to engage in the kind of pattern bargaining that took place in the other crafts. Nevertheless, some observers have argued that the unions representing these workers have been less combative not merely because their members lack bargaining power but also because the unions themselves lack resources, many of them being independent of any large, national union.

Airline bargaining with agents and other clerical employees has received relatively little attention in the period since deregulation in part because there is little of it, given the low level of unionization. Labor costs even for the unionized clerical employees were closer to market levels than the costs for the other crafts, and so there has been less room to cut costs. Nevertheless, clerical unions at all the struggling carriers have made concessions and typically made concessions similar to those made by the other crafts. The most important work rule change they have conceded is that allowing part-time employees, and every carrier has now secured this concession. And some carriers are even using split shifts of clerical workers.

Returning again to table 6–9 we find that increases in hourly earnings have declined among agents and other clerical employees. Again the decline in earnings lagged deregulation and the industry's financial nadir. Nominal wage increases actually turned negative in 1983–84 primarily because five carriers succeeded in cutting pay. The largest pay cuts were at Continental and Eastern, both of which have no clerical union. TWA also cut the pay of its clerical employees, who also were nonunion; partly in response to that action TWA's agents and clerical employees petitioned for a representation election.

In sum, nonunion agent and clerical employees have given up at least as much as the other crafts have, and they may in general have been worse off because without a union they had little, if any, say in the give backs. As a group, but especially among those with no union representation, these employees took greater cuts than the other airline crafts in the hard times following deregulation, but they nevertheless seem to have done much better than the other crafts when business improved. The lack of union protection has obviously made pay for this class much more sensitive to the demands of the individual carriers. One additional development among both the agent and clerical group and the mechanic group has been the employers' use of lump-sum payments as a partial substitute for annual pay increases. This practice, borrowed from labor settlements in manufacturing, restrains the growth of the base pay upon which benefits are calculated and the next round of pay increases are based. Lump-sum payments have been most prevalent at Northwest, Pan Am, and Piedmont.

Summary. The differences in bargaining experience among the airlines are most obvious in the cases where concession bargaining takes place across crafts at the same carrier. The various unions at Western, for example, agreed in 1983 to a 12 percent reduction in labor costs, but the mechanics achieved that cut entirely through work rule changes that led to layoffs, whereas, as noted above, the pilots achieved it entirely through pay cuts that preserved existing employment. Western's flight attendants and agents and clerical employees chose some combination of the two. It is the labor market circumstance of each of these groups that best seems to explain these different choices.

Finally, a special set of problems worthy of note is that created when the same union represents more than one of the crafts at the same carrier. The special labor market and bargaining circumstances of each craft then come into conflict with the pressure for consistent treatment within the union. The Teamsters, for example, represents all the major crafts at World. In bargaining with World over the concessions demanded of each craft, the union had to struggle with the tension between the principle of equal sacrifice across employees and the fact that some crafts, notably the mechanics, were much more able to resist concessions than others.

Issues for the Future

Problems Facing Unions. The changes in airline labor relations adopted since deregulation have created a series of problems for labor that go beyond concessionary bargaining. First, the pressure to make wage cuts has increased tensions between the union locals, whose members' jobs are at stake, and the internationals, whose leaders are concerned with protecting the pattern of compensation across the industry. In the beginning of this concessionary period the IAM pursued one extreme—preventing local concessions—while ALPA pursued the other—letting locals operate with almost complete independence. Since then both unions have moderated their positions.[69]

Recent developments have also led to the forging of new alliances between unions and between crafts. Unions in air transport have historically offered each other little cooperation, in particular, by routinely crossing one another's picket lines. Before deregulation the AFL-CIO had established a coordinating committee for airline unions that mainly dealt with lobbying efforts, but deregulation has since rallied support for cooperation in bargaining itself. Cooperation has been most evident at carriers facing bankruptcy, where the unions typically have been pressed to work together, often with banks and other outside parties, to reach agreements that will keep the airline in business. Collaborative efforts have been strongest at beleaguered Eastern, where the IAM has taken the lead in representing a coalition of union interests.[70]

More urgent pressures for interunion cooperation have arisen at those carriers that no longer simply shut down during a strike but instead try to operate using other personnel. Before this change unions could violate one another's picket lines without much effect; now such actions break strikes (as in the ALPA and IAM strikes at Continental in 1983 and in the flight attendants' strike at TWA in 1986). The unions have therefore pursued various strategies to encourage the honoring of picket lines (see the discussion below of the United strike), but airline labor still has a long way to go to claim a truly coordinated effort.

Mergers and Acquisitions. Perhaps the most pressing problems facing unions are those posed by mergers and acquisitions. Mergers are on the rise as the carriers try to develop regional networks to feed their hubs. More importantly, the prevalence of hub and spoke systems, the defensive pricing associated with them, and the shortage of additional airport capacity have combined to make it very difficult to enter markets without a merger. Indeed, the industry may be in the process of being oligopolized by a handful of major carriers, and if other carriers do not grow now, they will not be able to in the future.

Under the restrictions of the Railway Labor Act mergers bring with them the possibility of losing a union or, if merging with a nonunion carrier, of losing all the existing unions (typically, the representational status of the combined carrier is that which existed at the larger carrier). With the loss of labor protection provisions union members now also face loss of their seniority and other rights when mergers occur.

Mergers to acquire regional markets usually do not result in labor problems because they involve acquiring small, nonunion, commuter airlines. Sometimes these acquisitions are operated as independent carriers—Henson under Piedmont, American Eagle under American—but they can raise the threat of an alter ego operation. The more threatening mergers are those between large carriers. Five of the most significant mergers or acquisitions ever were arranged during one six-month period in 1985–86: United's purchase of Pan Am's overseas routes; Carl Ichan's takeover of TWA and the airline's subsequent acquisition of Ozark; People's purchase of Frontier, Provincetown-Boston, and Britt; Northwest's purchase of Republic; and Texas Air's acquisition of Eastern and then of People Express. Airline unions have learned through this not only that the choice of a merger partner is crucial for their interests, but also that they may be able to influence that choice by selectively manipulating labor cost prospects for different buyers.

To the extent that unions can influence the prospects of future labor costs for different merger candidates, they affect the relative value of the carrier to those candidates, the price they are willing to pay, and in turn which candidate will make the winning bid. Unions at TWA followed this pattern and negotiated directly with Carl Ichan, offering 25 percent wage concessions (in return for his promise not to sell the carrier off), and in turn threatened that if Texas Air bought the airline, there would be no concessions and possibly labor trouble as well. Of course, unions can use this tactic only if there is more than one suitor. Upon learning of Texas Air's intention to buy out their employer, Frontier's unions met this hurdle by actively seeking out a second buyer. They found one in People Express. Using an offer of future concessions as an enticement to People they received in return the promise that Frontier would continue to operate independently of People for four years.

The unions at TWA and Frontier not only determined the merger candidate but also secured some future labor protections in the process. Unions elsewhere are seeking similar protections against possible adverse consequences of mergers in the future through collective bargaining agreements with their current employers. The Teamsters union, for example, has secured seniority protections and other rights if mergers occur at Western and PSA; no doubt unions elsewhere will follow.

These merger strategies are no guarantee, however. Eastern's unions failed to prevent a takeover by Texas Air (which, as noted, has a bad reputation with labor) in 1986, partly because they could find no other merger candidates and partly because the takeover was made at the last minute under the threat of both strike and merger deadlines that came due before the unions could come to agreement among themselves. More specifically, all the unions would have had to approve an alternative to Texas Air, giving each union the equivalent of veto power over the entire process. The mechanics held all the cards because they were the last to give their approval; they eventually vetoed the survival plan perhaps because they had the most bargaining power of all the crafts and the least to lose from a change in ownership.

The Union Response: New Bargaining Demands. These attempts by unions to influence mergers, as well as the recent contract restrictions on double-breasted operations demonstrate how the bargaining demands of the airline unions have changed to protect their interests against the new set of problems unleashed since deregulation. As these examples illustrate, many of these threats operate outside of collective bargaining through management's business decisions. Nonetheless, the airline unions are seeking protections against such decisions through provisions secured in collective bargaining. Especially at the ailing airlines, management has an interest in gaining labor's approval of changes in business operations and thus has demonstrated some willingness to give something in return. It would be counterproductive to offer unions quid pro quos that raise current labor costs, but other offers can be attractive—contingent compensation, employment security, gains in union recognition clauses, and influence in business decisions, among others.

Table 6–10 illustrates the range of quid pro quos that airline unions have secured in return for making concessions. Again, the business decisions and circumstances of individual carriers determine what kind of offers management is willing to make; only carriers with good growth prospects are likely to offer employment security, for example, whereas only those in severe need of union concessions are likely to offer benefits that improve union bargaining power in the future. One obvious and common union gain at the struggling carriers has been the employee stock ownership plan, which offers

Table 6–10
Union Contract Gains Received through 1985 in Return for Wage and Work Rule Concessions, by Airline

Airline	Clause in Contract Requiring Some Form of:			
	Job Security	Employee Stock Ownership Plan (ESOP)	Profit- Sharing Plan	Union Member(s)(#) on Company Board of Directors
American	*		*	
Continental			*	
Eastern	*	*	*	4
Frontier		*		
Ozark	*			
Pan American		*		1
Republic	*	*	*	1
Trans World	*			
United	*			
Western		*	*	4

Sources: AIRCon contract files and the popular press.

Notes: Only those airlines whose unions have succeeded in obtaining these gains are included here. In each case an asterisk indicates that at least one of the unions representing employees of the airline have secured the plan or arrangement in question. Where profit-sharing plans exist, they cover virtually all the union members at the airline.

airlines an expeditious means to generate capital through wage cuts. In return, unions receive company shares, albeit usually nonvoting shares.

On the other hand, quality of work life (QWL) programs are rare in airlines because the employees are scattered geographically, rarely working together in stable groups, and because traditional rule-based management styles are reinforced by FAA regulations. Only American, Pan Am, Republic, and Western have QWL programs, and evidence from those programs is too sparse to know how extensive or successful these have been.

Industrial Conflict

In the first eight years after deregulation the number of strikes rose and then fell sharply. Before deregulation strikes were a routine occurrence because they posed less of a threat to the survival of the carriers. The industry's strike insurance plan (the MAP) and the protection of carriers' routes from new entrants during a strike—both of which ended with deregulation—had enabled carriers simply to shut down operations during strikes without serious threat to their long-term financial stability. Immediately following deregulation, between 1978 and 1981, the industry was still relatively healthy and strike levels remained high (14 at the 13 major carriers). Indeed, 1979, a year of industry expansion, had one of the highest strike rates of all time. But as the industry began to falter in 1981, it became clear, at least at the ailing carriers, that unions could not use their considerable bargaining power to strike because doing so would drive the carrier out of business. There was only one strike in 1982, one in 1983, and none in 1984.[71] Informal discussions with the parties and with mediators revealed, however, that in this ostensible peaceful period negotiations were far from harmonious and more often than not ran right up to the strike deadline before a settlement was reached.

And as the industry began to pick up again, strikes also increased; there were four strikes in 1985, three of which were long. Formal cooperative arrangements between management and labor that have recently become popular in other industries are relatively rare in airlines. Only Eastern and Western have pursued formal arrangements for cooperative problem solving of basic conflicts, and relationships at Eastern seem to change at least yearly. Most carriers have achieved at best only temporary rapprochements with their unions since deregulation.

Few if any of the strikes since deregulation could be claimed as a union victory—until ALPA's strike at United in 1985. United had secured two-tier wage agreements from its mechanics and flight attendants, but United's pilots had still not accepted them after more than a year of negotiations. (United argued that it needed a two-tier pilot pay plan to remain competitive with

American, which had negotiated such a plan in 1983.) In the meantime United had taken on 500 pilot trainees to help staff an immediate expansion, but management had refused to put the trainees on the payroll—and hence into the union and the bargaining unit—until ALPA signed a contract. The trainees therefore served as an important management bargaining chip: 500 new members for ALPA if agreement was reached, but 500 potential strike breakers if ALPA went on strike.

On May 17 ALPA struck United.[72] The carrier's flight attendants and some of its mechanics supported the strike, but the IAM did not. What was unusual about the strike was the success of ALPA's measures to ensure solidarity not only among its members but also with the trainees and flight attendants. United, which normally carried 15 percent of all domestic passengers, was reduced to operating at from 5 to 14 percent of its normal capacity (union and managements estimates differed, and both varied over time). ALPA estimated that only one percent of United's pilots, two percent of its flight attendants, and 2 of the 500 trainees crossed the picket lines and reported for work (*Philadelphia Inquirer* 1985b). Although the trainees were not yet ALPA members, the strike issue—two-tier pay rates—was essentially their problem, giving them a good reason to heed ALPA's request that they support the strike.

ALPA's strike campaign is memorable in large measure because of the new techniques the union employed in waging the strike: multimedia, videotaped presentations to members on specific issues (which apparently were packaged very similarly to the presentations previously used in negotiations by management); national teleconferences to link geographically separate pilot groups and establish solidarity; a toll-free national hotline for information on the strike; family and financial support programs during the strike; and systems of peer support that some have likened to Alcoholics Anonymous groups.[73]

A tentative agreement on May 25 called for a two-tier plan that merged into one wage scale in five years, but negotiations broke down over back-to-work issues. The strike continued until July 5 when United agreed to recall 650 low-seniority flight attendants who had lost their jobs to new hires during the strike.[74] ALPA challenged in court United's decision to give "superseniority" to pilots who had worked during the strike and its apparent decision not to hire the trainees who had refused to cross ALPA picket lines. Again, this dispute had its historical precedents. Southern Airways had hired replacements in its 1961 strike, granted them superseniority, and refused to bargain over it. In litigation taken by the union the courts held in favor of Southern (Kahn 1971, 477), but in 1985 they held for ALPA against United on both issues. In appeals, however, the court allowed United's decision against the trainees, asserting that they were not yet United employees.[75]

Even though the agreement represents a union concession at United (perhaps less so relative to industry practices), the strike was important for ALPA for several reasons. First, it introduced successful new techniques for organizing a strike; second, it represented the first successful effort by a union to shut down a carrier determined to fly since deregulation; and third, ALPA managed to achieve some solidarity among other unions at United and tried to protect employees outside of its own bargaining unit in the process. Interestingly, it was after its disastrous showing in the Continental strike of 1983 that ALPA had begun to evolve into the effective bargaining agent that later emerged at United. Just as the Century Air reorganization and pay cuts in 1931 had led to the formation of ALPA, the Continental reorganization and strike provided the shock that helped transform ALPA into a union able to function within the new environment of deregulation.

Conclusions

To anyone with an interest in industrial relations, airline deregulation was not a carefully considered experiment. The industry's experience in the 1920s and 1930s before governmental regulation had demonstrated that competitive markets generated considerable strain on labor relations, but the advocates of deregulation in the 1970s did not consider its effects on labor relations. The system of airline labor relations that had begun in 1938 adapted to the governmental regulations, and it is not surprising to find that system floundering, at least temporarily, now that those regulations have been removed.

One general conclusion that can be drawn from the airlines' experience since deregulation is that competitive markets do not necessarily have a uniform influence on collective bargaining. The market's influence is tempered not only by the business response of each individual firm but also by the existing collective bargaining structure and the various labor market circumstances operating at the time. In this industry the rapid spread of concessionary bargaining seems the result not simply of competitive market pressures but also of the particular response to those pressures made by a decentralized system of collective bargaining that offers no protection against them. The decentralized collective bargaining structure that worked to the unions' advantage when the market was protected turned on them completely when the market became competitive. The sensitivity of union wages to market forces therefore seems greatly dependent on the bargaining structure.[76] In other words, the bargaining experience across the airline crafts suggests that different types of union organization and labor market circumstances can influence the extent to which competitive pressures from the product market make themselves felt in labor relations.

In addition to the economic and financial pressures facing airline unions, it is important to note how many of their new challenges since deregulation have been the result of new corporate strategies. Virtually all of those strategies can be traced to Texas Air: alter ego operations, Chapter 11 maneuvers, and, in particular, mergers. It would be a mistake, therefore, to focus exclusively on deregulation and the resulting market pressures in any attempt to understand recent changes in airline labor relations.

Corporate restructuring and instability in the market for air transport should continue for some time, and so will the pressures to reorganize labor relations. As in other industries management has been able to use these pressures to win concessions from unions. The question for the airline unions is how best to regain the protections from market forces that deregulation took away. Part of the answer may be to make a greater effort to take wages out of competition by modifying the decentralized bargaining structures inherited from the period of regulation. Airline unions seem to have made greater strides than other unions in addressing the effects of business strategy decisions by placing contractual restrictions on such changes as alter ego operations. This process of change will certainly produce unions with different structures and different agendas that are pursued with different tactics. It seems clear, however, that the evolving system will span a broader range of issues and will give us plenty of things to study in the years ahead.

Notes

1. For a history of the fledgling air transport industry, see Spencer (1941), Warner (1938), and Kahn (1971).

2. As Panzar (1980) argued, routes offered carriers joint-product monopolies (mail and passengers), and some carriers were submitting ridiculously low mail bids to secure the route and then exploit the monopoly it gave on passenger traffic. Eastern Airlines, for example, bid zero on some routes for that reason.

3. For a firsthand account of New Deal arguments and the rule-setting that followed under the National Industrial Recovery Act of 1933, see Johnson (1935).

4. Pilot associations did exist at the time, and there were occasional job actions, mainly over the issue of flying in bad weather. For historical accounts of pilot labor relations, see Northrup (1947), Kahn (1953), Hopkins (1971; 1982), Baitsell (1966), and Kahn (1971).

5. See Kahn (1953) and Caves (1962) for an account of the early system of airline regulations.

6. For a thorough analysis of the act, see Rehmus (1977); see Rehmus (1985) for a short history of the act and the NMB.

7. As Northrup (1971) noted, the occupational basis for bargaining units does not always fit well with the industry's occupational structure. Ground crews, for example, comprise a wide range of jobs and are linked by no common craft or skills, and yet they have been lumped together in the same bargaining units under RLA. Moreover, Craft-based unions in the industry are particularly threatened by technological

change, as the elimination of some jobs as the result of an innovation often meant the elimination of entire unions (see Kahn 1971 for examples).

8. I have calculated this figure from NMB annual reports. The case establishing the decertification procedure was Alitalia Airlines, Inc. v. International Association of Machinists and Aerospace Workers, NMB CR-5432, May 18, 1983, in NMB (1983, 331–32).

9. The recommendations can be turned over to Congress, which can enforce them legislatively, but this has never happened in the airline industry.

10. Cullen (1977) credits Secretary of Labor George P. Schultz with having halted the practice during the Nixon Administration. There have been a total of 34 airline emergency boards in the years since passage of the RLA.

11. The Domestic Passenger Fare Investigation by the CAB in 1973 created a formula that based fares on average costs and distance. See Taneja (1976) on the development of CAB fare regulations.

12. During the two decades before deregulation the rate of return on investment averaged around 2 to 3 percent, roughly half of what it was in manufacturing. As a result of this stability, it was easy for carriers to secure debt financing; the high level of debt many had established would create problems in the 1980s when interest rates climbed.

13. Airline mergers were easier to arrange in those years because even debt-ridden carriers "owned" their routes, which were desirable assets for other carriers.

14. Among all of the LPPs those that became known as the Allegheny-Mohawk provisions (resulting from that merger) are generally viewed as providing the most complete protection for employees and the greatest burden for carriers seeking to merge. See Cotter (1967) for an analysis of the LPPs.

15. The figure for flight attendants, for example, is about 4 percent (calculated from CAB Form 41 data).

16. The main exception to these generalizations was criticism from small carriers and potential carriers, which were excluded from the trunk markets and wanted in. See U.S. Senate (1975) for the legislative debate that preceded deregulation.

17. For example, such plans would require carriers to arbitrate any outstanding issues at the request of the unions. See Unterberger and Koziara (1980) for details. The MAP was already showing signs of trouble as both Pan Am (in 1974) and Eastern (1975) had withdrawn as a quid pro quo for union concessions.

18. For a case-by-case rundown of these CAB decisions, see Mahoney (1983).

19. USAir and Piedmont voluntarily complied with the program before the above rules were issued (Duffy 1983).

20. See Duffy (1985) for a description of these cases.

21. See Kyle and Phillips (1985) for a discussion of the role of academic arguments in deregulation.

22. See Baumol (1982) for a description of the theory and Bailey and Panzar (1981) for an application to the airline industry.

23. See Bailey, Graham, and Kaplan (1985, 4).

24. Midway was the first of the major new carriers in 1979, followed by New York Air and then Muse and People Express in 1980. World and Capital Airlines were formerly charter carriers; and PSA, Southwest, and Air Florida were intrastate carriers; Piedmont and USAir were local service carriers.

25. This calculation excludes Delta from the nonunion group, for the reasons noted above, and also excludes commuter markets. See table 6–2.

26. Southwest, the original nonunion, low-cost carrier, is now unionized and purchased Muse in 1985.

27. In some cases, the fare cuts have generated so much additional demand that the established carriers gain some business (albeit at a lower fare). Some markets entered by People Express, for example, have shown traffic increases of 200 percent or more (McKinnon 1983).

28. The new, nonunion carriers' low-cost structures are the result of lower labor costs and more uniform fleets—generally B-737s, which are fuel efficient, operate with two-person crews, and were often purchased at a discount from a distressed trunk carrier. These carriers also subcontract many operations—maintenance, almost without exception, and often ground support and reservation services as well.

29. See Parenti (1983) and Schlesinger (1983; 1985) for descriptions of People's human resource policies.

30. In general, these reservation systems charge other carriers a fee to list their schedules but display more prominently the schedules of their owners. American, United, TWA, and Delta each own the biggest systems. See GAO (1986) for arguments about the competitive advantages such systems grant.

31. Carriers can discriminate in pricing even on the same flight because passengers cannot efficiently resell seats to one another. This characteristic makes airline pricing like that of a public utility.

32. Frequent flyer plans give bonuses of extra flying miles to the traveler, even though it is often the business traveler's employer that paid for the trips. The plans thus encourage loyalty to the carrier among business travelers.

33. Both Graham, Kaplan, and Sibley (1983) and Bailey, Graham, and Kaplan (1985) found, for example, that fares were not reduced by potential entry. This is not to suggest that the theory is wrong but rather that the assumptions necessary for it are not met in the airline case. For example, the theory requires that entry into and exit from markets be costless and that prices cannot be set below marginal costs (Baumol 1982), both of which assumptions, as noted above, do not hold for airlines.

34. ALPA v. Texas International Airlines, Inc., 850 U.S. Court of Appeals, (2d Cir. 1981).

35. Eight carriers had formed holding companies previously for reasons other than double-breasted strategies. Transamerica did form an international subsidiary, but it was unionized.

36. The CAB subsidy formula provided financial support to hard-pressed carriers even when the cause of the trouble was a strike. The CAB tried to prevent paying subsidies for strike losses, but the courts held for the carriers in 1949 during the American Overseas Airline strike (Kahn 1971).

37. The committee later evolved into the Airline Industrial Relations Conference (AIRCon), an industry clearinghouse for labor information.

38. The strike stopped 60 percent of domestic traffic, and the emergency board's recommendations went all the way through the Senate before the strike ended after 43 days (Cullen 1977).

39. The plan was initiated to prop up Capital Airlines, which was engaged in a long strike by the IAM over issues of industry wide concern. Because it is an inter-

airline agreement, the MAP required approval by the CAB under the Civil Aeronautics Act of 1938.

40. At its most generous, the plan compensated struck carriers for most of their revenues lost and, in turn, vastly increased the ability of carriers to resist strikes. Northwest made particularly extensive use of the plan to help hold its labor costs down. Indeed, the fact that Northwest was able to operate at healthy profit levels while using the plan helped swing opinion against it and eventually bring about its downfall, as discussed below.

41. For example, the decision to eliminate flight engineers beginning in 1961 and the decision to allow management greater latitude to increase pilot hours in 1965 also followed this pattern. See Kahn (1971) for details.

42. The comparison was mainly of trunk carriers to commuter, intrastate, and supplemental carriers. One of the important aspects of this study is that it considers the range of avenues through which regulations can increase union gains.

43. Industry calculations suggest, for example, that the ubiquitous $99 transcontinental fare could make money only if the planes flew at 150 percent of capacity. Cutting prices to fill empty seats draws passengers away from competitors, forces them in turn to cut fares, and in this manner has been the start of every major fare war in the industry. There have always been route-specific fare wars when new competitors enter markets, but the first systemwide fare war was that in 1979, when United cut fares to fill empty seats after its 59-day mechanic's strike. Eastern started the second systemwide war on transcontinental routes in 1981 when the company sought summer markets for the L10-11s it flew for winter traffic to Florida. TWA, American, and United (the transcontinental carriers) started the next war, this time in the Florida routes, when they sought winter markets for their planes used for transcontinental summer vacationers. Finally, American initiated the 1985 fare war in an effort to fill empty seats during the slack periods between the winter holidays.

44. The 1981 Professional Air Traffic Controllers Organization (PATCO) strike and the subsequent dismissal of the strikers probably prevented even worse bloodletting in the industry by artificially restricting capacity for two years until the government could train and hire new controllers. During that time the CAB imposed a freeze on new entrants at major airports and reduced schedules for the established carriers. See Northrup (1984) for an account of the PATCO strike and BNA (1981) for an assessment of the impact on individual carriers.

45. For example, hard times at Eastern in 1975 convinced the union to accept a variable earnings plan according to which pay would decline with a decline in net earnings below a specified figure. In 1979 United had secured a reduction from three- to two-member crews on its Boeing-737s in return for a no-layoff guarantee for pilots during the two-year agreement. (With the decline in business United paid an estimated $20 million in salary to pilots it would otherwise have laid off over those two years; *Business Week* 1981).

46. See Cappelli (1985a).

47. All information on airline contracts cited here and elsewhere comes from AIRCon files that summarize contract changes. Concessionary bargaining may best be thought of as a process (Cappelli 1983). The analysis here focuses on concessionary outcomes, however, which are defined as a cut in pay or benefits or a management work rule gain without an offsetting gain to the union in some other area of the contract.

48. The six healthiest airlines were American, Delta, Frontier, Northwest, TWA, and United.

49. The takeover process involved decisions by several courts, the California legislature (where Continental was incorporated), the CAB, and President Reagan, as well as much political intrigue, and one suicide (among management). See Weinberg (1985) for an account of the decision making at Continental.

50. Braniff achieved roughly the same reductions, but through negotiations with its unions.

51. The unions had trouble maintaining solidarity among the strikers in part because in the merger of Texas International and Continental employees were assigned to new locations and union representation changed. Continental's flight attendants switched unions and its clerks and agents lost representation.

52. In June 1984 the U.S. Bankruptcy Court upheld Continental's unilateral alteration of its agreement with ALPA (U.S. Bankruptcy Court for Southern District of Texas, Houston Division, 1985: Continental Airlines, Inc., 83-04019-H2-5; Continental Airlines, Inc., 83-04020-H1-5; Texas International Airlines, Inc., 83-04020-H1-5; Texas International Airlines Holdings Corp., 83-04022-H3-5). Other issues—such as whether actions by Continental or by its unions violated the RLA and which union (if any) should represent some of the bargaining units—remain unresolved.

53. I am indebted to Charles Pasciutto, Vice President of Industrial Relations at American, for the material from which this account was drawn. The fact that pilots at American are not part of ALPA no doubt made it easier to secure these changes.

54. Some newly hired pilots at American, for example, formed an association to press for an increase in the lower, or "B", pay scale. Perhaps partly in response to this (and no doubt also in response to a relative shortage of entry-level pilots), American recently raised the "B" scale and specified that it merge with the original scale after 15 years.

55. A more complete discussion of the relationships between airline responses and diversity in labor relations practice appears in Cappelli (1985b).

56. Three carriers—Eastern, Pan Am, and Hawaiian—restored the previous wage cuts in 1985. These data are from the AIRCon contract file.

57. The typical military applicant came to the industry after retiring from the military with 20 years' service (when military pensions are vested). The ideal candidate was not a fighter pilot but a military transport flyer.

58. Unpublished figures from the Air Transport Association.

59. Some of this training can be done using flight simulators, but small carriers often do not have simulators and must tie up their planes to provide all of flight training—clearly an expensive process. Of course, the attraction of eventually getting a position at a major carrier does help create the supply of trainees for both the military air forces and the commuter airlines.

60. These are the work rules at Braniff, Continental, Midway, New York Air, and People Express.

61. Boeing 727s, DC-10s, L10-11s, and Boeing 747s currently require three-member crews; the third officer, the most junior position, is a flight engineer.

62. For a description of the demands of the occupation, see Hochschild (1984).

63. Some observers believe the ALSSA was forced to split from ALPA largely because the coming of jumbo jets, which increased the ratio of flight attendants to

total flight crews, would have made the pilots a minority within the ALPA organization. It formed the Association of Flight Attendants which retains some informal affiliations with ALPA.

64. For an interesting history of flight attendant labor relations, see Nielsen (1982).

65. One obvious reason for this is that under the previous work rules attendants (all of whom at the time were women) had to resign if they married or when they reached the job's restrictive age standard. Recent reports suggest that early retirement programs and the numbers of new hires now possible under the two-tier pay plans are temporarily reducing average seniority levels among flight attendants.

66. Data on attendants' increases in 1984–85 are not yet complete because both Eastern's and TWA's contracts remain open.

67. A prime example was the international's decision to take Braniff to court to prevent Braniff's local from making concessions.

68. See, for example, Murphy (1983) and Nance (1985).

69. For example, the IAM has since approved some concessions, and ALPA has taken steps to limit the spread of concessions across carriers; ALPA's constitution was amended in 1985 to give the president approval power over all contracts (the same arrangement as at the IAM); and ALPA's development of a substantial strike fund combined with its new tactics at United signal a harder position in bargaining.

70. For a discussion of the coalition, see *Labor Research Review* (1984).

71. The pilot and flight attendant strikes at Continental in 1983 occurred outside of contract negotiations and therefore are not included here.

72. Before the actual date of the strike, 155 flights were canceled because of pilot "sick outs" (*Philadelphia Inquirer* 1985a).

73. For an account of these techniques, see *Wall Street Journal* (1985).

74. The final agreement called for renegotiating the two-tier agreement after five years and arbitration if the parties could not at that time agree.

75. Air Line Pilots Association v. United Air Lines, Inc., U.S. Court of Appeals (7th Cir.), nos. 85-2726 and 85-2833.

76. See Cappelli (forthcoming). The choice of bargaining structures may in some cases be a function of market forces, as Hendricks and Kahn (1982) have noted.

References

ATA. 1985. *Air Transport 1985: The Annual Report of the Scheduled Airline Industtry*. Washington, D.C.: ATA.

Aviation Daily. 1985. Status of Airline Labor Contracts. October 10, p. 220.

Bailey, Elizabeth, David R. Graham, and David P. Kaplan. 1985. *Airline Deregulation*. Cambridge, Mass.: MIT Press.

Bailey, Elizabeth, and John C. Panzar. 1981. The Contestability of Airline Markets During the Transition to Deregulation. *Law and Contemporary Problems* 44 (Winter): 125–47.

Baitsell, John M. 1966. *Airline Industrial Relations: Pilots and Flight Engineers*. Boston: Graduate School of Business Administration, Harvard University.

Baumol, William J. 1982. Contestable Markets: An Uprising in the Theory of Industrial Structure. *American Economic Review* 72 (March): 1–15.

BNA (Bureau of National Affairs). 1981. PATCO Strike Hits Pilots. *Daily Labor Report* 160 (September 11): A-6.

———. 1984. Machinists' Concessions at Braniff Held Binding. *Daily Labor Report* 176 (September 30): A-9.

———. 1986. Displaced Workers Hiring Priority Rights, Regulations Issued by DOL. *Daily Labor Report* 251 (December 31): A-7.

Business Week. 1981. United Takes on the Upstarts. October 4, p. 94.

———. 1982. Six Airlines: Gaining a Bit of Altitude. November 15, p. 68.

Cappelli, Peter. 1983. Concession Bargaining and the National Economy. In *Proceedings of the Thirty-Fifth Annual Meeting, December 28–30, 1982, New York,* ed. Barbara Dennis, 362–71. Madison, Wis.: Industrial Relations Research Association.

———. 1984. Union Gains under Concession Bargaining. In *Proceedings of the Thirty-Sixth Annual Meeting, December 28–30, 1983, San Francisco,* ed. Barbara Dennis, 297–305. Madison, Wis.: Industrial Relations Research Association.

———. 1985a. Airline Industrial Relations in Transition. In *Proceedings of the Thirty-Seventh Annual Meeting, December 28–30, 1984, Dallas,* ed. Barbara Dennis, 437–46. Madison, Wis.: Industrial Relations Research Association.

———. 1985b. Competitive Pressures and Labor Relations in the Airline Industry. *Industrial Relations* 24 (Fall): 316–38.

———. 1985c. Plant-Level Concession Bargaining. *Industrial and Labor Relations Review* 39 (October): 90–104.

———. Forthcoming. Market Forces, Bargaining Structure, and Wage Outcomes in the British Coal Industry *Industrial Relations.*

Card, David. 1986. The Impact of Deregulation on the Employment and Wages of Airline Mechanics, working paper. Princeton: Industrial Relations Section, Princeton University.

Caves, Richard E. 1962. *Air Transport and Its Regulators.* Cambridge, Mass.: Harvard University Press.

Clark, John O'Brien, Jr. 1985. Testimony. In *Airline Mergers and Acquisitions: The Question of Labor Protection,* Hearings of the Subcommittee on Aviation, U.S. Senate, 99th Cong. 1st sess. Washington, D.C.: GPO, p. 52.

Commons, John R. 1909. American Shoemakers, 1648–1895: A Sketch of Industrial Evolution. *Quarterly Journal of Economics* 24 (November): 39–84.

Cotter, Francis J. 1967. Civil Aeronautics Board and Labor Jurisdiction. *Journal of Air Law and Commerce* 33 (Spring): 335–50.

Cullen, Donald E. 1977. Strike Experience under the Railway Labor Act. In *The Railway Labor Act at Fifty: Collective Bargaining in the Railroad and Airline Industries,* ed. Charles M. Rehmus, 187–208. Washington, D.C.: National Mediation Board.

Duffy, Capt. Henry A. 1983. Testimony. In *Review of Airline Deregulation and the Sunset of the CAB,* Hearings of the Subcommittee on Aviation, U.S. House of Representatives, 98th Cong., 2d sess., p. 528. Washington, D.C.: GPO, p. 528.

————. 1985. Testimony. In *Airline Mergers and Acquisitions: The Question of Labor Protection,* Hearings of the Subcommittee on Aviation, U.S. Senate, 99th Cong. 1st sess., pp. 22–32. Washington, D.C.: GPO.

Dunlop, John T. 1985. Trends and Issues in Labor Relations in the Transport Sector. *Transport Research News* (May-June): 1–8.

GAO (General Accounting Office). 1985. *Increased Competition Is Making Airlines More Efficient and Responsive to Consumers.* Washington, D.C.: GPO.

————. 1986. *Airline Competition: Impact of Computerized Reservation Systems.* Washington, D.C.: GPO.

Graham, David R., Daniel P. Kaplan, and David S. Sibley. 1983. Efficiency and Competition in the Airline Industry. *Bell Journal of Economics* 14 (Spring): 118–38.

Hendricks, Wallace E., Peter Feuille, and Carol Szerszen. 1980. Regulation, Deregulation, and Collective Bargaining in the Airlines. *Industrial and Labor Relations Review* 34 (October): 67–81.

Hendricks, Wallace E., and Lawrence M. Kahn. 1982. The Determinants of Bargaining Structure in U.S. Manufacturing Industries. *Industrial and Labor Relations Review* 35 (January): 181–95.

Hopkins, George E. 1971. *The Airline Pilots: A Study in Elite Unionization.* Cambridge, Mass: Harvard University Press.

————. 1982. *Flying the Line: The First Half Century of the Air Line Pilots Association.* Washington, D.C.: ALPA.

Hochschild, Arlie Russell. 1983. *The Managed Heart: Commercialization of Human Feeling.* Berkeley: University of California Press.

Johnson, Hugh. 1935. *The Blue Eagle from Egg to Earth.* New York: Garden City Press.

Kahn, Mark L. 1953. Wage Determination for Airline Pilots. *Industrial and Labor Relations Review* 6 (April): 317–36.

————. 1971. Collective Bargaining on the Flight Deck. In *Collective Bargaining and Technological Change in American Transportation,* ed. Harold M. Levinson, Charles M. Rehmus, Joseph P. Goldberg, and Mark L. Kahn, 423–605. Evanston, Ill.: Transportation Center, Northwestern University.

Kyle, Reuben, III, and Lawrence T. Phillips. 1985. Airline Deregulation: Did Economists Promise Too Much or Too Little? *Logistics and Transportation Review* 21 (March): 3–25.

Labor Research Review. 1984. Up Against the Gloom and Doom. Vol. 4 (Winter): special issue.

Mahoney, William G. 1983. Testimony. In *Review of Airline Deregulation and the Sunset of the CAB,* Hearings of the Subcommittee on Aviation, U.S. House of Representatives, 98th Cong., 2d sess., p. 228. Washington, D.C.: GPO.

May, Daniel F. 1983. Testimony. In *Review of Airline Deregulation and the Sunset of the CAB,* Hearings of the Subcommittee on Aviation, U.S. House of Representatives, 98th Cong., 2d sess., p. 528. Washington, D.C.: GPO.

McKinnon, Dan. 1983. Testimony. In *Review of Airline Deregulation and the Sunset of the CAB,* Hearings of the Subcommittee on Aviation, U.S. House of Representatives, 98th Cong., 2d sess., p. 528. Washington, D.C.: GPO.

Molloy, 1985. *The U.S. Commuter Airline Industry: Policy of Alternatives.* Lexington, Mass.: Lexington Books.

Murphy, Patrick V., Jr. 1983. Testimony. In *Review of Airline Deregulation and the*

Sunset of the CAB, Hearings of the Subcommittee on Aviation, U.S. House of Representatives, 98th Cong. 2d sess. p. 27. Washington, D.C.: GPO.

National Mediation Board. 1983. *Determinations of the National Mediation Board.* Washington, D.C.: GPO.

Nance, John J. 1985. *Blind Trust.* New York: William Morrow.

New York Times. 1986. Pilot Hirings Surge at Airlines. January 1, p. 1.

Nielsen, Georgia Panter. 1982. *From Sky Girl to Flight Attendant: Women and the Making of a Union.* Ithaca, N.Y.: ILR Press, Cornell University.

Northrup, Herbert R. 1947. Collective Bargaining by Airline Pilots. *Quarterly Journal of Economics* 21 (August): 533–76.

———. 1971. The Railway Labor Act: A Critical Reappraisal. *Industrial and Labor Relations Review* 25 (October): 3–31.

———. 1977. Airline Strike Insurance: A Study in Escalation; Comment. *Industrial and Labor Relations Review* 30 (April): 364–72.

———. 1984. The Rise and Demise of PATCO. *Industrial and Labor Relations Review* 37 (January): 167–85.

Panzar, John C. 1980. Regulation, Deregulation, and Economic Efficiency: The Case of the CAB. *American Economic Review* 70 (May): 311–15.

Parenti, Harold. 1983. Testimony. In *Review of Airline Deregulation and the Sunset of the CAB,* Hearings of the Subcommittee on Aviation, U.S. House of Representatives, 98th Cong. 2d sess., p. 61. Washington, D.C.: GPO.

Philadelphia Inquirer. 1985a. UA and Pilots Are Stalled in Efforts to Avoid Strikes. May 17, p. 17–A.

———. 1985b. UA, Pilots to Meet with Mediator. May 20, p. 7–A.

Rehmus, Charles M. 1985. *The National Mediation Board at Fifty: Its Impact on Railroad and Airline Labor Disputes.* Washington, D.C.: National Mediation Board.

Rehmus, Charles M., ed. 1977. *The Railway Labor Act at Fifty: Collective Bargaining in the Railroad and Airline Industries.* Washington, D.C.: National Mediation Board.

Ross, Arthur M. 1948. *Trade Union Wage Policy.* Berkeley: University of California Press.

Schlesinger, Leonard. 1983. *People Express,* case study. Boston: Harvard Business School.

———. 1985. *People Express: Update,* case study. Boston: Harvard Business School.

Spencer, Francis. 1941. *Airmail Payment and the Government.* Washington, D.C.: Brookings Institution.

Taneja, Nawal K. 1976. *The Commercial Airline Industry.* Lexington, Mass: Lexington Books.

Unterberger, S. Herbert, and Edward C. Koziara. 1975. Airline Strike Insurance: A Study in Escalation. *Industrial and Labor Relations Review* 29 (October): 26–45.

———. 1980. The Demise of Airline Strike Insurance. *Industrial and Labor Relations Review* 34 (October): 82–90.

U.S. Department of Labor, Bureau of Labor Statistics. 1985. *Handbook of Labor Statistics.* Washington, D.C.: GPO.

U.S. Senate. 1975. *Oversight of CAB,* Hearings of Committee on Judiciary Oversight, 94th Cong. 2d sess. Washington, D.C.: GPO.

Wall Street Journal. 1985. Pilots' Bitter Strike Against Continental Changed Their Union. March 17, p. 1.

Warner, Edward. 1983. *The Early History of Air Transportation.* Northfield, Vt.: Norwich University.

Weinberg, Martha. 1985. *Continental Airlines,* case study. Boston: Harvard Business School.

7
Professional Sports

James B. Dworkin

Th, his chapter examines the salient characteristics of collective bargaining in a unique corner of the working world—the professional sports industry. According to *The Living Webster Encyclopedic Dictionary of the English Language,* a professional is "a member of any profession, but more often applied, in opposition to *amateur,* to persons who make their living by arts or sports in which others engage as a pastime." Thus, we are concerned here only with those who earn their livelihoods in sports, either as owners or as players. These individuals are viewed as being a part of the entertainment industry.

The chapter is further restricted in its focus primarily on teams, team owners, and players who have achieved major league status. Minor league and women's teams, though they meet most of the definition of professionalism cited above, are excluded here for reasons of scope.

Finally, the analysis presented here covers only the four sports of baseball, basketball, football, and hockey. Major league status for teams in these sports is defined by their membership in the National League of Professional Baseball Clubs, the American League of Professional Baseball Clubs, the National Basketball Association, the National Football League, the United States Football League, or the National Hockey League.

The Bargaining Environment

The Technological Environment

The basic output of a professional sports league is a game or match between two of the clubs that are members of the league. Although many, if not most, other industries have recently witnessed major technological changes that have greatly altered production processes and industry outputs, professional sports leagues continue to produce the same outputs—sporting events—in much the same way as they always have. And although in most other industries a product can be produced by a single firm, the same cannot be said for professional sports. A team must have an opponent to produce a game. Intra-squad games may generate some interest during practice seasons, but the real sporting challenge is only in the competition with another league club.

As Demmert (1973, 10–15) has pointed out, the stream of economic utility resulting from the combined inputs of two competitive teams can be separated into three elements. First, each game has associated with it an uncertainty of outcome. Games attract more fans when the outcome is highly uncertain, that is when the two teams are evenly matched. Nonetheless, even when two teams appear to be very unevenly matched, the nature of sporting events is such that the underdog may rise to the occasion and pull off an upset. Even the best teams lose every once in a while. Thus, uncertainty of outcome makes the game attractive to the potential ticket purchaser and the television viewer.

Second, games are said to possess entertainment value over and above the value of interest in their uncertain outcome. Spectators may flock to a New York Knickerbockers basketball game because, for example, they are particularly interested in watching one of the team's star players, Patrick Ewing. Or fans may attend what would seem to be a lopsided contest in anticipation of seeing a record set by either a team or a player. Thus, sports fans have many reasons for purchasing their tickets other than simply their interest in the uncertain outcome of the game.

The third utility accruing to spectators at sporting events is their pleasure in witnessing a victory by the team they support. That is not to say there are no sold-out stadiums for losing teams, but simply that fans do identify with winning clubs.

Teams generate revenues from their outputs (games) through the sale of tickets to spectators and through the sale of broadcast rights to radio and television stations. The major costs of operating a team are player development and salaries. More will be said later about these revenues and expenses, with particular reference to several strikes that have occurred in baseball and football over the issue whether the players receive a fair portion of the returns to their teams' coffers.

Each season the sports leagues publish an advance schedule of games. The typical arrangement is for each team to play other league teams an equal number of times at home and away as a visitor. The ultimate goal of every team is to win a league championship. In baseball this is accomplished by winning the World Series; in football, the Super Bowl; in basketball, the NBA playoffs; and in hockey, the Stanley Cup playoffs.

The skills required to operate a franchise in one of the major professional sports leagues are of two basic varieties. First, clubs require managerial talent to be successful. The typical image of management in professional sports is of a head coach like Tom Landry of the Dallas Cowboys or a baseball manager like Tommy LaSorda of the Los Angeles Dodgers. Head coaches are important, but teams also need a bevy of talented scouts, assistant coaches, and business managers. With more attention being paid these days to the financial successes—and failures—of sports clubs, it is safe to predict that business managers will assume an even larger role in the future. Thus, all professional sports demand two kinds of managerial talent: the manager who knows the game, and the manager who knows how to manage the team as a business enterprise.

The second type of skill required to operate a successful professional team is, obviously, trained athletic talent. Managerial skills may be important, but as the National Football League Players Association (1981) aptly put it, "We are the game." Despite the numbers of people who engage in sports recreationally, only a handful possess the talent and ability to "make it" in the big leagues.

The two basic sources of trained athletic talent are colleges and minor league (farm) systems. Baseball and hockey tend to rely on their well-developed farm systems, but they also look to star college players when attempting to fill their rosters. Football and basketball teams typically do not have minor league systems and thus rely almost exclusively on colleges in recruiting new players. It is interesting to note that football and basketball clubs are thereby able to avoid many of the training costs associated with operating a minor league system to develop new talent. Their counterparts in baseball and hockey regularly spend large sums of money on these player development activities. That financial burden will be shown below to be an important antecedent to some of the product market and labor market restrictions that have been established in those two sports. A description of those restrictions is essential to understanding the motivation of the players' to form unions and engage in collective bargaining activities.

The Economic Environment

Professional sports leagues have typically engaged in a host of anticompetitive practices in both the product market and the labor market. In the product market, all the major sports leagues have developed practices aimed at restricting entry into their leagues. It is virtually impossible to start up a team and expect to be accepted into one of today's major leagues. Even if a group of investors has more than enough money to devote to running a major league franchise, many hurdles must first be passed over. Take the case of baseball. The major leagues continue to talk about the possibility of expanding into new cities. Cities across the country line up with proposals to attract this sport that annually generates over 500 million dollars in revenue and draws over 45 million people to stadiums. They go to great lengths, constructing stadiums in anticipation of a franchise and even selling season tickets to demonstrate the interest of the populace. But, for the present, talk is all that is happening. No new franchises have been awarded. Each sports league jealously guards entry through a series of rules and regulations published in its by-laws and constitution.[1] The obvious aim of the owners in each league is to restrict product market competition. Too many teams dilute the talent on each team and could cause sports devotees' interest to wane, since the new teams are typically stocked initially from the rosters of the already existing teams. In short, the product market in professional sports is decidedly noncompetitive, and together the owners enjoy a complete monopoly over the production of major league games.

Given this situation, what options are available to a city or to investors who wish to enter the professional sports industry as a franchise owner? There are three basic ways to proceed. The first has already been described: To make out an application to the existing league and go through the formal process of attempting to obtain an expansion franchise. As already noted, the odds of gaining entry into the established league in this manner are very slim. A second method is to woo an established team away from its home site, as Indianapolis did in 1984 with the Baltimore Colts. A third, and historically common, route in all four major sports has been to work outside the rules of the established leagues and form new professional clubs in a *new* league, although no new league has survived.

The common theme underlying all of the rival leagues has been the desire to participate in a restricted, and elite, fraternity—the professional sports business. The problem all teams face boils down to a basic shortage of player talent. The rival leagues have invariably bid player salaries up for a short time to entice established stars from the older leagues to jump to the newer franchises. But the risks of taking those leaps are all too obvious to the players. How long will the new league survive? If my team files for bankruptcy, do I still get paid? Will I be blacklisted by the established league for life because I left it? These and other such questions have typically held the number of players jumping leagues to a minimum. Moreover, clubs in the established leagues typically respond to the new leagues by matching or bettering the contracts offered to star players by the new league.

Lesser talent and ability in the rival leagues has been a constant source of economic hardship. Without superstars, they lose fans. More important, without a devoted following, television and radio contracts are hard to come by and teams suffer further. In the end, the new league usually goes out of business after only a short period of operation. It is not unusual, however, for the most financially secure of the clubs in the new league to be absorbed into the existing league as part of a merger agreement at the time of the breakup of the rival league. The most obvious example of this is the peace treaty between the National Football League and the American Football League in 1970 that led to the present divisional structure under the umbrella of just one league, the NFL. The point is that even though entering a rival league is a risky business, it may be a useful strategy for *eventually* gaining entry into the established league. In fact, entry in this manner may be much more expeditious than waiting for the mature league to make an expansion decision on its own.

A similar set of anticompetitive rules can be found in the labor market of every professional league. But things were not always thus, and it is instructive to explore the development of these monopsonistic practices using an example from the oldest of the professional sports, baseball.[2]

In the early days of the National League, every player on every team was free to change teams at the end of each baseball season. This process, which we would refer to as free agency today, was referred to as "revolving" in the 1870s. Revolving was associated with two principal evils, according to club owners of the time. First and foremost, players were able to receive much higher salaries as clubs bid to acquire their services for the next season. The owners disliked having to pay players more money because of these bidding wars. Second, the constant switching of teams by star players was viewed as deleterious to fan loyalty. The owners alleged that fans identified themselves with certain star players on each team and that the loss of those players would most certainly cause the fans to stay home or spend their leisure time—and money—elsewhere. Thus, the owners decided to take action to protect the fans and themselves from the serious consequences of revolving.

That action was to be a forerunner of the labor market restrictions employed in all of the professional sports leagues to this day. On September 30, 1879 the owners instituted the first reserve rule, by which each player became the property of the club he had played for in the previous season. The reserve rules were easily enforced because each club realized that if it did not approach other clubs' players with lucrative contracts, those other clubs would in turn leave its players alone. A player no longer had the right to change teams at will. Instead, he had to play for the same team he had played for in the previous season unless he was either traded or sold outright. The reserve rule almost instantly brought spiraling salaries under control and forced star players to remain with their clubs, much to the pleasure of the loyal home fans. A player's only options were to accept his club's salary offer or retire from the game. When faced with these two extremes, the usual course of action was for the player to accept his club's salary offer and hope to increase his pay next year through stellar performance in his trade.

This first reserve rule eventually became a part of every individual player contract in each of the professional sports leagues. Every standard player contract in the National Hockey League, for example, contained the following language:

> The player hereby undertakes that he will at the request of the club enter into a contract for the following playing season upon the same terms and conditions as this contract save as to salary which shall be determined by mutual agreement.[3]

To give just one more example, basketball players were forced to sign player contracts that contained the following language:

> On or before August 1 next following the last playing season covered by this contract and renewals and extensions thereof, the Club may tender to the Player a contract for the next succeeding season by mailing the same to the Player at his address shown below, or if none is shown, then at his address last known to the Club. If the Player fails, neglects or omits to sign and return such contract to the Club so that the Club receives it on or before September 1st next succeeding, then his contract shall be deemed renewed and extended for the period of one year, upon the same terms and conditions in all respects as are provided herein, except that the compensation payable to the Player shall be the sum provided in the contract tendered to the Player pursuant to the provisions hereof, which compensation shall in no event be less than the compensation payable to the Player for the last playing season covered by this contract and renewals and extensions thereof.[4]

Predictably, the players were quite unhappy with the monopsonistic labor market situation they faced. A player had to sign with the team holding his contract. Failure to do so meant that his future in professional sports was at best uncertain. And once he had signed his initial contract, reserve rules and procedures effectively bound him to that one team *into perpetuity*. The players viewed this as a type of slavery, whereas the owners believed that the reserve system was a necessary means of protecting their investments in the development of superior playing talent.

Needless to say, a storm was brewing over the imbalance in bargaining power fostered by the reserve system's labor market restrictions. The players' later turn to collective action was precipitated by, more than any other single factor, their extreme disgruntlement with the player reserve system. In each sport, the story of unionization is different; and I will expand on those stories later in this chapter. But let us consider here an example of what would happen if a player refused to sign a standard contract. Would this player later become a free agent? Would any player dare attempt such a bold move? Would any league, club, or commissioner allow such an action to occur? And finally, how would the courts view forcing a player to sign a contract which in effect bound the player for life to one particular team?

Many of these questions were answered by the case of a star football quarterback, Joe Kapp. In 1970, Kapp did play the entire season with the New England Patriots without having signed the standard NFL player contract. He did so with the approval of NFL Commissioner Pete Rozelle. When Kapp tried to do so again in 1971, however, he was denied permission and asked to leave New England Patriot's training camp. In a subsequent lawsuit against the NFL, Kapp charged that the reserve system and the so-called Rozelle rule constituted a restraint of trade in violation of federal antitrust laws.[5] The Rozelle rule was a compensation formula NFL owners had adopted in 1963 to protect clubs that had lost players to free agency, as was the case when R.C. Owens played out his option with the San Francisco Forty-Niners and switched to the Baltimore Colts in 1962. Specifically, the rule read as follows (NFL 1975):

> Any player, whose contract with a League Club has expired, shall thereupon become a free agent and shall no longer be considered a member of the team of that club following the expiration date of such contract. Whenever a player, becoming a free agent in such manner, thereafter signed a contract with a different club in the league, then unless mutually satisfactory arrangements have been concluded between the two League Clubs, the Commissioner may name and then award to the former club one or more players from the Active, Reserve or Selection List (including future selection choices) of the acquiring club as the Commissioner in his sole discretion deems fair and equitable; any such decisions by the Commissioner shall be final and conclusive.

Professional sports leagues had sought to eliminate free agency through the reserve system. But when players were successful in changing teams in spite of the system, leagues adopted punitive compensation schemes to further hamper player movement from team to team. As we shall see, the long baseball strike of 1981 was essentially over the issue of compensation for teams' losing players to free agency. Baseball had never had a meaningful compensation system, and the owners' attempt to adopt such a system precipitated the 1981 strike.

The court in the Kapp case ruled that the option (reserve) clause, along with the Rozelle rule, did have the effect of perpetually restraining a player from pursuing his occupation; thus, the beginning of the end was at hand for the Rozelle rule. The final blow was to come in the Mackey case.[6] Here, the court ruled that the Rozelle rule did constitute a per se violation of the nation's antitrust laws. The rule could no longer be imposed upon the players against their will. But the court did note that some types of restrictions on player movement from team to team might be desirable from an economic standpoint, stating

> It may be that some reasonable restrictions relating to player transfers are necessary for the successful operation of the NFL. The protection of mutual interests of both the players and the clubs may indeed require this. We encourage the participants to resolve this question through collective bargaining. The parties are far better situated to agreeably resolve what rules governing player transfers are best suited for their mutual interests than are the courts.[7]

This prompting by the court did in fact set the stage for a compromise agreement reached through collective bargaining. The precise nature of the compromise and its effect on player movement will be discussed at a later juncture.

To conclude these comments on the economic environment, I should note that the professional sports industry is not one of high employment growth. As noted earlier, all leagues seek to restrict entry and thereby preserve their desired product market monopolies. Great expansion, therefore, will probably never occur. Nonetheless, where cities hold out the promise of large population centers that could add to the general wealth of the sport without detracting from the economic position of any particular league club, some expansion is bound to occur. Moreover, rival leagues may again challenge the established order, although their chances for survival seem to be rather slim. It seems safe to conclude that professional sports leagues will neither stagnate nor decline in the foreseeable future, but growth, if any, will probably be sporadic and most likely in revenues, not in employment.

The Legal Environment

There are no bargaining statutes that apply solely to the professional sports industry as a whole. Rather, the National Labor Relations Act, as amended, is the statute under which collective bargaining in the industry is conducted. Professional athletes are private sector employees, and they work in an industry that has a substantial element of interstate commerce associated with its operation. The National Labor Relations Board has also asserted jurisdiction over officials in professional sports.[8]

Because of the product and labor market restrictions described earlier, professional sports leagues have come under frequent congressional scrutiny. Many bills have been introduced and many legislative hearings have been held looking into the question whether some special regulatory agency is required in professional sports or, alternatively, whether the various professional sports leagues should be allowed to continue to operate by themselves.

Typical of these congressional committees was the House Subcommittee on the Study of Monopoly Power, which issued a long report on baseball in 1952 (U.S. House of Representatives 1952). The basic concern of those hearings was baseball's reserve clause and the antitrust exemption baseball had been granted in 1922.[9] The committee came up with five possible choices for action: legislation to outlaw the reserve clause; legislation granting baseball unlimited exemption from the antitrust laws; enactment of a comprehensive baseball code to be enforced by a new governmental agency; a limited antitrust exemption for the reserve clause; or no legislation of any kind dealing with baseball's reserve clause (U.S. House of Representatives 1952, 25). The House chose the last option and enacted no special legislation governing baseball. As noted above, this same scenario has been played out several times and undoubtedly will be again in the future.

But although no federal legislation governing sports has been passed, the industry has been involved in a number of key legal cases that have had important influences on the development of collective bargaining in each of the sports considered here. The legal challenges by the players have tended to revolve around the issue of the reserve system developed in each sport. Players have challenged the system on the grounds that it violates antitrust laws. The argument has typically been that reserve procedures allow teams to prevent players from moving from team to team and thus enable the owners to hold salaries at artificial levels below what players would earn in a more competitive labor market. The cases have been too numerous to describe in detail here; however, table 7–1 summarizes the key decisions on this issue.

Table 7–1
Key Antitrust Cases Brought by Players

Case	Sport	Year	Decisions
1. Federal Baseball Club	Baseball	1922	Baseball exempted from federal antitrust law
2. Gardella v. Chandler	Baseball	1949	Stare decisis
3. Toolson v. New York Yankees	Baseball	1953	Stare decisis
4. Flood v. Kuhn	Baseball	1972	Stare decisis
5. Lemat v. Barry	Basketball	1969	Player free to jump leagues
6. Central v. Barnett	Basketball	1971	Player free to jump leagues
7. Robertson v. NBA	Basketball	1975	Suit settled out of court; parties negotiated modification to reserve system
8. Radovich v. NFL	Football	1957	Football subject to federal antitrust laws
9. Kapp v. NFL	Football	1974	Option clause and Rozelle rule unreasonable
10. Mackey v. NFL	Football	1976	Rozelle rule illegal; parties negotiated a compromise
11. Boston v. Cheevers	Hockey	1972	Player free to jump leagues
12. Nassau v. Hampson	Hockey	1972	Player free to jump leagues
13. Philadelphia World Hockey Club, Inc. v. Philadelphia Hockey Club, Inc.	Hockey	1972	NHL reserve clause illegal

Sources: Citations for cases 1 through 13 are 1: 259 U.S. 200; 2: 172 F.2d 402; 3: 346 U.S. 356; 4: 407 U.S. 258; 5: 275 Cal. App. 2d 671; 6: 19 Ohio Op. 2d 130; 7: 389 F.Supp. 867 (S.D.N.Y.); 8: 352 U.S. 445; 9: 390 F.Supp. 73 (N.D. Cal.); 10: 407 F.Supp. 1000 (D. Minn.); 11: 348 F.Supp. 261 (D. Mass.); 12: 355 F.Supp. 733 (D. Minn.); 13: 351 F.Supp. 462 (E.D. Pa.).

Of the 13 cases summarized in the table, the scorecard reads nine victories for the players versus four victories for the professional sports clubs and leagues. In fact, the only league in which management has prevailed is in baseball. Here, the courts have consistently relied upon an early decision (case 1 in the table) in which baseball was ruled to be a sport and not a business. Thus, baseball has since 1922 been specifically exempt from the U.S. antitrust laws. Players attempting to abolish baseball's perpetual reserve system through antitrust challenges have been unsuccessful. Danny Gardella, George Toolson, and, most recently, Curt Flood all had their cases dismissed as the courts relied on the earlier *Federal Baseball Club* decision. As we shall soon see, in baseball, the demise of the reserve system was to come through the process of collective bargaining and not because of legal challenges to the reserve clause brought under the federal antitrust laws.

Such was not to be the case in the other sports leagues, however. All sought but failed to achieve the same antitrust immunity granted to baseball. The courts were willing to take a closer look at the reserve practices employed in each of the other sports because they lacked the protective umbrella of the 1922 baseball decision. Again, as shown in table 7–1, the courts consistently ruled that such practices were in violation of the law. Given these court mandates, the parties then employed collective bargaining to reach compromises on questions of player reservation. Before delving into those agreements, I will first take a closer look at the parties involved in collective bargaining in sports.

The Parties

Unions

Baseball players have experimented with unionization since the earliest days of the National and American Leagues. Not surprisingly, players formed unions to create an organized front to represent them in their fight to abolish the reserve system.[10] The first players union, the National Brotherhood of Professional Baseball Players, was formed in 1885 to give players a chance to air some of their dissatisfactions with their employment conditions. In addition to the reserve rule, players disliked the salary maximums enforced by the National League and the blacklisting of ballplayers who were strong union sympathizers. Those early players even went so far as to form their own Players League in direct competition with the National League in 1890. The two leagues eventually declared a truce, but many of the players' grievances were yet to be resolved.

Table 7–2 lists the various unions formed over the years in baseball, basketball, football, and hockey. In each major sport the athletes formed their union in the 1950s. The unions were primarily social organizations

Table 7–2
Unions and First Negotiated Contracts in Professional Sports

Union	Years in Operation	Year First Contract Negotiated
National Brotherhood of Professional Baseball Players	1885–1890	None
League Protective Players' Association (baseball)	1900–1902	None
Baseball Players' Fraternity	1912–1918	None
American Baseball Guild	1946	None
Major League Baseball Players Association	1954–present	1968
National Basketball Players Association	1953–present	1976
National Football League Players Association	1956–present	1968
National Hockey League Players Association	1957–present	1975
Major League Umpires Association (baseball)	1969–present	1977
National Association for Basketball Referees	1976–present	1977

at first; it was only after they hired professional leaders, such as Marvin Miller in baseball and Edward Garvey in football, that collective bargaining became the main thrust of the associations and contracts with the clubs were negotiated.

As noted above, and in the table, both baseball umpires and basketball referees later also formed unions. Officials in both sports have engaged in work stoppages to highlight their demands for better pay and working conditions.

In sum, in each professional sport one principal union represents all the players for the purposes of collective bargaining. Each of these unions has its own interesting history. Baseball unionism is by far the oldest, with active unionization attempts dating back over 100 years. As noted, the most recent union activity in professional sports has been in organizing sports officials in both baseball and basketball. Whether this activity will expand to football and hockey referees is an interesting question for debate.

Employers

Just as the players in each sports league have formed themselves into a single union for bargaining purposes, the team owners have likewise formed joint bargaining councils to deal with the players' unions. Although there is no collaboration across the various leagues, all bargaining within the confines of a particular league is done on a multiemployer basis. No individual teams bargain with the players' association over wages, hours, and other terms and conditions of employment. But since there is no collective bargaining over salaries (except to set minimum levels), it is true that each team must bargain with every one of its players over individual salaries for the ensuing season.

The typical arrangement is for the owners to set up an organization (separate from the league organization) to deal with labor relations matters; in baseball it is the Player Relations Committee. Such a committee is usually headed by an outside (of the game) labor relations expert, with representatives from several clubs serving more or less in an advisory capacity. As of this writing, Lee MacPhail, former President of the American League, is serving as the head of the Player Relations Committee. This is the first time for some while that the baseball owners have selected a baseball insider to oversee their labor relations business.

The only other aspect of ownership that deserves some mention at this juncture is the role of the league commissioner in labor relations and the collective bargaining process. The commissioner is an employee of the owners who typically has broad powers to take action against any club owners—or players—whose activities are judged, as is the phrase in baseball, to be "detrimental to the best interests of the game." The commissioner's charge raises some interesting questions. For example, is unionization in the best interests of the game? If players engage in a strike, should they be punished? What role should the commissioner have in resolving disputes between labor and management? As alluded to earlier with respect to football, Commissioner Rozelle once had extraordinary powers to make compensation awards to teams that had lost free agent players to other league clubs. Was that a proper exercise of a commissioner's authority? As already noted, the courts' answer to these questions was no; they struck down the Rozelle rule as being in violation of the Sherman Antitrust Act.

In general, as of late, league commissioners have tended to disagree over their proper role in labor relations issues. Former Commissioner of Baseball Bowie Kuhn was severely criticized for his inactivity during the long baseball strike of 1981. Peter Ueberroth, his successor, seems to be taking a much more active role in labor relations, particularly in having urged the owners to open their financial books in the 1985 negotiations and in promoting mandatory testing for drug use among players. In fact, when recently asked to list his most courageous actions in his first year as commissioner, Ueberroth was quick to mention these two actions (Nightingale 1986a, 44).

The Structure of Bargaining

Bargaining Units

Unlike many of the other industries covered in this volume, the professional sports industry is unremarkable in the structure of its bargaining arrangements. The conduct of bargaining has been described above. Each league has one management association for bargaining, and each league has one and only one union that represents every player on every league club. Those unions bargain collectively with management representatives over wage minimums, hours, and other terms and conditions of employment. The one unusual feature of bargaining in sports is that wages are negotiated separately between each club and every one of that club's players. In their last negotiations football players tried to establish a salary schedule based on years of experience, but that schedule was to be tied to a percentage of the gross revenues of the game, a concept management was unwilling to accept. In basketball the owners and players have agreed to a salary cap. For the 1985–86 NBA season the cap per team for salary expenses was set at 53 percent of gross NBA revenues, or $4.233 million per team. Although each team continues to negotiate salaries individually with each of its players, the salary cap has the effect of limiting what the club might be able to offer any particular player.

Pattern Bargaining

Professional sports leagues do not feature pattern bargaining as this term is commonly used in the labor relations field. That is, since all clubs bargain jointly with only one union, there is no one key settlement that then sets a pattern for other negotiated settlements to follow.

Nevertheless, there are several elements of pattern following that surface from time to time. For example, it is widely acknowledged that baseball players enjoy the broadest labor market freedoms of all professional athletes. When players in basketball, football, and hockey see how the free agency system has worked for the players in baseball, they seek to emulate this system in their own leagues. In fact, much of the labor-management strife that has occurred in these other sports can be attributed to the fact that the players have sought to follow the pattern of free agency set by their counterparts in baseball. And to turn the tables around a bit, it is also widely accepted that strong compensation systems for teams' losing free agent players tend to discourage employers from any attempts to lure players away from other teams. When faced with the loss of several star players or high draft choices, team owners think twice about going after free agents. The baseball owners' attempts to infuse an element of compensation into their sport in 1981 and 1985 can be interpreted as an effort to follow the pattern set in other sports, where such compensation has largely eliminated free agency.

A final area where patterns are important is salary bargaining. One thing that is very common in professional sports, with the possible exception of hockey, is for high draft choices to set a pattern for salary bargaining by all the other players signed on in a given year. Premier first round draft choices are usually the first to sign contracts, giving other first round and lower round picks an idea of the type of salary arrangement they can expect to negotiate. The same is basically true for free agents in baseball. After one club has made an offer to a free agent, other clubs have an idea of what the pattern of offers will look like. The other clubs can then either choose to drop out of the bidding cycle or make the same or a better offer to the prospective player. It has also been argued that final-offer arbitrators in baseball use the pattern of salaries set in the free agency process in rendering their final and binding salary awards. Thus, although professional sports demonstrate no pattern bargaining as this term is typically defined, one can argue that patterns of wages and other terms and conditions of employment are closely scrutinized in professional sports and can have a major effect on subsequent decisions.

The Bargaining Process

Historical Background

Although unions have been around for a long time in some sports like baseball, the actual process of collective bargaining has a much shorter history in every sport, including baseball. Team owners were in no hurry to embrace collective bargaining any sooner than they had to; like management in many other industries, they saw no need for unionization and thus were not likely to recognize a union of their employees until forced to do so.

Baseball owners were quick to form a steering committee to study the state of the game's employment relations after the demise of the American Baseball Guild in 1946. The committee's recommendations, referred to as the MacPhail Report, stated in part:

> . . . attempts to organize players represented our most pressing problem. If we were to frustrate Murphy and protect ourselves against raids on players from the outside, we deemed it necessary that the uniform players' contract be revised, and our players satisfied, at least to such extent as is feasible and practical. A healthier relationship between club and player will be effective in resisting attempts at unionization—or raids by outsiders.[11]

Based on these recommendations the owners established a representation plan, which they believed would eliminate the need for formal unionization. Players would henceforth be allowed to present grievances directly to their club's management, and they were provided two seats on the league's ruling body, the Executive Council. This representation plan contained two major flaws, however, from the perspective of the players. First, the players did have two seats on the Council, but these were *nonvoting* seats. But more important, the players realized that under this plan, club management retained the right to make a final and binding decision on each and every issue in dispute. Players soon tired of this "meet and confer" philosophy imposed upon them by their clubs. They came to the decision that what they needed instead was real collective bargaining.

The players soon took steps to achieve that goal. First, in 1953 they hired legal counsel in the person of J. Norman Lewis to advise them on topics of pressing concerns. And second, in 1954, during the All-Star break in Cleveland, 16 player representatives voted to establish a new association, which they named the Major League Baseball Players Association (MLBPA).

At first, the Association kept a low profile and did not act much like a union at all. In fact, the first President of the MLBPA, Bob Feller, was quoted as saying, "You cannot carry collective bargaining into baseball" (*New York Times* 1956, 52). But things were soon to change.

In the mid 1960s, sentiment arose for the MLBPA to become more active. Certain players of the day, such as the influential Curt Flood, were openly critical of the MLBPA as a company union that provided players with little or nothing in the way of benefits (Flood 1972). Many players, such as Robin Roberts, thought the MLBPA needed to have a full-time executive director. Roberts went so far as to ask Professor George Taylor of the Wharton School for his suggestions on a leader for the union. Taylor strongly recommended Marvin Miller, an assistant to David MacDonald, president of the steelworkers' union. Miller actively sought the job and was hired in the middle of the 1966 championship season. It is from this date that we can mark the beginning of real collective bargaining in professional sports in America. Baseball's first collective bargaining contract was signed in 1968, soon to be followed by labor agreements in basketball, football, and hockey (see table 7–2).

Bargaining Issues

The process of collective bargaining opened up a host of different discussions on issues in professional sports. Recall that before 1968 the owners unilaterally made all decisions on every aspect of employment in the industry. Once bargaining began the players could address such issues as minimum salaries, expense allowances, moving allowances, player shares of the proceeds from league championship games, pensions, and scheduling. To discuss fully all of those issues would require many more pages than are allotted to me here.

I therefore want to concentrate on the single issue that was most responsible for precipitating unionism in the first place—the player reserve system—and trace how the players in each sport have dealt with this problem through the process of collective bargaining.

To begin with, recall that the players disliked reserve clauses in their contracts because their teams could arguably pay much lower salaries than they would have had to pay in a more competitive labor market. Without some

Table 7–3
Average Player Salaries and Gross League Revenues, by Sport, in 1970, 1980, 1982, and 1985

	Average Nominal Player Salary (Average Real Salary, in 1967 Dollars)				Gross Revenues in 1982 (millions)
Sport	1970	1980	1982	1985	
Baseball	$29,000 (24,936)	$150,000 (60,728)	$235,000 (81,006)	$371,157 (117,716)	$400
Basketball	40,000 (34,394)	190,000 (76,923)	215,000 (74,112)	300,000 (95,147)	120
Football	34,000 (29,751)	70,000 (28,340)	95,000 (32,747)	165,000 (52,331)	550
Hockey	25,000 (21,496)	110,000 (44,534)	120,000 (41,365)	140,000 (44,402)	120

Sources: The salary data are from *Business Week*, February 22, 1982. Salary data for 1985 are from the *Wall Street Journal*, March 25, 1985, p. 31. Gross revenue estimates are from *U.S. News and World Report*, October 11, 1982.

freedom to switch teams, players believed they were underpaid and at the mercy of the club holding the rights to their contract. Consider the data presented in table 7–3 on average player salaries across the four professional leagues. These data clearly demonstrate that player salaries have grown substantially in both nominal and real terms since the advent of collective bargaining. (Unfortunately, reliable data on average player salaries before the advent of collective bargaining are not available.) Note that from 1970 to 1985 the real salaries of baseball players have increased more than fourfold, while basketball players have seen their real salaries almost triple. In the two other leagues, football and hockey, the percentage increases in average real salaries from 1970 to 1985 have not been as great. An interesting question is why the data across these four sports look so different. Much of the answer lies in the collectively bargained procedures each sport has adopted in response to player complaints about the reserve system. As we will see, some of the procedures have worked much more to the players' advantage than have others.

One final issue is worth noting with regard to table 7–3. The data on gross revenues in 1982 show that of all the sports football received the most revenues in that year, followed fairly closely by baseball, with hockey and basketball lagging far behind. A question that typically comes up in sports bargaining is what percentage of gross revenues ought to be allocated to player salaries. There is probably no one correct answer to this question. Obviously, players will seek a higher percentage, while owners will seek a lower one or, as was done in football, refuse to embrace this concept altogether. But simply for the purposes of information, note that in 1982, baseball clubs spent approximately 38 percent of their gross revenues on player salaries (650 players × $235,000/$400 million). The corresponding percentages in basketball, football, and hockey were 45, 22, and 45, respectively. The 1983 basketball labor pact specifically pegged player salary costs at 53 percent of gross revenues beginning with the 1984–85 championship season. The interesting comparison here is that the richest sport in terms of gross revenues, football, pays out the smallest fraction of its revenues for player wages.

Let us now focus our attention on how players in each sport have employed collective bargaining to formulate solutions to their number one problem, the reserve system.

Baseball. Baseball teams and players were in a unique situation because of the sport's exemption from federal antitrust laws. Yet despite the sport's insulation from antitrust prosecution, baseball players today enjoy perhaps the most liberal system of free agency and, as was shown in table 7–3, the highest average salaries of all professional athletes. How did this situation come about? Much of this story centers around a rather famous grievance arbitration case.[12] Since contract administration has played such a large role in the demise of baseball's perpetual reserve system, I will hold discussion of the baseball situation until the next section of this chapter.

Basketball. As already discussed above, professional basketball players all had to sign contracts Paragraph 22 of which allowed each club to renew a player's contract for a period of one year. It may seem that this was a fairly liberal system, since after the first year, free agency was theoretically possible. Nonetheless, basketball players hoping to switch teams under these rules faced a serious problem in the form of team compensation. To be specific, when a team lost a player to free agency, the team signing the player and the former team were to meet to work out a compensation arrangement for the player's former team. Failure to agree on a compensation formula meant that the NBA commissioner would become involved. The commissioner was empowered to set a compensation award that could include cash, player(s), draft choices, or a combination of any or all of these. As a result, team owners were afraid to sign free agent players for fear of the compensation award that might be meted out by the commissioner.

The players' lot improved considerably after the out-of-court settlement of the Oscar Robertson lawsuit. Through collective bargaining the owners agreed to modify the reserve and compensation systems in the following manner: First, Paragraph 22 was no longer to be automatically included in player contracts; and second, a "first refusal" process was adopted to replace the commissioner-determined compensation system. This new process went into effect in the 1981–82 season. The first refusal system allows free agent players to test the open market and receive an offer from any team interested in acquiring their services. An offer sheet then has to be presented to the player's present team. If the player's present team decides to match this offer, the player has to continue to play for his team; but if his team fails to match the offer, the player is free to sign with the team. Under this system, there is no compensation for teams that lose free agent players in this manner.

As might be expected, this new system of free agency has led to higher player salaries. Whether a player is allowed to switch teams or not, he is guaranteed the higher salary as reflected in his offer sheet. Predictably, the owners decided that they needed to have some control over the escalation of player salaries. The idea they came up with in negotiations with the players was a salary cap. Agreed to on March 31, 1983, this salary cap ties player salaries to gross NBA revenues. As noted earlier, the percentage figure agreed upon was 53 percent. Thus, as gross revenues continue to increase as television contracts grow more lucrative and ticket prices rise, player salaries will also be guaranteed to rise.

Indeed, player salaries have risen substantially. Table 7–4 presents the 1985–86 salaries of the 20 highest paid athletes in the NBA. Thirteen players

Table 7–4
The Twenty Highest Paid Professional Basketball Players, 1985–86

Player	Team	Salary
1. Magic Johnson	L.A. Lakers	$2,500,000
2. Moses Malone	Philadelphia	$2,145,000
3. Kareem Abdul-Jabbar	L.A. Lakers	$2,030,000
4. Larry Bird	Boston	$1,800,000
5. Jack Sikma	Seattle	$1,600,000
6. Julius Erving	Philadelphia	$1,485,000
7. Patrick Ewing	New York	$1,250,000
8. Ralph Sampson	Houston	$1,165,000
9. Mitch Kupchak	L.A. Lakers	$1,100,000
10. Otis Birdsong	New Jersey	$1,100,000
11. Marques Johnson	L.A. Clippers	$1,100,000
12. Albert King	New Jersey	$1,035,000
13. Kevin McHale	Boston	$1,000,000
14. Wayman Tisdale	Indiana	$987,000
15. Kelly Tripucka	Detroit	$971,000
16. Adrian Dantley	Utah	$950,000
17. Bill Cartwright	New York	$925,000
18. Buck Williams	New Jersey	$915,000
19. Sidney Moncrief	Milwaukee	$884,000
20. Akeem Olajuwan	Houston	$882,500

Source: *Sporting News,* January 6, 1986, 35.

earned over a million dollars that season, with quite a few others just below the million dollar mark. In comparison, as recently as 1981, no player earned over a million dollars.

Both sides seem to be satisfied with the salary cap to date. For the 1984–85 season the cap was set at 3.6 million dollars per team, but teams already above the cap were exempt from that maximum. Club owners like the idea of being able to predict future labor costs relatively accurately. And, with the exception of the handful of teams already above the cap, club managers like the idea of competing with one another on an equal footing. In turn, the players like the idea of being able to claim for themselves a fixed percentage of the game's gross revenues. When revenues increase, so does the cap.

In the 1985–86 season, for instance, the salary cap per team was set at $4.233 million per team. Table 7–5 presents the player payrolls of all 23

Table 7–5
NBA Team Payrolls and Performance, 1985–86

Payroll Rank/Team	Payroll	Winning Percentage (Rank)
1. L.A. Lakers	$8,579,750	.839 (1)
2. Philadelphia	$6,860,500	.606 (5)
3. New York	$6,651,500	.324 (21) tie
4. Boston	$6,110,000	.781 (2)
5. New Jersey	$5,785,500	.600 (6)
6. Seattle	$5,238,333	.394 (16)
7. Detroit	$4,633,666	.441 (14) tie
8. Chicago	$4,421,000	.389 (17)
9. L.A. Clippers	$4,290,000	.324 (21) tie
10. Houston	$4,259,000	.647 (4)
11. Golden State	$4,255,833	.333 (18) tie
12. Washington	$4,231,383	.500 (11) tie
13. Phoenix	$4,189,500	.333 (18) tie
14. Sacramento	$4,184,000	.333 (18) tie
15. San Antonio	$4,068,846	.594 (7)
16. Portland	$3,978,500	.568 (9)
17. Dallas	$3,932,346	.500 (11) tie
18. Indiana	$3,758,200	.313 (23)
19. Cleveland	$3,620,666	.441 (14) tie
20. Atlanta	$3,616,250	.531 (10)
21. Denver	$3,420,500	.586 (8)
22. Milwaukee	$3,347,332	.667 (3)
23. Utah	$2,919,500	.486 (13)

Source: *The Sporting News,* various issues.

Note: Winning percentages are as of January 5, 1986; by that date most teams had completed approximately 40 percent of their regularly scheduled games for the 1985–86 season.

NBA franchises for 1985–86, along with midseason performance standings in the league. Two observations are in order here. First, there is a wide disparity in total payrolls, ranging from a high of $8.5 million for the Los Angeles Lakers to a low of just under $3 million for the Utah Jazz. (Teams above the cap have been grandfathered, as noted above.) Second, spending a lot of money on player salaries does not necessarily translate into victories on the court. Many factors enter into determining a team's winning percentage; for example, in the season in question the New York Knicks were beset with a host of injuries to key players. Interestingly, some low-payroll teams (Milwaukee, Denver, and Atlanta) were performing well, while several high-payroll teams were having poor or mediocre seasons (New York, Seattle, and Detroit).

Thus, the NBA owners and players have replaced the former commissioner-determined system for free agency compensation with a first-refusal system and a salary cap. Both of these new procedures have had their problems and will likely be the focus of future negotiations between the parties. But for the time being, the parties seem reasonably well satisfied with their collectively bargained solution to the problem of player reserves.

Football. In 1947 the NFL inserted a one-year option rule (paragraph 10, Standard Player Contract) into every player's contract. As mentioned earlier, no problem with this rule came about until R.C. Owens played out his option and changed teams in 1962. The owners feared a wholesale movement toward free agency on the part of the players and thus promulgated the well-known Rozelle rule. Just as was the case in basketball, this rule allowed the football commissioner to make compensation awards to teams losing free agents. And just as in basketball, the owners' fears of the potential compensation award virtually put an end to the free agency market.

Players like Joe Kapp and John Mackey challenged this system in court and won a victory for all football players. The Rozelle rule was found illegal, and the parties were charged with bargaining collectively over a replacement for the former free agency system.

The procedure eventually agreed to in football resembled that in basketball in that it was of the first-refusal variety; however, the agreement, reached on March 1, 1977, contained one crucial element not found in basketball, a precisely specified compensation formula (NFL and NFLPA 1977, Art. XV). Recall that the basketball owners and players had eliminated the idea of compensation altogether. In football, however, the uncertainty of the commissioner's award has been replaced with the certainty of precise contract language specifying the compensation due to teams' losing free agent players to other league clubs. For example, a team signing a free agent player to a salary of over $200,000 would owe that player's former team two first round draft picks as compensation. Because this penalty is a stiff one for the teams to bear, it has severely hampered the mobility of the players. Although this system was agreed to through bargaining, the situation of the players is now, in effect, no better than it was under the old Rozelle rule.

Entering the 1982 negotiations, the players desperately wanted to abolish the compensation system and adopt a fixed wage scale based on 55 percent of the gross revenues in the sport. The football strike of 1982 was essentially over these two issues. This strike will be discussed in more detail later. Suffice it to say for now that the players failed to achieve their goals. The free agency system in football still contains the element of precise compensation; and naturally, it has hampered player mobility and has held salaries down. As was shown in table 7–3, professional football players are paid much less than their counterparts in baseball and basketball, especially in light of the larger gross revenue base in football. Table 7–6 provides data on NFL team payrolls for the 1984 season. It is interesting to note how these payrolls in some cases are lower than those for professional basketball teams presented in table 7–5. This is especially noteworthy in light of the fact that football squads have approximately four times the number of players found on the roster of a professional basketball team.

To summarize, football players have used bargaining to revamp the former Rozelle rule on free agency. Nevertheless, the route taken has maintained a strong element of compensation for teams losing free agents. Teams therefore are still leery of signing free agents because of the stiff penalties for doing so specified in the collective bargaining agreement. Moreover, observers argue that the revenue-sharing practices of professional football team owners serve as a disincentive for owners who are contemplating spending money on free agents. In other words, whether a team finishes first or last has little effect on the club's revenues. Thus, unless an owner values winning for its own sake, he or she has little or no incentive to spend huge amounts of money to purchase free agents. Players are clearly dissatisfied with the workings of this revised free agency procedure. It is a safe bet that they will strive to create free movement for players from team to team in future rounds of bargaining. A key element of such a strategy will have to be an attack on the existing compensation procedure.

Hockey. As noted previously, every player in the NHL was required to sign a Standard Player Contract that contained a reserve clause in its Paragraph 17.[13] Hockey players were none too successful in combating this perpetual reserve system until the establishment of a rival professional league, the World Hockey Association. Talented players like Gerry Cheevers, Derek Sanderson, and Edward Hampson were enticed to the rival league by higher salaries. The NHL responded by taking these players to court, seeking to enforce Paragraph 17 of the standard contract. The owners were to lose all of their cases, as was shown in table 7–1 above. The final blow to the NHL's reserve system

Table 7–6
NFL Team Payrolls and Performance, 1984

Payroll Rank/Team	Payroll	Final Winning Percentage and Rank
1. New York Jets	$12,800,000	.438 (17) tie
2. Green Bay	$11,300,000	.500 (14) tie
3. San Francisco	$11,200,000	.938 (1)
4. New England	$10,800,000	.563 (9) tie
5. Washington	$10,600,000	.688 (5) tie
6. Tampa Bay	$10,600,000	.375 (21)
7. Buffalo	$10,400,000	.125 (28)
8. New Orleans	$10,100,000	.438 (17) tie
9. Cincinnati	$10,000,000	.500 (14) tie
10. Dallas	$10,000,000	.563 (9) tie
11. Kansas City	$9,700,000	.500 (14) tie
12. L.A. Rams	$9,500,000	.625 (7) tie
13. Detroit	$9,300,000	.281 (23)
14. New York Giants	$9,100,000	.563 (9) tie
15. Cleveland	$9,000,000	.313 (22)
16. St. Louis	$8,700,000	.563 (9) tie
17. Seattle	$8,600,000	.750 (4)
18. L.A. Raiders	$8,100,000	.688 (5) tie
19. Pittsburgh	$7,900,000	.563 (9) tie
20. Philadelphia	$7,800,000	.406 (20)
21. San Diego	$7,800,000	.436 (19)
22. Chicago	$7,600,000	.625 (7) tie
23. Miami	$7,300,000	.875 (2)
24. Atlanta	$7,200,000	.250 (24) tie
25. Indianapolis	$7,200,000	.250 (24) tie
26. Denver	$7,100,000	.813 (3)
27. Minnesota	$6,400,000	.188 (26) tie
28. Houston	$5,900,000	.188 (26) tie

Sources: For payroll data, *Rocky Mountain News,* July 11, 1985, 22; for the winning percentage data, *Sporting News,* January 7, 1985, 18.

came in the *Philadelphia World Hockey Club* case. The court found that the reserve clause did violate the Sherman Antitrust Act by allowing the owners unilaterally to impose a system on the players that prevented them from exercising their right to move from team to team.

Owners and players in professional hockey reached a compromise agreement over free agency in 1975 (NHL and NHLPA 1975, 34–37). Players won the right to become free agents after the completion of an option year. The clubs retained the principle of compensation for teams losing free agent players. The term *equalization* is used in hockey to describe the payment due to a team for losing a free agent. The original contract provided that the equalization payment be decided upon by a neutral arbitrator if the two clubs involved were unable to reach a mutually agreeable settlement.

In the 1982 negotiations the parties decided to drop the use of equalization arbitration. Players 33 years old and older won the right of total free agency without compensation for the former team. But the owners won the right of first refusal. All younger free agents are faced with a compensation scheme much like that described in football. That is, for free agents signed to contracts in excess of $200,000, the compensation due to the player's former team is two first round draft picks. Based on recent events, it seems like this price is too steep to pay for most clubs. Not one younger player has been able to change teams under this free agency system since it was adopted in 1982, and a battle over this issue is now taking shape. Players are angry about their low salaries and ineffective free agency procedure. When the collective bargaining contract expires in September 1986 (after this writing), it is a certainty that the number one issue at the table will be none other than free agency.

Contract Administration

Players in the four professional sports examined here have all been successful in negotiating comprehensive grievance arbitration clauses into their collective bargaining contracts. Details of those grievance procedures can be found in Dworkin (1981a, 119–36, 176–86, 229–86).

Many different types of issues have been processed through those grievance procedures, as detailed in Wong (1986). I will focus here on one particular case that was responsible for helping baseball players dismantle the perpetual reserve system in their sport. But before delving into this case, we first need a little background information.

First, recall that baseball was exempted from antitrust prosecution in 1922 and still retains that exemption today. Player attempts to have the reserve system ruled illegal were totally unsuccessful (see table 7–1). Thus, another route would have to be found to the players' goal, free agency. This mechanism was to be collective bargaining but, in the first instance, the grievance arbitration process itself. Here is what happened.

The first labor agreement between owners and players in baseball was signed in 1968. Before then the closest thing baseball players had to a grievance system was the representation plan discussed earlier. The 1968 contract did include a grievance procedure, but the arbitrator empowered to make binding decisions in unresolved cases was none other than the then Commissioner of Baseball, William Eckert, who of course was an employee of the owners. Thus, management retained the right to make the final decision in all disputes. This situation was not to last long. The very next contract, signed in 1970, replaced the commissioner with a permanent, impartial arbitrator. The parties' agreement to this clause was to be a key event in the history of labor relations in baseball.

A second key event occurred in the 1973 negotiations. It was at this juncture that the owners and the players decided to incorporate the Uniform Player Contract into the collective bargaining agreement (*National League of Professional Baseball Clubs* 1973, 37, §10[a]). This contract contained such items as the player's salary, several rules and regulations, and, most important, the *reserve clause* in Paragraph 10(a). By inserting this Uniform Player Contract into the collective bargaining agreement, all provisions of the player contract, including the reserve rule, were opened to challenges through the grievance arbitration mechanism. The stage was now set for the players to challenge management's interpretation of the reserve rule as being perpetual in nature.

The challenge came within two years. In the 1975 season players Andy Messersmith and Dave McNally refused to sign contracts and were forced to play for their respective clubs under the reserve procedure entailed in Paragraph 10(a) of their player contracts. After the 1975 season ended each of the two players claimed he was a free agent. Having been reserved for one year, they both stated that they had no further obligation to their teams. The owners had a much different interpretation of Paragraph 10(a). Their view was that Messersmith and McNally were the property of their respective clubs for as long as the clubs wished to retain their services—in perpetuity.

The two players filed grievances and processed them to the final step of the grievance procedure. The "permanent" arbitrator at the time was Peter Seitz. At the arbitration hearing held on November 21 and 24, 1975, the club owners argued that (1) the grievances of the two players were not arbitrable; and (2) even if the grievances were found to be arbitrable, the grievances should be denied based on the merits of each case. Arbitrator Seitz ruled against the owners on both of these counts.[14] His ruling, issued near the end of that year, was to be the beginning of the end for baseball's perpetual reserve system. The Seitz decision did *not* say that the reserve system in baseball was illegal, but rather that the owners' interpretation that the reserve clause existed into perpetuity was wrong. A player could be reserved for *one* season, but after that season the reservation clause was no longer to be in effect. Just as several courts had done earlier, Seitz made a strong recommendation in his award that the two parties come together and use collective bargaining to mold a compromise reserve system, stating:

> The parties are still in negotiation . . . and continue to have an opportunity to reach agreement on measures that will give assurance of a reserve system that will meet the needs of the clubs and protect them from the damage they fear this decision will cause, and, at the same time, meet the needs

of the players. The clubs and the players have a mutual interest in the health and integrity of the sport and in its financial returns. With a will to do so, they are competent to fashion a reserve system to suit their requirements.[15]

The parties were quick to take up this challenge. They were able to negotiate a six-year reserve system that contained elements of both free agency and reservation. Players were bound to their teams for a period of six years. After serving that time, they were eligible to become free agents and negotiate with a number of teams interested in acquiring their services. Very important to the success of this system from the players' standpoint was the minimal amount of compensation that was built into the procedure. Unlike the situations in hockey and football, baseball teams signing free agent players would lose only very little: only one draft choice in the regular phase of the June Amateur Player Draft. And so in baseball this minimal amount of compensation has not dissuaded clubs from offering huge sums of money to valuable free agent players, and the sport's monopsonistic labor market had become much more competitive. As was demonstrated in table 7–3, baseball players are the highest paid of today's professional athletes, averaging over $370,000 per season. A further breakdown of average player salaries per club for 1985 is presented in table 7–7. As can be seen, the New York Yankees earned the highest salaries, followed closely by players for Atlanta and Baltimore. At the other end of the scale, players for Seattle earned the least, an average of $169,694 per year.

Determined to head off this salary spiral, baseball owners entered the contract negotiations in 1980 and again in 1985 with an eye toward revamping the collectively negotiated free agency system. Both of these sets of negotiations resulted in strikes by the players, the one in 1981 forcing the cancellation of 714 scheduled games. Relating the story of these two strikes in baseball will bring us up to date on baseball's free agency system.

Labor-Management Conflict

Historical Background

Most sports fans can readily recall the baseball strikes of 1981 and 1985 as well as the football strike of 1982, but few are aware of the fact that labor-management conflict in professional sports traces far back into the early years of this century.

The first strike in baseball was called in the spring of 1912 and has become known as the Ty Cobb incident, after the famous—and infamous—ballplayer. Cobb was constantly being heckled by a New York reporter

Table 7–7
Average Baseball Player Salaries, by Club, 1985

Salary Rank/Team	Average Player Salary
1. New York Yankees	$546,346
2. Atlanta	$540,988
3. Baltimore	$438,256
4. California	$433,818
5. Milwaukee	$430,843
6. Los Angeles	$424,273
7. Chicago Cubs	$413,765
8. Detroit	$406,755
9. San Diego	$400,497
10. Philadelphia	$399,728
11. Pittsburgh	$392,271
12. New York Mets	$389,365
13. Boston	$386,597
14. St. Louis	$386,505
15. Toronto	$385,995
16. Kansas City	$368,469
17. Houston	$366,250
18. Oakland	$352,004
19. Chicago White Sox	$348,488
20. Cincinnati	$336,786
21. San Francisco	$320,370
22. Montreal	$315,328
23. Minnesota	$258,039
24. Texas	$257,573
25. Cleveland	$219,879
26. Seattle	$169,694

Source: *The Sporting News,* December 16, 1985.

named Claude Lueker whenever Cobb's Detroit Tigers played in New York. On one such occasion, Cobb became so enraged that he leaped into the stands and attacked Lueker. As Cobb biographer John McCallum (1975, 86) described it,

The New York Fans were so amazed and startled that nobody moved a muscle until Cobb had finished with Lueker. Nobody could believe what they had just seen. No ballplayer had ever dared hop into the stands that way. As Cobb finished, they began to rise in rage. Ty had to fight his way back down to the playing field. All his teammates, led by Wahoo Sam Crawford, stood along the field brandishing bats. They were certain the fans would storm on the field and mob Cobb. They almost did.

American League President Ban Johnson suspended Cobb for his actions, and this precipitated a strike by his Detroit teammates. This first baseball strike ended peacefully when Johnson lifted Cobb's suspension.

A second baseball strike was narrowly avoided in June 1946. Earlier that spring, Robert Murphy had organized baseball's fourth union, the American Baseball Guild (*New York Times* 1946, 16). Murphy decided to present his demands for union recognition and collective bargaining to the owners of the Pittsburgh Pirates on the evening of June 7, 1946. He threatened that a strike would occur if the owners failed to recognize the players' union. In a tense locker room scene before the game, the players voted in favor of a strike by the slim margin of 20 to 16; however, a previous arrangement had been made that the strike vote would require a two-thirds majority in order to carry. Thus, for the lack of four votes, a second strike in baseball nearly took place (Gould 1946, 134–36).

The next labor action in baseball was not until 1972. At the start of the season, the players announced their intention to strike over the issue of pensions. The strike lasted 13 days and forced the cancellation of 86 games at the beginning of the season. In the end the players did achieve their pension goals, but they agreed to forfeit the wages they would have earned during the period of the strike.[16] The final agreement, signed on February 28, 1973, is also remembered as the one in which the players and owners agreed to implement the final-offer salary arbitration procedure.[17]

The 1976 round of negotiations was also marked by a major confrontation. Those negotiations were conducted after the players had won a favorable arbitration award in the Messersmith and McNally grievances discussed above. In an attempt to cause the players to settle quickly, the owners locked the players out during spring training. After 17 days had passed, Commissioner Kuhn ordered the owners to reopen the camps. Thereafter, the parties were able to reach the accord on free agency that was also described earlier.

Players in professional hockey and basketball have yet to engage in any strike activity. Football players have participated in only one major strike, in 1982.

Patterns of Conflict

The three recent strikes in baseball and football have involved all the players in these professional leagues, and two of the three have been lengthy, by historical standards. As reported earlier, the baseball strike of 1981 lasted for 58 days and forced the cancellation of 714 games; the football strike of 1982 lasted a full seven weeks. The 1985 baseball strike was very short, lasting but two days.

It was widely reported after that most recent baseball strike that players in all of the other sports were keeping a very close eye on the baseball situation. Simply put, players in football want what baseball players have, real free agency. The current football contract expires after the 1986 season, and Gene Upshaw, executive director of the NFL Players Association, is also predicting tough bargaining over the free agency issue.

Sources of Conflict

Baseball. The issue that precipitated the 1981 baseball players strike was none other than the owners' attempt to revise the free agency plan (Dworkin 1981b). This was to be baseball's first ever midseason work stoppage.

Club owners in baseball were aware of the dampening effect that compensation had on the free agency systems in both hockey and football. Their goal was to institute a similar form of compensation in baseball for teams losing free agents. The owners proposed that a roster player from the acquiring club be awarded to the team that had lost a free agent player. The players wanted no part of this system and instead sought to keep intact the system first negotiated in 1976.

Both sides seemed to realize that a confrontation was inevitable. Players were advised to save money in order to withstand a strike. The owners purchased strike insurance that guaranteed each team $50,000 for every cancelled game after a 153-game deductible. The strike began on June 12, 1981. A settlement was reached on July 31, 1981, with the season set to resume on August 9, 1981. It is interesting to note that the owners' strike insurance policy was exhausted as of August 8, 1981.

The settlement reached did provide additional compensation for teams losing free agent players. Free agent players were henceforth to be ranked based upon a complex performance formula. Teams that lost Type A players, ranked in the top 20 percent of all players in the league at a particular position grouping, would receive compensation in the form of one amateur draft choice and one professional player to be selected from a pool contributed to by all clubs. Teams that lost Type B players, ranked between the twentieth and thirtieth percentiles, would receive compensation in the form of two amateur draft choices. Compensation for teams that lost nonranked free agents remained what it had been: one amateur draft pick.

Both sides claimed victory after this settlement. Any impartial observer would have to note, however, that player salaries continued to climb as free agency operated almost exactly as it had in the past. It is true that a new form of compensation was added, but it was nowhere near as severe as that found in other sports. In fact, it is quite possible under this system that the team signing a free agent will forfeit nothing. This is because the team that loses a free agent (Type A) selects a professional player from a pool of players contributed to by *all teams* that choose to participate in the free agency process. Thus, for example, if Cincinnati signs on a Type A free agent from the Pittsburgh roster, the Pirates may well decide that the best available player in the compensation pool is currently on the roster of the San Diego Padres. If the Pirates select that player as compensation, Cincinnati loses nothing. And thus, this newly created compensation system has simply not been able to put a damper on the appetite of professional baseball teams for free agents.

And again in the 1985 baseball strike it appeared that free agent compensation was to be the major stumbling block. As time progressed, however, it turned out that the owners' major target was going to be the final-offer salary arbitration procedure. The owners believed this procedure was out of hand because arbitrators were looking to the high salaries paid to free agents in determining their awards for the junior players eligible to use arbitration. One suggestion raised was to limit the arbitrator's award to a maximum of double the player's salary in the previous season. The players, on the other hand, were happy with the workings of the final-offer system and therefore sought to maintain it without change.

After a two-day strike, a settlement was reached, in which the players agreed to increase the number of years of professional experience required to be eligible for arbitration. By increasing that number from two to three years, the number of players eligible to use salary arbitration will be reduced in the future.

In baseball the two major factors responsible for improving player salaries and mobility were salary arbitration and free agency. Both procedures were bilaterally agreed to by the parties. Both procedures tremendously increased player bargaining power, and, as we have seen, salaries have reached unprecedented levels. The last two rounds of negotiations in baseball have featured attempts by the owners to retrieve some of the power they had surrendered to the players in the past. The success of those attempts is yet to be measured. But it is interesting to note that in the 1985 negotiations the owners went so far as to open up their financial books to the players to impress upon them the serious economic situation facing many of the teams. In the past, owners had raised complaints of losing money—only to turn right around and offer huge guaranteed contracts to free agent players. Players and fans alike thus had found it hard to believe that teams in such poor financial conditions were able to proffer such lucrative contracts.

Interestingly, the two most attractive players in the 1986 crop of free agents, Kirk Gibson and Donny Moore, were pursued only by their present clubs, the Detroit Tigers and the California Angels, respectively. In previous years, players of their calibre would have been sought by several clubs in both leagues. Just what is happening?

The players are using words such as collusion and conspiracy to describe the latest events, while Commissioner Ueberroth has been quoted as saying,

"I don't think there's any kind of conspiracy or collusion at all" (Chass 1985). It is too early to tell what is actually going on. But it is clear that the owners have been searching for a way to hold down player salary increases. And the players are just as adamant in their desire to maintain a smoothly operating free agency system in which movement from team to team is not merely a theoretical possibility but a practical reality.

It has already been noted that salary arbitration is likely to be another source of conflict between baseball owners and players for some time to come. To this list of critical issues, one should also add the issue of drug testing. The current positions of the players and the owners are far apart on this sensitive topic, and it seems likely that this will be the basis for major confrontations in the future. Club owners would like to impose mandatory drug testing "for the good of the game," while players hold that indiscriminate testing violates their right to privacy. Baseball has had a much publicized problem with drugs lately, and so team owners will most likely continue to push for testing.

Basketball. Basketball players have never engaged in a strike. The only strikes that have occurred in this sport have involved the officials. (Baseball umpires have also engaged in several strikes.)

The sport of professional basketball seems to be enjoying something of a rebirth. It was but a few years ago that the NBA was considered dormant, and several of its franchises were in danger of collapsing. But then things started to turn around. In 1985 most of the teams made money and the NBA enjoyed a record attendance—10,506,355 fans. New star attractions such as Ralph Sampson, Akeem Olajuwon, Michael Jordan, Patrick Ewing, and Manute Bol have upped the league's television ratings and also have enabled the league to negotiate a substantially more lucrative television package (Taaffe 1986, 20).

The players and owners in basketball have reached negotiated agreements on a drug program and a salary cap. Early signs are that both parties seem satisfied with those new agreements. Although relations seem placid for now, the players are certain to want to respond to the improving financial health of the game. When the current collective bargaining pact expires in 1987, the players are certain to ask for a larger share of the game's expanding wealth. Whether they will seek a larger percentage of gross revenues or an elimination of the salary cap remains to be seen. Larry Fleischer, general counsel for the NBA Players Association has also stated that free agency will be high on the list of items for renegotiation in 1987. He explains the decrease in offer sheets to free agents in recent years by pointing to signs of collusion among the NBA clubs. Of course, league officials deny any such coordinated effort among the teams. Thus, although labor relations in basketball are calm at present, the heat is sure to be turned up after the 1986–87 championship season.

Hockey. Professional hockey players have also never gone on strike. They are nonetheless frustrated these days with what they perceive to be a very ineffective free agency system and with the low salaries paid to hockey players as compared to those paid other professional athletes. As noted earlier, the bargaining agreement between the players and the owners expires in September 1986. The two issues foremost in the minds of the players are sure to be money and free agency. Those issues are complementary, as a free agency system that encourages player movement from team to team also has the effect of raising salaries.

Brian Trottier, president of the NHL Players Association, has stated several times that he believes hockey players will have to go on strike to achieve concessions from the owners. No free agents have been able to switch clubs because of the stringent compensation system built into the current collective bargaining contract. Teams simply are not willing to lose two first round draft picks when they sign a top free agent player. And this means that no players are likely to be able to use the free agency procedure. Without a doubt, this issue will come to a head when the current labor contract expires.

Football. On July 15, 1982, the third collective bargaining contract between the National Football League Players Association and the National Football League expired. The basic issue in the dispute that followed was the low salaries paid to professional football players as compared to baseball and basketball salaries. The players argued (NFLPA 1981, 3) that they were not paid on the basis of performance but rather

> The owners operate in secret sessions to set wages. With few exceptions, an individual player has no chance against that system. Since we have examined all player contracts, there is no doubt that management establishes your salary by (1) the round you were drafted in, (2) your position, and (3) your years in the league. Salaries are not determined by your merit or your value to a team.

The players believed that merely to liberalize the free agency procedure would not solve the problem because all the owners would simply act in concert and not sign free agent players. Thus, the players demanded that the NFL give them 55 percent of the gross revenues in the sport to be used for salaries and other compensation. In particular, their union proposed setting up a self-administered wage scale based on years of experience in the league.

The owners had no interest in agreeing to the percentage-of-gross concept. Jack Donlan, chief negotiator for the NFL Management Council was quoted as saying, "Giving away a percentage of the gross is a concept alien to America. It's a control issue, and the owners aren't going to give up control" (*Newsweek* 1982).

The strike began on September 21, 1982 and was to last over 60 days, forcing the cancellation of seven weeks of the 1982 season (Ahlburg and

Dworkin 1983). The players were not to succeed. Team compensation for the loss of free agents remains an integral part of the free agency system. The players did not receive a fixed percentage of the gross revenues, nor did they obtain the wage scale they had demanded. They finally settled for a series of minimum salaries tied to years of seniority in the league (NFL Management Council 1982).

The NFL now faces several other critical issues. Television ratings have plunged for several years, although there were signs that interest in the game was beginning to increase in 1985. The NFL owners are also worried about the potential impact of the $50 million in damages awarded to Los Angeles Raiders owner Al Davis, who sued the NFL over its efforts to stop his moving the team from Oakland (Lancaster 1985). And finally, the Players Association still believes that the clubs are taking in enormous revenues that should be shared more equitably with the players. The next opportunity the players will have to press this point will be in August 1987, when the current labor contract expires.

Conclusions

Salient Features of Bargaining

Professional athletes have participated in true collective bargaining activities for a much shorter time than workers in the traditionally organized industries in the United States. Although unionism in baseball dates back over 100 years, the first collective bargaining contract in the sport was not signed until 1968. In basketball, football, and hockey, labor pacts were first signed in the mid-1970s.

Those labor agreements contain many of the traditional items, such as recognition clauses, grievance arbitration procedures, and pension systems. On the other hand, they also contain many arrangements that are unique to the game itself and its requisite travel schedule, such as regulations on travel scheduling, meal allowances, post-season pay, pre-season pay, and moving allowances.

One item that is conspicuous in its absence is a contractual salary arrangement. Most sports do use collective bargaining to set minimum salaries. In football, as we have learned, the collective bargaining contract contains a series of minimum salaries set by year of seniority. Other than that, however, there is no collective bargaining over player wages. Every season, unless a multiyear contract has been signed, individual owners must bargain with their individual team members over salary. Thus, professional sports leagues use *collective bargaining* to work out arrangements regarding hours and other terms and conditions of employment, but they also employ *individual bargaining* to decide salary matters. The fact that bargaining occurs at these two levels is one of the most particularistic features of labor relations in the professional sports industry, although it is a feature that has close parallels in some segments of the entertainment industry, such as the performing arts and broadcasting.

A second interesting feature that has been revealed in this chapter is the fact that much of the players' bargaining effort has been directed toward modifying existing anticompetitive labor market practices, specifically the reserve system. Though many economists are wont to judge unions as monopolies and denounce them for *their* actions restricting the free market, in professional sports, unionism has actually been associated with the gradual demise of the *owners'* monopsony powers and a movement to a more competitive labor market. Player mobility has not increased equally in every sport as a result, but the mobility that has been achieved can trace its roots to collective bargaining in the industry.

Evaluation of the Overall Performance of Bargaining

Collective bargaining has provided tremendous gains to the players in baseball and basketball. Those players now earn very high average salaries and also have the right either to free agency or to first refusal. Additionally, they have won many other rights commonly associated with unionism, such as the ability to challenge through a standard grievance arbitration procedure managerial decisions perceived as arbitrary, capricious, or discriminatory. Those players must certainly be pleased with the improvement in their situations brought about in a large part through collective bargaining.

Hockey and football players have also been able to improve their employment situation through collective bargaining, but they remain frustrated in their inability to achieve workable free agency systems like those enjoyed by their counterparts in baseball and basketball. They would probably be less enthusiastic in their endorsement of collective bargaining.

The owners in all four sports would likely prefer a return to the days of yesteryear, when they were able to control players' careers indefinitely through the reserve procedures they themselves had established. But such a return to the past will not occur. Owners are also disturbed by the record of strikes in the professional sports industry. When viewed in the context of the strike record in many other industries, however, strikes in professional sports have certainly not had unduly pernicious effects. Team management is also concerned about profits and losses, and rightly so. With the necessity of spending more money on player salaries, sharp business minds are becoming a greater necessity today than ever before in the operation of a professional sports franchise. Perhaps unionism will have a "shock effect" and ultimately promote the adoption of more modern management practices in professional sports.

As time goes by, managers have had to get used to the idea of unionism. Indeed, going from a system of unilateral control to one of bilateral determination takes some getting used to on the part of both sides. Although the owners are not enamored of the process of bargaining, they are likely soon to arrive at the conclusion that it can be used to the benefit of both parties.

What do the consumers—the fans—think about the overall performance of the collective bargaining system in professional sports? Most fans are tired of hearing about potential strikes, actual strikes, and who is and is not a free agent. Fans naturally also dislike having sports seasons disrupted by strikes. But the evidence is overwhelming that spectators do return to the game after a strike is over, usually in record numbers. The average fan has a hard time understanding how a person who earns $300,000 a year playing a "game" could ever be dissatisfied and think of going on strike. The thing he forgets to consider is that for the professional athlete (as well as for the owner) the game is no longer recreational activity. Rather, it is a serious business for the athletes; it is the way they earn their livings and support their families. Moreover, playing careers are typically brief. Once the fans come to understand the game as a profession and not as a recreational activity, they are likely to be more understanding of the players' bargaining goals and activities.

Finally, how does an academician such as I feel about the overall performance of the collective bargaining system in professional sports? Things are not perfect! They never have been and are not likely to be so. But the system is working, and that is very important. The fact that is most salient in my mind is that through unionism and bargaining, players have been able to move into a freer labor market. Players today are paid more in line with what they are worth to their teams and are no longer exploited through unilaterally established reserve procedures. Thus, because of the competitiveness that has been infused into the professional sports labor market since the advent of collective bargaining, I would have to rate the overall performance of the system favorably.

Predictions for the Coming Decade

I have mentioned many of my predictions for the future throughout this chapter. I will therefore only briefly recap here what I think will be the major events in bargaining over the next decade.

First, the primary issue of concern at the bargaining table will continue to be free agency and player mobility. In baseball, in particular, the owners will be on the offensive in an attempt to impose a compensation scheme that will slow the escalation of player salaries. It will be the players in football and hockey who will aggressively pursue the elimination of compensation for teams losing free agents. If they succeed, we can look for player salaries in both sports to increase sharply. Obviously, other issues such as drug testing, salary arbitration, amd grievance procedures will be important. Nonetheless, free agency is the single issue that has had and will continue to have the largest impact on the financial future of both the owners and the players in professional sports. Thus, it will continue to dominate the labor relations news coming out of this industry.

Second, the bargaining over this issue augers to be extremely difficult, producing major confrontations between owners and players. Strikes are likely in professional hockey and in football as well. Baseball players have also shown a willingness to strike, and if pushed in the compensation area, they may well resort to that tactic again. But although labor leaders in basketball speak of their unhappiness with the current free agency system, the tradition of peaceful relations in that sport makes a strike there much less easy to predict.

Finally, I would like to note that the process of collective bargaining has been a constructive mechanism for resolving all types of problems in the professional sports industry. Solutions have not always come easily and have not always been perfect in nature. But solutions have been reached and the process of collective bargaining has worked for both sides. I predict that this trend will continue into the future. We are not likely ever to return to the days of the perpetual reserve system. But it is just as unlikely that players and their unions will ever take control of the industry in which they operate. Instead, through collective bargaining, the players and the owners will continue to reach compromises on issues of the employment relationship in professional sports.

Notes

1. For just one example, see NFL (1975).

2. A complete treatment of this issue can be found in Dworkin (1981, 8–21).

3. See *National Hockey League* (1975) and comments about this reserve clause feature in *Philadelphia World Hockey Club, Inc., v. Philadelphia Hockey Club, Inc.,* 351 F.Supp. 462 (E.D. Pa. 1972), p. 479.

4. See *National Basketball Association Uniform Player Contract,* paragraph 22. Examples of standard player contracts from all leagues can be found in Blackman (1976).

5. *Kapp v. National Football League,* 390 F.Supp. 73 (N.D. Cal. 1974).

6. *Mackey v. National Football League,* 407 F.Supp. 1000–7 (D. Minn. 1975).

7. *John Mackey et al. v. National Football League et al.,* No. 76-1184, United States Court of Appeals, Eighth Circuit (October 18, 1976).

8. *The American League of Professional Baseball Clubs and Association of National Baseball League Umpires,* 180 NLRB 190 (1969).

9. *Federal Baseball Club of Baltimore, Inc. v. National League, et al.,* 259 U.S. 200 (1922).

10. See Dworkin (1981a, 10–23) for a description of five separate attempts at unionization by professional baseball players.

11. Quoted in Gregory (1956, 194).

12. *Professional Baseball Clubs,* 66 LA 101 (December 23, 1975).

13. See *Standard Player Contract for the National Hockey League,* paragraph 17.

14. *Professional Baseball Clubs,* 66 LA 101 (December 23, 1975).

15. Ibid. at 117–118.

16. For an interesting update on player pension issues in baseball, see Nightingale (1986b, 13–16).

17. For an update on the final offer salary arbitration procedure, see Dworkin (1986, 63–69).

References

Ahlburg, Dennis A. and James B. Dworkin. 1983. Player Compensation in the National Football League, Industrial Relations Center Working Paper 83-04. Minneapolis: University of Minnesota.

Blackman, Martin E. 1976. *Representing the Professional Athlete.* New York: Practicing Law Institute.

Chass, Murray. 1985. Free-Agent Freeze-Out? *Sporting News,* December 9, p. 2.

Demmert, Henry G. 1973. *The Economics of Professional Team Sports.* Lexington, Mass.: Lexington Books.

Dworkin, James B. 1981a. *Owners versus Players: Baseball and Collective Bargaining.* Boston: Auburn House.

———. 1981b. Results of the Professional Baseball Players' Strike of 1981. *Texas Business Review.* November-December, pp. 268–71.

———. 1986. Salary Arbitration in Baseball: An Impartial Assessment After Ten Years. *Arbitration Journal* 41 (March): 63–69.

Flood, Curt. 1971. *The Way It Is.* New York: Pocket Books.

Gould, Paul. 1946. Unionism's Bid in Baseball. *New Republic* 115: 134–36.

Gregory, Paul. 1956. *The Baseball Player: An Economic Study.* Washington, D.C.: Public Affairs Press.

Lancaster, Hal. 1985. NFL Faces Some Tough Seasons If TV Ratings Don't Improve Soon. *Wall Street Journal,* September 6, p. 15.

McCallum, John. 1975. *Ty Cobb.* New York: Praeger.

National Basketball Association Uniform Player Contract. In author's possession.

National Hockey League—National Hockey League Players Association Collective Bargaining Agreement, September 15, 1975. In author's possession.

National Football League Players Association. 1981. *Why a Percentage of Gross? Because We Are the Game.* In author's possession.

National Football League, *Constitution and By-Laws,* 1975. In author's possession.

National Football League and the National Football League Players Association Collective Bargaining Contract, March 1, 1977. In author's possession.

National League of Professional Baseball Clubs and American League of Professional

Baseball Clubs and Major League Baseball Players Association, Basic Agreement Between, January 1, 1973. In author's possession.

Newsweek. 1982. They're Playing for Keeps. September 20, pp. 70–79.

New York Times. 1956. Players Ask Joint Meeting. December 11, p. 52.

————. 1946. Minimum of $7,500 in Majors Sought. May 3, p. 16.

NFL Management Council and NFLPA. 1982. *1982 Collective Bargaining Agreement,* effective date, July 16, 1982. In author's possession.

Nightingale, Dave. 1986a. Ueberroth's First Year. *Sporting News.* January 6, pp. 44–45.

————. 1986b. Fattest Feline in Sports: Some Reforms Are Needed in Baseball's Overfunded Pension Plan. *Sporting News.* May 12, pp. 13–16.

Taaffe, William. 1986. TV To Sports: The Buck Stops Here. *Sports Illustrated*, February 24, pp. 20–27.

U.S. House of Representatives. 1952. *Organized Baseball: Report of the Subcommittee on the Study of Monopoly Power of the Committee on the Judiciary.* H.R. 2002, 82 Cong., 2d sess.

Wong, Glenn M. 1986. A Survey of Grievance Arbitration Cases in Major League Baseball. *Arbitration Journal* 41 (March): 42–62.

8
Higher Education

Samuel B. Bacharach
Timothy P. Schmidle
Scott C. Bauer

Higher education in the United States is big business: annual current fund expenditures by all U.S. institutions of higher learning averaged $70 billion in the early 1980s, a figure that was on a par with the individual contributions to the gross national product made in those years by the automobile, telecommunications, and petroleum processing industries (Meisinger and Dubeck 1984).[1] It is also a diverse enterprise, its institutions varying greatly in their size, mission, structure (single- versus multicampus), location (rural versus urban), and prestige. Colleges and universities also vary in their administrative control (public versus private, secular versus religious) and in the type of education they offer (two-year versus four-year and advanced degrees). Table 8–1 offers evidence on the scale and diversity of the higher education institutions in this country.

Unionism in higher education well reflects the industry's diversity. In particular, unionism by college and university faculty and staff members exhibits dramatic differences between the public and private sectors, as it does between two- and four-year institutions. In fact, the diversity of bargaining in the industry is one of its more salient features.

We will focus in this paper primarily on faculty collective bargaining, partly because this occupational group, unlike nonacademic employees, has unique goals and practices in forming unions and conducting collective bargaining, and partly because more is known about faculty bargaining than about bargaining among nonacademic employees. Moreover, we also focus more of our attention on faculty unions and unionization than on the bargaining process, unlike many of the other chapters in this volume. Because collective bargaining is a relatively new phenomenon in higher education, and because academic researchers have slighted study of their own backyards in favor of other industry studies, evidence on the actual process of bargaining in higher education is still scant.

Table 8-1
Number and Enrollments of Higher Education Institutions, by Type and Source of Administrative Control, 1981

	All Institutions		Universities		All Other Four-Year Institutions		Two-Year Institutions	
	Number	*Enrollment*	*Number*	*Enrollment*	*Number*	*Enrollment*	*Number*	*Enrollment*
Public institutions	1,498	9,647,032	94	2,152,474	464	3,013,850	940	4,480,708
Percentage of all institutions	46%	78%	3%	17%	14%	24%	29%	36%
Percentage of public institutions			6%	22%	31%	31%	63%	46%
Private institutions	1,755	2,724,640	62	748,870	1,359	1,740,267	334	235,503
Percentage of all institutions	54%	22%	2%	6%	42%	14%	10%	2%
Percentage of private institutions			4%	27%	77%	64%	19%	9%
Public and private institutions	3,253	12,371,672	156	2,901,344	1,823	4,754,117	1,274	4,716,211
Percentage of all institutions			5%	23%	56%	38%	39%	38%

Source: Percentages calculated from Grant and Snyder (1983, 104).

The Bargaining Environment

Public Policy

Statutory support for collective bargaining in public higher education is relatively recent. Most of the existing legislation allowing bargaining in public colleges and universities was passed in the early 1970s, when nineteen states enacted their initial legislation (provisions in five states predated that period), as shown in table 8–2. Collective bargaining in the twenty remaining states without enabling legislation is rare.[3]

Table 8–2
Legislation Allowing Collective Bargaining in Public Institutions of Higher Education

State	Date of Legislation or Amendment
Alaska	1972
Arizona	Governing boards*
California	1975 (2-yr.); 1978 (4-yr.)
Connecticut	1975
Delaware	1970
District of Columbia	Governing boards*
Florida	1974
Hawaii	1970 (amend. 1975)
Illinois	1983
Iowa	1974
Kansas	1970 (2-yr.) (amend. 1974)
Maine	1974 (2-yr. voc. tech.) (amend. 1975) 1975 (all other)
Maryland	Governing boards*
Massachusetts	1974
Michigan	1973 (amend. 1976)
Minnesota	1971 (amend. 1976, 1980)
Montana	1973 (amend. 1975)
Nebraska	1972
Nevada	Governing boards*
New Hampshire	1975
New Jersey	1974 (amend.)
New York	1967 (amend. 1975)
Ohio	1983
Oregon	1963 (2 yr.) (amend. 1975)
Pennsylvania	1970
Rhode Island	1958 (amend. 1973)
South Dakota	1969 (amend. 1974)
Vermont	1972 (amend. 1975)
Washington	1973 (2-yr.)
Wisconsin	1966 (2-yr.) (amend. 1974) (teaching assistants 1985)

Source: Douglas with Kotch (1986, 113).

*"No legislation. Governing boards enacted policy enabling collective bargaining at institution. Not general for state institutions of higher education as a whole."

The market for unionization in jurisdictions with favorable collective bargaining laws may be almost saturated. In some states—Connecticut, Delaware, Hawaii, Massachusetts, New Jersey, New York, and Rhode Island—almost all public higher education institutions are organized. In several others—Michigan, Minnesota, and Pennsylvania—all but the major research institutions are organized (Garbarino and Lawler 1977). Legislation passed in 1983 in Illinois and Ohio should foster union growth, as evidenced by recent organizing activity in both states. The 1980s otherwise, however, have been marked by a dearth of legislation affecting collective bargaining in higher education, although several states have considered new provisions. In 1983, for example, both chambers in the Washington state legislature passed a bargaining bill, but the governor vetoed it. In the remaining states that introduced legislation—Indiana, Maryland, Missouri, North Dakota, Virginia, West Virginia, and Wisconsin—the proposed bills were defeated in a floor vote or in committee (Douglas 1984a). In 1984 legislation was reintroduced in Maryland, Washington, and Wisconsin; and Colorado also discussed a bill supportive of faculty bargaining. None of those measures was adopted (Douglas with Kotch 1985).

Neither the presence nor the absence of bargaining legislation guarantees that bargaining will or will not take place, however. The influence of the legislation is subject to three qualifications. First, although the presence of legislation has been identified as an inducement to collective bargaining, the relationship between faculty unionization and the relative support for bargaining provided by the law, or its "strength," has not been explored. Second, the absence of legislation does not preclude bargaining—as in the cases of Illinois and Ohio before 1983. Third, administrative agencies can decline their jurisdiction over the industry, as was the case in National Labor Relations Board (NLRB) decisions before 1970. Up to that time the board had declined to extend its jurisdiction under the National Labor Relations Act (NLRA) to nonprofit educational institutions. In December 1951 the NLRB received a representation petition from the Community and Social Agency Employees, a CIO affiliate, which sought to represent clerical workers in Columbia University libraries. The board denied the petition, stating, "We do not believe that it would effectuate the policies of the [NLRA] for the Board to assert its jurisdiction . . . when the activities involved are noncommercial in nature and intimately connected with the charitable purposes and educational activities of the institution."[4]

Eighteen years later several nonfaculty occupational groups at Cornell University sought union recognition under New York's labor relations statute, termed "one of the few little Wagner Act[s] applicable to private educational institutions" (Carr and Van Eyck 1973, 25). Cornell University petitioned the NLRB to hold the representation election, preferring coverage under the federal statute to the state law, which did not prohibit union unfair labor practices. After reviewing the growth in universities' budgets, their increasingly "commercial" nature, and the federal government's expanding role in higher education, the board overturned the *Columbia University* decision.[5] A year later, in 1971, the NLRB held that faculty members "qualify . . . as professional employees under Section 2(12) of the [NLRA], and are therefore entitled to all the benefits of collective bargaining if they so desire."[6] But despite these administrative rulings union organizing at private colleges and universities enjoyed no great success throughout the 1970s.

The 1980 Supreme Court ruling in *NLRB v. Yeshiva University*[7] has done much to ensure that collective bargaining in higher education remains a public sector phenomenon. In a five-to-four decision the court declared that Yeshiva University faculty members possessed sufficient influence over university governance as to be deemed "managerial" employees, and as such they were without rights under the NLRA. Justice Powell, writing for the majority, stated:

> The controlling consideration in this case is that the faculty of Yeshiva University exercise authority which in any other context unquestionably would be managerial. To the extent the industrial analogy applies, the faculty determines within each school the product to be produced, the terms upon which it will be offered, and the customers who will be served.[8]

The *Yeshiva* Decision has not affected public sector unionization, as the courts have ruled against the small number of employers that have sought a similar decision (Franke 1984). Furthermore, recently enacted laws in Ohio and Illinois have demonstrated that states can preclude *Yeshiva* challenges to faculty organizing.[9] Nonetheless, *Yeshiva* has seriously hampered faculty organization in private colleges and universities. Over 50 schools have taken claims under *Yeshiva* to litigation, and to date, faculty unions have lost almost every case (Douglas 1984b, 1). New organizing activity in private institutions has been practically nonexistent (Douglas with Kotch 1986).

Faculty unions in private colleges and universities may gain some solace from the fact that by January 1985 very few new claims under the *Yeshiva* decision were being litigated (Douglas with Kotch 1985, 5). Moreover, there is the possibility—however remote in the immediate future—of federal action to override the decision. In 1980 and again in 1984 amendments to the NLRA were introduced, albeit unsuccessfully, to extend the act's coverage to faculty members (see Zirkel 1981 and U.S. Congress, House 1985).

The Economic Environment

Higher Education Budgets. The 1960s were boom years for higher education. Faculty employment grew from 381,000 in the school year 1950–60 to 825,000 in 1969–70 (Tuckman 1976). Building construction and expansion took place on a large scale, with the institutions expending $21.5 billion for buildings and improvements over the decade. And 702 new institutions were founded, of which 534 were public (Stadtman 1980).

The schools paid a price for their expansion, however. Many were charged with having mortgaged their futures by financing their expansion with debt (Carnegie Foundation 1975, 22). Beginning in the late 1960s and early 1970s operating costs took a sharp increase as the result of inflation, higher faculty salaries, greater student aid, and the expansion of academic activities. At the same time, the institutions witnessed declining growth in federal support, gifts and grants, and endowment income.

The schools' financial difficulties were exacerbated by the severe recession and steep increase in fuel costs of 1974–75. College administrators looked with hope at the improved fiscal position of the states in 1976, but subsequent taxpayer revolts diminished their expectations. In 1978, 2,294 presidents of public and private institutions were asked to identify the problem of greatest concern to them. The 45 percent who responded "financing" outnumbered, by a three-to-one margin, those who cited "decreasing enrollments," the second most frequently mentioned concern (Stadtman 1980, 89).

The fiscal problems of higher education have been attributed in part to the shortsightedness of the institutions' administrators, whose "lax financial and academic management" during the 1970s led to deficits (Keller 1983, 4). Bowen (1980, 20–21) formulated five "laws of higher educational costs" to describe this shortsightedness:

1. The dominant goals of institutions are educational excellence, prestige, and influence.
2. In quest of those goals institutions place virtually no limit on the amount of money to be spent for seemingly fruitful educational ends.
3. Each institution raises all the money it can.
4. Each institution spends all the money it raises.
5. The cumulative effect of these four laws is an administrative "policy" of ever-increasing and unchecked expenditures.

Throughout this period over the 1970s of unchecked spending, the cushion provided higher education by the federal government also began to slip. The federal portion of higher education institutional funding decreased from 19 percent in 1970–71 to 13 percent in 1981–82, although in actual dollars the federal portion doubled (Plisko and Stern n.d.). Reagan administration efforts to decrease the federal deficit of the 1980s could result in large-scale cuts in spending for higher education. Responsibility for the provision of new funds is likely to shift from the federal level to state governments.

Despite these threats to funding, higher education institutions have remained fairly durable. Attrition rates have been modest: From 1940 to 1970 0.5 percent of all schools merged or closed each year, and in the 1970s that rate increased only to 0.8 percent (Carnegie Council 1980). Although closings probably will not become rampant, schools nonetheless are facing two threatening issues in particular: a debilitating reduction of revenues from state and federal sources; and a critical need to reallocate resources within the institution (Meisinger and Dubeck 1984, 122).

Student Enrollment. Higher education institutions in the 1980s are also facing declining demand for their services. In 1983, 61 percent of all college students were 18 to 24 years old and almost 80 percent of undergraduates were less than 25 years old (Plisko and Stern n.d., 77). The U.S. population in this age bracket is expected to decline 18 percent between 1983 and 1993. This decrease will not result in a drop of comparable magnitude in student enrollment, as schools are already taking steps to attract more students and maintain enrollment levels; nonetheless, full-time equivalent employment is projected to decline 4 percent by 1990, which is expected to result in a 6 percent decrease (to 589,000) in full-time equivalent instructional staff (Frankel and Gerald 1982a, 77).

Efforts to attract more students have taken a number of forms, including lowering admission standards; increasing student financial aid; adopting more aggressive recruiting strategies, some of which target "nontraditional" students; and introducing and expanding programs that are popular with students (Carnegie Council 1980). As the competition among schools for the diminishing pool of students increases, "consumer sovereignty" will also increase. Marketing—and marketability—may become the primary concern of college administrators, who may begin to use marketability as a prime criterion in deciding on the educational products to be offered by their institutions. Faculty members are therefore becoming concerned that their job security will come to depend not only on students' choice of a college, but also on their selection of a major. A department's continued existence may well hinge on its attractiveness to students. In fact, enrollment shifts in academic majors have already led to some 920 faculty layoffs and terminations nationwide (Begin and Lee, 1985, 9).

Faculty Unions

Unions and Union Membership

As the data in tables 8–3 and 8–4 demonstrate, there are three major unions in higher education: the American Association of University Professors (AAUP), the American Federation of Teachers (AFT), and the National Edu-

Table 8–3
Number of Faculty Members Represented by a Certified Bargaining Agent, by Type of Institution, 1985

Type of Institution	AAUP	AFT	NEA	Independent	AAUP/AFT	AAUP/NEA	AFT/Ind.	AFGE	AFSCME	Other	Total
Public											
Four-Year	18,655	31,826	15,474	1,577	19,521	18,000	0	126	0	4,850	110,029
Two-Year	780	33,069	34,318	7,648	117	285	0	0	80	0	76,297
Total	19,435	64,895	49,792	9,225	19,638	18,285	0	126	80	4,850	186,326
Private											
Four-year	2,944	2,766	2,329	414	0	0	26	0	0	23	8,502
Two-Year	180	194	123	245	0	0	0	0	0	0	742
Total	3,124	2,960	2,452	659	0	0	26	0	0	23	9,244
All											
Four-Year	21,599	34,592	17,803	1,991	19,521	18,000	26	126	0	4,873	118,531
Two-Year	960	33,263	34,441	7,893	117	285	0	0	80	0	77,039
Total	22,559	67,855	52,244	9,884	19,638	18,285	26	126	80	4,873	195,570

Source: Douglas with Kotch (1986, 109).

Note: The figures include both full-time and part-time faculty members included in the certified bargaining unit. No distinction is made with respect to union membership. AFGE is the American Federation of Government Employees, and AFSCME is the American Federation of State, County and Municipal Employees.

Table 8–4
Number of Bargaining Agents and Bargaining Agreements, by Type of Institution, 1985

| Union | Number of Recognized Bargaining Agents, 1985 | | | | | | | | | Number of Collective Bargaining Agreements, 1985 | | | | | | | | |
| | Public Institutions | | | Private Institutions | | | All Institutions | | | Public Institutions | | | Private Institutions | | | All Institutions | | |
	4-yr.	2-yr.	Total	4-yr.	2-yr.	Total	4-yr.	2-yr.	Total	4-yr.	2-yr.	Total	4-yr.	2-yr.	Total	4-yr.	2-yr.	Total
AAUP	23	3	26	17	1	18	40	4	44	22	3	25	17	1	18	39	4	43
AFT	22	85	107	21	5	26	43	90	133	20	78	98	17	4	21	37	82	119
NEA	17	173	190	14	5	19	31	178	209	16	166	182	11	5	16	27	171	198
Independents	9	25	34	10	2	12	19	27	46	6	23	29	7	2	9	13	25	38
AAUP/AFT	2	1	3	0	0	0	2	1	3	2	1	3	0	0	0	2	1	3
AAUP/NEA	1	1	2	0	0	0	1	1	2	1	1	2	0	0	0	1	1	2
AFT/Independents	0	0	0	1	0	1	1	0	1	0	0	0	1	0	1	1	0	1
AFGE	2	0	2	0	0	0	2	0	2	2	0	2	0	0	0	2	0	2
AFSCME	1	1	2	0	0	0	1	1	2	1	1	2	0	0	0	1	1	2
Other	2	1	3	1	0	1	3	1	4	2	1	3	0	0	0	2	1	3
Total	79	290	369	64	13	77	143	303	446	72	274	346	53	12	65	125	286	411

Source: Douglas and Kotch (1986, 105–6)

cation Association (NEA). In 1985 the AFT independently represented 67,855 faculty members; the comparable figure for the NEA was 52,244 and for the AAUP, 22,559. These figures must be augmented by those encompassing joint representation arrangements between the organizations. Coalitional representation in higher education arose in part to enhance the unions' prospects of victory in representation elections and in part to avoid the interunion rivalries and divisiveness entailed in choosing a single union (Garbarino 1975, 101).

The AAUP was founded in 1915 by a group of faculty members, who envisioned a professional organization, not a labor union, for college teachers. From the outset the organization has been concerned with academic freedom (Ladd and Lipset 1973, 5) and other academic and administrative issues, promulgating its views through a series of policy statements. In 1940, for example, the association issued a *"Statement of Principles on Academic Freedom and Tenure."* If the AAUP subsequently receives complaints that a college or university violated the standards outlined in one of its statements, it may formally investigate the charges and publicly censure the institution. To support faculty demands for pay raises, the AAUP also initiated, in the 1950s, an annual nationwide survey of faculty salaries.

The AAUP's acceptance, albeit gradual, of the concept of collective bargaining began in the mid-1960s. In 1966 its Special Committee on Representation of Economic Interests issued a statement that declared, in part, "If a party feels compelled to seek representation through an outside organization, the Association believes itself . . . to be best qualified to act as representatives" (Lindeman 1973, 87). A "Statement on Collective Bargaining," which declared that the organization would "pursue collective bargaining as a major additional way of realizing its goals in higher education," was adopted at AAUP's 1972 annual meeting (Carnegie Foundation 1973, 223). This transition has fractionalized the organization; published accounts of a membership split over the concept of, and commitment to, collective bargaining as the organization's primary vehicle for achieving its goals appear regularly (see, for example, Mortimer and McConnell 1978; Watkins 1982; Banner 1984).

The National Teachers Association, the predecessor of the NEA, was founded in 1857 to "evaluate the character and advance the interests of the profession of teaching . . . and promote the cause of popular education in the United States" (Mortimer and McConnell 1978, 72). The NTA and a public school superintendents' association merged in 1870 to form the National Education Association. The NEA established a higher education department in 1872; 80 years later the department was renamed the American Association of Higher Education (AAHE). During the 1960s the relationship between the NEA and the AAHE became estranged over the issue of faculty unionism. Opposed to collective bargaining in higher education, the AAHE severed its ties with the NEA in 1971. The NEA had earlier (in 1967) established the National Faculty Association of Community and Junior Colleges and (in 1968) the National Society for Professors. In 1974 those two groups merged to become the NEA Higher Education Council.

In 1916 the American Federation of Labor granted a charter to the American Federation of Teachers, whose original charter locals consisted of primary and secondary school teachers in Chicago, Gary, New York, Scranton, and Washington, D.C. (Kolodny 1975). In the 1930s several AFT locals for faculty members were established (Carr and Van Eyck 1973), and when the union established a higher education department in 1967, there were some 50 AFT college locals (Garbarino 1975).

The most notable distinction among the three organizations (as shown in tables 8–3 and 8–4) is the NEA's dominance at the two-year educational institutions. Table 8–4 shows that in 1985 the NEA had 171 contracts at those schools, while the AFT had only 82 and the AAUP had only 4. Nevertheless, as shown in table 8–3 the number of faculty members represented at two-year colleges is roughly the same for the NEA and the AFT.

It is otherwise difficult to draw distinctions among the major faculty organizations because of a dearth of available data.[10] An empirical analysis of faculty union agreements negotiated between 1967 and September 1975 found no significant difference among contracts that could be attributed to the union involved; in other words, the contracts negotiated by the NEA, AFT, and AAUP contained similar terms (Bognanno, Estenson, and Suntrup 1978, 199). A later comparison of various provisions in NEA, AFT, and AAUP contracts—including provisions on management rights, tenure, nonrenewal, appointment, promotion, financial retrenchment, and long-range planning—revealed "some interesting variations" but again no "truly marked differences" (Chandler and Julius 1979, 55).

Union Growth

As of the 1985–86 school year there were some 700,000 faculty members employed full- or part-time in colleges and universities. Of those, 195,570, or 27.9 percent, were represented in bargaining units. Of the faculty members in public institutions 186,326, or 36.8 percent, were covered by collective bargaining contracts, and of their counterparts in private colleges and universities 9,244, or only 4.7 percent, were unionized. At two-year colleges 38.1 percent of the teachers were covered by labor agreements, whereas 23.8 percent of four-year college faculty members were organized (Douglas with Kotch 1986).

Collective bargaining in higher education began in 1963 in a public two-year college, the Milwaukee Technical Institute. The institute, part of a district of elementary and secondary schools, negotiated with a local association of faculty members in the district. In 1966 the United States Merchant Marine Academy was the first four-year institution to be organized. Unionization expanded in the late 1960s and the early 1970s particularly in state colleges and universities. St. John's University was among the first of the private institutions to engage in bargaining. By the end of the 1971–72 academic year bargaining agents had been chosen by faculty members at 33 four-year colleges and universities nationwide and at six multicampus systems: the City and State universities of New York, Rutgers—The State University of New Jersey, and the state college systems in Nebraska, New Jersey, and Pennsylvania (Carr and Van Eyck 1973). Table 8–5 gives an overview of the development of faculty collective bargaining over the past decade.

As shown in the table the number of faculty bargaining agreements has almost doubled since 1974. Although data to help explain faculty unionization are sparse, we will examine some more indirect evidence that traces faculty unionism to teachers' dissatisfaction with their compensation; the growing bureaucratization of colleges and universities; and individual demographic factors.

Dissatisfaction with Compensation. Dissatisfaction with compensation is probably the most frequently cited explanation for faculty unionization in the 1970s and 1980s. As noted earlier the 1960s had been boom years for higher education. As colleges and universities expanded, so did their demand for

Table 8–5
Faculty Union Growth, 1974–85

Year	Number Bargaining Agents at:			Number of Collective Bargaining Agreements at:		
	Two-Year	*Four-Year*	*All*	*Two-Year*	*Four-Year*	*All*
1974	180	97	277	145	66	211
1975	190	111	301	150	68	218
1976	218	125	343	158	76	234
1977	224	119	343	176	90	266
1978	251	131	382	208	93	301
1979	261	145	406	219	118	337
1980	276	151	427	236	123	359
1981	284	138	422	268	114	382
1982	286	137	423	268	109	377
1983	283	134	417	275	118	393
1984	291	138	429	278	117	395
1985	303	143	446	286	125	411

Source: Douglas with Kotch (1986, 103).

teachers. Total faculty compensation in constant dollars rose 41.2 percentage points from 1959–60 to 1969–70, an increase greater than that of any previous decade — save the 1920s (Carnegie Council 1980). Faculty members' real purchasing power (annual salary adjusted for inflation) rose every year from 1960–61 to 1968–69, ranging from a low of 1.7 percent (1968–69) to a high of 5.9 percent (1964–65) (Carr and Van Eyck 1973).

But as we have seen the 1970s were not as auspicious. Fewer new academic positions were opening up (Tuckman 1976); and average faculty salary in real terms initially remained constant (1970–71 to 1971–72), rose slightly (by 0.1 percent), and then decreased for each of the academic years from 1972–73 to 1980–81 (Hansen 1985). From 1972–73 to 1980–81 the declines in real faculty incomes fluctuated from a low of – 1.0 percent (1974–75 to 1975–76, and 1975–76 to 1976–77) to a high of – 5.5 percent (1978–79 to 1979–80). There were slight increases (0.3 to 2.0 percent) during the early 1980s; table 8–6 provides salary and compensation data for 1986–87.

There is counterintuitive anecdotal evidence that institutions with high compensation levels (relative to other schools) were among the first organized (Bennett and Johnson 1979), which suggests that the decline in faculty salaries relative to *other* professionals' pay may also have contributed to their pay dissatisfaction (Lindeman 1973). Faculty members' compensation relative to that of other professionals has continued to worsen; longitudinal data indicate that real salary increases for other professionals exceeded those in academia over the entire 1971–84 period (Hansen 1985).

Bureaucratization. Increased bureaucratization in higher education, which alters administrator-faculty relationships and affects faculty interactions and autonomy, may also have contributed to union growth. The expansion of bureaucracy during the period of faculty unionization resulted in part from the dramatic rise in school enrollments. Campuses with over 10,000 students accounted for only 25 percent of all enrollments in 1955, whereas they accounted for about 50 percent in 1977 (Carnegie Council 1980). In 1958 only 10 campuses had total enrollments in excess of 20,000 and claimed only 8 percent of the total U.S. student population. By 1969, 65 campuses had enrollments of more than 20,000 and claimed 27 percent of the total student population. And of those campuses 26 had over 30,000 students, accounting for 15 percent of national enrollment. These developments prompted observers in *Science* magazine to remark: "The 'community of scholars' has . . . undergone a radical transformation: in sheer size, the modern multiversity resembles medieval London rather than Oxford" (Gallant and Prothero 1972, 381).

The increasing role of the state government in higher education also altered educational organizations. The states' contribution to the operating income of public colleges and universities rose from $490 million in 1950 to

Table 8–6
Faculty Members' Weighted Average Salaries and Average Compensation, by Academic Rank and Type of Institution, 1986–87
(N = 322,174 faculty members at 1,875 institutions)

Academic Rank	Average Salary				Average Total Compensation			
	All Institutions	*Public*	*Private Independent*	*Private Religious*	*All Institutions*	*Public*	*Private Independent*	*Private Religious*
Professor	$45,530	$45,280	$50,270	$37,620	$55,300	$54,770	$61,820	$45,990
Associate	33,820	34,170	34,910	30,090	41,460	41,810	43,180	36,830
Assistant	27,920	28,470	28,310	24,600	33,090	34,900	34,420	29,560
Instructor	21,330	21,810	20,440	19,900	26,040	26,860	24,510	23,610
Lecturer	24,930	24,730	26,410	24,080	30,690	20,550	32,190	28,970
All Ranks	35,470	35,790	37,760	29,670	43,250	43,580	46,350	36,060

Source: *Academe* (1987, 9).

Notes: The sample excludes two-year colleges that do not use standard academic rankings.

$17.6 billion in 1970. And from 1950 to 1980 enrollment in public institutions increased from 1.1 million to 9.0 million. The number of public colleges and universities doubled over those years, and during the 1960s two-year colleges were established at the rate of nearly one per week (Carnegie Foundation 1982). As the states spent more on higher education, they became more involved in campus governance, through increasing centralization and state regulation.[11] Faculty collective bargaining, it is argued, resulted in part from the teachers' loss of autonomy as decision making became more centralized under state regulation and multicampus systems. But on the other hand, it is also argued that collective bargaining tends to exacerbate centralization (Birnbaum 1980, 9) by creating single, systemwide bargaining units in state college and university systems.

Governance. Unionization may also have been fostered by dissatisfaction with the faculty role in college governance. Interestingly, 70 percent of 234 college and university presidents surveyed in 1973 believed that giving faculty a greater role in decision making would diminish the prospects of unionization (Odewahn and Spritzer 1976). It is important to keep in mind, however, the significant structural variations among institutions noted at the outset of this chapter. In many community, state, and private liberal arts colleges "ideas of faculty participation in governance and shared collegial decision-making have always been fictional, for the institutions were actually managed by strong administrators and trustees" (Kemerer and Baldridge 1975, 29). This pattern may also apply to predominantly black institutions, church-affiliated schools, and former teachers' colleges, but it does not hold for research universities (Keller 1983).

Faculty influence varies, of course, by structure within as well as among institutions. Teachers may participate in decision making at any of a number of levels in their colleges, such as in departments, schools within universities, and faculty senates. Departments, for example, may play an important role in curriculum, hiring, and promotion decisions (Lee 1978). Indeed, faculty members believe that they play a significant role in college governance at the departmental level. A 1969 study found that 60 percent of the respondents to a survey of faculty members believed they had "a great deal or quite a bit" of "opportunity to influence departmental policy" (Carnegie Foundation 1973, 45), and 60.8 percent of respondents replied in a similar manner to a 1984 Carnegie Foundation survey (*Chronicle of Higher Education,* 1985, 25–28).

Faculty members may believe they can influence departmental decisions, but they are also concerned with participating in decision making beyond their department's doors. The AAUP, in its 1966 "Statement on Government of Colleges and Universities," declared: "Agencies for faculty participation in the government of the college or university should be established at each level where faculty responsibility is present. An agency should exist for the presentation of the views of the whole faculty" (Carnegie Foundation 1973, 213). Thus, we can assume, for lack of evidence to the contrary, that if college professors have no faculty senate or are dissatisfied with the one they have, they may turn to unions as a means to exert their influence.[12]

The establishment of a faculty senate is contingent upon trustee or administrative approval, and its powers are delegated by these same officials. No dues are collected; rather, the senate is funded by the college or university. Its officers serve in a part-time, unpaid capacity, and its membership usually encompasses some administrators.

Several investigations of the extent of senates' influence over college affairs have been undertaken. The AAUP surveyed chief administrative officers and AAUP chapter presidents at 970 institutions (of which some 800 were four-year schools) in 1969–70. (Two-year colleges were underrepresented, suggesting that the results overstate the average degree of faculty participation in the population as a whole; Garbarino 1975, 35). The survey delineated five degrees of faculty participation—determination, joint action, consultation, discussion, and none—in three types of decisions: personnel, academic, and administrative. The median degree of participation was slightly below "consultation," which was defined as "a formal procedure for recommendations, a vote or other expression of opinion." Of the three types of decisions, respondents indicated faculty had the greatest influence in academic affairs. Faculty participation in the other two types of decisions was decidedly weaker. For example, 66 percent of the responses indicated no participation, or participation through discussions only (expressions of opinion), in deciding personnel and administrative matters, such as faculty salary scales; and 75 percent indicated the same low level of participation in individual salary decisions.

In another survey presidents of nonunion colleges and universities indicated that their faculty senate's influence was greatest over decisions on the curriculum and on degree requirements. Senate participation in economic decisions, such as faculty salaries and work loads, was rated much lower (Kemerer and Baldridge 1975).

All told these findings have raised the criticism that academic senates "do not really lead to where the power is—namely, to that place and time in the budget process where fundamental decisions and allocations are made. Not only the size of one's salary but the fundamental expression of values and priorities are at issue there" (Boyd 1972, 121).

Individual Characteristics. Interest in faculty unionization may also be associated with certain individual characteristics, although the evidence to date is sparse. There is some evidence that younger faculty members, for example, may be more supportive of collective bargaining (Boyd 1972; Lindeman 1973). But there is also evidence that more senior faculty members turn to unions in reaction against their junior colleagues (Carr and Van Eyck 1973, 57–58):

> At a former teachers college, vocational school, or experimental college, which had a limited purpose and program, but has been undergoing rapid growth and development into a college of arts and sciences or a regional university, a movement toward collective bargaining may be led by older faculty members who find themselves competing for salary increases and program support with . . . young faculty members.

Kemerer and Baldridge (1975, 65) have also observed that older faculty members, interested in preserving their status, may initiate organizing efforts.

As should be obvious now, the existing research has not sufficiently modeled the possible factors leading to faculty unionization. Nonetheless, some promising *indirect* evidence on faculty attitudes toward bargaining does shed some light on this complex issue.

Although each of the statistical analyses mentioned below examined only one school, save for Gress (1976), their findings on faculty attitudes toward collective bargaining are fairly consistent. In particular, they suggest that satisfaction with salaries and fringe benefits is negatively associated with interest in unionization. Faculty members who believe their pay increases are only weakly linked to their performance are more supportive than others of unionization. Satisfaction with supervision and promotional opportunities is inversely related to union support, as are age, academic rank, tenure, and current salary level (Allen and Keaveny 1981; Bigoness 1978; Gress 1976; Grossnickle 1980).[13]

But, as noted, attitude surveys provide at best only indirect explanations for union growth, as general support for collective bargaining does not necessarily translate into support for a particular union in a specific bargaining election (Garbarino and Aussieker 1974, 264). The linkage between support for bargaining and actual voting behavior is examined next.

Individual differences in voting patterns among faculty members have unfortunately also received little scrutiny. In one study individual demographic measures—of academic rank, gender, tenure, status, and salary—showed no power to predict voting behavior in union representation elections; but certain attitudes—distrust in administrative decision making and dissatisfaction with work content—did predict votes in favor of union representation (Hammer and Berman 1981). Faculty demographic characteristics again were found to have had no statistically significant relationship with voting behavior in two elections conducted at New York University; however, not surprisingly, voting against union representation was positively associated with satisfaction with six conditions: financial benefits, personnel policies, academic freedom, working conditions, participation in governance and educational policy determination (Bornheimer 1985). Other studies of faculty representation elections consist of descriptive case studies, from which it is difficult to generalize. One study attributed support for unions to dissatisfaction with compensation and governance (Carey 1978), while another attributed union defeats in part to the emergence of anti-union factions of faculty members and administration opposition to unions (Bodner 1974). The importance of these last factors were echoed in a review of 28 elections in which the faculty rejected collective negotiations (Mortimer, Johnson, and Weiss 1975).

Part-Time Faculty

Colleges and universities have always employed a fair number of part-time teachers which continues to pose a difficult challenge for faculty unions. The term *part-time faculty,* which has been defined in a variety of ways, refers "in a general way to any appointment for which there is less than a normal range of assigned duties, and the terms of employment recognize the fractional involvement of the worker" (Leslie, Kellams, and Gunne 1982, 1; also see Gappa 1984). In 1961, 35 percent of all postsecondary instructional staff were part-timers; and 20 years later the same proportional distribution existed.[14] In the intervening years, however, employment of part-time faculty declined (during the 1960s), and then dramatically escalated (during the 1970s). Between 1972 and 1977 the number of part-time instructors at two-year schools increased 83.6 percent, whereas the number of full-time faculty at those institutions rose only 12.9 percent. During the same period part-time employment at universities increased 11 percent, while full-time employment rose only 2.6 percent; at the remaining four-year schools, part-time employment jumped 61.2 percent, while full-time employment increased 22.1 percent (Scott 1983). In 1976 part-timers constituted over one-half of all faculty members in two-year institutions (Leslie, Kellams, and Gunne 1982, 19).[15]

Faculty unions have demonstrated a fairly explicit concern that part-time teachers jeopardize the job security of full-time teachers; part-timers often receive less pay and fewer fringe benefits than full-timers, making them an economical alternative work force for colleges and universities. At the same time, however, faculty unions have also been concerned to improve employment conditions for their part-time members.[16] The ambivalent position unions have adopted is typified by the following statement, a resolution approved in 1985 by the NEA Representative Assembly (National Education Association 1985, 230):

> E.16. Misuse of Part-time Faculty. The National Education Association believes that part-time faculty should be employed only when an educational program requires specialized training or expertise not available in the full-

time faculty and when the need for such training and expertise does not justify more than half-time employment. Part-time faculty should receive the same salary and fringe benefits as full-time faculty, prorated according to the workload. The Association also believes that part-time faculty should not be employed for the primary purpose of reducing instructional budgets or for the purpose of reducing the number of full-time positions.

Colleges and universities offer several justifications for the use of part-time faculty. First, part-timers allow administrators greater flexibility in curriculum design and course scheduling (Friedlander 1980). Second, part-timers who possess skills not held by the full-time faculty can be employed to expand the number of courses offered by the institution. Thus can colleges hire such professionals as musicians and performing artists, as can community colleges draw upon local experts for vocational classes (Leslie, Kellams, and Gunne 1982). Furthermore, as previously noted, higher education institutions are now seeking to offset enrollment declines by attracting a more diverse student body. They often turn to part-timers to teach older, part-time students who demand classes scheduled evenings and weekends at off-campus locations — outside the normal workday of the full-time instructors. Third, schools may hire part-time faculty for new courses, those in which enrollment patterns are uncertain, and then summarily dismiss the instructors if the demand is insufficient. Finally, as noted at the start of this discussion, part-timers are quite simply a cheap source of labor. The financial advantage of employing part-time faculty members may be offset, however, by a significant disadvantage — that of diminished educational quality.[17]

Thus, it appears that part-time employment among college faculty is a given. Unions may respond to this fact in the future by stepping up their attempts to organize part-timers, but in their attempts to date, unions have encountered several difficulties. High turnover rates among part-timers make it difficult to identify, and maintain, their union support. Part-timers have infrequent contacts with one another and thus do not have the opportunity to share mutual experiences and concerns (Abel 1984). Moreover, their other job obligations off campus constrain any commitment to union activity they might like to make. Finally, the heterogeneity of the part-time work force poses yet additional problems for union organizers.

More specifically, these faculty members may have a range of motivations for part-time work, which undoubtedly translates into a diverse range of interests. Economic concerns may be primary for some; intrinsic rewards may be sufficient for others; long-term career development may preoccupy a third group (Leslie, Kellams, and Gunne 1982, 41). Identifying a mutuality of interests may be difficult for union organizers. Nonetheless, they cannot overlook the importance to part-timers of finding a means to increase their job security, fringe benefits, salary increments, and support services, as well as their pay (Abel 1984; Gappa 1984; Leslie, Kellams, and Gunne 1982)—and unionization is one very obvious means. All told, then, it is likely that the employment of part-time faculty members, and the potential for organizing them, will be among the most heated topics in higher education unionism over the next few years.

The "Quality School" Debate

Critics of faculty unionism, and others, have often asserted that it is the schools adhering to a lower standard of academic excellence that are most susceptible to unionization. Three now-dated studies gave credence to that assertion.

The 1969 Carnegie Commission survey asked faculty members to agree or disagree with the (not particularly illuminating) statement that "collective bargaining by faculty members has no place in a college or university" (Carnegie Foundation 1973, 42). Their responses were categorized by "school quality," which was measured by admissions standards and by expenditures (total and for research only) per student (Ladd and Lipset 1973, 13). Just over half of the respondents from the "elite" schools disagreed with the statement, a rate that progressively increased as "school quality" declined. Ladd and Lipset attributed this pattern of responses, in part, to faculty members' greater role in school governance and their greater compensation levels at the better quality institutions.

In the second study Aussieker and Garbarino (1973) classified four-year schools on the basis of their quality ratings in *The Gourman Report*.[18] The authors computed the number of unionized institutions in each of the quality categories, calculations they believed supported "the correctness of the common assumption that unionism has been concentrated in relatively low-quality institutions" (p. 124). Nonetheless, Aussieker and Garbarino also suggested that school quality served as a proxy for other factors in the decision to unionize, such as faculty participation in school governance, academic work loads, and academic status.[19]

The third study (Garbarino 1975) classified four-year institutions by quality (measured by a different rating system than the *Gourman* system), locus of control (public or private), and the legal environment (legislation allowing collective bargaining in the public sector). Although acknowledging the small number of observations in his analysis, Garbarino nevertheless concluded that there was a "clear-cut tendency for unionization to be concentrated in the institutions that [were] in the lower . . . tiers of the quality distribution" (p. 75). The author noted two significant aberrations from this tendency: The high-quality public schools in states with legislation favorable to collective bargaining were highly unionized, while low-quality private schools were very sparsely unionized. Another, more recent empirical study found that the greater the "organizational effectiveness" of a college or university, the less unionized its faculty members were.[20]

These studies of the linkage between school quality and faculty unionization may have a twofold value to union organizers. First, if there is indeed a linkage—whatever the underlying reasons for it—unions may best be able to increase their memberships by focusing their organizing efforts on the lower echelon schools. Second, if unions hope to organize a broad range of schools, they will need to tailor their efforts to the individual school. If, for example, school quality measures are simply a proxy for faculty satisfaction with compensation and governance, union organizers will have to identify other issues of importance to teachers in the more elite schools; they will also have to dissuade these professors from their belief that unionism is the exclusive province of lower quality ("unprofessional") faculties. In other words, issues such as compensation and governance may be more salient in the "lower quality" schools, and issues such as comparable worth and tenure may be more salient at the "elite" schools.

Unions of Nonfaculty Employees

College and university employees who are not faculty members constitute another group of the potentially organizable in higher education, but little is known about the extent of nonfaculty organizing. An analysis of representation elections conducted in private institutions soon after the 1970 *Cornell University* decision indicated that most organizing activity focused on *nonteaching* staff.[21] More recently, unions such as the United Automobile, Aerospace and Agricultural Implements Workers (UAW), the Service Employees International Union (SEIU), and the American Federation of State, County and Municipal Employees (AFSCME) have organized nonacademic staff at Columbia, Stanford, and the University of California (Heller 1985).

The most visible recent manifestation of unionism among nonfaculty employees was the ten-week strike by Yale University clerical and technical workers in the autumn of 1985. The strike was conducted by Local 34, New England Hotel and Restaurant Employees (AFL-CIO), which represents all permanent hourly (nonsalaried) Yale staff who work more than 20 hours a week, except for hourly maintenance and service workers. At the time of the strike the unit covered some 2,600 employees with 250 job titles; the clerical and technical staff was 85 percent women (Coulson 1985).

The Yale experience well illustrates that organizing nonfaculty personnel can be a difficult task. Previous organizing drives by the Office and Professional Employees International Union (OPEIU) and the UAW had failed. Local 35's margin of victory in the May 1983 representation election was only some 30 votes. Its success has been attributed to its "grassroots" approach to organizing, whereas the previous campaigns had been "efforts . . . by outside groups with little base to work from and with little knowledge of Yale" (Coulson 1985, 54).

What was notable about the Yale strike, for our purposes here, was the extent of support for the strike evidenced by Yale faculty members. Their receptivity to the labor dispute took three forms: support, opposition, and indifference (Kagan 1985). Some faculty members conducted classes off-campus to avoid picket lines. Two motions in support of the union were defeated in separate votes of the Yale faculty, although on neither occasion was a majority of the faculty present. A comment by a Yale administrator suggests that the interests of faculty members and unionized nonteaching staff do not coincide (Lorimer 1985, 2):

> A primary goal of the faculty for the university's negotiating agenda was pre-servation of their ability to pick the most qualified members of the clerical and technical unit without bumping provisions or seniority restraints so they could assure themselves of top-notch research groups or outstanding secre-tarial support.

The continued existence of a nonfaculty labor force that is predomi-nantly nonunion raises several questions for the AFT, AAUP, and NEA:

1. To what extent should union resources be devoted to organizing non-faculty employees?

2. How should the organizing campaign be conducted? Would, for exam-ple, a campaign among secretaries be directed as much against the alleged abuses of their immediate supervisors—faculty members who are already members of the union—as it would be against the school admin-istration?

3. Would successful organizing among nonfaculty employees serve as an inducement for teachers to unionize, or would professors perceive it as further evidence that unionism is unprofessional?

The nonteaching staff thus represents another potentially organizable group, albeit one for which the industrial union model may be more applic-able than it is for the faculty group. The nonfaculty staff is a diverse group, though, encompassing as it does nonteaching professional employees, sup-port staff, maintenance staff, campus police, and so on. It is hard to predict common interests, much less organizing success, among this population.

Employers and Bargaining Structure

The structure of collective bargaining in higher education only partly reflects the heterogeneity of the employing institutions. As was previously noted, in 1983–84 there were 3,284 higher education institutions in the United States, 1,803 of which were privately funded and 1,481 of which were in the public sector. And, as noted, the institutions also vary by type: four-year multicampus and single-campus universities, four-year comprehensive colleges, four-year specialized colleges, two-year colleges, and institutions that offer postsecondary education but do not confer a two-year degree. Given this heterogeneity one might think that bargaining structure is largely a function of institutional type.

The key determinant of bargaining structure is not type, however, but the governing body administering the institution — whether it is public or private and, if public, which administrative body is deemed the "employer" for purposes of collective bargaining. If, for example, the state government's executive office serves as the employer, the body that negotiates the faculty contract could be a representative of the governor's office, a postsecondary education commission, or a board of regents. Hawaii, with a single faculty bargaining unit encompassing both two- and four-year institutions, has a centralized structure (Garbarino 1976), as do other two-year and four-year college and university *systems* that bargain a single contract with faculty union representatives from institutions throughout the system. The State University of New York system, for example, has a single bargaining unit covering faculty members in all the state's four-year colleges and universities and two-year agricultural and technical schools; and the Community College System of Minnesota has a single contract for 14 community colleges.[22] It has been argued, interestingly, that under this arrangement college and university presidents function in the collective bargaining process merely as "middle managers" (Haak 1985).

Less centralized bargaining structures exist if the employer is a county or local government. In New York state, for example, a county or group of counties acts as the employer, negotiating contracts with unionized faculty members in the community college receiving the county funding. Another example is state-sponsored schools that negotiate their own contracts with individual union locals; in this case the employer is the board of trustees of the school. Michigan follows this approach; eight of the state's four-year institutions negotiate their own agreements (Garbarino 1976).

Thus, it is difficult if not impossible to identify a primary bargaining structure in public higher education. Whether two-year or four-year institutions are considered, it is virtually useless to examine the characteristics of institutions to predict bargaining structure. Differing historical and legal developments in the various state and local governments that control public institutions make for a broad range of entities deemed the "employer" for collective bargaining purposes. In short, the structure of bargaining appears entirely contingent on the locus of decision making authority in publicly controlled institutions.

Most institutions in the private sector have but one campus (Benewitz 1975), and therefore the appropriate bargaining unit designated by the National Labor Relations Board (NLRB) usually encompasses only one campus. But even when considering privately controlled institutions, the issue of bargaining structure is not clear-cut. In private institutions with several campuses, bargaining may occur either at each campus or on a systemwide basis. The NLRB established, for example, a separate bargaining unit for each of Long Island University's three campuses but one inclusive unit for Fairleigh Dickinson University's three campuses (Benewitz 1975; Hankin 1979; Kennedy 1974).

The Bargaining Process

In turning now to the process of collective bargaining in higher education we will examine common and emerging issues addressed in faculty bargaining—compensation, salary increases, pay equity, school governance, and job security—and then move on to brief discussions of contract administration and strike activity.

Bargaining Issues

Overall Compensation. Recent research suggest that unionized faculty members are more satisfied with their pay than are their nonunion counterparts (Gomez-Mejia and Balkin 1984). Nevertheless, whether faculty unions have actually raised the pay of their members over that of nonmembers is hard to say; empirical research on the question has produced decidedly mixed results. Birnbaum (1974) contrasted pay levels at 88 unionized schools with those at the same number of institutions without collective bargaining (as of 1972–73). The author matched pairs of union and nonunion schools by similarities in administrative control (public, independent, church related); program level (highest degree conferred); compensation level in the base year; and, when possible, the number of full-time faculty members and geographic location. Among the sample as a whole the unionized schools paid more in both of the two years examined. (The average differentials were $47 in 1968–69 and $824 in 1972–73.) Birnbaum also found statistically significant differentials in 1972–73 for two subsets of the sample: public universities and public four-year colleges. In a subsequent study Birnbaum (1976) identified a statistically significant union-nonunion average annual pay differential of $1,144 for 70 matched schools in the 1974–75 academic year.

Morgan and Kearney (1977) also used the matching procedure; their sample of 46 four-year schools in 1974–75 revealed an average union wage effect of $625. As part of the same study a stepwise regression analysis indicated that the presence of a union was the best among six predictors of faculty compensation change over the years 1969–70 to 1974–75.

Two subsequent studies found different union effects, however. Brown and Stone (1977) contrasted growth rates for faculty salary and compensation nationwide between 1970–71 and 1975–76 with those on 32 campuses that had initial contracts effective between 1971–72 and 1975–76. Collective bargaining did not have a statistically significant impact on compensation or salaries for any faculty rank. And the Guthrie-Morse, Leslie, and Hu (1981) regression analysis of 30 matched pairs of four-year schools found an insignificant union effect on average compensation for the 1970–78 period.

The contradictory findings on faculty unions' effects on pay may be a function in part of methodological problems. Each of the studies cited here drew from a small sample of schools. Furthermore, the matching procedure used called for subjective judgments by the researchers about appropriate pairings (Begin 1979; Marshall 1979). The most comprehensive investigation of collective bargaining's impact on faculty pay, one that employed AAUP survey data in longitudinal and cross-sectional regression analyses, concluded (in part) that unionism had raised faculty pay; however, the degree of the effect varied greatly depending on the estimating model used and the time period covered (Freeman 1978, 28–29).

Salary Adjustments. Although the impact of research activity and other factors on academic earnings has been empirically investigated by numerous authors,[23] the relationship between unionism and salary adjustments such as merit pay has received little attention. The available information is dated. One study of 61 faculty bargaining agreements found that 47 percent contained terms governing merit pay, but the agreements examined were negotiated 10 to 18 years ago (Bognanno, Estenson, and Suntrup 1978). A more recent investigation of four-year schools noted that 36 percent of the 88 agreements analyzed contained a merit pay provision (Johnstone 1981). A more recent examination of merit pay provisions in four-year state colleges in New Jersey revealed a wide range in the extent to which the concept as embraced; but the authors nonetheless noted that union opposition to merit pay was "considerable" (Hollander and Turnbull 1984, 95). Another analysis, of 207 faculty contracts, found that 80 percent did not mention merit pay. This finding, according to the author, lent "support to those who claim that merit pay is still too controversial and [subjectively determined] to be widely accepted by faculty organizations" (Douglas 1983b, 8).

Another salary adjustment issue of concern to faculty union members is the market differentials paid to professors in certain disciplines. Over the years 1976–77 to 1984–85 faculty members who taught courses in high demand—business, computer science, engineering, and law—received the largest percentage increases in average salaries of faculty in all the academic disciplines (Hansen 1985). In fact salaries in those disciplines were already relatively high in 1976–77, and disciplines that offered comparatively low salaries in 1976–77 showed only small percentage increases over the period. Hence, there has been a widening of salary differentials across disciplines over the decade 1976–85. The union response to administrators' bargaining demands for "market" pay differentials was recently investigated; the findings were that only 16 contracts, or less than 14 percent, of the 117 collective bargaining contracts studied addressed the issue.[24] Nonetheless, we would expect to see this issue addressed more often in the future as higher education institutions face ever-growing competition for other organizations recruiting persons with highly technical skills.

Pay Equity. Although faculty and nonfaculty unions representatives have become increasingly concerned with issues of pay equity and comparable worth (equal pay for comparable work in different jobs), faculty members have not been successful in comparable worth lawsuits (Begin and Lee 1985). A recent suit settled in out of court negotiations did result in pay raises for some 6,000 AFSCME members who were nonfaculty employees at the University of Washington, as well as for several thousand other Washington state college and university staff members.[25] The university employees affected were for the most part nurses and clerical workers.

The details of *AFSCME v. State of Washington* are instructive because the case is one of the few that have dealt directly with the issue of comparable worth. The state decided to negotiate a settlement, even though the U.S. Court of Appeals had overturned the District Court's decision in favor of the union's claims (Fields 1985). District Court Judge Jack Tanner had ruled that Washington state's failure to adjust salary levels, after the university had "conducted comparable worth studies showing . . . [a] 20 percent disparity in salaries between predominantly male and predominantly female job classification" violated Title VII of the Civil Rights Act of 1964.[26] The Ninth Circuit declared that "a study which indicates a particular wage structure might be more equitable should not categorically bind the employer who commissioned it"[27] Thus, despite the fact that the parties settled their dispute in favor of the union's members, the appeals court decision leaves the future of pay equity disputes still in question.

Governance. Unionization has not significantly altered the preexisting college and university governance structures, at least in the four-year institutions, where departmental autonomy remains intact (Lee, 1978). Furthermore, collective bargaining has not led to the demise of faculty senates (see, for example, Begin 1974). Faculty members have simply embraced a dualistic concept of school governance, with their senates addressing academic issues while their unions address economic issues. The senates retain their influence over curriculum and degree requirements, while the unions have their largest influence, as we have seen, over faculty compensation, and working conditions (Kemerer and Baldridge 1981). Nevertheless, it is not always easy to distinguish between the two sets of issues (Garbarino 1975; Wollett 1975); and as faculty unions gain in influence, faculty senates may lose some of theirs.

Job Security. As previously noted, various studies suggest that younger, nontenured faculty members are the most favorably disposed toward unionization. But if, as a result, union organizers focus their efforts primarily on this group, they risk alienating the more senior, tenured staff. To increase their membership, faculty unions must obviously identify issues of mutual concern to both groups. Recent threats to the job security of both groups may make this a more salient bargaining issue in the future, while at the same time enhancing the value of collective bargaining to all faculty members.

Approximately 85 percent of all colleges and universities have tenure systems, and these schools employ around 95 percent of all faculty members (Chait, 1975). The percentage of tenured faculty members in four-year institutions has risen sharply, from 50 percent in 1969–70 to 75 percent in 1980–81 (Carnegie Foundation 1980). College and university officials have responded to this increase by imposing tenure quotas,[28] which obviously pose a direct threat to the job security of the nontenured teaching staff. Because unions have succeeded in blocking the establishment of these quotas at a number of institutions, they may find greater appeal among nontenured faculty members in the future (Chait 1975, 61). And administrative attempts to establish new types of nontenured employment, such as those requiring renewable contracts, may also stimulate union involvement in issues of job security for the nontenured group.

The job security of tenured faculty members may also become increasingly threatened, as budgetary retrenchment becomes more and more of an issue.[29] Challenges to the job security of the tenured staff may serve as an inducement to unionism, as faculty organizations have shown they can provide assistance in addressing this issue as well. The AAUP, for example, has recommended that its locals seek inclusion of a "financial exigency" clause in their bargaining agreements to bolster the job security of tenured faculty members.[30]

Unions have negotiated other job security protections for tenured faculty members. Some faculty bargaining agreements specify that professors be involved in decision making on budgetary issues, and some outline procedural rights to review budgetary decisions and rights in layoffs and recalls.

Thus, unions can take advantage of the universal concern with job security to bridge divergent views toward unionism and collective bargaining issues among nontenured and tenured faculty alike. This does not mean, of course, that the interests of the two groups necessarily mesh, but merely that the two may be willing to accommodate each other's interests. Finally, they may have no trouble agreeing that the greatest threat to their job security lies in the employment of part-time instructors, an issue we have already discussed earlier in this chapter.

Contract Administration

Contract administration procedures in higher education are similar in many respects to those in the industrial sector. Over 90 percent of bargaining agreements in higher education call for the use of grievance procedures, and 74 percent specify binding arbitration (Douglas 1985a).

On the other hand, dispute resolution during the course of faculty contracts also exhibits several distinguishing features. Grievances, for example, may be limited to allegations of procedural violations only, particularly in four-year institutions (Begin 1979). Thus, arbitrators often are prohibited from analyzing the substantive merit of "academic judgments," as, for example, in tenure and termination grievances (Lee, 1978). Differentiating academic judgments from due process considerations, however, can be a difficult undertaking. And the authority of the arbitrator is constrained in another respect: "Even if the arbitrator finds a violation, he is seldom empowered, as he would be in the industrial sector, to reinstate or promote an employee or to grant . . . tenure" (Berkowitz 1981, 64). In cases of dismissals or denials of tenure the arbitrator can stipulate only that the matter be reconsidered by the appropriate institutional group.

An additional peculiarity in administering faculty contracts is that grievances are frequently brought against personnel decisions made by the grievant's *peers*—other faculty members—and not just against *administrators'* decisions (Begin 1979). This may be a contributing factor in the relatively small number of grievances filed by faculty members. Although precise data are not available, general indications suggest their use of grievance procedures has been limited (Begin 1979; Lee 1978).

Strike Activity

Not only do faculty members file few grievances, they also seldom go on strike. The 119 strikes by faculty unions that took place over the years 1966–

84 involved (on an annual average) only 2.6 percent of all unionized institutions and only 2.8 percent of their faculty members (Aussieker 1985). Walkouts predominated in the public sector, particularly in community colleges—which is not surprising given the greater unionization and strike opportunities (single campus negotiations) in those schools.[31] Strike activity in the United States has dropped precipitously in recent years, but faculty strikes have always been infrequent events, suggesting that faculty unions' bargaining power has not fluctuated dramatically in response to macroeconomic trends—perhaps because it never was large.[32]

The Outlook for Faculty Unionism

If dissatisfaction with compensation and other aspects of work is one of primary reasons faculty members turn to unions, recent survey data indicate the current conditions for faculty unionization are favorable. The Carnegie Foundation concluded from its 1984 nationwide survey of some 5,000 faculty at two-year and four-year schools that the professoriate is "deeply troubled" (Carnegie Foundation 1985, 31). Over two-thirds of the respondents characterized faculty salary levels as fair or poor, and 60.7 percent similarly rated their own salary (*Chronicle of Higher Education* 1985). With the statement "I feel trapped in a profession with limited opportunities for advancement" 28.1 percent were able to agree; and 38.1 percent predicted they might leave teaching within five years. Furthermore, 62.2 percent believed that collective bargaining was "likely to bring higher salaries and improved benefits."

The Carnegie study yielded several other findings, however, that should caution against predicting a ground swell of support for faculty unionization. For example, 36.4 percent of the respondents agreed that "collective bargaining by faculty members has no place in a college or university." And even though faculty dissatisfaction with pay and working conditions was greater in the 1984 survey than that expressed in the 1975 Carnegie Council survey, support for collective bargaining apparently diminished over those years: 77 percent of the 25,000 respondents in the 1975 survey said they believed collective bargaining would improve compensation; but as noted above, only 62 percent in the 1984 survey so indicated. The proportion in 1984 agreeing that collective bargaining has no place in academia increased more than 8 percentage points over the proportion—28 percent—in 1975 (Jacobson 1985).

Since neither survey identified specific reasons for the lack of support for unionism, we can only speculate on what those reasons are. We will hazard to say that it is ironic, in a working environment supposedly populated by a "community of scholars," that a lack of solidarity may be a contributing factor. Numerous observers have asserted that faculty members' strongest ties extend well beyond their department and school and lie instead with other members of their particular academic discipline across the globe (Gerry 1978; Schuster and Bowen 1985).

Over twenty years ago, Burton Clark (1963, 70–73) remarked:

> As campuses increase in size, complexity, and internal specialization, there is less chance that the faculty will be able to operate effectively as a total faculty in college affairs, or as the governmental body we have in mind when we speak of a community of scholars. The decision-making power and influence of the faculty is now more segmented—segmented by subcollege, by division, and particularly by department. . . .
>
> The campus is a holding company for professional groups rather than a single association of professionals

Clark also asserted that this fragmentation was accompanied by an increase in the "personal authority" of each professor, as greater specialization within narrow areas of expertise and a favorable job market enhanced each scholar's status. Clark recognized the existence of a "professor-entrepreneur" who regularly obtained his or her own funding from foundations and the federal government.

But conditions have changed. The academic job market has tightened considerably, federal support has tapered off, and the choices—and bargaining power—of the individual faculty member have diminished. Nonetheless, the ethos of individualism, and individual effort, may continue to pervade academia. If collective bargaining is to become more widespread in higher education, unions will have to demonstrate that they present an attractive alternative in an environment that has dramatically changed over the past two decades.

Notes

1. In defining *higher education* for the purposes of this chapter, we adopt the following Carnegie Foundation (1975, 1) definition:

> "Higher education" is defined here as the "collegiate sector" of postsecondary education—that is, public and private community colleges, four-year liberal arts colleges, comprehensive colleges and universities, and universities and professional schools. This commentary does not attempt to cover the "non-collegiate sector" of postsecondary education: proprietary occupational schools, other postsecondary institutions (recreational and occupational schools not eligible for federal student aid), and "other learning opportunities" (such as those offered by churches, corporations, and labor unions)

2. Of the 3,284 higher education institutions existing in 1983–84, 1,481 were

public and 1,803 were private; two-year schools constituted 38.7 percent of the total (Broyles and Fernandez 1984).

3. Colorado (with two contracts), Missouri (two contracts), and Virginia (one contract) are exceptions (Douglas with Kotch 1986).

4. *Trustees of Columbia University,* 97 NLRB 427 (1951).

5. *Cornell University,* 183 NLRB 41 (1970); 74 LRRM 1272 (1970).

6. *Long Island University,* 189 NLRB 110 (1971); 77 LRRM 1003 (1971).

7. 444 US 672, 103 LRRM 2526 (1980).

8. Ibid., 2532.

9. Specifically, the Ohio statute specifies: "Heads of departments or divisions are supervisors; however, no other faculty member or group of faculty members is a supervisor solely because the faculty member or group of faculty members participates in decisions with respect to courses, curriculum, personnel, or other matters of academic policy" (Ohio Senate Bill no. 133, quoted in Douglas 1984b). According to the Illinois statute, in order to be deemed a supervisor, a faculty member has to spend a "preponderance" of employment time on supervisory duties (Malin 1985).

10. The Carnegie Foundation conducted an extensive survey of the three unions' members in 1969 (see Ladd and Lipset 1973, 44–45, but more recent profiles have relied on much smaller samples (Muczyk, Hise, and Gannon 1975; Rhodes 1977), preventing any reliable generalization about the unions in recent years.

11. According to Jones (1985, 180–81) centralization and regulation were justified as:

"necessary to prevent service duplication; exercise quality control over degree programs, curricula, and advertising by institutions; control capital planning, construction, and institution-siting decisions; establish and maintain state and institutional master plans and planning processes; adjudicate disputes between segments and institutions; influence resource allocation decision making; influence employment practices, hiring decisions (for example, affirmative action), and the provision of specific services to selected clientele groups."

12. In the 1969 Carnegie Commission survey 60 percent of the respondents gave a "fair or poor" rating to their faculty senate or council.

13. Two studies produced results diverging somewhat from the above findings. Bergmann and Hills (1979) failed to identify any association between support for collective bargaining and, respectively, income, age, and academic rank. Kazlow and Giacquinta (1977) identified greater interest in unionization among tenured faculty members than among their junior colleagues, echoing the hypothesis of Kemerer and Baldridge (1975).

14. These percentages were computed from Grant and Snyder (1983, 103) and Plisko and Stern (n.d.). *Instructional staff* as used here includes "faculty members with the title of professor, associate professor, assistant professor, instructor, lecturer, assisting professor, adjunct professor, or interim professor (or its equivalent). Excluded are graduate students with titles such as graduate or teaching fellow who assist senior staff." Plisko and Stern (n.d., 110).

15. The National Center for Education Statistics estimates that part-time employment of instructional staff will decrease from 245,000 in 1981 to 220,000 in

1993 and that full-time faculty employment will decline from 452,000 to 415,000 (Plisko and Stern n.d., 110). Thus, part-time teachers will still constitute 35 percent of higher education faculties in 1993. This projection is not surprising; it is premised on the assumption that the recent percentage distribution will remain in effect (Frankel and Gerald 1982b, 28).

16. This concern by faculty unions could also, of course, be construed as an attempt to create an economic disincentive to hire part-time instructors. A passage from the AFT's "Statement on Part-Time Faculty Employment" similarly illustrates the balancing of interests (Levenstein 1980, 2):

> Many faculty frequently perceive part-timers as a threat—an attitude not without foundation—and resent their presence in the department; others may be concerned by the unjust disparity between their salaries and employment situation and those of exploited part-time faculty.

17. Data from three nationwide surveys of faculty members, conducted between 1975 and 1978, revealed that part-time faculty (relative to full-time faculty) had fewer academic credentials and less teaching experience; used fewer instructional media; had fewer out-of-class interactions with their students, colleagues, or administrators; read fewer journals; and had less influence over course content, textbook selection, and curriculum development. Extensive employment of part-timers may therefore threaten the quality of educational programs offered by colleges and universities (Friedlander 1980, 35). Nonetheless, because part-time faculty members work without direct supervision and are seldom evaluated, a more direct assessment of their impact on the educational "product" of schools is not possible. In fact, the indirect measures of their performance cited above may create a double standard. Tenure decisions for full-time faculty are based on their demonstrating academic excellence, with standards established through peer review, whereas part-time instructors often are simply reappointed, or not, by administrators, on the basis of performance that has to be only "adequate" (Leslie, Kellams, and Gunne 1982, 61).

18. *The Gourman Report* (first edition) used several measures of quality, among which were admissions standards, physical facilities, finances, research, and teaching quality (Gourman 1977, 3–4).

19. Aussieker and Garbarino's distribution of unionized schools simply mirrored that of the total population of schools (Gold 1974). According to one estimate, in 1968–69 there were 43 high-quality, 141 medium-quality, and 176 low-quality universities. The comparable numbers for four-year colleges were 110, 248, and 997, respectively (Finkelstein 1984). When Gold calculated the proportion of schools organized, the predicted unionism–school quality linkage was not apparent. She suggested that subsequent research on faculty unionism forgo reliance on general quality standards and use instead more readily quantifiable independent variables, such as enabling legislation and public versus private control.

20. Cameron (1982) evaluated the "effectiveness" of 41 four-year institutions, using a measure computed from administrator and faculty ratings of student educational satisfaction; student academic, career, and personal development; faculty quality; system openness; ability to acquire resources; and organizational health. The author was unable to determine whether unionism was a response or a contributor to organizational ineffectiveness.

21. Of the 76 elections held between July 1970 and March 1972, 63 did not involve faculty members. The disaggregated figures are as follows: clerical, 13 elections; food service, 3; crafts, 3; "industrial," 15; maintenance, 24; guards, 1 (computed from Schramm 1972). Furthermore, in only two of the 76 cases was one of the three major faculty unions actively involved in the nonteaching staff election. (The remarks in this section do not concern *nonteaching professionals,* some of whom are in bargaining units with faculty members.)

22. We are able to identify 66 public higher education *systems* that have faculty unions. Among those, 36 are community college districts; several mix two- and four-year schools (for example, the City University of New York, the State University of New York, and the University of Hawaii). Some statewide units allow for individual agreements and differences in particular contractual terms. The University of Alaska Community College system, for instance, allows salary minimums and maximums to differ among campuses. Nonetheless these "permissive" approaches appear to be an aberration, as contractual terms usually apply uniformly to all faculty members within a statewide system.

23. Hamermesh, Burton, and Weisbrod (1982); Johnson and Kasten (1983); Katz (1973); Marsh and Dillon (1980); Siegfried and White (1973); Tuckman, Gapinsky, and Hagemann (1977).

24. Only 16 of the 117 agreements addressed these pay differentials. Three limited the effective time periods for market pay adjustments; four indicated that a faculty member had to initiate the request for an adjustment; seven placed responsibility for initiating the adjustment in the administration or the academic department (Douglas 1985b).

25. American Federation of State, County and Municipal Employees v. State of Washington, 38 FEP 1353 (1985). See Fields (1986) for a discussion of the settlement.

26. 33 FEP 809 (1983).

27. 38 FEP 1360 (1985).

28. In 1972, 5.9 percent of all higher education institutions had tenure quotas; this percentage increased to 9.3 in 1974 (Chait and Ford 1982). Thirty percent of four-year institutions with tenure systems had the quotas in 1985 (Watkins 1985).

29. Fiscal retrenchment led to the termination of 103 faculty members at the State University of New York (SUNY) between September 1974 and September 1976; of those, 62 were tenured (34 later obtained positions elsewhere within SUNY). In Wisconsin 88 of the state's tenured faculty members were laid off as a result of the legislature's cuts in the personnel budget for 1973–74 and 1974–75; and 34 additional tenured faculty members were also subsequently laid off (Mortimer 1981, 154–55).

30. In a 1976 statement the AAUP defined *financial exigency* as "an imminent financial crisis which threatens the survival of the institution as a whole and which cannot be alleviated by less drastic means [than termination of appointments]" (Fellman 1984, 14). As explained in the following excerpt from the statement (quoted in Gray 1983, 39), inclusion of this standard in a collective bargaining agreement may enhance the job security of tenured employees:

> If your particular agreement includes a financial exigency provision and if it also incorporates the AAUP's 1976 Recommended Institutional Regulations (RIR) "survival" definition of financial exigency, then the courts probably will not allow termination of tenured faculty unless there is an imminent financial crisis threatening the

survival of the institution as a whole that cannot be alleviated by less drastic means. The court may indeed force the institution "as a whole" to face near bankruptcy before it will allow the termination of any tenured faculty member, regardless of the need for programmatic change.

In litigation involving the interpretation of faculty contracts that do not include the AAUP's standard, the courts have been reluctant to use the "survival" criterion in evaluating whether a financial exigency exists (Gray 1981).

31. Of the 117 faculty strikes that occurred between 1966 and 1983, 68 were called by the AFT; 24, by the NEA; and 23, by AAUP affiliates (Douglas 1983a).

32. The existence of dispute resolution mechanisms does not appear to provide an alternative explanation for infrequent strikes because faculty contracts specify neither conventional nor final-offer arbitration. Furthermore, the fact that unions in higher education are predominantly in the public sector (see table 8–3), where strikes for the most part are prohibited, also does not explain the strike rate, since other governmental employees—most notably, primary and secondary school teachers—have often engaged in work stoppages.

References

Abel, Emily. 1984. *Terminal Degrees: The Job Crisis in Higher Education.* New York: Praeger.

Academe. 1987. The Annual Report on the Economic Status of the Profession. 73 (March–April): 3–79.

Allen, Robert, and Timothy Keaveny. 1981. Correlates of University Faculty Interest in Unionization: A Replication and Extension. *Journal of Applied Psychology* 66 (October): 582–88.

Aussieker, Bill. 1985. The Changing Patterns of Faculty Strikes in Higher Education. *Journal of Collective Negotiations in the Public Sector* 14: 349–57.

Aussieker, Bill, and Joseph W. Garbarino. 1973. Measuring Faculty Unionism: Quantity and Quality. *Industrial Relations* 12 (May): 117–24.

Banner, James, Jr. 1984. The Schism in the American Professoriate That Could Jeopardize Academic Freedom. *Chronicle of Higher Education,* May 30, p. 72.

Begin, James. 1974. Faculty Governance and Collective Bargaining: An Early Appraisal. *Journal of Higher Education* 45 (November): 582–93.

———. 1979. Faculty Bargaining and Faculty Reward. In *Academic Rewards in Higher Education,* ed. Darrell Lewis and William Becker, 245–96, Cambridge, Mass.: Ballinger.

Begin, James, and Barbara Lee. 1985. Collective Bargaining in Higher Education: A Look Ahead. *Journal of the College and University Personnel Association* 36 (Summer/Fall): 6–14.

Benewitz, Maurice. 1975. Bargaining in Higher Education. In *Proceedings of New York University Twenty-Seventh Annual Conference on Labor,* ed. David Raff, 43–68. New York: Matthew Bender.

Bennett, James, and Manuel Johnson. 1979. *Demographic Trends in Higher Educa-*

tion: *Collective Bargaining and Forced Unionism?* Los Angeles: International Institute for Economic Research.

Bergmann, Thomas, and Frederick Hills. 1979. Departmental Affiliation as a Determinant of Professors' Attitudes Toward Collective Bargaining: A Case Study. *Journal of the College and University Personnel Association* 30 (Summer/Fall): 48–55.

Berkowitz, Maurice. 1981. Arbitration in Higher Education: Is Academic Arbitration *Sui Generis?* In *The Legal and Economic Status of Collective Bargaining in Higher Education, Proceedings, Ninth Annual Conference,* 61–66. New York: The National Center for the Study of Collective Bargaining in Higher Education and the Professions.

Bigoness, William. 1978. Correlates of Faculty Attitudes Toward Collective Bargaining. *Journal of Applied Psychology* 63 (April) 228–33.

Birnbaum, Robert. 1974. Unionization and Faculty Compensation. *Educational Record* 55 (Winter): 29–33.

———. 1976. Unionization and Faculty Compensation: Part II. *Educational Record* 57 (Spring): 116–18.

———. 1980. *Creative Academic Bargaining.* New York: Teachers College Press.

Bodner, Gerald. 1974. *The "No Agent" Vote at N.Y.U.: A Concise Legal History,* special report 9. Washington, D.C. Academic Collective Bargaining Information Service, August.

Bognanno, Mario, David Estenson, and Edward Suntrup. 1978. Union-Management Contracts in Higher Education. *Industrial Relations* 17 (May): 189–203.

Bornheimer, Deane. 1985. Conditions Influencing Faculty Voting in Collective Bargaining Elections. *Research in Higher Education* 11 (3): 291–305.

Bowen, Howard. 1980. *The Costs of Higher Education.* San Francisco: Jossey-Bass.

Boyd, William. 1972. Collective Bargaining in Academe: Causes and Consequences. In *Labor Relations in Higher Education,* 117–31. New York: Practicing Law Institute.

Brown, William, and Courtenay Stone. 1977. Academic Unions in Higher Education: Impacts on Faculty Salary, Compensation and Promotions. *Economic Inquiry* 15 (July): 385–96.

Broyles, Susan, and Rosa Fernandez. 1984. *Education Directory, Colleges and Universities, 1983–84.* Washington, D.C.: GPO, February.

Cameron, Kim. 1982. The Relationship Between Faculty Unionism and Organizational Effectiveness. *Academy of Management Journal* 25 (March): 6–24.

Carey, Sheridan. 1978. Reasons Why Faculty Members Accept or Reject Unions in Higher Education: The University of Massachusetts Experience. *Journal of Law and Education* 7 (January): 79–86.

Carnegie Council on Policy Studies in Higher Education. 1980. *Three Thousand Futures: The Next Twenty Years for Higher Education.* San Francisco: Jossey-Bass.

Carnegie Foundation for the Advancement of Teaching. 1973. *Governance of Higher Education.* New York: McGraw-Hill.

———. 1975. *More Than Survival: Prospects for Higher Education in a Period of Uncertainty.* San Francisco: Jossey-Bass.

———. 1982. *The Control of the Campus.* Washington, D.C.: Carnegie Foundation for the Advancement of Teaching.

————. 1985. The Faculty: Deeply Troubled. *Change* 17 (September/October): 31–34.

Carr, Robert, and Daniel Van Eyck. 1973. *Collective Bargaining Comes to the Campus.* Washington, D.C.: American Council on Education.

Chait, Richard. 1975. Faculty Unions and Academic Tenure: On a Collision Course. In *Collective Bargaining in Higher Education, Proceedings, Third Annual Conference,* ed. Thomas Mannix, 60–67. New York: National Center for the Study of Collective Bargaining in Higher Education, Baruch College, City University of New York, April.

Chait, Richard, and Andrew Ford. 1982. *Beyond Traditional Tenure.* San Francisco: Jossey-Bass.

Chandler, Margaret, and Daniel Julius. 1979. *Faculty vs. Administration: Rights and Issues in Academic Collective Bargaining.* New York: National Center for the Study of Collective Bargaining in Higher Education, Baruch College, City University of New York.

Cheit, Earl. 1971. *The New Depression in Higher Education,* A General Report for the Carnegie Commission on Higher Education and the Ford Foundation. New York: McGraw-Hill.

Chronicle of Higher Education. 1985. Who Faculty Members Are, and What They Think. December 18, pp. 25–28.

Clark, Burton. 1963. Faculty Organization and Authority. In *Governing Academic Organizations,* ed. Gary Riley and J. Baldridge, 64–78. (Reprinted from *The Study of Academic Administration* [Berkeley: Center for the Study of Higher Education, 1963]). Berkeley: McCutchan, 1977.

Coulson, Crocker. 1985. Labor Unrest in the Ivy League. *Arbitration Journal* (September): 53–62.

Douglas, Joel, 1983a. Faculty Work Stoppages in Higher Education: 1966–1983. *Newsletter* (National Center for the Study of Collective Bargaining in Higher Education and the Professions [NCSCBHEP]) 11 (December): 1–6.

————. 1983b Salary and Compensation Methodology in Academic Collective Bargaining. *Newsletter* (NCSCBHEP) 11 (January/February): 1–8.

————. 1984a New Bargaining Legislation—1983. *Newsletter* (NCSCBHEP) 12 (January/February): 4–8.

————. 1984b. "Yeshivawatch"—Year Five. *Newsletter* (NCSCBHEP) 12 (July/August): 1–10.

————. 1985a. An Analysis of the Arbitration Clause in Collective Bargaining Agreements in Higher Education. *Newsletter* (NCSCBHEP) 13 (March/April): 1–8.

————. 1985b. Market Process/Market Equity Provisions in Faculty Contracts. *Newsletter* (NCSCBHEP) 13 (September/October): 1–8.

Douglas, Joel, with Elizabeth Kotch. 1985. *Directory of Faculty Contracts and Bargaining Agents in Institutions of Higher Education,* vol. 11. New York: NCSCBHEP, January.

————. 1986. *Directory of Faculty Contracts and Bargaining Agents in Institutions of Higher Education,* vol. 12. New York: NCSCBHEP, January.

Fellman, David. 1984. The Association's Evolving Policy on Financial Exigency. *Academe* 70 (December): 678–92.

Fields, Cheryl. 1985. Appeals Court Overturns "Comparable" Pay Order for Washington State Employees. *Chronicle of Higher Education,* September 11, p. 19.

———. 1986. Accord Is Reached on Pay Disparities in Washington State. *Chronicle of Higher Education.* January 9, p. 19.

Finkelstein, Martin. 1984. *The American Academic Profession: A Synthesis of Social Scientific Inquiry Since World War II.* Columbus: Ohio State University Press.

Franke, Ann. 1984. Two Trends in Academic Collective Bargaining: A Faculty Representative's Perspective. *Journal of Law and Education* (October): 651–68.

Frankel, Martin, and Debra Gerald. 1982a. *Projections of Education Statistics to 1990–91,* Vol. 1: Analytical Report. Washington, D.C.: GPO.

———. 1982b. *Projections of Education Statistics to 1990–91,* Vol. 2: Methodological Report. Washington, D.C.: GPO.

Freeman, Richard B. 1978. *Should We Organize? Effects of Faculty Unionism on Academic Compensation,* National Bureau of Economic Research Working Paper no. 301. Cambridge, Mass.: NBER, November.

Friedlander, Jack. 1980. Instructional Practices of Part-Time Faculty. In *Using Part-Time Faculty Effectively,* ed. Michael Pasons, 27–36. San Francisco: Jossey-Bass.

Gallant, Jonathan A., and John W. Prothero. 1972. Weight-Watching at the University: The Consequences of Growth. *Science* 175 (January 28): 381–88.

Gappa, Judith. 1984. *Part-Time Faculty: Higher Education at a Crossroads,* ASHE/ERIC Higher Education Research Report no. 3. Washington, D.C.: Association for the Study of Higher Education.

Garbarino, Joseph W. 1975. *Faculty Bargaining.* New York: McGraw-Hill.

———. 1976. State Patterns of Faculty Bargaining. *Industrial Relations* 15 (May): 191–205.

Garbarino, Joseph W., and Bill Aussieker. 1974. Creeping Unionism Revisited. In *Proceedings of the Twenty-Sixth Annual Winter Meeting,* December 28–30, 1973, ed. Gerald Somers, 259–66. Madison, Wis.: Industrial Relations Research Association.

Garbarino, Joseph W., and John Lawler. 1978. Faculty Union Activity in Higher Education, 1977. *Industrial Relations* 17 (February): 117–18.

Gerry, Frank. 1978. Reflections on Faculty Unionization: Academic Implications. *Liberal Education* 64 (May): 171–81.

Gold, Lois. 1974. Measuring Faculty Unionism: Quantity and Quality. *Industrial Relations* 13 (October): 325–31.

Gomez-Mejia, Luis, and David Balkin. 1984. Faculty Satisfaction with Pay and Other Job Dimensions Under Union and Nonunion Conditions. *Academy of Management Journal* 27 (September): 591–602.

Gourman, Jack. 1977. *The Gourman Report,* 2d. ed. Los Angeles: National Education Standards.

Grant, W. Vance, and Thomas D. Snyder. 1983. *Digest of Educational Statistics, 1983–1984.* Washington, D.C.: GPO, December.

Gray, John. 1981. Legal Restraints on Faculty Cutbacks. In *Challenges of Retrenchment,* 171–93. San Francisco: Jossey-Bass.

———. 1983. Financial Exigency and Contract Law. In *Collective Bargaining in a*

Period of Retrenchment, Proceedings, Eleventh Annual Conference, ed. Joel Douglas, 36–44. New York: National Center for the Study of Collective Bargaining in Higher Education and the Professions, Baruch College, City University of New York, April.

Gress, James. 1976. Predicting Faculty Attitudes Toward Collective Bargaining. *Research in Higher Education* 4 (1976): 247–56.

Grossnickle, William, Rosina Lao, and Timothy Apple. 1980. Psychological Variables Related to Faculty Attitudes Toward Collective Bargaining. Paper presented at the Southeastern Psychological Association Convention, March.

Guthrie-Morse, Barbara, Larry Leslie, and Teh-Wei Hu. 1981. Assessing the Impact of Faculty Unions: The Financial Implications of Collective Bargaining. *Journal of Higher Education* 52 (May/June): 237–55.

Haak, Harold. 1985. Collective Bargaining in the Year 2000: A President's Perspective. *Journal of the College and University Personnel Association* 36 (Summer/Fall): 21–25.

Hammer, Tove Helland, and Michael Berman. 1981. The Role of Noneconomic Factors in Faculty Union Voting. *Journal of Applied Psychology* 66 (August): 415–21.

Hamermesh, Daniel, George Johnson, and Burton Weisbrod. 1982. Scholarship, Citations and Salaries: Economic Rewards in Economics. *Southern Economic Journal* 49 (October): 472–81.

Hankin, Joseph. 1979. Unit Determination: Basic Criteria in Federal and State Jurisdictions. In *Landmarks in Collective Bargaining in Higher Education,* ed. Aaron Levenstein, 91–100. New York: National Center for the Study of Collective Bargaining in Higher Education and the Professions, Baruch College, City University of New York, April.

Hansen, W. 1985. Salary Differences Across Disciplines. *Academe* 71 (July/August): 6–7.

Heller, Scott. 1985. Clerical Workers Gaining Attention Through Unions. *Chronicle of Higher Education,* January 23, pp. 1, 28.

Hollander, Ted, and Judith Turnbull. 1984. The Merits of Merit Pay: Where's the Merit in Merit? In *Structural Reform in Higher Education Collective Bargaining, Proceedings, Twelfth Annual Conference,* ed. Joel M. Douglas, 86–96. New York: National Center for the Study of Collective Bargaining in Higher Education and the Professions, Baruch College, April.

Jacobsen, Robert. 1985. New Carnegie Data Show Faculty Members Uneasy About the State of Academe and Their Own Careers. *Chronicle of Higher Education,* December 18, pp. 1 and 24.

Johnson, Marvin, and Katherine Kasten. 1983. Meritorious Work and Faculty Rewards: An Empirical Test of the Relationship. *Research in Higher Education* 19 (1): 49–71.

Johnstone, Ronald. 1981. *The Scope of Faculty Collective Bargaining.* Westport, Conn.: Greenwood Press.

Jones, L.R. 1985. *University Budgeting for Critical Mass and Competition.* New York: Praeger.

Kagan, Donald. 1985. The Strike at Yale: A Faculty Perspective in Support of the University Administration. *Newsletter* (National Center for the Study of Collective Bargaining in Higher Education and the Professions) 13 (July/August): 7–8.

Katz, David. 1973. Faculty Salaries, Promotions, and Productivity at a Large University. *American Economic Review* 63 (June): 469–77.

Kazlow, Carole, and Joseph Giacquinta. 1977. Tenure, Support of Collective Bargaining, and Unionism in Higher Education: Some Challenging Findings. *Research in Higher Education* 6: 45–63.

Keller, George. 1983. *Academic Strategy*. Baltimore: Johns Hopkins University Press.

Kemerer, Frank, and J. Victor Baldridge. 1975. *Unions on Campus*. San Francisco: Jossey-Bass.

———. 1981. Senates and Unions: Unexpected Peaceful Coexistence. *Journal of Higher Education* 52 (May/June): 256–64.

Kennedy, Ralph. 1974. NLRB and Faculty Bargaining Units: The Charting of an Uncharted Area. In *Collective Bargaining in Higher Education, Proceedings, Second Annual Conference,* ed. Thomas Mannix, 35–50. New York: National Center for the Study of Collective Bargaining in Higher Education and the Professions, Baruch College, April.

Kolodny, Jules. 1975. The American Federation of Teachers. In *Collective Bargaining in Higher Education,* ed. Judith Vladeck and Stephen Vladeck, 129–51. New York: Practicing Law Institute.

Ladd, Everett, Jr., and Seymour Lipset. 1973. *Professors, Unions, and American Higher Education*. Berkeley: California Commission on Higher Education.

Lee, Barbara. 1978. *Collective Bargaining in Four-Year Colleges: Impact on Institutional Practice,* AAHE-ERIC Higher Education Research Report no. 5. Washington, D.C.: American Association for Higher Education.

Leslie, David. 1975. *Conflict and Collective Bargaining,* AAHE-ERIC Higher Education Research Report no. 9. Washington, D.C.: American Association for Higher Education.

Leslie, David, Samuel Kellams, and G. Manny Gunne. 1982. *Part-Time Faculty in American Higher Education*. New York: Praeger.

Levenstein, Aaron, ed. 1980. Focus on the Part-Timer. *Newsletter* (National Center for the Study of Collective Bargaining in Higher Education and the Professions) 8 (December): 1–3.

Lindeman, Lynn. 1973. The Five Most Cited Reasons for Faculty Unionization. *Intellect* 102 (November): 85–88.

Lorimer, Linda. 1985. The Strike at Yale: Administration Perspective. *Newsletter* (National Center for the Study of Collective Bargaining in Higher Education and the Professions) 13 (July/August): 1–3.

Malin, Martin. 1985. Implementing the Illinois Educational Labor Relations Act. *Chicago Kent Law Review* 61 (1): 101–47.

Marsh, Herbert, and Kristine Dillon. 1980. Academic Productivity and Faculty Supplemental Income. *Journal of Higher Education* 51 (September/October): 546–55.

Marshall, Joan. 1979. The Effects of Collective Bargaining on Faculty Salaries in Higher Education. *Journal of Higher Education* 50 (May/June): 310–22.

Meisinger, Richard, and Leroy Dubeck. 1984. *College and University Budgeting*. Washington, D.C.: National Association of College and University Business Officers.

Mingle, James. 1981. Challenges of Retrenchment. In *Challenges of Retrenchment,* ed. James Mingle, 1–15. San Francisco: Jossey-Bass.

Morgan, David, and Richard Kearney. 1977. Collective Bargaining and Faculty Compensation: A Comparative Analysis. *Sociology of Education* 50 (January): 28–39.

Mortimer, Kenneth. 1981. Procedures and Criteria for Faculty Retrenchment. In *Challenges of Retrenchment,* ed. James Mingle, 153–70. San Francisco: Jossey-Bass.

Mortimer, Kenneth, Mark Johnson, and David Weiss. 1975. "No Representative" Victories in Faculty Collective Bargaining Elections. *Journal of the College and University Personnel Association* 26 (January/February): 34–47.

Mortimer, Kenneth, and T.R. McConnell. 1978. *Sharing Authority Effectively.* San Francisco: Jossey-Bass.

Muczyk, Jan, Richard Hise, and Martin Gannon. 1975. Faculty Attitudes and the Election of a Bargaining Agent in the Pennsylvania State College System—II. *Journal of Collective Negotiations in the Public Sector* 4 (2): 175–89.

National Education Association. 1985. *NEA Handbook, 1985–86.* Washington, D.C.: National Education Association.

Odewahn, Charles, and Allan Spritzer. 1976. Administrators' Attitudes Toward Faculty Unionism. *Industrial Relations* 15 (May): 206–15.

Plisko, Valena, and Joyce Stern. N.d. *The Condition of Education, 1985 Edition.* Washington, D.C.: GPO.

Rhodes, A. Louis. 1977. Some Characteristics of Faculty Union Memberships and Their Implications. *Social Problems* 24 (April): 463–68.

Schuster, Jack, and Howard Bowen. 1985. The Faculty at Risk. *Change* 17 (September/October): 13–21.

Schramm, Carl. 1972. Effects of NLRB Jurisdictional Change on Union Organizing in Private Colleges and Universities. *Labor Law Journal* 23 (September): 572–83.

Scott, Barbara. 1983. *Crisis Management in American Higher Education.* New York: Praeger.

Siegfried, John, and Kenneth White. 1973. Financial Rewards to Research and Teaching: A Case Study of Academic Economists. *American Economic Review* 63 (May): 309–15.

Stadtman, Verne. 1980. *Academic Adaptations.* San Francisco: Jossey-Bass.

Tuckman, Howard. 1976. *Publication, Teaching, and the Academic Reward Structure.* Lexington, Mass.: Lexington Books.

U.S. Congress, House, Committee on Education and Labor, Subcommittee on Labor-Management Relations. 1985. *Hearing on Collective Bargaining at Private Educational Institutions and in the Performing Arts,* 98th Cong., 2d sess., September 18, 1984. Washington, D.C.: GPO.

Watkins, Beverly. 1982. AAUP as a Union: The Tensions Endure. *Chronicle of Higher Education* July 7, pp. 1, 8.

———. 1985. Colleges Urged to Re-Examine Hiring Practices for Tenure-Track Positions and Part-Time Jobs. *Chronicle of Higher Education,* December 4, pp. 1, 28.

Wollett, Donald. 1975. Self-Governance and Collective Bargaining for Higher Education Faculty: Can the Two Systems Co-Exist? In *Collective Bargaining in Higher Education: The Developing Law,* 33–51. New York: Practicing Law Institute.

Zirkel, Perry. 1981. In Search of the Meaning of *Yeshiva, Research Currents* (AAHE-ERIC/Higher Education (April): 7–10.

9
Police

John Thomas Delaney
Peter Feuille

I n 1919 the Boston police conducted a famous but abortive strike that had two lasting effects: It helped propel Massachusetts Governor Calvin Coolidge into the White House; and it sparked among the public a strong backlash against police unionism that was to persist for nearly 50 years. Not until the late 1960s did police officers embrace unions on a large scale, and even then the ghost of the Boston strike was regularly invoked to condemn police unionism. But by the 1970s police officers had become one of the most highly unionized of all public sector occupations. In this chapter we will analyze the structure, process, and outcomes of police labor relations in the United States. First, though, we will analyze the environment within which the police labor relations system operates, beginning with a discussion of how the outputs of the police industry are measured.[1] As we will see, the structure, process, and outcomes of police bargaining are directly influenced by the characteristics of the external environment and by the nature of the police industry itself.

The Bargaining Environment

Police Outputs

In most private sector industries outputs are clear: automobiles, processed meats, tires, tractors, financial services, and so on. In many public agencies — such as schools, research institutes, sanitation, and defense — outputs are difficult to measure, although there is general agreement on what the outputs are. The local police represent an unusual public agency, however, because there is no clear consensus within the industry as to what outputs or products the industry should or does produce.[2]

We are grateful to Nancy Bartter and Nancy Fisher for helpful research assistance and to Hervey Juris and David Lewin for their valuable comments on this chapter.

We may say that the police produce (or attempt to produce) safety. But *safety* is such a general and all-inclusive term that it does not usefully describe police outputs; that is, saying that the police try to maximize safety is like saying that consumers try to maximize utility: both statements may be true but neither tells us how those objectives are achieved. A more useful approach is to look at what police officers actually do at work. If we put aside such administrative and housekeeping tasks as roll-call briefings, report writing and filing, and equipment maintenance, we can classify police activity into three basic categories: law enforcement, order maintenance, and social service. Law enforcement work comprises response to calls of crimes in progress, investigation of crimes, surveillance of suspects, arrests, and processing of arrestees (officers often refer to these kinds of activities as "real police work" to distinguish them from other duties). Work to maintain public order includes such activities as crowd control at public gatherings, traffic control, intervention in family or neighborhood disturbances, and patrolling to display a police presence. Finally, police engage in a wide variety of social services to help persons in need of assistance, such as alcoholics, the mentally ill, lost motorists, lost children, evicted tenants, and persons needing medical care. Although much of this last form of work has little direct connection with the law enforcement responsibilities of police officers, they perform these functions because theirs is one of the very few governmental agencies that is accessible to the average citizen 24 hours a day, seven days a week.

As these descriptions imply, there are no clear dividing lines between these categories, and some tasks could be classified in more than one category; for example, intervening in a violent fight between a husband and a wife may involve enforcing the assault and battery laws, keeping order in the neighborhood, and providing family counseling. Although some law enforcement tasks (such as arresting a notorious fugitive after a chase) are glamorous, research has shown that only a small portion of the average patrol officer's time (usually less than one-fifth) is spent on law enforcement duties. Instead, the average police officer's workday seldom brings him or her in contact with crime and criminals (Reiss 1971, 63–120). In fact, the patrol officer's typical tour of duty is marked by a considerable amount of monotonous patrolling punctuated by various kinds of encounters with citizens, many of which encounters are messy or unpleasant and a few of which are dangerous. Moreover, the police succeed in solving only a fraction of the crimes reported to them (in 1978 only about one-fifth of the serious crimes reported were cleared by arrests; U.S. Department of Justice 1981, 367); and a majority of victimization incidents are never even reported to the police, so that these incidents never become official "crimes" (U.S. Department of Justice 1981, 228). The police are therefore limited in their ability to deal with crimes, and they are extremely limited in their ability to prevent crimes from occurring. Nonetheless, these prosaic workplace statistics have done little to detract from the popular image of the police as "crime fighters."

As in many service industries, it is difficult to distinguish between police industry outputs and the work done by police industry employees. More specifically, it is not always clear what police inputs are (hours worked, patrol car miles driven, responses to calls for assistance?) or what police outputs are (crimes cleared by arrest, traffic citations issued, citizen stops made?). For example, are reported crimes an input (that is, a measure of the demand for police) or an output (that is, a measure of police effectiveness)? In fact, in the absence of a production function with a maximization objective, the police regularly rely on quantitative measures that include both inputs and outputs to justify their performance (and budget requests).

There are several other characteristics of police work that are pertinent to an understanding of outputs in this industry. First, the police have a license to use coercive force against all other citizens, and it is this societally sanctioned capacity to use even deadly force that gives police their special status in the community and underlies all their interactions with other citizens (Bittner 1970). Second, the police have an unusually large amount of discretion to decide how they will perform their duties. They have that discretion because of the reactive, contingent, and unsupervised nature of most police work: The police generally react to requests for assistance rather than initiating contacts; the situations they encounter involve considerable uncertainty; and they perform their work away from the eyes of a supervisor. Their discretion is most apparent in their frequent underenforcement of the law, as any errant motorist who has received an oral warning instead of a written citation can attest.

Third, these two work characteristics—license to use coercive force and substantial discretion—have defined the special organizational features of police departments: They are strictly governed by myriad regulations that circumscribe the behavior of officers; they rely heavily on the threat of punishment to induce appropriate work behavior (McNamara [1967] termed police departments "punishment-centered bureaucracies"); and they are organized in a military fashion, with a "command" staff of well-defined ranks and an emphasis on obedience and hierarchical authority. These organizational features tend to make rank-and-file employees wary, not only of their supervisors, but also of the larger society. The socially divisive nature of much police work fosters an "us versus them" mentality among police officers that makes the police bureaucracy as a whole suspicious of outsiders and resistant to change. And these features will also help explain some of police officers' reasons for joining the unions.

In short, the police serve in an industry that emphasizes its law enforcement outputs but in fact devotes most of its resources to order maintenance and social service functions. Nonetheless, the distinctions among these multiple outputs are seldom clear, and often there are strong disagreements among the police and other segments of society over how these outputs should be provided.

Police Product Markets

In the United States the police industry is part of the system of local government. The most obvious characteristic of the industry, then, is its extreme decentralization. In 1978 there were about 20,000 state and local law enforcement agencies nationwide (U.S. Department of Justice 1981, 3, 53), and about two-thirds of these were municipal police departments. The large number of employers in the industry does not, however, as in the private sector, lead to product market competition. In fact, the second most obvious characteristic of the industry is the absence of product market competition. Each local police agency has an almost complete product market monopoly that is defined both geographically (by, for example, the city limits or the county line) and functionally (that is, by the type of offense). This monopoly is reinforced by the absence of capital mobility in this industry: Local governments cannot relocate outside of their districts; and the police function is not a candidate for contracting out to the private sector. Coupled with this official monopoly, though, is a keen unofficial competition for status among police agencies; as they compete with one another for greater law enforcement prestige, police departments bolster their demands for larger budgets.

As an agency of city government, municipal police departments are controlled by a mixture of elected and appointed city officials: the mayor, city council, city manager, city budget director, police chief, city civil service commission, city police and fire commission, and so on. City hall usually exerts year-to-year financial control over the police department, and the annual police budget is adopted on an incremental basis (that is, one year's police budget is an incremental adjustment over the previous year's). Funds for police operations come from the city's general revenues, and police outputs are provided on an unpriced basis (although many cities seem to view the officers assigned to traffic and parking control duties primarily as revenue collectors rather than as law enforcement personnel). Day-to-day operational control over the department rests with the police chief and the command staff.

Thus, U.S. police departments operate under local control. Although there may be some state regulation (of such matters as pension rights, civil service rules, crime definitions, and crime reporting), each city or county is free to provide whatever mix of police services its citizens want. And although police agencies share a great deal of information among themselves, each agency jealously guards its autonomy. As Wilson (1968) has shown, police agencies use their autonomy to offer a different mix of services in different localities. Research on police service techniques may be funded by federal agencies (usually in the Department of Justice) and information about policing innovations may be widely disseminated, but local police agencies are nonetheless under little competitive product market pressure to modify the delivery of their police services in response to developments in other jurisdictions.

Together, the lack of direct product market competition, the lack of any attainable output maximization objective, and the control by local government officials all mean that many decisions regarding police service delivery are made on a political basis (in the nonpejorative sense of that term). In any community there will be divergent views about how police services should be delivered. How many police officers should we have? Should parking ordinances be vigorously enforced in commercial areas? Should the department use two-officer patrols on certain shifts? Should black or Hispanic officers be assigned to work primarily in the black or Hispanic sections of the city? Under what circumstances may the police use deadly force? What weapons should officers carry? Should certain areas be patrolled by officers on walking beats? Should a board of civilians review incidents of questionable police behavior? It is rare indeed that there is one and only one answer to any of these questions of service delivery, and the decision is ultimately made or approved by elected officials. As a result, the decision is often made in response to community political pressure of one sort or another, including pressure brought to bear by the police themselves, usually through their union.

Police Labor Markets

The diversity represented in the thousands of U.S. police departments makes any labor market generalization hazardous. What follows is a portrayal of the central tendencies of external and internal police labor markets.

The external police labor market is characterized by local recruiting; state, regional, and national recruiting efforts are rare. Most departments require only a valid driver's license and a high school education, though many cities give preference to applicants with some college education. Two decades ago police officers were men recruited primarily from blue-collar backgrounds and occupations. This statement is less true today because of the recent influx of female officers and because of the relatively higher salaries officers now command (most medium-size and large cities pay their officers between $20,000 and $35,000 per year; Hoetmer 1985). In most cities these days there is a queue, and sometimes a long one, of applicants seeking police jobs.

Despite the minimal entry requirements, in most departments the selection process is a lengthy one in which the successful applicant must pass a battery of written, physical, and psychological tests. The tests are used to weed out applicants who appear ill-suited to the mental, physical, and psychological stresses of police work, but, again, the agencies rarely require a specified set of skills.

Once the successful applicant has joined the internal labor market, he or she is sent to the police academy for a formal training program, which lasts from 10 to 26 weeks in most departments. The training covers the laws to enforce, arrest procedures, domestic dispute intervention, report writing, firearms use, hand-to-hand fighting, and driving techniques, among other things. The formal program is complemented by on-the-job training through assignment to patrol duty with veteran officers (not surprisingly, Van Maanen [1975] reports that the "street smarts" the veterans convey to the rookies are often at odds with the formal training lessons at the academy). In most departments the probationary period for rookies is one year, and during that time many new officers quit or are dismissed.

The large majority of officers are assigned to the patrol division (which includes traffic control in departments without separate traffic divisions); the balance are assigned to detective work and administrative work. Most new officers must endure the rigors of night shift and weekend work, and in those departments that assign shifts based on seniority many years will elapse before the rookie can bid onto the day shift.

Police departments, like the armed forces, are stratified by rank. A medium-size department usually has the ranks of patrol officer, sergeant, lieutenant, captain, deputy chief, and chief.[3] Up through captain, these "superior officer" ranks are filled by civil service promotions; ranks beyond captain are usually filled at the discretion of the police chief or local government officials. Promotions are made based on exam scores, seniority, performance evaluations, and managerial preference (Shimberg and diGrazia 1974). Except at the level of chief, all promotions are from within; there is no lateral entry in the police industry. In fact, the personnel eligible for promotion to any rank are most often those at the next lower rank, and so the labor market competition for vacant superior officer jobs is restricted to a small group. Management training for personnel in the superior officer ranks is usually only modest.

As noted earlier, to elicit proper performance police bureaucracies rely on punishment or the threat of punishment for errant behavior rather than on rewards for good behavior. As a result, police officers are quick to avoid blame when something bad happens ("running for cover" is a well-recognized response in most departments). Another result of the reliance on punishment is the ubiquitous police disciplinary process. The administration of discipline is a much more complex affair in police departments (union or nonunion) than in almost any other type of organization. Today most departments have internal affairs units (or officers with those responsibilities) to investigate charges against officers; elaborate rules (often collectively bargained with the union) regarding the interrogation of officers under suspicion; formal disciplinary proceedings (almost always involving a formal—and sometimes quite legalistic—hearing) against officers charged with misconduct; and appeal rights for officers found guilty in those proceedings. Disciplinary actions range from a letter of reprimand to discharge (or resignation in lieu of discharge). A prime day-to-day objective of most officers is to avoid becoming ensnared in the police disciplinary process.

Police officer performance is monitored in two ways. The first is by conducting periodic (annual or semiannual) performance appraisals, and the importance attached to those appraisals varies substantially across departments (as does the usefulness of the appraisals). The second and more important method is by calculating daily "activity" indicators, such as the number of arrests made, tickets issued, or calls answered. Because police officers cannot be directly supervised as they work, police management regularly imposes activity standards on nonsupervisory officers. For instance, several years ago in one large midwestern city officers assigned to traffic duty were expected to issue ten tickets per eight-hour shift, and regular patrol officers were expected to write one ticket per shift. In a small midwestern city in another state police detectives in 1986 were expected to make four arrests each week. No police agency ever admits (at least publicly) that it imposes quotas like these on its officers, but all agencies have written or unwritten "norms," "targets," "standards," or "benchmarks" that officers are expected to meet. Officers who deviate from the standards for any significant length of time will incur the disfavor of their superiors. These output norms serve as very useful indicators of activity for police agencies under pressure to "do something" about maintaining law and order; and to record the necessary data, departments produce reams of performance statistics that are also used to help justify police budget requests.

This analysis shows that police product and labor markets are extremely decentralized and local in nature. Police outputs are delivered locally, and police labor inputs work within the strict boundaries of the municipality. Although the police industry should be considered national in scope, it is divided into thousands of noncompeting units delivering local services. As we will see, the structure and practice of police labor relations reflect this localized character of the police industry.

The Economic Environment

From the end of World War II through 1980 local government was a growth industry in terms of both employment and expenditures, and policing was no exception. For instance, in 1972 local governments in the United States employed 411,361 persons on a full-time basis in "police protection" (this figure includes both sworn and civilian police employees but mostly the former), and they spent a total of $5.1 billion providing police services in that year. By 1983 full-time police employment had increased to 514,000 (a 25 percent increase over 1972), and expenditures had grown to $15.3 billion (these are nominal rather than real dollar figures) (U.S. Department of Commerce 1985).

These data indicate that the size of the police industry has grown faster than the general population (by comparison, the nation experienced a 12 percent increase in population between 1972 and 1983). Nevertheless, these national statistics mask considerable state-by-state and city-by-city variation. Census figures show, for example, that Michigan local governments employed 17,220 full-time police protection employees in 1972 and 18,034 such employees in 1982 (or only 4.7 percent more), whereas Texas local governments employed 19,747 such employees in 1972 and 31,173 in 1982 (or 57.9 percent more) (U.S. Department of Commerce 1985). If those two states accurately represent, respectively, the heavily unionized Frost Belt and the lightly unionized Sun Belt, these figures suggest that the lion's share of the growth in policing has taken place in the rapidly expanding population centers of the South and not in the comparatively stable or dwindling centers of the North. And among all local governments in 1982, 52 percent of full-time police protection employees were unionized; but in some southern and western states very few police officers were unionized, while in some northern states more than 80 percent of the local police were organized (U.S. Department of Commerce 1985).

Much of the reason for increasing expenditures on police protection has been the relative increase in police salaries during the postwar years (that is, police pay relative to the pay of other workers). Table 9–1 presents pay index data comparing the increase in the average weekly pay of private, nonfarm,

Table 9–1
A Comparison of the Indexed Pay Levels of Police and Private Sector Employees, 1950–78

Year	Index of Average Weekly Pay for Private, Nonagricultural, Nonsupervisory Employees (1967 = 100)	Index of Annual Maximum Salary of Police Officers in Cities of 100,000 or More (1967 = 100)
1950	52	45
1955	66	58
1960	79	72
1965	94	89
1970	118	128
1975	161	180
1978	200	215
1950–78	A 284% increase	A 378% increase

Sources: Private sector pay information is from U.S. Department of Labor (1985, 204). Police pay information is from U.S. Department of Labor (1980, 301).

nonsupervisory employees with the increase in average annual salary maximums of police officers in large cities during the years 1950–78 (note that the data in the table are index values, not actual dollar amounts). Over that period police pay increased at a faster rate than did the pay of rank-and-file employees in the private sector, and the largest disparity was during the 1965–70 period, during which time police pay increased 44 percent, while private pay increased 26 percent. The late 1960s were the years when "law and order" became a salient issue in political campaigns as voters grew concerned with rising crime rates and racial and student unrest; and the figures in table 9–1 indicate that the police benefited economically as a result. In addition, those were also the years when large numbers of police officers began to unionize, and police collective bargaining may have played a role in the relative surge of police pay in the late 1960s (as we will discuss in more detail later). Nonetheless, this upsurge came to a halt after that; during the years 1975–78 the pay of private sector employees increased faster than police pay.

In private industry technological innovation enables a smaller number of employees to produce a greater volume of output. In policing, labor-saving productivity improvements have been almost nonexistent. To be sure, there have been continual innovations in weaponry, protective clothing, communications devices and techniques, and police administration, including computer analyses of crime patterns and patrol beats. But those innovations have not been the labor-saving kind seen in the private sector, for no one has invented gadgetry to replace the cop on the beat or the detective investigating crimes. The only certain way cities can save police labor is by reducing police services (by, for example, assigning one officer instead of two to a patrol car, reducing the number of patrol beats in a sector of the city, increasing the caseload of each detective, or eliminating less essential services, such as minor traffic accident reports).

Police administrators have, however, tried to make more effective use of their available sworn officers by "civilianizing" many police department tasks. For instance, there is no reason why fingerprinting, dispatching, laboratory, crime analysis, parking control, clerical, and custodial duties must be performed by a gun-carrying sworn police officer with arrest powers. During the past 15 or so years many police departments have therefore placed civilian employees in these kinds of positions—at times over police union opposition (Juris and Feuille 1973, 125–50)—either because civilian wages are lower than those of sworn officers in many of these jobs or because specially trained civilians have greater expertise to handle these jobs. The displaced sworn officers have then been placed in the patrol, detective, or traffic positions that require police training and expertise. For instance, International City Management Association data for cities with populations over 25,000 show that an average of 13 percent of all police department positions were filled by civilians in 1971, whereas an average of 19 percent of those positions were so staffed in 1981 (Delaney, Feuille, and Hendricks 1986, 106). Even so, however, the increase in total police employment in recent years probably balances the civilianization of departments, enhancing their productivity but not necessarily reducing the demand for sworn officers.

In sum, the police industry in this country has been characterized by steady growth for many years. There have been no technological innovations, no introduction of competing products, and no government deregulation of police product or labor markets to cause any sudden shift in the demand for or supply of police services. There has, however, been considerable variation in police employment and expenditure patterns around the country, with the result that the economic environment for collective bargaining has been buoyant in some localities and stringent in others. Because of the extreme unevenness in local economies around the nation, this variation is likely to continue.

The Legal Environment

The same type of variation in the economic environment also exists in the legal environment within which police bargaining occurs. Some states have passed legislation strongly encouraging and protecting police collective bargaining, whereas others have no bargaining legislation of any kind and a few have prohibited all public employers from engaging in collective bargaining.

The legal environment for police collective bargaining in each state is summarized in table 9–2, which details the police bargaining legislation in effect in 1985; the year the first bargaining law covering police was enacted by the state; and the year any arbitration law covering police was enacted by the state. For purposes of comparison the table is divided into two parts: one listing the states with some bargaining legislation; and the other, those with none. It is important to keep in mind that the information displayed here refers only to bargaining and arbitration laws that apply to police and not necessarily to other occupational groups; therefore, a table applicable only to teachers or firefighters would be somewhat different (see, for example, Freeman 1986, 47).

Table 9–2 shows that by 1985, 25 states and the District of Columbia had duty-to-bargain laws and three states had meet-and-confer laws (a weaker form of the duty to bargain) covering the police. Those laws give police unions the statutory right to be recognized as the representative of police officers in a specified bargaining unit and to bargain collectively on behalf of the members of the bargaining unit. The scope of bargaining (the subject matter of negotiations) varies, however, as do the impasse procedures and the enforcement mechanisms prescribed in each state's law. Consequently, the strength of the statutory protection of police bargaining is not uniform across states. Further, although most of the police bargaining and arbitration laws have been on the books for many years (as shown in the second and third columns of table 9–2a) there is little likelihood that greater statutory uniformity will emerge in the foreseeable future. As of this writing, only two states, Ohio and Illinois, have passed a police bargaining or arbitration law in the 1980s, and there is no evidence to suggest that any new laws are in the offing.

As indicated in the fourth and fifth columns of table 9–2a, by 1981 the percentage of cities with populations over 25,000 that practiced police collective bargaining (measured by the presence of a written police contract) was much higher in most states than the percentage ten years earlier. Among all those large cities, 332 of 944 (or 35.2 percent) bargained with police unions in 1971, whereas 703 of 1,015 cities (or 69.3 percent) bargained with police unions in 1981 (Feuille, Hendricks, and Delaney 1983, 16). Because this growth in police bargaining happened during the period in which police bargaining rights were being statutorily established, the results in the table imply that those bargaining laws contributed to the growth of police bargaining. This implication has been confirmed in a multivariate analysis by Ichniowski (1986, 26), who found that the passage of a police bargaining law led to a great deal of police bargaining. He also found that most states with no bargaining legislation for police experienced little police bargaining.

Legislation effecting compulsory interest arbitration among police also has contributed to the growth of police unions. Those arbitration laws mandate that impasses in negotiations between cities and police unions be resolved by a binding award issued by a neutral third party. To be eligible to use the arbitration procedure mandated, however, police officers have to be unionized and engaged in a collective bargaining relationship with city hall. In other words, the presence of a police arbitration statute creates an incentive to unionize over and above the incentive created by bargaining legislation alone. This incentive is borne out in the results from the survey on which the table 9–2 results are based: In 1981, 382 of the 388 cities located in arbitration states (or 98.5 percent) bargained with police, while only 321 of the 627 cities located in nonarbitration states (or 51.2 percent) did so (Feuille, Hendricks, and Delaney 1983). These results imply that the passage of a police arbitration law leads to growth in police unionization over and above the growth spurred by passage of a police bargaining law. In fact, in a multivariate analysis Ichniowski (1986) found that arbitration laws were more predictive of growth in police collective bargaining than were bargaining laws (though the difference was not large).

The data in table 9–2, and other data (U.S. Department of Labor, LMSA 1981), suggest that the legal environment for police bargaining in different states can be categorized as falling into one of four climates: strongly favorable, moderately favorable, moderately unfavorable, and strongly unfavorable. A strongly favorable climate is one in which the state has passed laws both protecting bargaining and requiring interest arbitration (examples being

Table 9–2
An Overview of Police Collective Bargaining and Arbitration Legislation

a. States Having Legislated Bargaining Rights by 1985

State	Law[a]	Year First Bargaining Law Enacted	Year Arbitration Law Enacted	Percentage of Cities (Pop. 25,000+) Bargaining in:[b] 1971	1981
Alaska	DTB	1972	1972	33.3%[c]	66.7%[c]
California	MC	1961	—	58.7	96.4
Connecticut	DTB	1965	1975	88.9	100.0
Delaware	DTB	1965	—	66.7[c]	100.0[c]
District of Columbia	DTB	1970	1980	0[c]	100.0[c]
Florida	DTB	1974	—	0	69.8
Hawaii	DTB	1970	—	0[c]	100.0[c]
Illinois	DTB	1985	1985	24.4	58.2
Iowa	DTB	1974	1974	0	100.0
Kansas	MC	1971	—	0	40.0
Maine	DTB	1969	1974[d]	100.0[c]	100.0[c]
Massachusetts	DTB	1965	1974–81[e]	68.3	100.0
Michigan	DTB	1965	1969	79.5	97.6
Minnesota	DTB	1971	1973	33.3	100.0
Montana	DTB	1973	—	20.0	100.0
Nebraska	DTB	1968	1968	20.0	80.0
Nevada	DTB	1969	—	20.0	80.0
New Hampshire	DTB	1975	—	0[c]	66.7[c]
New Jersey	DTB	1968	1977	53.7	100.0
New York	DTB	1967	1974	82.4	94.7
Ohio	DTB	1984	1984	24.5	68.0
Oklahoma	MC	1971	—	0	73.3
Oregon	DTB	1971	1973	42.9	100.0
Pennsylvania	DTB	1968	1968	89.7	100.0
Rhode Island	DTB	1968	1970	77.8	100.0
South Dakota	DTB	1969	—	0[c]	100.0[c]
Vermont	DTB	1973	—	100.0[c]	100.0[c]
Washington	DTB	1967	1973	55.6	94.4
Wisconsin	DTB	1959	1972	85.7	100.0

b. States with No Legislated Bargaining Rights as of 1985

State	Percentage of Cities (pop. 25,000+) Bargaining in:[b] 1971	1981	State	Percentage of Cities (pop. 25,000+) Bargaining in:[b] 1971	1981
Alabama	0	12.5%	Missouri	0	11.8%
Arizona	0	25.0	New Mexico	14.3	25.0
Arkansas	0	25.0	North Carolina	0	0
Colorado	6.3	25.0	North Dakota	0[c]	0[c]

Table 9–2 continued

Georgia	0	0	South Carolina	0	0
Idaho	0	40.0	Tennessee	9.1	18.2
Indiana[f]	14.0	52.4	Texas[f]	0	14.8
Kentucky[f]	0	22.2	Utah	0	16.7
Louisiana	0	18.2	Virginia	0	0
Maryland[f]	16.7	33.3	West Virginia	14.3	28.6
Mississippi	0	14.3	Wyoming	33.3[c]	33.3[c]

Sources: Information on bargaining and arbitration laws was obtained from the state laws as reported in Bureau of National Affairs (n.d.). City bargaining data were calculated from a survey conducted by the authors in 1981.

[a]DTB = duty to bargain law; MC = meet and confer law; and a dash = no statewide arbitration law.

[b]The percentages in these two columns are based on cities whose bargaining status we were able to identify (which included more than 90 percent of all cities).

[c]These percentages were calculated from data on fewer than five cities in the state.

[d]The Maine arbitration law is binding only for nonwage bargaining subjects.

[e]The Massachusetts arbitration law was repealed indirectly when Proposition 2 1/2, a property tax limitation referendum, was passed in November 1980.

[f]Indiana passed a collective bargaining law in 1975 that was declared unconstitutional by the state supreme court in 1977. Kentucky, Maryland, and Texas have enacted collective bargaining laws that are restricted to specific communities or require citizen approval in a referendum election.

Illinois, New York, and Ohio). In these states police unions have a legally protected right to bargain and a legally protected mechanism to seek bargaining outcomes favorable to the union. (Later in this chapter we will show that arbitration seems to favor union interests more than management interests.) A moderately favorable climate is one that grants police unions a legally protected right to bargain (including "meet and confer" states) but does not require police arbitration (as in California, Delaware, and Florida). In these states police have no statutory right to insist on arbitration as a means of resolving negotiating impasses.

In contrast, a moderately unfavorable legal climate neither protects bargaining nor mandates arbitration but does allow police bargaining to occur (either by common law, referendum, or an attorney general's opinion). This "bargaining permitted" category includes such states as Indiana, Kentucky, and Louisiana, and in some of these states bargaining is limited to those cities that have adopted their own local bargaining procedures. Finally, the strongly unfavorable category is limited to those few states that expressly prohibit police collective bargaining (Georgia, North Carolina, and Virginia). In these states police officers have only an informal voice in determining their terms of employment.

In short, the legal environment for police bargaining varies substantially from state to state. Not surprisingly, the data show that states with favorable legal climates for police bargaining also have a great deal of police bargaining. Indeed, as shown in table 9–2a, many of these states have police bargaining in all of their large cities. In contrast, states with an unfavorable legal environment for bargaining tend to have only a modest amount of police bargaining, and the relatively few bargaining relationships that do exist in those states tend to be concentrated among the larger cities. As noted earlier, we see nothing on the horizon to indicate that this variation in legal environments will change in the foreseeable future.

Finally, it is important to mention that, to our knowledge, no state has granted police officers a legal right to strike. In the years since 1970 ten states (Alaska, Hawaii, Illinois, Minnesota, Montana, Ohio, Oregon, Pennsylvania, Vermont, and Wisconsin) have granted the statutory right to strike to some groups of public employees, and in 1985 a California court decision extended that right to most of its public employees. But, to date, no state has extended strike rights to police. Because most communities dread the consequences for public safety of any police strike, it would seem that any protection of police officers' right to strike will be a long time in coming. As we will see in a later section of this chapter, however, this state of affairs has not prevented a number of police unions from striking.

The Bargaining Structure and the Parties

Bargaining Structure

As amply illustrated in the preceding section, police bargaining is extremely decentralized. This decentralization is mirrored in the shape of police bargaining units. Membership in a police union is almost always limited to police department personnel; that is, it is extremely rare for any other city employees to be members of a police union. Moreover, the ranks of police unions are filled by sworn police officers; civilian employees in the police department, if they are unionized, are usually members of a bargaining unit separate from the sworn officers' unit (though there are some exceptions to this rule for groups such as dispatchers). In some cities the unit includes patrol officers only (rank-and-file officers); more commonly the unit includes one or more levels of superior officers in addition to patrol officers. In large cities there may be one unit for patrol officers and a separate unit for superior officers (New York City has five separate police units: patrol officers, detectives, sergeants, lieutenants, and captains). In a 1981 sample of 461 police contracts we collected from around the country, 26 percent of the contracts specified a patrol officers–only bargaining unit, and the rest specified a unit consisting of patrol officers and other police employee groups.

The number of "law enforcement or security employee" bargaining units in local governments across the country stood at 3,795 in 1982 (U.S. Department of Commerce 1985). Those units do not cross administrative boundaries: city police have their own units, county deputy sheriffs have their units, and the state police have theirs. Multiemployer police bargaining arrangements exist almost nowhere (the only well-established arrangement of this type we have found is in the suburbs of Minneapolis–St. Paul). Although there are substantial labor market incentives for police employers in a particular metropolitan area to engage in such coordinated bargaining (such as to avoid whipsawing or reduce transaction costs), there are no product market incentives to do so. Because each employer and local union pair jealously guards its bargaining autonomy, the police industry has no such thing as a master contract with standard terms that cover large parts of the industry.

This local locus of bargaining authority is anything but accidental. Because each city controls its own finances and its own operating affairs, and because each has a monopoly on general-purpose police services within its own boundaries, it makes sense for police contracts to be negotiated within the bounds of each municipality (although, again, employers across localities and states do share a great deal of information on police administration, including police bargaining). Expressed another way, the locus of product market power determines the locus of bargaining; the locus of the police product market is the locality; and thus police bargaining is controlled locally. As a result, the average police contract covers fewer than 100 employees, and that average is not likely to change as long as the political divisions of the nation remain the same.

The Parties

Employers. In the police industry the employers are city, county, and state governments. In the cities this means that the "employer" for bargaining purposes is a representative of city hall who usually reports to the mayor or city manager; thus, bargaining in most cities is handled by the executive rather than legislative branch. Executive control also exists at the county and state levels, although at all three levels of government the legislative body must approve the economic expenditures called for by the negotiated contract. The vast majority of tentative agreements negotiated by the representatives of the executive branch are ratified by the legislative branch, but periodically a city council or county board of supervisors may reject a tentative settlement for reasons of political advantage. Such an event, though rare, illustrates that public sector employers do not have the same unitary authority to make decisions that private sector employers have.

Although city hall negotiates police contracts and is ultimately responsible for administering them, the police chief (and his command staff) is responsible for the day-to-day management of the police department. In some cities the police chief's representative is a direct participant in contract negotiations; in others police management does not sit at the bargaining table. City hall representatives often are ambivalent about the value of police management's participation in negotiations: on the one hand, police management zealously seeks to protect managerial prerogatives, and thus police managers are very useful for evaluating the union's noneconomic proposals; but on the other hand, the salaries of police management usually increase in direct proportion to the rank-and-file pay increases negotiated by the union, and thus police management's sympathies usually lie with the union on the economic issues. Because of their divided loyalties, police managers are only a partial partner on the employer side of the negotiating table in most cities.

Nonetheless, because police management must operate its department within the constraints imposed by the police contract, there does need to be (and usually is) close coordination between police managers and the city hall labor relations staff when administering the contract. The police command staff is responsible for processing grievances through the lower steps of the grievance procedure, but city hall usually retains control over the last step, arbitration (including any grievance settlements negotiated to prevent the use of arbitration).

Unions. There is no single dominant union in this industry, an unsurprising result considering the local nature of police product markets and bargaining structure. Instead, there is a very large number of police unions,[4] many of which are local organizations, many others of which are affiliated with a state police organization, and yet others of which are affiliated with a national organization. The national unions are of two types: police only, such as the Fraternal Order of Police; and mixed in occupations, such as the Teamsters or AFSCME. Table 9–3 lists local and membership data for the five main national unions that have police locals.

The extent to which police are represented by different types of police unions is illustrated by the unions listed in our 1981 sample of 461 police contracts. In that sample 258 contracts specified an independent, local association (that is, no state or national affiliation was specified, though some may have existed), and 36 contracts specified that the local was affiliated with a state association (such as the Police Officers Association of Michigan). Among the locals affiliated with a national union, 91 contracts were negotiated by Fraternal Order of Police (FOP) lodges, 32 by International Brotherhood of Police Officers (IBPO) locals, 18 by American Federation of State, County and Municipal Employees (AFSCME) locals, 18 by International Brotherhood of Teamsters locals, and eight by affiliates of the International Union of Police Associations (IUPA). In other words about 36 percent of the

Table 9–3
Police Locals and Membership in National Unions

National Union	Number of Locals	Number of Members
1. Fraternal Order of Police (FOP): Independent	1,458	170,000
2. International Union of Police Associations (IUPA): AFL-CIO	250	13,000
3. International Brotherhood of Police Officers (IBPO): a division of the National Association of Government Employees (NAGE), which is affiliated with the Service Employees' International Union (SEIU), AFL-CIO	228	13,000
4. American Federation of State, County and Municipal Employees (AFSCME): AFL-CIO	n.a.	10,000
5. International Brotherhood of Teamsters, Chauffers, Warehousemen and Helpers of America (Teamsters): Independent	n.a.	n.a.

Source: Local union and membership data are from figures supplied to us by each union.

Note: All membership and local union figures are approximate calculations as of the spring of 1986. They refer only to members who were city police officers and county deputy sheriffs; they do not refer, for example, to corrections officers or probation officers. The figures also do not include members of the national unions who were in other occupations, such as truck drivers or county clerical staff.

police contracts in our sample were negotiated by affiliates of national unions that represent police.

This percentage of national affiliations should not be confused with a national, as opposed to a local, locus of police bargaining activity. The fact that a local police union is affiliated with a national organization does not mean that bargaining is controlled or even much influenced by higher level union officials. The national unions that have police affiliates generally have small national staffs and limited resources, and they allow their locals a great deal of bargaining autonomy. To the extent that the locus of internal union power is reflected in the allocation of union dues money, an example may illustrate the degree of local control over the bargaining process. A midwestern FOP local, or "lodge," charges each of its members $130 per year in dues (there are about 35 members in the bargaining unit). Of that amount, $3 is forwarded to the national office (the "Grand Lodge"); $11 is forwarded to the state lodge (some which goes toward a modest life insurance policy for each member); and thus the local lodge keeps $116, or 89 percent, of the dues money it collects. The lodge uses this money for, among other things, contract negotiations and administrative purposes. The local can purchase contract negotiations and administrative services from the state lodge at an annual cost of about $72 per member, but this particular lodge has decided not to do so. As a result, the local union is free—and has the resources—to handle collective bargaining as it sees fit. If this example is representative, and we believe it is, it illustrates how local police unions manage to retain their bargaining autonomy when they affiliate with a national union such as the FOP.

Furthermore, as table 9–3 indicates, police officers have not demonstrated allegiance to any single national union, as firefighters have with the International Association of Fire Fighters. Instead, police affiliations with one or another national union tend to be strong in some regions and almost nonexistent elsewhere. The FOP, for example, has many lodges in Pennsylvania and Illinois but few on the West Coast, while the IBPO has strongholds in New England and many Teamster police locals can be found in Michigan. On the other hand, many (perhaps most) local police unions maintain some kind of affiliation with a statewide group (even though that affiliation may not be listed in their contract), but they do so primarily to lobby the state legislature and to exchange bargaining information and mutual assistance with other locals in the state. All told, then, the modest nature of these state and national affiliations does not restrict the bargaining autonomy of local police unions. We therefore cannot overemphasize the degree of local union bargaining control in the industry. As the decentralized nature of the product and labor markets determined the decentralized bargaining structure in the industry, so too have all three brought forth highly individualistic bargaining processes—the outcomes of which vary by locality, as we shall see in the next section.

The Bargaining Process

Table 9–2 has demonstrated that police collective bargaining has become a fact of life in the United States, at least in cities with populations over 25,000. Although police unionism trailed private sector developments by about three decades, during the past 20 years cities and police unions have acquired considerable experience handling and resolving the issues that have appeared on the bargaining table.

Bargaining Issues

Nonwage Contract Provisions. In this section we return to our sample of police contracts to analyze the types of issues addressed in police bargaining.

Later in this section and in the next we supplement these contract data with data from 343 police interest arbitration awards we collected covering the 1970–83 period (for details on this sample of contracts, see Feuille, Hendricks, and Delaney 1983). Our contract sample is probably overrepresentative of arbitration states (states with compulsory arbitration statutes covering the police) because we originally designed the survey to study interest arbitration. Recall that arbitration states offer police unions the most favorable legal environment for bargaining. As a result, the contracts we collected probably contain more provisions that are favorable to the union than would a randomly selected sample of police contracts. Nonetheless, as one of the largest such samples ever collected, it provides much useful information about police bargaining.

Before we examine the contract data, we should explain a few of the measures we used to draw our conclusions. To assess the favorableness to the union of the multiplicity of clauses in police contracts, we first developed a contract scoring index composed of 130 nonsalary terms (salaries were analyzed separately) that might be found in the contracts. (Each index item was constructed to rate the contract term on a scale ranging from zero points for least favorable to the union to ten points for most favorable to the union, with the intermediate values (of equal interval) for the intermediate degrees of favorability.) A contract that contained all 130 items, each of which was given the maximum value, would thus have received a total score of 1,300 points. In fact, our highest individual contract score was 783.4 points. Based on research by Kochan and Block (1977) we grouped each of the 130 index items into one of the following six categories: fringe benefits (such as insurance, retirement, and holidays); pay supplements (overtime pay, longevity pay, shift differential pay); working conditions (scheduling, equipment); individual security (primarily seniority); union security (recognition, dues checkoff, membership requirements); and equity (grievance procedures, disciplinary procedures, performance appraisals).[5]

The top part of table 9–4 shows how the contracts in the 1981 sample scored on these six categories of provisions, their total scores, and the average number of contract provisions in each category. (The table does not portray provisions not in the index.) The results show that almost half (28 of 60) of the indexed provisions in the average contract addressed monetary issues—either fringe benefits or pay supplements—but keep in mind that this tally excludes salaries. The bottom part of table 9–4 shows that there is considerable variation in the strength of police contracts across the country. For instance, contracts negotiated in Michigan cities were scored almot twice as high on the index as those negotiated in California cities. A quick look at the asterisked states also suggests that contracts negotiated in arbitration states were more favorable to the unions than contracts negotiated in other states. We have found further evidence of this apparent advantage to the union of bargaining in an arbitration state in a multivariate analysis that showed that

Table 9–4
Police Contract Provisions Evaluated by an Index of Favorability to the Union, 1981

a. Provisions in and Scores for the Average Contract

Index	Number of Provisions in the Average Contract	Average Index Score
Index of all provisions	60	449.3
Index of:		
Fringe benefit provisions	16	116.8
Pay supplement provisions	12	88.0
Equity provisions	11	91.8
Union security provisions	11	83.0
Working condition provisions	6	39.2
Individual security provisions	4	30.5

b. Average Total Scores, by State

State (Number of 1981 Contracts)	Average Score	Standard Deviation
*Michigan (26)	633.3	68.4
*Connecticut (16)	568.1	93.1
*Oregon (6)	547.7	58.4
Nevada (4)	500.0	136.9
*Iowa (15)	498.6	80.4
*New Jersey (35)	495.8	90.1
Montana (5)	493.8	42.6
*Rhode Island (7)	491.7	51.4
*New York (32)	490.9	77.8
*Massachusetts (42)	487.8	73.3
*Minnesota (18)	479.9	52.6
Florida (23)	475.2	81.4
*Washington (9)	472.6	58.0
Ohio (22)	459.6	136.1
Texas (5)	459.0	95.0
Oklahoma (6)	441.3	60.5
*Wisconsin (14)	429.0	94.9
Illinois (26)	425.5	102.4
*Pennsylvania (19)	403.7	133.4
Colorado (4)	395.0	142.5
Indiana (9)	353.7	126.4
California (90)	322.5	109.9

Notes: For both parts of the table, N = 461 contracts. In the lower part, the numbers in parentheses indicated the number of cities in the state for which we have 1981 contract data. We included in the table only those states for which we have at least four 1981 contracts.

*States with compulsory interest arbitration laws.

1981 police contracts were 19 percent (or 65 index points) more favorable to the union's interests in arbitration states than elsewhere (after controlling for other influences on contract strength; Feuille, Delaney, and Hendricks 1985b). The standard deviations shown in table 9–4 also imply that within some individual states there is considerable variation in contract favorability, while in others there is little. Taken together, the figures in this table indicate that the contractual protections enjoyed by police officers vary considerably from state to state and even from city to city in the same state.

Without examining the full range of issues addressed in police contracts, we can learn much about police bargaining by examining three types of issues in particular that appear in most: seniority applications, union security, and law enforcement. The first two are common in union contracts in most industries, while the third type involves issues specific to police employment. We chose these three because employees are especially interested in seniority rights; unions, in contractually protecting their organizational security; and society, in the extent to which law enforcement issues are resolved by collective bargaining, rather than by police management or through the political process. Furthermore, these three issues are broadly representative of the range of noneconomic issues that are addressed in police bargaining.

Table 9–5 shows the extent to which the 1981 police contracts required seniority to be used as either a criterion or the controlling criterion for making such personnel decisions as filling job vacancies, making shift assignments, and determining layoffs. For most of these types of decisions, the typical contract said nothing explicit about seniority (although seniority may nevertheless carry great weight in management's actual decision making on these issues; Juris and Feuille 1973). Seniority carried little contractual weight in the filling of job vacancies and promotions. It was most influential in vacation selection, layoff, and shift assignment decisions. But in light of the fact that many police departments allowed officers to select vacation times by seniority in the era before police unionism and the fact that relatively few departments actually conduct layoffs, the data in table 9–5 indicate that relatively few personnel decisions regarding the allocation of officers to jobs are made on the basis of strict, contractually required seniority.

Table 9–6 examines the prevalence of union security provisions in the 1981 contracts. An open shop existed in 65 percent of the contracts (assuming that "no provision" is the functional equivalent of an explicit open shop provision); an agency shop existed in almost one-third; and union shops and maintenance-of-membership requirements were rare. The prevalence of open shops is probably less bothersome to police unions than it is to other unions because most police departments are highly cohesive, resulting in voluntary membership rates exceeding 90 percent. Nonetheless, as agency shop clauses become more common in the public sector as a whole, and as they come to

Table 9–5
Seniority Provisions in Police Contracts, 1981
(N = 461 contracts)

	Contracts with the Provision	
Application of Seniority	*Number*	*Percent*
Job vacancies and promotions		
None	228	49.5%
Excluded	147	31.9
Included	79	17.1
Governs	7	1.5
Shift assignments		
None	237	51.4
Excluded	92	20.0
Included	49	10.6
Governs	83	18.0
Involuntary transfers		
None	327	70.9
Excluded	91	19.7
Included	32	6.9
Governs	11	2.4
Voluntary transfers		
None	326	70.7
Excluded	75	16.3
Included	51	11.1
Governs	9	2.0
Layoffs		
None	225	48.8
Excluded	58	12.6
Included	35	7.6
Governs	143	31.0
Vacation selection		
None	156	33.8
Excluded	54	11.7
Included	74	16.1
Governs	177	38.4

Legend:
  None   = No seniority provision in the contract.
  Excluded = Provision excludes seniority as a criterion.
  Included = Provision includes seniority as a criterion.
  Governs = Provision states that seniority governs as a criterion.

receive judicial and legislative approval as well, they should begin to appear in a growing portion of all police contracts.

Dues checkoff arrangements appeared in about three-fourths of the 1981 contracts. In contrast, a contractual requirement for pay parity with firefighters was rare. As a result, to the extent that pay parity exists in the 461 cities studied, it exists because of political custom, management decision, or a pay parity requirement in the firefighters' contract—not in the police contract.[6]

Table 9–6
Union Security Provisions in Police Contracts, 1981
(N = 461 contracts)

	Contracts with the Provision	
Union Security Provision	*Number*	*Percent*
Union membership		
No provision	109	23.6%
Open shop	191	41.4
Maintenance of membership	4	0.9
Agency shop	144	31.2
Union shop	13	2.8
Dues checkoff		
No provision	118	25.6
Voluntary	323	70.1
Automatic unless employee objects	3	0.7
Mandatory	17	3.7
Pay parity with firefighters		
No provision	445	96.5
Some provision	16	3.5
Released time for union business		
No provision	134	29.1
Time off for grievances	52	11.3
Time off for grievances and negotiations	45	9.8
Time off for grievances, negotiations and other business	230	49.9

Finally, more than 70 percent of the contracts permit union members some amount of released time to handle union business.

A subject of great interest to police unions, employers, and industrial relations observers is the extent to which law enforcement matters are addressed in police contracts. Because the police have license to use force, and because most officers work on an unsupervised basis, police departments have a plethora of rules that regulate such matters as firearms carried, ammunition used, the qualifications to use firearms, and the conditions under which deadly force and less-than-deadly force may be used. Cities and police departments also have rules governing other types of issues that have direct implications for law enforcement, such as staffing requirements, officer rights in citizen complaints and internal investigations, and officer residency requirements. Because the union perspective on these law enforcement issues may diverge from the management perspective (especially that of the elected officials in city hall), there is some reason to be concerned that successful union attempts to negotiate these issues into the police contract will have the effect of determining important aspects of a community's law enforcement policy behind the closed doors of the negotiating room.

Table 9–7 contains some figures about the extent to which these kinds of law enforcement issues were negotiated into the sample of 1981 police contracts. These figures show that the most frequently negotiated law enforcement issues were those that established some due process rights for officers who are the subject of citizen complaints and internal investigations, but even those rights appeared only in fewer than half of the contracts. Firearm issues appeared in fewer than 20 percent of the contracts, and use-of-force provisions were almost nonexistent. About 16 percent of the contracts placed some contraint on where an officer had to reside in relation to the community served, and about 13 percent of the contracts contained staffing requirements (for example, a requirement that two officers be assigned to each squad car during the evening shift). Taken together, the data in table 9–7 indicate that law enforcement issues have not been widely negotiated into police contracts, and thus these issues remain within management's prerogative in most jurisdictions. In our separate analysis of police interest arbitration awards, we reached a similar conclusion: law enforcement issues were rarely submitted to arbitrators for resolution; instead, it was economic issues (salaries and benefits) that were grist for the arbitration mill (Delaney and Feuille 1984).

Table 9–7
Law Enforcement Issues Covered in
Police Contract Provisions, 1981
(N = 461 contracts)

	Contracts with the Provision	
Provision	*Number*	*Percent*
Officer rights in citizen complaints	195	42.3%
Officer bill of rights in internal investigations	185	40.1
Firearm qualification	80	17.4
Type of sidearm carried	58	12.6
Type of ammunition used	50	10.8
Residency requirement Residency required within a specified radius of community	46	10.0
Residency in community required	29	6.3
Staffing Minimum levels specified	39	8.5
Some provision without minimum levels	19	4.1
Must carry gun off duty	16	3.5
Armament in squad cars	10	2.2
Use of deadly force	3	0.7
Use of less-than-deadly force	3	0.7
Firearm review board	3	0.7

Before leaving this topic, however, it is important to note that many bread-and-butter issues in police contracts can have law enforcement implications. In the years before police unionism police management commonly required officers to work more than their regular 40-hour week for off-duty court appearances, call-ins, and standby orders, usually for no increase in pay (or for compensatory time off, which managers often persuaded the officer not to take). Police unions have put a stop to such practices by requiring that all work over and above the basic workweek receive extra compensation, usually at an overtime rate (that is, these personnel practices are now costly rather than free; Juris and Feuille 1973). As a result, police contracts are now replete with numerous pay provisions governing overtime, call-ins, off-duty court appearances, standby duty, roll calls, shift differentials, and special assignments. These supplemental pay requirements may affect the allocation of officers to specific jobs depending on the price tag involved; for example, parades and political demonstrations may be less thoroughly policed now than in the past because of the higher staffing costs demanded by the contracts. Moreover, some of these requirements may give officers an incentive to perform their duties in a particular manner; for example, with off-duty court appearances requiring a pay rate at time-and-one-half and a minimum time off of four hours, night shift officers have an incentive to make arrests. Similarly, as we saw in table 9–5, seniority provisions often influence shift assignments. To the extent that the more-senior officers select the day shift, the evening and night shifts—when most crimes occur and most calls for assistance are received—may be populated by rookies and other less experienced officers. And a contractual requirement that two officers be assigned to each patrol car can limit the number of cars the city is able to put on the streets. Consequently, even without provisions specifically regulating the conduct of law enforcement, many police contracts contain provisions that may affect the delivery of police services to the community, and, at least in theory, some of those effects could be detrimental to the quality of those services. Nevertheless, we have no hard evidence to suggest that any detrimental service delivery effects have resulted from police contract terms.

All together, the results reported in tables 9–4 through 9–7, and some additional contract analysis results reported elsewhere (Delaney and Feuille 1984), indicate that the issues that survive the bargaining process to be included in police contracts are primarily the traditional bread-and-butter issues historically addressed by all American trade unions: pay, pay supplements, and fringe benefits. Other police contract provisions deal with the standard noneconomic concerns of unions: working conditions, individual security, and equity. In addition, many police unions have succeeded in protecting their institutional interests by negotiating union security provisions, particularly those granting police officers far greater protection against arbitrary, inconsistent, or harsh managerial actions than they had before they joined unions. Officers' pay supplements and fringe benefits have been increased and contractually guaranteed, officers are compensated for work beyond their regular workweek, they have achieved some explicit rewards for their seniority, they have contractual due process protections in disciplinary matters, and most have a grievance procedure to appeal claims of unfair treatment. These contractual protections have forced police managers to manage their personnel more effectively and fairly than in the past (sometimes to management's chagrin). These changes have been especially noteworthy considering the emphasis on rule-following and on punishment as the principal modus operandi of police command staffs. Despite all these changes, however, our data indicate that only a modest proportion of the provisions in police contracts involve the law enforcement topics that are unique to the police service. Consequently, our data do not support a conclusion that the police unions of the United States have, through the collective bargaining process, come to play any determining role in municipal law enforcement itself.

Salaries. As noted above, the most frequently negotiated items in police contracts are the salaries of bargaining unit members. Because patrol officer salaries are the benchmark rates for all other rates, we will examine these carefully.

Police officers are hired at an entry-level patrol salary and usually reach the top step of patrol salaries three or four years later, through automatic annual movements up the patrol officer salary schedule. The difference between the entry-level and top-level patrol salaries is usually in the range of 20 to 25 percent. As a result, during the first few years on the job officers receive hefty annual increases through a combination of upward movement through the patrol officer salary schedule and negotiated across-the-board increases; but in subsequent years they receive only the negotiated increases plus any longevity payments to which they are entitled (for example, $500 after 10 years of service, $750 after 15 years, and so on). Additional pay raises are possible only through promotion or through transfer to the detective ranks (which usually commands a modest stipend over the patrol rate). Some cities have developed senior patrol officer or master patrol officer titles, with modestly higher pay, to provide a longer career ladder for officers who want to remain in patrol (and those slots are usually filled based on the officer's education and experience).

Police unions have had only a modest influence on this salary structure. Many unions, for example, have not attempted to negotiate a single rate for all officers irrespective of experience on the job, but some others have succeeded in reducing the number of steps between the entry- and top-level salaries. Similarly, unions have usually not opposed efforts to create senior or master patrol classifications, although they often emphasize the experience component of any such classification more than does management (so that upward movement will be more automatic than it would be otherwise). In addition, most departments had some form of longevity pay before unions came along, but unions have regularly sought to increase the frequency and amount of those longevity payments.

Consistent with the local nature of police product and labor markets, the variation in police salaries both across states and within states is substantial. In 1984, for instance, the highest maximum patrol officer salary reported in a national salary survey (excluding Alaska) was $36,360 (in Santa Clara, California), and the lowest maximum salary reported was $10,500 (in Arkadelphia, Arkansas) (Hoetmer 1985). Similarly, within Illinois in that year the maximum patrol officer salary in Peoria was $30,647, while in Marion it was $16,640 (Hoetmer 1985). In another multivariate analysis, within-state police salary dispersion was shown to be only modestly smaller in 1981 than in 1971, and neither collective bargaining nor interest arbitration exhibited much effect on salary variation (Delaney, Feuille, and Hendricks 1984). In other words, there is no reason to believe that either bargaining or arbitration will create intercity uniformity in police salaries, a conclusion that, again, is consistent with the very localized structure of police bargaining.

Further multivariate analyses show that patrol officer salaries are higher in cities where the police bargain collectively than where they do not and that—independent of this bargaining effect—salaries are higher in cities located in states with compulsory interest arbitration statutes for police than in states without those laws (Feuille and Delaney 1986; Delaney, Feuille, and Hendricks 1986). For example, Feuille and Delancy (1986) have shown that cities that bargain collectively with their police and cities located in arbitration states pay minimum and maximum patrol officer salaries that are several percentage points higher than the salaries paid in cities that do not bargain with their police or are located outside of arbitration states. Moreover, these bargaining and arbitration effects were measured independently of each other; thus, the total salary effects of unionization are greater in arbitration states than in states with no arbitration laws. In other words, the analyses show that it pays for the police to unionize, and it pays even more to be unionized in an arbitration state.

In sum, police salaries are the key issue in police bargaining (and in police arbitration proceedings as well). Police unions have successfully pushed salary levels above those prevailing in nonunion locations, other things equal, and the favorable bargaining environment created by arbitration statutes has enabled police unions to obtain even higher salaries. It is important to bear in mind, however, that studies suggest that the impact of police unions on wages is smaller than the 10 to 30 percent differentials reported in studies examining private sector unionism. In addition, it also is important to note that police salaries are substantially influenced by a wide variety of market characteristics (such as city size, city location within or outside a metropolitan area, region of the country, city wealth, and local manufacturing wages), some of which are, in fact, far more influential than police collective bargaining (Feuille and Delaney 1986).

Contract Administration

Grievance Procedures. As previously shown in table 9–4, the average contract in our sample of 1981 police agreements contained, in addition to salary items, 60 nonsalary provisions (as we counted them) covering a wide variety of substantive issues. How do police unions and employers resolve disputes over the interpretation of those contractual items? The increasingly common method is to use a grievance procedure that culminates in arbitration (not to be confused with interest arbitration, or the arbitration of negotiations impasses). For instance, in our 1981 sample of 461 contracts, 392 contracts (or 85 percent) contained a grievance procedure, and 320 of those procedures (69 percent of the total sample, or 82 percent of the contracts with procedures) culminated in arbitration, whereas only 53 percent of our sample of 1975 contracts called for grievance arbitration. It is therefore quite likely that grievance arbitration is even more widespread in police contracts today than it was in 1981.

We do not have data on the issues grieved and how those issues are resolved at the pre-arbitration steps of the grievance procedure. We can draw some inferences, however, from our analysis of 600 police grievance arbitration awards reported in the *Labor Arbitration in Government* series during the 1971–85 period (American Arbitration Association). As long as we remember that arbitrated grievances may or may not be representative of all grievances filed, and that the American Arbitration Association has wide latitude to select for publication those police awards it deems noteworthy, these 600 police awards may be usefully analyzed for our purposes here.

The 600 awards involved police agencies and unions in 27 different states, but 82 percent of the awards came from only six states (Connecticut, Massachusetts, Michigan, New Jersey, New York, and Pennsylvania). The awards were issued by 297 different arbitrators, and about half of the awards involved police agencies serving jurisdictions with populations smaller than 50,000. The cases were brought by a wide range of local police unions, including those affiliated with the FOP, IBPO, AFSCME, and the Teamsters, as well as many independents (or at least local unions with no listed affiliation).

Table 9–8 portrays the subjects grieved in these cases and their disposition. By our count the 600 awards involved 637 separate decisions rendered by the arbitrators involved (for example, an award in which the arbitrator ruled that the grievance was arbitrable and then ruled on the merits of the

Table 9-8
Subjects and Disposition of Grievance Arbitration Cases, 1971–85
(N = 600)

| Type of Grievance[a] | Number (Percent) of all Grievances | Grievance Disposition | | | |
		Number (Percent) Sustained in Part	Number (Percent) Fully Sustained	Number (Percent) Denied	Number (Percent) Not Arbitrable
Denial of benefits	303 (47.6%)	7 (2.3%)	148 (48.8%)	147 (48.5%)	1 (0.3%)
Contract interpretation	155 (24.3)	2 (1.3)	62 (40.0)	90.0 (58.1)	1 (0.6)
Discipline	91 (14.3)	7 (7.7)	44 (48.4)	39 (42.9)	1 (1.1)
Discharge	41 (6.4)	4 (9.8)	22 (53.7)	15 (36.6)	0 (0.0)
Application of seniority	47 (7.4)	1 (2.1)	17 (36.2)	29 (61.7)	0 (0.0)
Total	637[b] (100.0)	21 (3.3)	293 (46.0)	320 (50.2)	3 (0.5)

Source: American Arbitration Association (1971–1985).

[a]"Denial of benefits" involves pay supplements or fringe benefits; these grievances almost always involve money or paid time off. "Discipline" and "discharge" cases are self-explanatory. "Application of seniority" involves all cases in which the grievant claimed a violation of seniority rights. "Contract interpretation" involves the cases that do not fit into the other four categories, including such examples as the use of performance appraisals in the promotion process, changing staffing assignments, and discrimination for union activity. Many of these cases involve challenges to unilateral managerial action.

[b]This total exceeds the number of cases (600) because some cases involved more than one issue being grieved.

grievance was counted as two decisions). The data in the table indicate that almost half of the decisions involved an alleged denial of contractual benefits, a quarter involved a dispute over the interpretation of some part of the contract, about one-fifth involved discipline and discharge, and about 7 percent involved seniority disputes. Overall, management won slightly more than half of these cases outright (the grievance was denied), while the unions won either full or partial affirmation of the grievance slightly less than half the time. Employers fared best in the seniority cases and worst in the discharge cases. But recall, however, that because we have no information about AAA's publication criteria, we have no way of knowing if this win-loss portrait accurately represents the disposition of all police awards.

Labor-Management Committees. The standard method of contract administration in police labor relations is the filing and processing of a grievance through the contractual grievance procedure. Nevertheless, almost half of the police unions and employers in our 1981 sample had adopted an alternate mechanism for addressing issues of mutual concern—the labor-management committee. Of the 461 contracts in our sample, 211, or 46 percent, specified at least one labor-management committee (together those 211 contracts called for 297 different committees). The committees were given the latitude to discuss such topics as issues of general workplace concern, safety, grievances, education, insurance, uniforms, and equipment. Most committees could recommend changes in these areas; only 21 of them could mandate changes. We have no way of knowing how many of the committees functioned effectively to address and resolve issues of mutual concern and how many were "paper" arrangements that served to accomplish little or nothing. Nonetheless, the mere fact that almost half of the contracts specified a labor-management committee indicates a fairly widespread willingness of police unions and employers to address at least some issues in a more cooperative and less adversarial fashion than is usually the case in traditional grievance processing.

Labor-Management Conflict

Strikes

Strikes have been the most controversial aspect of police collective bargaining ever since the 1919 Boston police strike, and the controversy continues today. There is unanimous agreement that police protection is essential to the maintenance of public safety, and most citizens today would emphatically endorse Calvin Coolidge's dictum that "there is no right to strike against the public safety." This consensus is reflected in the absence of any statutorily guaranteed right to strike for police officers in any jurisdiction in the United States.

Nevertheless, the absence of the legal right to strike means only that the police strikes that have occurred have been illegal. Indeed, as shown in table 9–9, the years 1970–80 witnessed 245 police strikes (unfortunately, because of federal budget cuts, reliable and comprehensive public sector strike statistics are not available for the years after 1980), with the annual number of strikes increasing steadily during the latter half of that period. Simply making police strikes illegal, then, has not prevented them from occurring, a conclusion supported by careful multivariate research (Ichniowski 1982). This conclusion does not mean, however, that police strikes are a standard feature of police bargaining. For instance, in 1980 there were 43 police strikes, but "law enforcement and security" bargaining units in state and (mostly) local governments numbered 3,912 in 1982 (U.S. Department of Commerce 1985). If we

Table 9–9
Police Strikes in the United States, 1970–80

Calendar Year	Number of Strikes	Number of Workers Involved	Number of Days Idle
1970	28	1,600	6,800
1971	22	23,800	111,300
1972	15	600	1,600
1973	5	600	1,700
1974	12	1,500	4,500
1975	14	3,600	11,800
1976	18	3,100	8,400
1977	24	2,700	9,100
1978	25	3,600	9,400
1979	39	13,000	63,000
1980	43	6,000	16,800
	245		

Sources: U.S. Department of Labor (1972, 1973, 1974) and U.S. Department of Labor (1976, 1978, 1980, 1981).

Note: The strike data include instances of simultaneous police and firefighter strikes.

assume that the number of units was roughly the same in 1980, the strike data indicate that only slightly over one percent of those units experienced a strike in that year. A similar finding was reported by Stern and Olson (1982), who found that strikes took place in 1.6 percent of police contract negotiations during the years 1975–77 (although they also found that the strike rate varied substantially across states depending on the police labor relations legislation in the state). Stern and Olson also found that the propensity to strike among police was less than the strike propensity of firefighters and well below that of teachers. Police strikes, therefore, can be considered rare events.

Rare as they may be, police strikes (which sometimes take the form of sickouts or the "blue flu") provoke strong feelings among police employers, the public, and police unions themselves. Unions frequently justify strikes as the bargaining tactic of last resort, one that is the only way to get management to pay attention to union demands, whereas employers and the public condemn them as posing a clear and present danger to the public safety. In fact, the desire to prevent police strikes is almost always the primary justification offered by proponents of interest arbitration laws. In other words, heated rhetoric about police strikes almost always subsumes the claim that such strikes are horrible events that will ultimately inflict great damage on innocent bystanders.

But what does the strike record itself show? We have been unable to uncover any carefully controlled analysis of the effects of police strikes. The few case studies of police strikes that exist (Juris and Feuille 1973; Ayres 1977; Bopp, Chignell, and Maddox 1977) indicate that no significant upsurge of criminal or disorderly activity was the result of those strikes. The belief that police strikes are horrendous presupposes that management is incapable of ensuring public safety during a police strike. In fact, the historical record shows that cities—especially those with contingency plans for police strikes—have been able to respond rather well to police walkouts. For instance, in January 1971 Milwaukee police management was able to put more squad cars on the street during a four-day strike than they normally would have, by deploying management personnel for extended shifts, among other things. More generally, cities have discovered that by canceling leaves, instituting 12-hour shifts, assigning superior officers to street duty, and entering into mutual aid pacts with other cities, they can create a sufficient police presence in the community to weather a police strike (although much routine work, such as record keeping, traffic accident reporting, and minor crime investigation, may have to be postponed during the strike). Expressed another way, it is extremely difficult to believe that the nation would have tolerated 245 police strikes over an 11-year period if those strikes had caused a genuine breakdown in law and order (as was seemingly the case in Boston in 1919 and in Montreal in 1969). Consequently, that police strikes are horrendous events is simply an unsubstantiated opinion, but it nonetheless remains most unlikely that this lack of substantiation will lead to any right-to-strike laws for police unions.

From the union's perspective the purpose of a police strike is to bring sufficient pressure to bear on the employer to compel management to meet the union's demands in order to end the strike. In other words, the strike is designed to increase management's costs of rejecting the union's demands. What form do these costs take? They are not economic, for a police strike does not shut off revenues to the city (that is, taxes are still collected), although sometimes police officers engage in "ticket strikes" by refusing to issue traffic tickets, thereby depriving the city of a minor source of revenue. In fact, the city will save the salaries of the strikers (minus any overtime wages paid to those employees who work during the strike). No, the cities' costs are political, to whatever extent the strike succeeds in inconveniencing or creating anxiety in the citizenry, in turn forcing management to seek an early end to the strike.

Do strikes achieve this objective? This question is very difficult to answer, for both unions and employers in any setting go to great lengths to portray themselves as winners of a strike, and it is extremely difficult to determine how the terms of a strike settlement differ from what would have been negotiated if no strike had occurred. Some police strikes end on terms favorable to the union, but others do not. History has shown that the strike may be a risky course for a police union to pursue: The citizens may get mad at the union and give their support to management; management may do an excellent job of coping with the strike and therefore may not increase its offer; and strikers may be disciplined for having taken part in an illegal walkout (and also may lose pay during the strike). In short, police strikes create pressure on the union and the strikers as well as on management, and for this reason the employer's ability to take a strike must be balanced against the union's ability to conduct a strike. As a result, a police strike is hardly a guarantee that police officers will achieve the bargaining demands that led them to strike in the first place.

In spite of the fact that the consequences of police strikes remain unproven, and in spite of the fact that police strikes are rare, they continue to be highly controversial events. As mentioned briefly above, one of the results of this controversy has been the passage of compulsory interest arbitration laws in many states, ostensibly for the purpose of preventing police (and other public employee) strikes.

Compulsory Interest Arbitration

As illustrated above in table 9–2, 16 states and the District of Columbia have compulsory interest arbitration (hereafter "arbitration") laws covering the police. (A few other states, such as Hawaii, Nevada, and Wyoming, have arbitration laws covering firefighters.) These arbitration statutes were designed to ensure that police negotiating disputes do not erupt in strikes by requiring that any unresolved disputes be submitted to an arbitrator for final and binding resolution. In other words, arbitration is employed as a form of no-strike insurance, a form of insurance that the alternative techniques, mediation and factfinding, cannot take.

The legislative histories of the various state arbitration laws show that almost all of them were passed as a result of union lobbying on their behalf, usually in the face of opposition lobbying by municipal management. The two primary reasons offered for such statutes are the need to protect the public from police strikes and the need to give police officers a dispute resolution mechanism that will require management to take union bargaining demands seriously. In practice, this second reason is the key to understanding why unions lobby for and cities lobby against the statutes: the unions believe they will be able to obtain more favorable results when they bargain under the umbrella of arbitration than they would otherwise, and city management believes precisely the same thing. Because each side is looking for a power advantage at the bargaining table, this lineup on either side of the arbitration question is hardly surprising.

Let us examine, then, the actual effects arbitration laws have had. First, although the available evidence indicates that arbitration is not a perfect form of no-strike insurance, a substantial body of evidence shows that far fewer police strikes have occurred where arbitration is mandated than where it is not (Ichniowski 1982; Lester 1984; Olson et al. 1981; Stern et al. 1975; Stern and Olson 1982). Thus, arbitration seems to have done an effective job of preventing strikes.

Second, arbitration seems to have done an even more effective job of advancing the workplace interests of police officers. We saw earlier (in our discussion of salary provisions in police contracts) that the availability of arbitration has enabled police officers to obtain higher salaries than they would have otherwise. And as was also noted earlier, researchers have found that police contracts in arbitration states contain more provisions favorable to the union than are contained in police contracts negotiated in other states (Feuille, Delaney, and Hendricks 1985b). Similarly, research has shown a positive relationship between the availability of arbitration and improved police fringe benefits, although this relationship is not consistent over time (Feuille, Delaney, and Hendricks 1985a). Taken together, these research findings indicate that the presence of an arbitration law enhances the ability of police unions to obtain improved salaries, benefits, and contractual protection for their members (for a summary of this research, see Delaney, Feuille, and Hendricks 1986).

Third, it is important to note that it is the *availability* of arbitration which is associated with outcomes favorable to the union; the research evidence indicates that the *use* of arbitration contributes relatively little to these outcomes. In states with arbitration laws there were no consistent differences over time between the salaries, fringe benefits, or contract scores that were arbitrated and those that were negotiated (Delaney, Feuille, and Hendricks 1986). This finding is very plausible, for it simply says that there is no long-term net advantage from actually using the arbitration process once we control for the availability of arbitration. If this were not the case—if arbitrated salaries, for example, were significantly higher (or lower) than negotiated salaries—we would expect to find that every police union (or every city) in every arbitration state in every year had insisted on using arbitration. Instead, for the years 1975–81 we found that only about one-fifth of the unions and cities in arbitration states in our sample actually used arbitration in any given year. In other words, it is the threat of arbitration rather than the actual use of the procedure that is associated with outcomes favorable to the union.

Fourth, as noted earlier, the presence of an arbitration law creates an incentive for police officers to unionize, for only police unions (not individual officers) are eligible to use the arbitration procedure. In our study of police labor relations, almost all of the sampled cities in the arbitration states bargained with police, whereas only about half of the cities in the nonarbitration states did so (Feuille, Hendricks, and Delaney 1983; see also Ichniowski 1986).

Fifth, arbitration influences the process of collective bargaining. We know, for example, that unions and employers alike view arbitration as a significantly less costly procedure than the strike, and thus they are willing to use arbitration more than the strike to resolve their negotiating disputes (Anderson 1981; Ponak and Wheeler, 1980). We also know that the type of arbitration makes a diffrence: arbitration cases that will be decided on a final-offer-by-package basis seem to encourage more negotiating behavior than do conventional arbitration cases (Delaney and Feuille 1984; Feuille 1977; Lester 1984). In addition, some cities and unions turn to arbitration frequently and repeatedly, while others rarely do. And recent research suggests that in some states there may be a "narcotic effect" (discouraging bargaining activity and encouraging the parties to use arbitration instead) in the first few years after an arbitration statute is passed but that in the long run no such effect is apparent (Chelius and Extejt 1985). Finally, arbitration states have many more negotiated agreements than arbitration awards; awards range from as low as five percent of all contract settlements (in Iowa) to as high as one-third of all contract settlements (in Pennsylvania) annually (Feuille, Hendricks, and Delaney 1983). Together these findings, all of which are based on other public employee groups as well as police, suggest that bargaining and arbitration are generally compatible, although the degree of their compatibility varies considerably across jurisdictions.

Sixth, arbitration may have some impact on the costs of delivering police services. Unionized police departments in arbitration states tend to employ more sworn police officers and fewer civilian employees (clerks, dispatchers, custodians, technicians) than their counterparts in other states (Delaney, Feuille, and Hendricks 1986). Cities in arbitration states also exhibit 5 to 23 percent higher police department costs (depending on the year and the sample of cities), in addition to any higher expenses resulting from higher compensation costs, than cities in other states (Delaney, Feuille, and Hendricks 1986). Our research on police service delivery was much more adept at identifying these costs than explaining why they exist. We therefore regard these findings as only tentative. But if they should withstand further scrutiny, these findings will clearly suggest that the costs of arbitration are substantial and extend far beyond any increases in police officer compensation accruing from arbitration awards.

Arbitration has been and continues to be controversial, with the unions solidly defending it and management strongly denouncing it. The supporters say that it is necessary to prevent strikes and equalize power at the bargaining table. If these objectives are as worthwhile as claimed, we wonder why most states have not passed arbitration laws. The critics say that arbitration is inimical to our democratic form of representative government because it grants binding authority to allocate scarce public resources to a third party, the arbitrator, who is appointed, not elected by the public, and thus is not directly accountable to the public. This critical view, however, is hard to reconcile with the lopsided record of constitutional approval of arbitration in state appellate courts and with the fact that no state legislature has ever rescinded an existing arbitration law (Delaney, Feuille, and Hendricks 1986). If arbitration is really such a perverse method for resolving negotiating disputes, it would not have been tolerated as long and as widely as it has.

The available evidence, therefore, indicates that arbitration is an acceptable and effective but costly method for resolving disputes between employees and employers that might otherwise erupt into overt conflict. Arbitration has received judicial approval in most states in which its existence has been challenged. It is clearly associated with a reduced level of strikes. It is also associated not only with higher salaries and more favorable contract provisions for police officers, but also with higher police department costs. As a result, the case for and the case against arbitration will depend on the relative importance of these different effects to the parties in the debate: those who believe that fewer strikes and improved employment terms are more important than the increased costs for the police department and city budget; and those who believe that the increased costs for the city outweigh any benefits accruing to the union members. Because there is no formula to assess the relative importance of those different values, compulsory interest arbitration will continue to be a controversial aspect of police and other public sector bargaining.

Finally, the focus in this section on police strikes and police interest arbitration as the two most visible methods of resolving negotiating conflicts should be kept in proper perspective. Each year only a tiny fraction of all police negotiations lead to a strike, and each year only a minority (less than one-fourth) of all police negotiations involve an arbitration award. In other words, the vast majority of police contracts are fashioned at the negotiating table rather than on the picket line or in the arbitral hearing room.

Conclusions

During the 1980–85 period private sector labor relations in the United States were turbulent and led to many changes in practices (as attested by many of the other chapters in this volume). Employers demanded and received substantial concessions from unions in many industries; large numbers of employers openly pursued expensive campaigns to remain nonunion; and the unions' share of the private sector labor force declined.

The turbulence in the private sector makes labor relations in the public sector seem like a sea of stability in comparison. Over the past decade union-management relations in government have matured considerably. Employers have learned that taking a strike can be an effective way to find support for their own position, and citizens have learned that public employee strikes do not necessarily result in chaos. Both unions and employers in the public sector have become adept at manipulating mediation, factfinding, and interest arbitration proceedings to their own advantage, and both have become increasingly willing to use grievance arbitration to resolve their contract interpretation disputes. In sum, collective bargaining in government has become stabilized, more mature, and unions and employers have learned how to live with each other. This general conclusion applies just as readily to police collective bargaining.

The salient features of police collective bargaining are fourfold (and the first three are applicable to bargaining in local government in general). First, police bargaining is highly decentralized because of the strongly local nature of police product markets, and it is extremely unlikely that the bargaining structure in this industry will ever include regional, statewide, or national negotiation units. In turn, we will continue to see substantial diversity in police salaries, benefits, and contract terms within and across state boundaries.

Second, the distribution of police bargaining relationships across the country is very uneven. Almost all cities in the Northeast, upper Midwest, and West Coast engage in police bargaining, but relatively few cities do in the Southeast, Southwest, and Rocky Mountain region. Much of this geographic variation is directly reflected in the variation in the support for police bargaining created by the presence or absence of police bargaining and arbitration laws. Because the states with such laws will continue to have them, and because the states without such laws will continue not to have them, it is likely that this uneven distribution of police unionization will persist. Further, because most of the growth in police employment will continue to occur in the lightly unionized areas of the country, the proportion of all police officers who are unionized may slowly decline.

Third, police union interests are squarely within the mainstream of American trade unionism. Expressed differently, the pecularities of law enforcement have not resulted in a brand of trade unionism unique to police bargaining. Our analysis of several hundred police contracts and arbitration awards showed that police unions have devoted most of their energies to the traditional bread-and-butter (salaries, pay supplements, fringe benefits) issues and noneconomic (working conditions, equity, individual security, union security) issues that have been near and dear to the hearts of U.S. trade unionists for decades. In other words, although few police locals are affiliated with the AFL-CIO, police unionism is very similar to unionism in other industries. Moreover, the law enforcement issues that are unique to the police service only infrequently appear in police contracts and awards, and thus there is no reason to believe that police unions have had much, if any, effect on law enforcement policy in this country.

Fourth, collective bargaining processes and outcomes are more strongly influenced by compulsory interest arbitration in the police industry than in any other industry. Compulsory arbitration is less prevalent among other public sector employees than among the police, and it is almost nonexistent in private industry, where even voluntary arbitration is rare. Consequently, much of our knowledge of interest arbitration and its effects has come from the police experience with it. That experience shows that compulsory arbitration is constitutionally compatible with our governmental system, that on balance it works to improve employees' employment terms, that it effectively prevents strikes, and that it appears to increase significantly the cost of delivering a given bundle of police services. Arbitration has proved to be an enduring phenomenon in almost all the states that have adopted it, but its longevity does not seem to have quieted the controversy between unions and employers over its appropriateness. Perhaps because of this controversy, it seems likely that arbitration laws will continue to cover the police only in selected states.

Our focus on the structure and process of collective bargaining should not hide the fact, however, that police union-management relations necessarily take place in a political environment (Juris and Feuille 1973). Police strike pressures are measured primarily in political rather than economic terms. Police unions have engaged in electoral politics to help elect friendly public officials, and they have lobbied their state legislatures to obtain such objectives as bargaining and arbitration laws, increased state aid to cities (so that cities can offer more money at the bargaining table), and changes in workplace conditions that are not determined at the bargaining table (such as pension and civil service regulations). But these political activities in turn should not obscure the fact that police unions devote most of their resources (time, energy, and money) to collective bargaining activities. The point here is simply that we cannot fully understand police union efforts to represent their members' interests unless we also take into account their political activities.

Perhaps more so in the police industry than in any other, observers of collective bargaining are most concerned with the impact of police unions on the employer—the police department. As noted earlier, to assess the overall impact of police unionism, we have to reach some agreement on the value of its different effects. Police unionism has increased the costs of delivering police services. But it has also resulted in granting police officers considerable protection from arbitrary, inconsistent, and inequitable managerial actions: Officers are no longer required to work extra hours for no pay, extra hours are compensated at overtime rates, fringe benefits are considerably improved, officers have due process protection in internal investigations and a grievance procedure to challenge managerial actions. Certainly the lot of unionized police officers today is much improved over their situation only some 20 years ago. And since police management remains in charge of police operations and law enforcement policy, the union presence has been much more keenly felt in police labor markets than in police product markets. In other words, police unionism has not influenced the speed with which a squad car responds to a call for emergency assistance, but it has strongly influenced the employment conditions of the officer behind the wheel of that car.

Notes

1. In this chapter we will focus primarily on police employed in municipalities; we will devote little attention to county deputy sheriffs or to state police, and we will say nothing about federal law enforcement officers (in, for example, the Federal Bureau of Investigation, the Drug Enforcement Agency, and the Bureau of Alcohol, Tobacco, and Firearms). Similarly, we will exclude from our analysis the other employees in the criminal justice system, such as corrections officers (prison guards), probation officers, prosecutors, and judicial employees.

2. A large body of literature analyzes the police function in American society. Among the more useful works are Bittner (1970), Bordua (1967), Goldstein (1977), Niederhoffer (1967), Reiss (1971), Rubinstein (1973), Skolnick (1966), and Wilson (1968). The material in this section of our chapter draws heavily from Goldstein's work.

3. Some occupational definitions: whatever their rank, all officers are sworn "police officers" (just as all university faculty members are "professors" irrespective of official rank), and these are the police department employees who have arrest powers and the authority to carry and use weapons in the performance of their duties (police department employees without arrest powers and weapons authority are "civilian" employees). The nonsupervisory rank is composed of "patrol officers" (in the days when only men were police officers this rank was often called "patrolman"), though in some cities this rank is titled "police officer." Most of the people in this rank wear uniforms while on duty; these are the officers who patrol the community and respond to most of the calls for assistance. Nonsupervisory officers who investigate crimes are called "detectives," "investigators," "inspectors," or "plainclothes officers," and they wear civilian clothes while on duty. In some cities this type of work may constitute a separate civil service rank; more frequently it is an assignment given to particular patrol officers (often carrying with it a slightly higher pay rate and almost always involving higher status than uniformed duty). "Superior officers" make up the ranks above patrol officer (the designation refers only to rank and not to competence); in most cities these civil service ranks include sergeant, lieutenant, and captain. These ranks are filled through civil service promotion procedures. The ranks above captain are discretionary; the occupants of these ranks serve at the pleasure of the police chief or the local government, or both. The number of separate ranks in any city varies directly with the size of the department.

4. Perhaps reflective of the public's fear of police strikes and thus perhaps of police unionism itself, most police unions renounce the word *union* and refer to themselves by some other name (usually *association*). In a booklet describing its organiza-

tion, the Fraternal Order of Police even denies that it is a union, although admitting to "labor relations" as one of its activities.

5. The complete index appears in Feuille, Hendricks, and Delaney (1983).

6. Concerns about parity, often a contentious issue in the traditional rivalry between police and fire units, cause each group to keep an extremely sharp eye on the other's negotiations.

References

American Arbitration Association. 1971–1985. *Labor Arbitration in Government* series. New York: AAA.

Anderson, John C. 1981. The Impact of Arbitration: A Methodological Assessment. *Industrial Relations* 20 (Spring): 129–48.

Ayres, Richard M. 1977. Case Studies of Police Strikes in Two Cities—Albuquerque and Oklahoma City. *Journal of Police Science and Administration* 5: 19–31.

Bittner, Egon. 1970. *The Functions of the Police in Modern Society.* Chevy Chase, Md.: National Institute of Mental Health.

Bopp, William J., Paul Chignell, and Charles Maddox. 1977. The San Francisco Police Strike of 1975: A Case Study. *Journal of Police Science and Administration* 5: 32–42.

Bordua, David J., ed. 1967. *The Police: Six Sociological Essays.* New York: Wiley.

Bureau of National Affairs. N.d. *Government Employee Relations Report Reference File.* Washington, D.C.: BNA.

Chelius, James R., and Marian M. Extejt. 1985. The Narcotic Effect of Impasse-Resolution Procedures. *Industrial and Labor Relations Review* 38 (July): 629–38.

Delaney, John, and Peter Feuille. 1984. Police Interest Arbitration: Awards and Issues. *Arbitration Journal* 39 (June): 14–24.

Delaney, John, Peter Feuille, and Wallace Hendricks. 1984. Police Salaries, Interest Arbitration, and the Leveling Effect. *Industrial Relations* 23 (Fall): 417–23.

———. 1986. The Regulation of Bargaining Disputes: A Cost-Benefit Analysis of Interest Arbitration in the Public Sector. In *Advances in Industrial and Labor Relations,* vol. 3, ed. David B. Lipsky and David Lewin, 83–118. Greenwich, Conn.: JAI Press.

Feuille, Peter. 1977. Final-Offer Arbitration and Negotiating Incentives. *Arbitration Journal* 32 (September): 203–20.

Feuille, Peter, and John Delaney. 1986. Collective Bargaining, Interest Arbitration, and Police Salaries. *Industrial and Labor Relations Review* 39 (January): 228–40.

Feuille, Peter, John Delaney, and Wallace Hendricks. 1985a. Police Bargaining, Arbitration, and Fringe Benefits. *Journal of Labor Research* 6 (Winter): 1–20.

———. 1985b. The Impact of Interest Arbitration on Police Contracts. *Industrial Relations* 24 (Spring): 161–81.

Feuille, Peter, Wallace Hendricks, and John Delaney. 1983. *The Impact of Collective Bargaining and Interest Arbitration on Policing.* Washington, D.C.: U.S. Department of Justice.

Freeman, Richard B. 1986. Unionism Comes to the Public Sector. *Journal of Economic Literature* 24 (March): 41–86.

Goldstein, Herman. 1977. *Policing a Free Society.* Cambridge, Mass.: Ballinger.

Hoetmer, Gerard J. 1985. Police, Fire, and Refuse Collection and Disposal Departments: Personnel, Compensation, and Expenditures. In *The Municipal Yearbook 1985.* Washington, D.C.: International City Management Association.

Ichniowski, Casey. 1982. Arbitration and Police Bargaining: Prescription for the Blue Flu. *Industrial Relations* 21 (Spring): 149–66.

———. 1986. Public Sector Union Growth and Bargaining Laws, National Bureau of Economic Research working paper no. 1809. Cambridge, Mass.: NBER, January.

Juris, Hervey A., and Peter Feuille. 1972. *Police Unionism.* Lexington, Mass.: D.C. Heath.

Kochan, Thomas A., and Richard N. Block. 1977. An Interindustry Analysis of Bargaining Outcomes: Preliminary Evidence from Two-Digit Industries. *Quarterly Journal of Economics* 91 (August): 431–52.

Lester, Richard A. 1984. *Labor Arbitration in State and Local Government.* Princeton: Industrial Relations Section, Princeton University.

McNamara, John J. 1967. Uncertainties in Police Work: The Relevance of Police Recruits' Backgrounds and Training. In *The Police: Six Sociological Essays,* ed. David J. Bordua, 163–252. New York: Wiley.

Niederhoffer, Arthur. 1967. *Behind the Shield: The Police in Urban Society.* Garden City, N.J.: Doubleday.

Olson, Craig A., James L. Stern, Joyce M. Najita, and June M. Weisberger. 1981. Strikes and Strike Penalties in the Public Sector, final report to the Labor-Management Services Administration. Washington, D.C.: U.S. Department of Labor.

Ponak, Allen, and Hoyt N. Wheeler. 1980. Choice of Procedures in Canada and the United States. *Industrial Relations* 19 (Fall): 292–308.

Reiss, Albert J., Jr. 1971. *The Police and the Public.* New Haven: Yale University Press.

Rubenstein, Jonathan. 1973. *City Police.* New York: Farrar, Strauss, and Giroux.

Shimberg, Benjamin, and Robert J. diGrazia. 1974. Promotion. In *Police Personnel Administration,* ed. O. Glenn Stahl and Richard A. Staufenberger, 101–24. Washington, D.C.: Police Foundation.

Skolnick, Jerome H. 1966. *Justice Without Trial: Law Enforcement in Democratic Society.* New York: Wiley.

Stern, James L., and Craig A. Olson. 1982. The Propensity to Strike of Local Government Employees. *Journal of Collective Negotiations in the Public Sector* 11: 201–14.

Stern, James L., Charles M. Rehmus, J. Joseph Loewenberg, Hirschel Kasper, and Barbara D. Dennis. 1975. *Final-Offer Arbitration.* Lexington, Mass.: D.C. Heath.

U.S. Department of Commerce, Bureau of the Census. 1974. *1972 Census of Governments, Compendium of Public Employment.* Washington, D.C.: GPO, November.

———. 1979. *1977 Census of Governments, Historical Statistics on Governmental Finances and Employment.* Washington, D.C.: GPO, November.

———. 1984a. *Governmental Finances in 1982.* Washington, D.C.: GPO, October.

———. 1984b. *Public Employment in 1983.* Washington, D.C.: GPO, June.

————. 1985. *1982 Census of Governments, Labor-Management Relations in State and Local Governments.* Washington, D.C.: GPO, May.

U.S. Department of Justice, Bureau of Justice Statistics. 1981. *Sourcebook of Criminal Justice Statistics—1980.* Washington, D.C.: GPO.

U.S. Department of Labor, Bureau of Labor Statistics, 1972, 1973, 1974. *Analysis of Work Stoppages.* BLS Bulletins 1727, 1777, 1813. Washington, D.C.: GPO.

————. 1980, 1985. *Handbook of Labor Statistics,* BLS Bulletins, 2020 and 2217.

————. 1976, 1978, 1980, 1981. *Work Stoppages in Government.* BLS Reports 453, 532, 582, BLS Bulletin 2110. Washington, D.C.: GPO.

U.S. Department of Labor, Labor-Management Services Administration. 1981. *Summary of Public Sector Labor Relations Policies.* Washington, D.C.: GPO.

Van Maanen, John. 1975. Police Socialization: A Longitudinal Examination of Job Attitudes in an Urban Police Department. *Administrative Science Quarterly* 20 (June): 207–28.

Wilson, James Q. 1968. *Varieties of Police Behavior: The Management of Law and Order in Eight Communities.* Cambridge: Harvard University Press.

10
Collective Bargaining in American Industry: A Synthesis

Clifford B. Donn
David B. Lipsky

T he preceding eight chapters deal with the current status of collective bargaining in eight U.S. industries. The differences between collective bargaining for police officers and auto workers or between professional athletes and college professors are obvious and illustrate the richness and variety of contemporary collective bargaining. Depite that diversity, however, the eight industries exhibit important similarities in collective bargaining. The common themes that link most, if not all, of the industries examined in this volume are perhaps less obvious, but a careful reading of the preceding chapters reveals that there have been a number of common factors affecting collective bargaining in these industries even though the responses of the different labor-management pairs have varied.

This chapter identifies and discusses some of the most important of the common themes that emerge from the study of these eight industries. The same general framework used to organize each of the industry studies—a modification of Dunlop's systems model—is again used here to examine those themes. Although most of the topics discussed below will be illustrated with examples from at least two of the eight industries, some references will also be made to the experience in industries not covered in this book. We conclude by discussing the future of collective bargaining in American industry.

The Bargaining Environment

Technology

Technological change has always been a major factor affecting collective bargaining relationships, and the 1980s were no different in that regard. Some recent technological changes had a direct effect on bargaining in the 1980s. Unions of office and clerical workers, for example, have negotiated special conditions for employees who spend substantial amounts of time working at computer terminals (Cornfield, forthcoming, and the references cited therein). In the maritime industry technological innovation has had a severe effect on employment: containerization has dramatically cut the need for labor in the loading and unloading of ships, and other innovations, ranging from corrosion resistant materials to larger vessel sizes, have dramatically reduced the number of workers required to deliver a given cargo a given distance (Donn 1986, and the references cited therein). Often, the effect of technological change has been more subtle. Most of the industries in this book have recently been touched in many ways by technological change. The rubber, telecommunications, and automobile industries may be the three where the changes were most far-reaching and thus had the most influence on bargaining relationships.

As Karper documents, the tire industry experienced dramatic changes when radial tires replaced bias-ply tires. This change required substantial retooling by the tire companies, but retooling was not the source of the greatest impact. Rather it was the increased durability of radial tires, which reduced the demand for replacement tires, just as a variety of other economic factors, such as economic recession and the steady growth of auto imports, all combined to reduce the demand for tires on new cars as well. Together with these other factors, the change to radial technology helped produce a massive contraction of employment in the industry.

Hendricks discusses the myriad technological advances that have had major effects on employment in the telecommunications industry. The modular assembly of telephone components has reduced the time and skills required for telephone repair. The change to electronic switching has reduced costs, automated many maintenance and operator functions, and reduced the need for central office technicians. The more profound effects of technological change, however, have arisen from changes in signal transmission technology, which have allowed the substitution of microwave transmission for traditional signal transmission over wires. As Hendricks emphasizes, these changes were instrumental in the deregulation of the industry because much of the technological argument for the preservation of a "natural monopoly" disappeared. Indeed, the development of this technology makes it feasible for large telephone users to by-pass local telephone companies entirely, which has had severe implications for the pricing structure of telephone services.

Katz has pointed to the role of technological change in the auto industry in promoting the internationalization of production in that industry. Standard cars can now be constructed of interchangeable parts manufactured all over the world. Management's consequent desire to negotiate more flexible work rules in the industry has also been prompted, in part, by its desire to make greater use of robotics and microelectronic technology.

A key to understanding the effect of technological change on collective bargaining is to recognize that technological change per se is seldom an issue negotiated directly by unions and employers. Some unions, such as those in the maritime industry and the printing trades, have in the past tried (and, in general, failed) to block the introduction of new technologies, but this kind of Luddite mentality is not characteristic of American unions. Most unions in the United States, including those examined in this volume, have been willing to give employers virtually a free hand in introducing new machines and new methods of production. Instead, they have focused on attempting to control the *effects* of technological change on their constituents, using two basic approaches to protect those workers adversely affected. First, they have negotiated work rules, staffing requirements, retraining programs, procedures to govern layoffs, transfers, and displacement, controls over "outsourcing" (subcontracting), and other procedural devices to mitigate the effects of technological change. Second, they have sought compensation, often in the form of severance pay, supplemental unemployment benefits, early retirement benefits, or income and job guarantees, to reimburse workers harmed by the new technologies (Slichter, Healy, and Livernash 1960, 342–71; Somers, Cushman, and Weinberg 1963; Kochan 1980, 435–38).

The Economic Environment

There is nothing new in economic instability and nothing new in that instability having an effect on collective bargaining. The ten years following 1975, however, were characterized by economic instability on a scale not witnessed since the 1930s. The long post–World War II period of relatively steady growth came to an end, with bargaining relationships having to face economic challenges more substantial than they had seen in more than 30 years.

The two most salient economic challenges to collective bargaining in the 1980s were the recession of the early part of the decade and the growth of foreign competition, which had resulted from growing international economic interdependence. The apparel and electrical products industries especially suffered, and the three manufacturing industries examined in this volume—automobiles, agricultural machinery, and tires—as well as the airline industry, all clearly showed the severe effect of recession on collective bargaining relationships. The three manufacturing industries also are good examples of industries hard hit by foreign competition.

In the early 1980s the automobile industry suffered its worst contraction of output in 40 years because of the combined effects of recession and foreign competition. Imports had long been a growing share of the automobile market in the United States, but the trickle of imports in the 1960s became a flood in the early 1980s just as the recession was shrinking the total size of the U.S. automobile market. As Katz explains, the industry responded in a variety of ways. Temporary protection from Japanese imports was obtained through "voluntary" quotas. Japanese manufacturers were subjected to pressures, not all of them subtle, to do more of their assembly work in the United States. American automakers enlisted foreign companies in a variety of joint ventures, ranging from selling foreign-produced vehicles in this country under the name of the U.S. manufacturer (Chrysler-Mitsubishi), to joint production ventures in the United States (General Motors-Toyota), to the virtual take-over of a U.S. company by a foreign company (American Motors-Renault).

Auto imports became the symbol of the public's unhappiness with the trade imbalance, especially that with Japan. The response of many of the foreign producers has been to move part of their production capacity to the United States. General Motors, Ford, Chrysler, and American Motors had been essentially the only domestic producers, but by the mid-1980s Volks-wagen, Nissan, Toyota, and Mazda all had facilities operating in this country or were committed to opening facilities in the near future at locations already identified. Some of those companies, such as Volkswagen and Mazda, have accepted union representation without strong opposition, while others, such as Nissan, have tried to avoid organization. The United Auto Workers has tried to meet with the latter producers to allay their fears and assure them that cooperative relationships are possible, but obviously the union has not persuaded all of them. The success or failure of the innovative UAW-GM Saturn agreement may play a key role in determining whether the foreign companies take the union's overtures of cooperation seriously.

The decline in auto sales alone would have made for difficult economic times in the tire industry, but along with the switch to radial technology noted above, the industry was also hit by the dramatic growth of foreign competi-tion. The Europeans (Michelin) and the Japanese (Bridgestone) gained large shares of the shrinking tire market. Again, the union, the United Rubber Workers, agreed to significant local concessions at the negotiating table, but that did not prevent most of the major companies from abandoning certain segments of the tire market and moving into other, sometimes unrelated, product lines. This change in the companies' production strategies placed even more pressure on the URW.

Agricultural machinery companies prospered during the 1970s when commodity prices and land values were increasing. But as Seeber explains, both of those trends reversed in the first half of the 1980s, causing a marked decline in the demand for new farm machinery. The agricultural machinery industry was also adversely affected by foreign competition and, perhaps to a greater degree, by the near-collapse of the farm economy in the mid-1980s. These two forces together reduced employment in the industry by over one-third between 1979 and 1984.

Airlines have long been especially sensitive to recession. Vacation trav-elers postpone or cancel plans and businesses reduce travel when they need to control costs. The recession of the early 1980s hit the airline industry, as Cappelli notes, at a time when changes in public policy designed to enhance competition in the industry had already disturbed long-standing bargaining relationships. Recession and deregulation combined to bring about the most dramatic bargaining concessions in American industry and at the same time, as in the case of Eastern Airlines, the appointment of union representatives to company boards of directors.

Another factor in the economic environment has been the growing competition of nonunion employers in a variety of industries. Sometimes nonunion competition takes the form of newly created domestic companies operating in industries that were once entirely or almost completely unionized, as in steel and telecommunications. At other times the source of nonunion competition is foreign producers that either export to the United States or build nonunion facilities of their own in this country, as in autos and electrical products. Deregulation has proven to be a factor that can open a previously unionized market to nonunion competition. Trucking is one example of an industry once dominated by unionized companies but now facing serious competition from nonunion employers (Levinson 1980; Mills and McCormick 1985, 423–63). The growing number of nonunion contractors in major segments of the contract construction industry has long been evident; unionized construction employers are now almost completely excluded from the residential building segment of the market and are losing their share of the commercial and even the industrial segments as well (Mills 1980; Mills and McCormick 1985, 90–92). Coal mining was once almost totally unionized, but more than half of all coal tonnage is now produced by nonunion companies, most of which are open pit operations west of the Mississippi (Navarro 1983). Among the industries studied here airlines, automobiles, and tires all provide examples of different forms of nonunion competition and different methods of addressing it.

The principal factor leading to the recent increase in nonunion competition in the airline industry has been deregulation, which has enabled the existing local carriers to expand into trunk routes and the new carriers to enter those routes as well. A number of the local carriers and new carriers have been nonunion, People Express constituting perhaps the archetypical example of the new nonunion company. Another employer strategy that has to some degree increased nonunion competition in the airline industry involves a technique long used in the construction industry, "double breasting." Cappelli notes that a few unionized carriers have spun off their own nonunion subsidiaries, which then compete with their unionized divisions.

Foreign competitors moving to the United States have been the principal source of nonunion competition in the tire industry. The United Rubber Workers, however, has not as yet had any success in organizing the new domestic facilities of Michelin, although the union does represent workers at Bridgestone. Of course, as Karper indicates, the domestic producers have also moved facilities out of their traditional base in Akron, Ohio. Goodyear, Firestone, General, and Uniroyal have all tried to avoid the organization of their new facilities. Other unions faced with similar circumstances, such as the United Auto Workers and the United Steelworkers, have reponded in part by seeking to organize workers in other industries, but the URW has decided to confine its organizing efforts strictly to the rubber industry. To date, the union's success has been limited at best.

Thus, the industry studies contained in this volume serve to illustrate how recession, foreign competition, and nonunion domestic competition undercut union bargaining power in the 1980s. In industries particularly hard hit by those developments, unions suffered the loss of many members. To stem the erosion of membership, the unions reluctantly granted wage and benefit concessions. In some cases (such as autos) those concessions seemed to stanch the loss of members, at least temporarily. But in others (such as rubber) union concessions did not sufficiently counter the opposing forces of the marketplace, and union power and membership continued to erode.

The Legal Environment

In the early years of the Carter presidency, the union movement mounted a major effort to persuade Congress to amend the Taft-Hartley Act, the major federal statute that directly regulates labor-management relations in the private sector. The union movement sought amendments to the statute that would expedite certification election procedures and increase the scope of remedies for unlawful employer activities. The business community, however, strongly opposed labor law reform, and the reforms died in the Senate in 1978. The subsequent opposition of the Reagan administration has effectively prevented the resurrection of labor law reform in the 1980s, with the consequence that the statutory framework governing labor relations in the private sector has remained basically unchanged since the Landrum-Griffin amendments were added to the Taft-Hartley Act in 1959 (Kochan 1980, 64–65; Kochan, Katz, and McKersie 1983, 40–45 and 230–36).

Nevertheless, changes in other federal statutes, and in state and local laws, and rulings and interpretations by administrative agencies and the courts significantly affected the public policy context of collective bargaining in many industries. For example, Cappelli notes the use of the bankruptcy laws by some airline companies to avoid the obligations of existing collective bargaining agreements. That strategy was not confined to airlines and was one factor that helped precipitate a significant reworking of the federal bankruptcy code. Since 1984 federal law requires that a company that files for bankruptcy must negotiate in good faith with its unions on changes in its labor contracts and, if it fails to reach agreement, cannot dissolve its contracts without the approval of the federal bankruptcy court (*New York Times* 1985a).

One public policy change that dominated all others in its influence on collective bargaining in the 1980s was deregulation. In a process that began in the 1970s and accelerated under the pro-market philosophies of the Reagan administration, numerous industries in which competition had been restricted found themselves exposed to at least some of the rigors of the market. Among our eight industries telecommunications and airlines provide excellent examples of bargaining relationships that have struggled to adjust to deregulation and have done so in different ways and with different degrees of success.

For 40 years the airline industry was closely regulated by the Civil Aeronautics Board, which controlled the routes flown by carriers, the prices they charged, and the entry of new carriers into the industry. Then in 1978 Congress passed the Airline Deregulation Act, which over the following several years virtually eliminated federal controls in the industry. Soon after passage of the act new carriers began to enter into competition with the existing carriers. Some of the new carriers (People Express, New York Air, Midway) were nonunion, but as Cappelli points out, the nonunion carriers still account for only a small portion of the industry's trunk markets. Price and route competition became much more prevalent than in the past, and a wave of mergers and acquisitions swept through the industry. The effects of deregulation on collective bargaining were dramatic, producing what are probably the most profound changes in bargaining relationships and practices of all those described in this volume.

Telecommunications began deregulation and divestiture more recently, in 1984, and so their full effects and even the direction of their effects are not yet as clear as in the case of airlines. The effects of deregulation on collective bargaining in the telephone industry need to be distinguished from the effects of divestiture. Only long distance telephone service has been substantially deregulated: Local service continues to be regulated by the states. AT&T's monopoly over long-distance service has ended, and the down-scaled company and its unions now face competition for the first time in their history. The parties' adjustment has not been easy; serious strikes occurred in both the 1983 and 1986 bargaining rounds. By contrast, the regional operating companies and their unions continue to be shielded from the full effects of competition. Divestiture has, however, allowed each operating company to pursue its own collective bargaining strategy, with some seeking cooperative relations and others taking a more aggressive stance toward their unions. The upshot of these changes is likely to be much more diversity in the terms of labor contracts covering workers in the telecommunications industry, although it is likely to be several years before this prediction can be verified by experience.

The legal environment of collective bargaining in the public sector is in marked contrast with the legal environment in the private sector. With the exception of the federal sector statutory regulation of public sector bargaining rests with the states. A majority of states passed statutes governing collective bargaining by state and local employees in the 1960s and early 1970s, and as Delaney and Feuille explain in their chapter on police, there is little uniformity in those statutes across states. The duty to bargain, the scope of bargaining, the right to strike, strike penalties, and the methods prescribed for resolving impasses all take different forms in different states. Some states encourage public sector bargaining; other states discourage or even prohibit it. Nevertheless, many of the statutes have been in place for more than a decade, so that our understanding of the effects on bargaining of alternative policy approaches is well advanced. A salient issue in the case of police is the effect of an interest arbitration statute on bargaining outcomes. Delaney and Feuille show that police salaries are higher in states with arbitration statutes than in states without. Clearly, this kind of evidence has implications not only for the policy decisions made in the public sector but also for those made in the private sector.

The Parties

Over the last two decades union membership contracted in manufacturing, mining, and transportation. One result of this contraction was the disappearance of many unions, mostly through merger with other, stronger unions. Union mergers affected bargaining in such industries as textiles and apparels, nonferrous metals, graphic arts, meatpacking, and the railroads (Janus 1978; Chaison 1980). Curiously, this trend did not surface in most of the industries included in this volume. Merger was not a strategy pursued by the UAW, URW, or CWA, or in education by the NEA and AFT.

At the same time that unionism was contracting in some sectors, it was expanding in others, notably in the public sector, retail trade, services, and education. The NEA, for example, grew to 1.9 million members and became the largest union in the United States. The AFT, the NEA's rival, reached 600,000 members. The United Food and Commercial Workers International Union—created, in the late 1970s and early 1980s, out of a series of mergers of unions in retail and wholesale trade, meatcutting, meatpacking, and insurance—became the largest AFL-CIO affiliate. The Service Employees' International Union, which organized clerical and service workers in both the public and private sectors, also experienced significant growth. The American Federation of State, County and Municipal Employees is another union that added significant numbers of new members. As a result the labor movement is no longer dominated by blue-collar workers; today union membership is much more heterogeneous, consisting of large numbers of government employees, clerks, service employees, and professionals (Gifford 1982; Kokkelenberg and Sockell 1985; *New York Times* 1985b).

Three of the chapters in this book examine occupations or sectors in which, until the 1960s, collective bargaining was either nonexistent or relatively unimportant but, now, is a major means of determining the terms and conditions of employment. For example, police officers are the one group of workers examined in this volume who are employed entirely in the public sector. Twenty-five years ago government employees were less highly unionized than employees in most other sectors of the economy; there was little statutory support for public employee collective bargaining; and most public employers were reluctant to engage in a process they viewed as tantamount to ceding their sovereignty. But in the 1980s the public sector, federal as well as state and local, is one of the most highly unionized "industries." About 55 percent of all police officers are unionized, making them one of the most highly unionized of the public sector occupations. Collective bargaining is widespread, albeit, as Delaney and Feuille make clear, not universal. As the chapter on police indicates, public sector collective bargaining is characterized by several unique problems of bargaining structure, legal framework, issues subject to negotiation, and dispute resolution.

University professors represent a group for whom collective bargaining is still in the relatively early stages of development. As Bacharach, Schmidle, and Bauer note, the legal environment has not been entirely supportive of bargaining in private universities and colleges; and potential faculty unionists often still evince skepticism about whether the traditional adversarial model of bargaining is suitable for them and, if not, whether unions are suitable means for faculty to pursue less confrontational forms of workplace governance.

Professional athletes are a group for whom collective bargaining is now widespread and of major importance. Again, the nontraditional nature of bargaining in this industry is apparent in Dworkin's chapter. For example, collective bargaining sets minimum salaries, but salaries above the minimum remain subject to individual player negotiation. Also particular to this industry is the restriction on the interteam mobility of athletes, which has been probably the most controversial and persistent issue in collective bargaining in professional sports.

On the employer side of the table corporate mergers, takeovers, and the reorganization of numerous U.S. companies have had a profound effect on bargaining relationships. The restructuring of corporations has implications for the coverage of collective bargaining agreements and for the obligation of the employer to bargain, because in the eyes of the law a change in the identity of the employer can alter or even eliminate a bargaining relationship. In this volume the airlines serve as an example of the serious adjustments in bargaining that are necessary when reorganization is widespread.

The companies' double-breasted strategy, for example, produced larger corporations operating both union and nonunion carriers under different names (such as the Texas Air Corporation, which operates a nonunion subsidiary, New York Air, and a unionized subsidiary, Continental). Cappelli points out, as well, that the competitive rigors of the market have led to serious financial difficulties for a number of airlines, some of which have responded by seeking purchasers or mergers. Frank Lorenzo, president of the Texas Air Corporation, has been particularly active in all phases of airline reorganization, engaging in double breasting, buyouts, and mergers. He has also been identified by the unions in the industry as an opponent of unionization and collective bargaining. When Texas Air tried to take over TWA, the unions went so far as to offer to negotiate concessions to an alternative buyer, Carl Icahn, in an effort to avoid a Lorenzo takeover.

The Structure of Bargaining

Bargaining structures closely reflect the make-up of the bargaining parties and, in turn, have much to do with the balance of power the parties bring to the bargaining table. The term *bargaining structure* refers to the size and scope of the units that engage in bargaining. Some bargaining structures encompass only a single department or a single plant, while others encompass two or more plants, or even an entire industry. Employers can bargain singly or collectively (for example, through a multi-employer association); and unions can bargain singly or in a coalition with other unions. Bargaining structure also refers to pattern setting and pattern following—that is, whether and to what extent a key agreement influences the terms of other agreements. Fundamentally, therefore, structural considerations in bargaining raise questions of power. Who has the power to make decisions in bargaining? If bargaining is at the plant level, one can surmise that a considerable amount of decision-making power will be in the hands of local company and union representatives. If bargaining is at the company or industry level, the balance of power is likely to shift to top union leaders and corporate officers (Weber 1967). Although the concept seems, at first blush, to be straightforward, on closer analysis bargaining structure can be quite subtle.

The sources of this subtlety are several. For example, although the National Labor Relations Board technically delineates the size and scope of bargaining units, the so-called appropriate bargaining units specified by the board for purposes of determining union representation questions are frequently not the basis on which negotiations or grievance administration occur. Even when appropriate bargaining units are plantwide or based on occupational groups within a plant, negotiations may be conducted on a companywide or even an industrywide basis. Basic steel is a good example of an industry that traditionally engaged in industrywide bargaining despite the fact that its appropriate bargaining units were technically plantwide in scope (Stieber 1980).

A second source of subtlety in bargaining structure is that different issues are often resolved at different levels of decision making. In many industries issues such as wages and fringe benefits may be negotiated at the company level, while others such as work rules are negotiated at the plant level. One of the best examples of how bargaining structure can exist on these multiple levels is the way grievances are handled in most bargaining relationships. Grievances are usually addressed initially at the department level and, if unsettled there, usually move to the plant and then to the company level. Accordingly, simple statements about the level at which collective bargaining occurs cannot be made in many cases. Unless the issue under discussion is identified, the level at which it will be decided cannot be known.

A third source of subtlety in bargaining structure arises from the patterns that are set and followed in much of bargaining. Employees' desire to achieve settlements that match what other comparable workers receive and employers' desire to pay no more than their competitors do are among the most powerful motivations in collective bargaining negotiations. Those factors, and other forces as well, induce the bargaining parties to look closely at other bargaining settlements in choosing their goals for the next round of negotiations. Sometimes these patterns are ill-defined because the parties take note of large numbers of settlements and their rough assessment of a common trend serves as a starting point for their negotiations. In other cases the patterns are well defined and obvious, as in the case of a company or industry that considers itself to be in tandem with another company or industry (Dunlop 1957; Ross 1948; Bourdon 1979).

The 1980s have brought significant changes in bargaining structures, both in the formal level at which negotiations and contract administration occur and in the traditional patterns that have been followed. Examples of both types of changes abound. The breakup of traditional industrywide negotiations in steel is one of the best examples of a major change in the formal structure of negotiations (*New York Times* 1986a; *Washington Post* 1986). The meatpacking industry is a good example of an industry in which traditional patterns have dissolved, with different companies achieving divergent settlements depending on their aggressiveness in negotiations and on their financial health.

Almost all of the industries studied in this volume have seen bargaining structure changes in response to changes in the technological, economic, and legal environments of the 1980s. Telecommunications, automobiles, tires, and airlines have all seen shifts in formal negotiating structures or traditional patterns, or both.

The bargaining structure in the telecommunications industry was not particularly stable even before the breakup of AT&T. As Hendricks explains, the union had sought nationwide bargaining for many years but had achieved it, at least in a formal sense, only in 1974. The spinoff of the Bell System's regional operating companies has left the new bargaining structure in doubt, but it seems clear that formal nationwide bargaining across the operating companies is over for the time being. The regional operating companies seem unanimous in their opposition to nationwide bargaining; and since the formal bargaining units were never altered to reflect the emergence of a de facto nationwide negotiating structure in the 1970s, it seems likely that the companies will be able to maintain that opposition. Whether a tight tandem relationship or pattern will emerge among the regional operating companies cannot be predicted at this point with any confidence.

In the automobile industry the changes in bargaining structure have been of great importance, but they have had little effect on either the formal bargaining units or on the level at which the parties actually face each other in negotiations. Rather, the changes have largely been reflected in the breakdown of traditional pattern relationships within the industry and in the accompanying new heterogeneity of contract terms across the companies and among the plants within companies. In the early 1980s the major elements of the compensation and benefits packages contained in General Motors, Ford, and Chrysler contracts at the national level were no longer indistinguishable. Differences in their compensation packages reflected differences in their financial positions and in the nature of their production processes. Similarly, traditional pattern relationships among the major auto producers and the numerous small supplier companies have been under strain. As Katz has documented, in 1982 and in later negotiations between the UAW and the parts supply companies, their settlements have substantially broken from the assembly company patterns. The breakdown in auto industry patterns has had major implications for several other industries as well, including steel, nonferrous metals, tires, and agricultural machinery—all of which have traditionally closely scrutinized the settlements in autos. In fact, the automobile settlements had traditionally established the key pattern for a significant portion of all manufacturing industries. Thus, auto settlements no longer serve as the pacesetters they once did.

In the tire industry, although the formal structure of national bargaining on a company-by-company basis remains, other aspects of the bargaining structure have changed. In particular, as Karper points out, the ten-year experiment of the major tire producers with mutual strike insurance ended with the 1976 negotiations. For many years negotiated settlements in this industry followed the automobile pattern closely. Once bargaining uniformity within the automobile industry broke down, it was impossible to find an auto pattern to follow. Bargaining in the tire industry also broke step under pressures caused by growing nonunion competition, growing factionalism within the URW, and the tire companies' new-found means of threatening the union economically with plant closings and layoffs.

The bargaining structures in the airline industry also broke down, in the 1980s, as previously local carriers and other new entrants joined the trunk markets. The Deregulation Act of 1978 also brought about changes in the industry's bargaining structure by another means. The act, as Cappelli points out, outlawed the Mutual Assistance Pact (MAP) the trunk carriers had used as strike insurance. This has reduced employer solidarity in the face of labor conflict, but it has also served to offset, at least to some degree, the diminution of bargaining power the airline employees suffered because of increased competition in the deregulated market. The elimination of the MAP has been the one feature of the new environment that has been favorable to the airline unions but, as Cappelli makes clear, it has not served to protect them from the rigors of the competitive market.

Police bargaining is a good example of a strictly local, or craft, structure of bargaining. Police officers almost never bargain with other municipal employees as one group, nor do the jurisdictions for which they work join forces with others in a multi-employer structure. By contrast, bargaining in professional sports is on an industrywide, multi-employer basis: All the owners in each sport band together for bargaining purposes, usually delegating the authority to make agreements to professional negotiators, and all sign contracts that apply uniformly to the teams and players in the league.

It is apparent that the dominant trend in bargaining structures in the 1970s and 1980s was toward more decentralized bargaining and a breakdown of previously robust patterns. One result of this trend was less standardization in labor contracts both within and across industries. Another result was a downward shift in decision-making power, from top industry and union leaders toward the regional and local representatives of the parties. In the 1980s, as in the years before World War II, the plant and the workplace became important arenas for the determination of critical bargaining issues.

The Bargaining Process

Bargaining Issues

Wages, fringe benefits, and work rules are always on the agenda in collective bargaining. The particular approaches the parties take to addressing these and other issues differ over time, however, depending on developments in the technological, economic, and legal environments within which bargaining occurs. The 1980s gave birth to a number of innovative contract provisions and agreements, especially but not exclusively those designed to promote greater cooperation between labor and management. Garnering much attention in the popular press, those experiments have included employee representation on company boards, greater use of joint union-management committees, greater reliance on profit or productivity sharing as a form of compensation, and the adoption of more flexible work rules, such as reducing the number of job classifications that may exist under a collective bargaining agreement (see, for example, Kochan and Barocci 1985, 15–28). Some groups of professional employees who are relatively new to collective bargaining, such as college faculty members, provided models for cooperative and consultative ventures. Among the industries examined in this volume automobiles and professional sports were perhaps the most innovative in the contract language they employed to address both the traditional bargaining issues and the more novel ones.

In automobiles one highly publicized development was the appointment of the president of the UAW to the board of directors of the Chrysler Corporation, a quid pro quo for the economic concessions that Chrysler so desperately needed in 1979 to secure government loan guarantees that were to keep the company from bankruptcy. All of the major auto companies now have some form of quality-of-working-life or employee participation scheme as well, and all of those schemes have been designed to reshape, at least in part, the old adversarial relationship between the union and the companies.

The automobile industry has also instituted pay systems that base compensation much more directly on company performance than was the case in the past. To some extent profit sharing has been the price unions have demanded for short-term wage concessions, but in other respects it has partially replaced other elements of the compensation package that based wages on formulas largely unconnected to company performance (for example, cost-of-living adjustments).

In addition, as Katz explains, the Saturn agreement between the UAW and General Motors represented a remarkable experiment in joint planning for the future. Reached in mid-1985 the agreement specified bargaining and other workplace arrangements for a plant that was still some five years away from production. Although some experts in labor law had doubts about the legality of the Saturn agreement (because at the time the agreement was signed, Saturn had no employees who might have chosen or rejected union representation under the National Labor Relations Act's certification procedures), other labor relations experts hailed the agreement—with its flexible work rules, broad job categories, and commitment to employee participation—as a fundamental improvement that augered well for collective bargaining as an institution.

It should be emphasized that the agricultural machinery industry, organized by the same union as autos and closely associated for many years with the auto pattern of settlements, has adopted virtually none of these innovative approaches. While the collective bargaining process in the auto industry has been in upheaval, the parties in agricultural machinery have dealt with their most critical issues in basically the same fashion they did 30 years before. Seeber notes that the result has been a high level of conflict in this industry.

Collective bargaining agreements in professional sports contain a cornucopia of unusual contract provisions that deal with the special employment circumstances of professional athletes. Dworkin explains in detail the kinds of provisions that have been negotiated in baseball, basketball, football, and hockey to deal with the issue of player mobility among teams. Reserve clauses, salary arbitration, option years, offer sheets, compensation caps, and several other innovative approaches have all been tried, but the issue still remains in the forefront of sports negotiations. Players in the major sports are not easily replaced because the fans identify with their favorite stars, making each player a unique commodity with some degree of monopoly power. Nevertheless, these contract provisions are not necessarily novel, since the same issue also arises in other segments of the entertainment industry.

Similarly, police collective bargaining agreements often contain unique language that reflects the unusual nature of the work police officers do. Some of the provisions that Delaney and Feuille have labeled as "law enforcement" provisions deal with topics, such as the use of firearms or restrictions on the location of an officer's residence, that are unheard of in most other labor contracts. As in professional sports these provisions are only new in the sense that collective bargaining is relatively new in the police industry.

In the 1980s unions and employers throughout American industry negotiated many innovative terms to address employment security issues. As industries faced recession, foreign competition, and deregulation, even employees high on seniority lists who had considered themselves immune to layoff faced the prospect of unemployment, and sometimes permanent displacement. With employers demanding a variety of economic concessions at the bargaining table, unions have often made some form of job protection the quid pro quo for their agreement on cost-saving provisions. Airlines, automobiles, telecommunications, and agricultural machinery have all reached agreement on job security innovations.

About half of the trunk airlines have granted some type of job security concessions, usually in exchange for union concessions that have lowered current labor costs. As Cappelli notes, the carriers most likely to grant job security concessions are those that do not believe those guarantees will prove costly, that is, those carriers that view themselves as having good growth prospects.

The automobile contracts contain a variety of new approaches to the issue of job security. Katz discusses the employment guarantees for workers with 15 or more years' seniority contained in the 1982 Ford and General Motors contracts. These provisions emphasize guaranteed income streams for senior workers. Much more comprehensive employment guarantees were included in those contracts on an experimental basis for a small number of plants. The companies also made concessions in their plant-closing and outsourcing practices.

As Hendricks explains, the telecommunications unions began to negotiate protection against anticipated employment changes before divestiture and deregulation actually came about. In their case the protections largely revolved around wages, benefits, and seniority for employees transferred within what was once the integrated AT&T system.

Seeber notes that job security concerns in the agricultural machinery industry have also given rise to a variety of solutions. For example, the UAW obtained agreement on the "domestic content" of the output at International Harvester, on group incentives that allow for some wage flexibility, and on early warnings of plant closings.

Perhaps the most widely publicized set of changes in bargaining issues during the late 1970s and, especially, the first half of the 1980s came in the form of concessionary bargaining. There is nothing new in the phenomenon of employers' coming to the bargaining table with their own strong demands, or of unions' conceding some of their terms and conditions of employment when the firm or the industry faces dire economic circumstances. The long post–World War II prosperity, however, had made such episodes the exception rather than the rule. Labor experts as well as workers had come to expect that the initiative in negotiations would be taken by unions and that the terms and conditions of unionized employees would steadily improve. The question of wage and benefit improvements was not if but how fast they would occur. The 1979 Chrysler agreement ushered in an era in which the "if" question came to the fore as large numbers of unions accepted wage reductions and work rule changes, initially to save financially strapped employers but later also to enable other employers to compete with those that had already won concessions. The steel and trucking industries witnessed substantial concessions by unions in the 1980s. Among the industries studied here, agricultural machinery, automobiles, and airlines all engaged in concessionary bargaining along these lines.

In the agricultural machinery industry concessions have almost exclusively taken the form of pay cuts. The UAW has been reluctant to grant concessions on work rules and has been willing, at least in the negotiations up to 1986, to engage in vigorous strike action to make that policy stick.

But the automobile industry provides an interesting contrast because here the UAW has been willing to agree to much more radical and innovative concessions, including substantial changes in work rules. Why the UAW has been willing to grant broad-ranging concessions in autos and not in agricultural machinery remains something of a mystery, although it is probably the result of differences in the personalities and dispositions of the UAW's auto and agricultural machinery leaders, the characteristics of the rank and file, the strategies of the employers, and the history and traditions of bargaining in the two industries. Certainly there have been wage and benefit concessions in automobiles, including the demise of the annual improvement factor, the shift of some COLA payments into health or pension funds, and the negotiation of contingent compensation schemes, such as bonuses and profit sharing. As Katz points out, however, work rule changes appeared not only in the experimental Saturn agreement, but also in many of the existing auto plants. Most of the work rule changes were negotiated in local UAW contracts, and in 1982 and 1984 the Ford and General Motors national agreements specifically authorized those local work rule negotiations.

Economic concessions may have been more widespread and substantial in the airline industry than in any other. One of the principal forms of concessions agreed to by the airline unions has been the adoption of two-tier wage plans in which new employees are paid on a scale lower than that of the existing employees. Some of the two-tier agreements allow new employees eventually to catch up to the more senior employees, while others do not. Those agreements have raised a host of strategic and legal questions, not the least of which is whether unions negotiating such agreements violate their duty of fair representation to new employees (*Harvard Law Review* 1985).

In the past union negotiators were always prepared to grant concessions, but only when employers could persuade them that exceptionally threatening circumstances required that they be made. Unions feared that once they granted concessions, even to an enterprise on the verge of dissolution, they would not be able to hold the line with healthier firms. Any concessions, it was thought, could conceivably cause a union's wage structure to come tumbling down like a house of cards. In effect, during hard times unions preferred to maintain wages and benefits and allow employers to reduce labor costs by means of employment cutbacks. But in the 1980s many unions seemed willing to reverse that preference. In the last decade unions accepted significant wage concessions in exchange for employment security provisions and employment guarantees. And if union wage structures have not collapsed, they have seriously eroded, especially in manufacturing. Whether wage concessions have on balance served to reduce employment losses is, however, a question that remains unanswered.

Labor-Management Conflict

Strike activity declined precipitously in the United States in the 1980s. To illustrate, in a typical year in the 1970s there were between 200 and 300 strikes involving 1,000 or more workers (in 1974 there were 424 such strikes), but in 1984 there were only 62 such strikes and in 1985 only 54 (U.S. Department of Labor 1986). (It might be noted that the government stopped collecting data on strikes involving fewer than 1,000 workers in 1981.) Did American collective bargaining enter an era of industrial peace?

It has been said in international relations that peace is not merely the absence of war. Similarly, in labor relations peace is not merely the absence of strikes. True industrial peace is characterized by a climate of accommodation (if not cooperation), by each party's recognition of the legitimacy of the other party in the relationship, and by a willingness to compromise on divisive issues. By this definition, many strike-free industries were not truly in a state of peace in the 1980s. Rather, the decline of strike activity is probably attributable to the realization by many unions that the strike weapon had lost much of its effectiveness in those years of economic decline, high unemployment, technological change, and conservative public policies. Historically, strike activity usually declined during recessions, and so the dramatic drop in strikes in the early 1980s might have been simply a cyclical response. When unemployment is high, union bargaining power is undercut because, among other reasons, employers have a ready supply of workers to replace strikers (see, for example, Kaufman 1981).

Also contributing to the decline, however, was the fact that many employers appeared more willing to continue to operate during a strike than they were before. Many of those that did continue operations during strikes permanently replaced some or all striking employees and succeeded in breaking the union. Others simply deployed supervisors and nonstriking employees in an attempt to wring more favorable settlements from the striking unions (Perry, Dramer, and Schneider 1982). The Reagan administration had set the tone for this development in 1981 when it replaced the striking air traffic controllers and decertified their union (Northrup 1984). The significance of that action was not lost on a large number of employers in both the public and the private sectors. Moreover, President Reagan's appointment of new members to the National Labor Relations Board, members who seemed less sympathetic to unions, also appears to have made employers more willing to deal aggressively with unions in strike situations. In airlines, for example, the employers began to operate during strikes in the 1980s.

Telecommunications is a good example of an industry in which modern technology allows production to continue relatively unhindered, at least during the early stages of a strike. Telephone companies have long sought to maintain service during strikes, and the advancing automation of telephone services has steadily increased their capacity to do so successfully. Although telephone installation and maintenance may have to be postponed during a strike, basic telephone service is now so completely automated and computerized that the great bulk of telephone services can be provided without the consumer noticing any change. Supervisory employees, for example, can be shifted to essential maintenance work to keep the system operating. These expediencies do put pressure on the employer, however, and that pressure increases as time goes on with backlogs of unattended administrative functions and service orders and with growing fatigue among the supervisory employees, who have to spend long shifts doing tasks that have become unfamiliar. Nonetheless, the companies' capacity to continue to provide basic services weakens the bargaining power of telecommunications employees in strike situations. Still, as Hendricks points out, increased competition among providers of long distance telephone service may have increased the vulnerability of AT&T to strikes. Competition raises the possibility that a strike may mean lost customers. Moreover, the breakup of the Bell System also means that the regional operating companies cannot draw on management and supervisory personnel from all over the country to assist them during a regional or local strike.

In contrast to telecommunications, the airlines' recent attempts to operate during strikes have often been expressly designed to rid the companies of their burden of dealing with the union. For example, the recession in the industry in the early 1980s and the ready supply of qualified pilots allowed Continental to replace nearly all of its unionized pilots. Even if their replacement did not succeed, in the end, in removing the pilots' union, the replacement of higher paid senior pilots with junior pilots substantially reduced Continental's operating expenses.

The Future of Collective Bargaining

The decade of the 1980s was a time of ferment for the institution of collective bargaining. Unions and employers had to respond to changes in the technological, economic, and legal environments that were unprecedented in the post–World War II period. Recession and economic stagnation, foreign and nonunion competition, deregulation and divestiture—all served to shift the initiative in collective bargaining from unions to employers. One result of this shift was a greater willingness of unions to grant concession on wages, benefits, and work rules. Somewhat overshadowed by concession bargaining was an equally significant development—the increased willingness of many employers and unions to enter into innovative arrangements in which issues formerly outside the scope of bargaining became the focus of their concern. If agreements that sought to improve the quality of working life, to promote union and employee participation in business decision making, to base pay on profits and other measures of employee and firm performance, to enhance the employment security of union members, and to experiment with other forms of workplace reform did not become the norm, they certainly became more commonplace in the 1980s. Those developments had the effect of broadening the scope of bargaining beyond the parties' traditionally narrow focus on wages, hours, and conditions of employment. In effect, many unions traded short-term economic concessions for an expanded role in the enterprise. Paradoxically, these trade-offs, the ostensible result of unions' weakness in the 1980s, might serve to strengthen their position in the long run.

The loss of members in traditional union strongholds caused the labor movement to undertake an intense self-appraisal. In 1982, for example, the AFL-CIO established the Committee on the Evolution of Work, consisting of top international union and AFL-CIO leaders, to assess the condition of workers and their unions and to make recommendations for the "renewal and regeneration" of the American labor movement. Among several noteworthy recommendations in the committee's 1985 report was a proposal to create new categories of union membership for workers not employed in organized bargaining units. Noting that the number of *former* union members in the labor force was greater than the number of *current* union members (27 million versus 20 million), the committee believed that a new category of membership might serve to bring those former members back into the union fold, even if circumstances prevented unions from representing them directly in collective bargaining (AFL-CIO 1985).

By the end of 1986 some 30 international unions had established, or were planning to establish, the category of "associate member." One of the first benefits offered to associate members was a consumer credit card that carried an interest rate significantly below the rate on other cards issued by the nation's banks. At the same time the AFL-CIO was laying plans to offer both associate and full members an array of financial and consumer services, such as discounts on consumer goods; inexpensive life, auto, and homeowner insurance; and money market and mutual funds designed especially for union members. All of those services, it should be noted, were to be financed or subsidized by the union movement itself, and not by employers through collective bargaining (*New York Times* 1986b and 1987; and discussions with AFL-CIO leaders in Washington, D.C., in November 1986). This historic shift in organizing strategy could mean that in the future labor will emphasize its collective *purchasing* power even more than its collective *bargaining* power. But it was the hope of the AFL-CIO that members attracted to the movement because of the new services would eventually recognize the advantages of collective bargaining as a method of improving their welfare.

As the 1980s drew to a close, the wave of corporate mergers, acquisitions, bankruptcies, and reorganizations continued without abatement in industries such as autos, steel, agricultural machinery, oil refining, and trucking. Those events disrupted many stable bargaining relationships. Many corporations continued to shut down their older, unionized facilities and open new, nonunion plants; move their production facilities overseas; form new, nonunion subsidiaries; or subcontract part of their work to nonunion or foreign producers. The effect of these corporate actions on collective bargaining is well documented in this volume's industry studies. Corporate reorganizations and relocations were clearly another factor that caused a shift in the balance of power in labor relations from unions to employers, and there is no sign that a reversal in this trend will occur in the near future.

In the 1940s and 1950s collective bargaining was the seedbed for many new employee benefits—pension plans, health insurance, vacation plans, and supplemental unemployment benefits—that later spread to nonunion workplaces. In some cases nonunion companies had first introduced such benefits in the 1920s or earlier, but it was the union movement that took the initiative in refining, improving, and diffusing wage and fringe benefit plans and personnel policies (with some important exceptions) in the years following World War II (see, for example, Slichter, Healy, and Livernash 1960).

It is not at all certain that the union sector continues to be the leader today. Increasingly during the 1980s the leadership role in developing innovative personnel and human resource policies was assumed by several nonunion companies (or companies that are primarily nonunion) such as IBM, Eastman Kodak, DuPont, Eaton, and several other companies in the high technology industries. Clearly, some nonunion employers adopted progressive human resource policies because of a conscious desire to avoid unionization, but for others union avoidance was not necessarily their sole motivation. These others based their policies on the belief that practices that enhanced employees' job satisfaction and job security were also the best means of improving job performance and of attracting and retaining the types of workers they needed. In other words, keeping a step ahead of the union sector made good business sense (see, for example, Kochan, Katz, and McKersie 1986, especially 47–80).

By the end of the 1980s some parts of the union sector were in the unaccustomed position of needing to catch up with the advances introduced by an elite group of nonunion firms. In some industries, such as autos, the parties continued to be on the cutting edge of workplace reforms. But the industry studies in this volume demonstrate that the innovations adopted by the UAW and the auto companies in the 1980s were not always matched in other unionized industries. In a significant number of bargaining relationships the parties continued to focus on traditional bread-and-butter issues.

Whether the union sector will, in the future, lead the way in developing and diffusing workplace reforms and new personnel practices is difficult to forecast. The question is closely linked to the future vitality of the institution of collective bargaining itself. The economic environment of bargaining relationships in the future will either foster or discourage efforts to keep collective bargaining alive and well. In the 1980s the parties in distressed and declining industries were often more worried about their own survival than about the vitality of their bargaining relationships. In general, now as in the past, collective bargaining thrives in stable or growing industries. Despite the bargaining innovations that have occurred in distressed industries, one can safely predict that collective bargaining will grow stronger in the future only if the macroeconomy in general and the unionized sectors of economy in particular experience healthy economic growth. But if the economy experiences periodic and prolonged recessions or economic stagnation and decline, collective bargaining (and its capacity to initiate workplace reforms) will suffer.

The future of collective bargaining will also depend on the direction of public policy. In the 1980s deregulation shook the roots of collective bargaining in several key industries. But now that deregulation has largely been completed, it is not likely to continue to have a critical influence on bargaining relationships. Collective bargaining was clearly weakened in deregulated industries, such as telecommunications, airlines, and trucking, but it did survive. And having survived, it is not likely to grow any weaker in those industries.

More important than regulatory policies to the future of collective bargaining in American industry will be the direction taken by the National Labor Relations Board and the courts. Having failed to achieve congressional approval of labor law reform in the 1970s, the union movement then saw itself as the victim of a long series of adverse decisions by those agencies in the 1980s. Whether those decisions were right or wrong, and whether they had the effect, as labor asserts, of weakening unions and collective bargaining, are questions that can be debated. It must be a significant sign, however, that labor's frustration with contemporary public policies grew to such heights that several important union leaders seemed prepared to see the Taft-Hartley Act scrapped and to return the "law of the jungle" (*New York Times* 1985c, quoting Lane Kirkland, president of the AFL-CIO). The future vitality of the union movement and collective bargaining, then, may very well depend on whether the public policy apparatus continues to be dominated by a conservative, pro-business ideology or turns in the direction of a liberal, more pro-union one. Any such turn will itself depend, of course, on the outcomes of future presidential and congressional elections and, ultimately, on public opinon.

Managerial attitudes and philosophies will also help determine the future of collective bargaining. Management ideologies have taken marked swings throughout the twentieth century. In the early part of the century, management opposition to unions was the norm, but by the 1950s the sociologist Daniel Bell was writing about "the end of ideology," which in industrial relations presumably meant managerial acceptance of unions and collective bargaining (Bell 1961). It was common—though perhaps only fashionable—for industry leaders in the 1950s to laud the value of collective bargaining in a free society. If a consensus among managers on the virtues of free collective bargaining ever did exist (and scholars still debate this point), it certainly fell apart in the 1960s and 1970s. In fact, in the 1980s it was difficult to find a manager who had a good word to say about unions or collective bargaining. Managerial attitudes tended in recent years to range from grudging acceptance of unions to aggressive opposition. At the extreme some managers, albeit a minority, were willing to violate the law (for example, by firing union sympathizers) to avoid unionization. If the dominant management values continue to be strongly anti-union, the prospects for a revitalization of collective bargaining do not appear to be promising (Kochan, Katz, and McKersie 1986).

Finally, the future of collective bargaining most certainly depends on the future vitality of the union movement itself, and particularly on the effectiveness and energy of union leaders. If the labor movement is able to generate fresh ideas and charismatic leaders, as it managed to do in the 1930s, all other obstacles to the regeneration of collective bargaining may fade in importance. A sign that renewed energies may be coursing through the labor movement was the AFL-CIO's adoption in 1985 of a new organizing strategy, discussed above. It might be contended that there is equally a need for labor to develop a new collective bargaining strategy. During most of the post–World War II period, union leaders like the UAW's Walter Reuther could be counted upon to generate new and creative ideas in collective bargaining. But by the 1980s many union leaders seemed to be suffering from a near exhaustion of ideas. The labor force of the future will consist not only of highly educated, skilled, white-collar workers but also of millions of less educated, less skilled workers, many of whom will be minorities and immigrants (see, for example, Kerr and Staudohar 1986, 36–72). Labor's challenge, therefore, will be to develop a bargaining strategy that will appeal to this variegated constituency.

The shape of an effective bargaining strategy can now be only dimly perceived. An indisputable premise is that an effective bargaining strategy must entail labor's energetic representation of its members' interests. Beyond that general statement lie murky waters. It is not likely that labor will abandon its traditional focus on bread-and-butter issues, although it may never again be as inflexible on those issues as it was before the concessionary era. It is also a fair guess that we shall witness the continued diffusion of workplace innovations throughout the unionized sector. But today's innovations will be old hat tomorrow. To revitalize collective bargaining the union movement will need to come up with even more creative strategies to suit the needs and desires of the workers in the next century.

All told, it is not surprising that scholars and practitioners alike have begun to debate whether collective bargaining in American industry had reached a historic turning point: Was collective bargaining permanently changed by the developments of the 1980s? Or did it merely experience a temporary detour from its historic path? Derber has called the former viewpoint the "new-stage theory" and the latter the "rerun theory" (Derber 1983; see also Cullen 1985). Clearly, collective bargaining was not as stable in the 1980s as it had been in the 1950s, nor was it as turbulent as it had been in the 1930s. There were, as this book amply illustrates, significant changes in the 1980s, and many of the changes will certainly have a lasting impact on the practice of collective bargaining. But on the other hand, nothing occurred in the 1980s that changed the fundamental character of collective bargaining in most American industries. The key features of the institution, which are aptly described by the systems framework used throughout this volume, remained unaltered by the developments of the last decade. In truth, in every era collective bargaining has been characterized by both stability and change. The institution was never as static as some believe it was. Similarly, since its inception in the nineteenth century collective bargaining has always had certain unchanging features. In the 1980s collective bargaining in American industry was, indeed, in a period of transition to a "new stage." But, we maintain, collective bargaining has always been a dynamic institution: It has always been in a state of transition from the knowable past to the uncertain future.

References

AFL-CIO Committee on the Evolution of Work. 1985. *The Changing Situation of Workers and Their Unions.* Washington, D.C.: American Federation of Labor–Congress of Industrial Organizations.

Bell, Daniel. 1961. *The End of Ideology.* New York: Collier Books.

Bourdon, Clint. 1979. Pattern Bargaining, Wage Determination, and Inflation: Some Preliminary Observations on the 1976–78 Wage Round. In *Unemployment and Inflation: Institutionalist and Structuralist Views,* ed. Michael J. Piore, 115–33. White Plains, N.Y.: M.E. Sharpe.

Chaison, Gary N. 1980. A Note on Union Merger Trends. *Industrial and Labor Relations Review* 34 (October): 114–20.

Cornfield, Daniel B. Forthcoming. Women in the Automated Office: Computers, Work, and Prospects for Unionization. In *Advances in Industrial and Labor Relations,* ed. David Lewin, David B. Lipsky, and Donna Sockell. Greenwich, Conn.: JAI Press.

Cullen, Donald E. 1985. Recent Trends in Collective Bargaining in the United States. *International Labour Review* 124 (May-June): 299–322.

Derber, Milton. 1983. Are We in a New Stage? In *Proceedings of the Thirty-fifth Annual Meeting, December 28–30, 1982, New York,* ed. Barbara D. Dennis, 1–9. Madison, Wis.: Industrial Relations Research Association.

Donn, Clifford B. 1986. Federal Subsidies, Technological Change, and Collective Bargaining in the Ocean-Going Maritime Industry, photocopy. Syracuse, N.Y.: LeMoyne College.

Dunlop, John T. 1957. Wage Contours. In *New Concepts of Wage Determination,* ed. George W. Taylor and Frank C. Pierson, 127–39. New York: McGraw-Hill.

Gifford, Courtney D. 1982. *Directory of U.S. Labor Organizations,* 1982–83 ed. Washington, D.C.: Bureau of National Affairs.

Harvard Law Review. 1985. Note; Two-Tier Wage Discrimination and the Duty of Fair Representation. Vol. 98 (January): 631–49.

Janus, Charles J. 1978. Union Mergers in the 1970s: A Look at the Reasons and Results. *Monthly Labor Review* 101 (October): 13–23.

Kaufman, Bruce E. 1981. Bargaining Theory, Inflation, and Cyclical Strike Activity. *Industrial and Labor Relations Review* 34 (April): 333–55.

Kerr, Clark, and Paul Staudohar, eds. 1986. *Industrial Relations in a New Age.* San Francisco: Jossey-Bass.

Kochan, Thomas A. 1980. *Collective Bargaining and Industrial Relations: From Theory to Policy and Practice.* Homewood, Ill.: Richard D. Irwin.

Kochan, Thomas A., and Thomas A. Barocci. 1985. *Human Resource Management and Industrial Relations: Text, Readings, and Cases.* Boston: Little, Brown.

Kochan, Thomas A., Harry C. Katz, and Robert B. McKersie. 1986. *The Transformation of American Industrial Relations.* New York: Basic Books.

Kokkelenberg, Edward C., and Donna R. Sockell. 1985. Union Membership in the United States, 1973–1981. *Industrial and Labor Relations Review* 38 (July): 497–543.

Levinson, Harold M. 1980. Trucking. In *Collective Bargaining: Contemporary American Experience,* ed. Gerald G. Somers, 99–150. Madison, Wis.: Industrial Relations Research Association.

Mills, D. Quinn. 1980. Construction. In *Collective Bargaining: Contemporary American Experience,* ed. Gerald G. Somers, 49–98. Madison, Wis.: Industrial Relations Research Association.

Mills, D. Quinn, and Janice McCormick. 1985. *Industrial Relations in Transition: Cases and Text.* New York: John Wiley.

Navarro, Peter. 1983. Union Bargaining Power in the Coal Industry, 1945–1981. *Industrial and Labor Relations Review* 36 (January): 214–29.

New York Times. 1985a. Troubled News Agency Seeks to Void Labor Pact. July 19, p. B5.

———. 1985b. U.S. Cites Continued Drop in Union Membership. February 8, p. B5.

———. 1985c. Workers Still Need Labor Law's Shield. July 21, p. 2F.

———. 1986a. Concessions and Company-by-Company Steel Talks. April 10, p. A10.

———. 1986b. Unionists to Get Low-Interest Credit Cards. July 2, p. A15.

———. 1987. Labor's Changing Outlook: Can Unions Achieve a Comeback? February 22, p. 8.

Northrup, Herbert R. 1984. The Rise and Demise of PATCO. *Industrial and Labor Relations Review* 37 (January): 631–49.

Perry, Charles R., Andrew M. Dramer, and Thomas J. Schneider. 1982. *Operating During Strikes.* Philadelphia: Industrial Research Unit, Wharton School, University of Pennsylvania.

Ross, Arthur M. 1948. *Trade Union Wage Policy.* Berkeley: University of California Press.

Slichter, Sumner H., James J. Healy, and E. Robert Livernash. 1960. *The Impact of Collective Bargaining on Management.* Washington, D.C.: Brookings Institution.

Somers, Gerald G., Edward L. Cushman, and Nat Weinberg, eds. 1963. *Adjusting to Technological Change.* New York: Harper and Row.

Stieber, Jack. 1980. Steel. In *Collective Bargaining: Contemporary American Experience,* ed. Gerald G. Somers, 151–208. Madison, Wis.: Industrial Relations Research Association.

U.S. Department of Labor, Bureau of Labor Statistics. 1986. Unpublished strike data.

Washington Post. 1986. Steel Firms Start Crucial Labor Talks. March 9, p. K1.

Weber, Arnold. 1967. Stability and Change in the Structure of Collective Bargaining. In *Challenges to Collective Bargaining,* ed. Lloyd Ulman, 13–36. Englewood Cliffs, N.J.: Prentice-Hall.

Index

Page numbers in italics indicate figures; page numbers followed by t indicate tabular material.

About the Contributors

Samuel B. Bacharach is professor in the Department of Organizational Behavior at the New York State School of Industrial and Labor Relations, Cornell University. He received the Ph.D. in sociology from the University of Wisconsin in 1974. He has published many scholarly articles and is the co-author of *Power and Politics in Organizations* (1980), *Bargaining: Power, Tactics, and Outcomes* (1981), and *Paying for Better Teaching: Merit Pay and Its Alternatives* (1984). Much of his recent research has concentrated on labor relations in education.

Scott C. Bauer is senior consultant at Organizational Analysis and Practice, Inc. (OAP), of Ithaca, New York. He received bachelor's and master's degrees from Cornell University and is now on leave from the doctoral program in organizational behavior at that institution. Bauer's recent research has included investigations of the design of teachers' jobs; teacher compensation and career development systems; and compensation of faculty and non-teaching professionals in higher education. He is now serving as OAP project leader for the design and implementation of a system for personal computers that will code provisions in faculty collective bargaining agreements.

Peter Cappelli is the Joseph Wharton Associate Professor of Management at the Wharton School, University of Pennsylvania. He received his doctorate in labor economics in 1983 from Oxford University, where he was a Fulbright Scholar. He has written extensively about contemporary labor relations, his recent publications including "Competitive Pressures and Labor Relations in the Airline Industry" (1985) and "Plant-Level Concession Bargaining" (1985).

John Thomas Delaney is assistant professor at the Graduate School of Business, Columbia University. The author of numerous articles on public sector labor relations and dispute resolution, he received the Ph.D. in labor and industrial relations from the University of Illinois in 1983. He is also the co-author of the third edition of *Public Sector Labor Relations: Analysis and Readings* (forthcoming.)

James B. Dworkin is associate dean of the Krannert Graduate School of Management and associate professor of organizational behavior and human resource management, both at Purdue University. He has published *Owners versus Players: Baseball and Collective Bargaining* (1981) and numerous scholarly articles on industrial relations, including "Polygraph Tests: What Labor Arbitrators Need to Know" (1986) and "Faculty Intentions to Unionize: Theory and Evidence" (1985). He also serves as an arbitrator, mediator, and factfinder in labor-management disputes in the private and public sectors. He received the Ph.D. in industrial relations from the University of Minnesota in 1977.

Peter Feuille is professor of labor and industrial relations at the University of Illinois at Urbana-Champaign. He received the Ph.D. in industrial relations in 1973 from the University of California, Berkeley. Having published widely in professional journals, he is also the coauthor of *Police Unionism* (1973) and of the third edition of *Public Sector Labor Relations: Analysis and Readings* (forthcoming). His main research interests are police labor relations, public sector collective bargaining, and union-management dispute resolution.

Wallace E. Hendricks is professor of economics and of labor and industrial relations at the University of Illinois at Urbana-Champaign. He received the Ph.D. in economics from the University of California, Berkeley, in 1973, and has been a consultant for many public and private institutions, including the U.S. Department of Energy, the Illinois Commerce Commission, Commonwealth Edison, and Continental Airlines. He is the co-author of *Wage Indexation in the United States: Cola or Uncola?* (1985), and his articles have appeared in numerous scholarly journals.

Mark D. Karper is director of the Institute of Industrial Relations and associate professor of industrial relations at Le Moyne College. Since receiving his Ph.D. in economics from the University of Cincinnati in 1980, he has served as an arbitrator on various panels and as a mediator and factfinder for New York state. His articles have appeared in the proceedings of the Industrial Relations Research Association and the *Monthly Labor Review*.

Harry C. Katz is associate professor at the New York State School of Industrial and Labor Relations, Cornell University. He received his Ph.D. in economics from the University of California, Berkeley, in 1977. He has published *Shifting Gears: Changing Labor Relations in the U.S. Automobile Industry* (1985) and has co-authored *The Transformation of American Industrial Relations* (1986) and the second edition of *Collective Bargaining and Industrial Relations* (forthcoming).

Timothy P. Schmidle is a doctoral candidate at the New York State School of Industrial and Labor Relations, Cornell University, where he is completing his dissertation on faculty unions, salaries, and budgetary allocations in higher education. He received the M.S. in labor relations from Cornell in 1984 and the Master of Public Administration degree from the Maxwell School of Citizenship and Public Affairs, Syracuse University, in 1979.

Ronald L. Seeber is associate director of Extension and Public Service at the New York State School of Industrial and Labor Relations, Cornell University. He received the Ph.D. in labor and industrial relations from the University of Illinois in 1981. His many journal articles and book chapters have included studies of union behavior, concessionary bargaining, and alternative forms of grievance settlement; and most recently he co-authored the second edition of *Collective Bargaining and Labor Relations* (1987).

About the Editors

David B. Lipsky is associate dean and professor at the New York State School of Industrial and Labor Relations, Cornell University. He received the Ph.D. in economics from the Massachusetts Institute of Technology in 1967. He has published widely in scholarly journals and is the author or editor of seven previously published books. Most recently, he co-authored *Paying for Better Teaching: Merit Pay and Its Alternatives* (1984) and co-edited *Advances in Industrial and Labor Relations,* volume 3 (1986). In addition to serving as a mediator, factfinder, and arbitrator in collective bargaining disputes, he is the former editor and associate editor of the *Industrial and Labor Relations Review.*

Clifford B. Donn is professor and chairman of the Department of Industrial Relations at Le Moyne College. He received the Ph.D. in economics from the Massachusetts Institute of Technology in 1980. He has published a number of scholarly articles on dispute settlement and on the Australian trade union movement, as well as *The Australian Council of Trade Unions: History and Economic Policy* (1983). He also serves as a mediator and factfinder in public sector collective bargaining disputes in New York state.